BETWEEN TWO FIRES

"A deeply reported account of what it's like to live in Putin's Russia, but it's not about Twitter bots or influencing foreign elections or even Vladimir Putin himself. . . . Yaffa gives us insight into Putin by helping us better understand the political culture that produced him."

—NPR

"Few journalists have penetrated so deep and with so much nuance into the moral ambiguities of Russia. If you want insight into the deeper distortions the Kremlin causes in people's psyches, this book is invaluable."

—Peter Pomerantsev, author of
Nothing Is True and Everything Is Possible

"Superb . . . [an] excellent new book . . . Yaffa has distinguished himself with his rigor, his acumen, and his nuanced voice. . . . His in-depth reporting consistently allows him to move beyond the headlines, revealing the deeper historical and sociological patterns that underpin that notoriously contradictory country."

—*Foreign Affairs*

"A wonderfully insightful book . . . well-told and neatly interlinked stories . . . It is to Mr. Yaffa's credit that in general he avoids simplifying. Even when he describes people who seek cynical advantage from the powerful, the picture is never completely dark; when he portrays moral heroes, he never presents them as infallible. That is how things are in life, perhaps nowhere more so than in Russia."

—*The Economist*

"Joshua Yaffa's portrait of a people is a triumph—a brilliantly original, deeply literate path through the moral struggles and calculations of a modern Russia he knows in his bones."

—Evan Osnos, author of *Age of Ambition*

"Yaffa skillfully weaves together perceptive descriptions of flesh-and-blood people with a balanced evocation of the wider political and historical context. As we follow these individuals, we come to understand many of the developments of the post-Soviet era . . . through the eyes of those who have lived through them. Yaffa has a good eye for colourful detail . . . and he proves attentive to the subtleties and ambiguities of Russian life."

—Tony Wood, *Financial Times*

"A fascinating and nuanced account that illuminates the myriad conflicting and often contradictory forces that have shaped the Russia of today." —Douglas Smith, *The Wall Street Journal*

"*Between Two Fires* is a study of compromise, opportunism, and the fraught moral choices available in Putin's Russia. In a series of carefully reported stories, Joshua Yaffa shows how people choose—

sometimes consciously and other times not—to adapt, change, and otherwise 'make do' in an authoritarian state."

—Anne Applebaum, author of *Red Famine* and *Gulag*

"[A] highly original and riveting account . . . Good and not-so-good men and women are forced to make difficult choices—and Joshua Yaffa's remarkable book is a guide to the pain and pleasure of their lives in the public arena."
—Robert Service, *Foreign Policy*

"In *Between Two Fires,* Joshua Yaffa brilliantly captures the complex choices and compromises that Russians make to survive, thrive, or remain true to their principles in Putin's Russia."

—Michael McFaul, former U.S. ambassador to Russia and author of *From Cold War to Hot Peace*

"Deeply reported and detailed . . . A fascinating exploration into the beliefs and psyches of Russians in many different career fields who reveal their souls to Yaffa, often to a surprising degree but with little apparent fear of reprisal."
—*San Francisco Chronicle*

"*Between Two Fires* stands a rank above most publications of its genre because of its effective shoe-leather reporting. Not content with analyzing media coverage or online debates, Yaffa has sought out and interviewed both his central characters and their friends, enemies, and former supporters."
—Greg Afinogenov, *Bookforum*

BETWEEN
TWO FIRES

BETWEEN TWO FIRES

TRUTH, AMBITION,
AND COMPROMISE
IN PUTIN'S RUSSIA

JOSHUA YAFFA

CROWN
NEW YORK

2021 Crown Trade Paperback Edition

Published in the United States by
Crown, an imprint of Random House,
a division of Penguin Random House LLC, New York.

CROWN and the Crown colophon
are registered trademarks of Penguin Random House LLC.

Originally published in hardcover by Crown, an imprint of Random House,
a division of Penguin Random House LLC, New York, in 2020.

Portions of this work were originally published in *The New Yorker* in different form.

LIBRARY OF CONGRESS CATALOGING-IN-PUBLICATION DATA
NAMES: Yaffa, Joshua, author.
TITLE: Between two fires / Joshua Yaffa.
DESCRIPTION: First edition. | New York : Tim Duggan Books, 2020 |
Includes bibliographical references and index.
IDENTIFIERS: LCCN 2019025918 (print) | LCCN 2019025919 (ebook) |
ISBN 9781524760601 (paperback) | ISBN 9781524760618 (ebook)
SUBJECTS: LCSH: Putin, Vladimir Vladimirovich, 1952– —
Public opinion. | Public opinion—Russia (Federation). |
Political culture—Russia (Federation). | Presidents—Russia
(Federation)—Election. | Russia (Federation)—Politics and government—1991–
CLASSIFICATION: LCC DK510.766.P87 Y34 2020 (print) |
LCC DK510.766.P87 (ebook) | DDC 947.086/2—dc23
LC record available at https://lccn.loc.gov/2019025918

Printed in the United States of America

crownpublishing.com

2nd Printing

FIRST EDITION

For my parents

CONTENTS

—

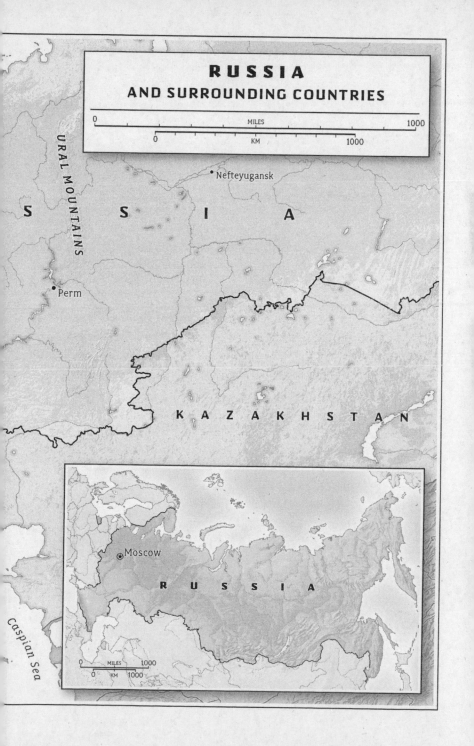

RUSSIA
AND SURROUNDING COUNTRIES

0   MILES   1000

0   KM   1000

URAL MOUNTAINS

S   S   I   A

• Nefteyugansk

• Perm

K A Z A K H S T A N

Caspian Sea

⊛ Moscow

R   U   S   S   I   A

0   MILES   1000

0   KM   1000

BETWEEN
TWO FIRES

THE WILY MAN

—

I N THE WINTER OF 1987, YURI LEVADA STUMBLED UPON A TAN-
talizing opportunity. Levada, then fifty-seven, with a gentle face
and a thin dusting of white hair, was a sociologist whose very field of
interest had long relegated him to the margins of the academy. For
decades, Soviet authorities dismissed sociology as bourgeois pseudo-
science. Official doctrine posited that essentially all one needed to
know about society was contained in the class-based system of Marx
and his notion of historical materialism. But in the mid-eighties, the
rise of Mikhail Gorbachev and his policy of perestroika—a rethinking of the Soviet economy involving an opening of the country's political and civic culture—created an opportunity for Levada and a
small number of like-minded colleagues.

Levada was known to be honest and sincere, with an alert mind
that stood out among the gray, dull plodders who dominated Soviet
academic circles. He was certainly no dissident: he existed within the
system, even if he never penetrated its inner realms, and his basic decency and outsize intellectual aptitude set him apart from those who
did. He and a circle of friends and onetime graduate students spent
years gathering after hours in the spare conference rooms of scientific
institutes, discussing taboo questions of sociological theory and the
country's sporadic outcroppings of avant-garde theater and poetry.

But now they were given control over a newly created body, the

All-Union Center for Public Opinion Research, VTsIOM for short, the first large-scale polling and social research center in the country's history. Gorbachev and his reformist allies in the politburo were aware that the Soviet system, if left unchanged, would soon reach its breaking point. And they were also aware of how little they understood about the citizens they ruled. It was in part due to this sudden tolerance for intellectual heterodoxy, but really a result of the general upheavals of the time, that VTsIOM was created. Levada was named head of its theoretical studies department, and took with him a handful of colleagues who had been his graduate students in the 1960s. At the new institute, Levada would have the resources and practical tools to test his ideas and gain a real, tactile feel for society. He could actually carry out surveys in the field.

The last time Levada had been given such a public platform, in 1966, things had not ended so well. He was in his mid-thirties, a young professor newly out of graduate school, when a sympathetic colleague at Moscow State University invited him to give a series of lectures on sociology in an auditorium on campus. The lectures quickly gained a following, oversubscribed by university students and sought out by members of Moscow's intelligentsia, who crouched in the hall's aisles and stood cramped in its doorways—"hanging from the chandeliers," as the Russian expression goes. On the surface, there was nothing transgressive or forbidden about Levada's lectures: he simply spoke of the central tenets of sociology, an academic science that emerged in France and the United States in the late nineteenth century as a response to the conundrums of modernity. Today's listener would struggle to find the sharp language of a dissident in Levada's talks. He avoided politics entirely and focused on various theories of social formation and the relations between individuals in social systems. It was straightforward and professorial, which also made it sensational.

Sociology gave Levada a portal to a language that was both open and plain, a way of examining Soviet society without the fogginess of official doctrine. "It's not easy to understand, but his simple, human view of things, not distorted by propaganda—it created a shocking effect," said Alexey Levinson, who, thanks to Levada, discovered sociology as a university student in the sixties. "He called a cat a cat, and a dog a dog." Few in the lecture hall had heard anyone speak like that before. "All of Moscow was running there, as we say," said Lev Gudkov, another promising student of Levada's. The lectures gave Levada a forum to begin to explore the questions that would consume him later in life: the Soviet individual's timidity and servitude before the state, which was a product both of the fear that came from repression and an inability to imagine oneself without the state—a paternalistic symbiosis.

But then came August 1968, when Soviet tanks put an end to the Prague Spring, a short-lived period of openness and reform in Czechoslovakia—"socialism with a human face," as Alexander Dubček, then the leader of the Czech Communist Party, summed up its guiding idea. After the violence in the streets of Prague, a reactionary campaign swept through Soviet culture and academia, ensnaring a number of artists and intellectuals who were accused of deviating, however minutely, from the accepted tenets of Soviet thought. The next year, in 1969, Levada was called to a hearing at the Academy of the Social Sciences. Over several hours, his interrogators charged him with all manner of ideological transgressions. They seized on a remark he had made that in modern society, the individual is subjected to all sorts of external pressure: from the state, mass culture, the market, even tanks. Levada had made the point in 1966, before the tanks rolled into Prague, but the image was deemed too incendiary to be accidental. Throughout the hearing, as Levada stood before his accusers, he carried himself with his customary restraint. He didn't plead for mercy or confront his tormentors head-on. At one point, when he realized his defense was futile, he simply closed his briefcase and took a seat.

The verdict was preordained, and the fact that the hearing resembled a political show trial was not accidental, given that up until a decade or so prior, many of the same men on this disciplinary panel had done their part in carrying out Stalin-era ideological repressions. "By then, their teeth and claws had been pulled out, they couldn't kill," Levinson said. "But they said the kinds of things about Levada that, a couple decades before, would have meant a person would be sent off to the camps and never return." Instead, Levada was stripped of his professorship and ordered to join an academic institute in a non-public, essentially anonymous position. As Anna Akhmatova, the grande dame of twentieth-century Russian poetry, might have put it, the times had become rather vegetarian. It was not the Gulag, but it was a form of exile, akin to how Dubček, after his arrest in the final days of the Prague Spring, was sent to work as a park ranger in a remote stretch of Slovak forest. Levada was cut off from the mainstream of Soviet science and barred from publishing new work or even being cited by other academics in their own articles. "Just me, all by myself, and that's how it was—by myself—for sixteen years," he later recalled.

All the while, at home and with small groups of friends and colleagues, Levada kept working through his understanding of what came to be called *Homo sovieticus:* a new species that appeared as a result of the Soviet Union's grand and terrible social experiment. For this species, Levada wrote, "the state is not just one of a number of historically formed social institutions . . . but a kind of superinstitution, universal in its functions and sphere of activities . . . of a pre-modern paternalistic type that penetrates into all corners of human existence. The project of the Soviet social state is by definition totalitarian, in that it does not leave a person with any independent space." And of no less importance, the subjects of that state must be not only dependent but grateful: "Care from those at the top should be met with appreciation from those at the bottom."

Partly out of residual fear, but also thanks to a combination of cleverness and resourcefulness, many Soviet citizens responded by grafting themselves onto the state—an institution they may not have trusted or respected, but couldn't imagine overcoming or living without. It began as a survival mechanism, in which citizen and state subconsciously worked together to ensure that the individual took agency in stifling his own freedom and chances for self-realization. At once resourceful and passive, untrusting and indifferent, Levada's Soviet Man intuitively understood that it was easier—and ultimately more profitable—to play one's own game within the system. Bravery took the form of passive resistance, as when the editor of *Questions of Philosophy,* a man considered to be a young, relatively progressive thinker, declared he would not allow any attacks against Levada to appear in his pages, even as he refused to publish Levada himself. "He kept his promise," Levada remarked, with a kind of begrudging appreciation.

It was Soviet Man whom Levada wanted to study when perestroika and his appointment to VTsIOM gave him the opportunity to carry out field research. He could see that many of the most malignant features of Soviet society were being stripped away, replaced with an inchoate culture of inquisitiveness and challenging long-held dogma. Levada was consumed by the question of whether, with the eventual withering of the Soviet system, *Homo sovieticus* would similarly disappear, or at least evolve.

In 1989, Levada set out to test the question by asking everyday people about their relationship with the state. It was an exhilarating prospect, and one that felt terrifyingly urgent. "The situation was developing turbulently," with little time for unhurried philosophizing, Levada said. By trying to make sense of Soviet society, he and his team at VTsIOM were "feeling the pulse of a sick person."

AT THE TIME, Communist governments were falling throughout Eastern Europe, the Soviet military was pulling out of Afghanistan, and Soviet society was witness to a turbulent realignment in the country's political course. Researchers gathered focus groups and handed out questionnaires at VTsIOM's fourteen regional offices around the Soviet Union. Far more material came from responses to a one-page survey printed in *Literaturnaya Gazeta,* a popular weekly that published poetry and literature and also dabbled in politics. Under the headline "What Do You Think?" the survey asked readers to answer questions on their expectations, fears, and relationship to the state. The public reaction was overwhelming. Levada's team received nearly two hundred thousand responses; some had been filled out by entire families, others by whole factory brigades. Postal workers would drop off heaving sacks of completed questionnaires, which gathered in awkward piles in the corridor of the Tourist Hotel on Leninsky Prospekt, where the researchers had their office. "Society was yelling, it wanted something," said Levinson. "We had this feeling that a new kind of person had appeared."

To Levada, it seemed that Soviet Man was in a stage of metamorphosis, leaving behind his fear, powerlessness, and instinctual obedience. The very fact that the survey had provoked such a vibrant response was itself a sign that the country's social order was shifting. As Levada and his team wrote in a report documenting their findings, "The formation of public opinion is one of the signs of the fall of totalitarian society" and the "herd instincts, phobias, images of the enemy" that were germane to it: "The ice has started to melt." The results showed falling levels of enthusiasm for a strong leader around whom the rest of the country should consolidate. A majority said they were ready for a more honest appraisal of their country's history, even if that history would be uncomfortable or unflattering in places. Most wanted closer relations with the West, and no longer feared war or encirclement by ill-intentioned enemies, a perennial phobia used to consolidate the population and ensure loyalty.

So much of Soviet life had been dictated by the two-way untruth perpetrated by both citizen and state: the citizen pretended to be an enthusiastic and loyal subject, and the state pretended to be both competent and interested in providing for individual well-being. A show of obedience was matched by a show of paternal care. This took on comedic form in an infamous Soviet-era joke: "We pretend to work, and they pretend to pay us." This was not especially fervent loyalty, but rather passive acquiescence, made palatable by all the ways a person could outsmart the system and eke out small, private victories against it. When Levinson and Gudkov were writing their dissertations, a department head at Moscow State University demanded they cite some "bourgeois" authors so as to criticize them. So they simply made up fake ones and attacked their work; the academic committee never noticed. "We both were proud of how we were able to deceive them," said Levinson. And why should they not have been?

The hope of perestroika, backed up by the results Levada's team was receiving by the bagful on Leninsky Prospekt, was that the country's citizens were changing, psychically distancing themselves from the state and taking on more personal responsibility. Society appeared on the verge of leaving behind its "pernicious, malignant, morally ruinous form of adaptation," said Levinson. Levada himself published an essay on this phenomenon, entitled "Outgoing Nature." Soon the Soviet Union would be gone entirely, collapsing in the way of all towering empires: at first slowly and imperceptibly, then quickly, in a flash no one saw coming. With it disappeared many of the structures and institutions that shaped Soviet Man: from the Communist Party's singular control over career advancement to the planned economy, which led to deficits of goods and the ability to access them based on favors and personal relationships. In hindsight, Levada's presumption that the Soviet collapse would herald the appearance of a new type of person seems like a mirror image of the utopian thinking the early Bolsheviks had imagined.

IT DIDN'T TAKE LONG, however, for it to become clear that a new citizenry would be much slower in coming. Under Levada, the team at VTsIOM continued to produce surveys and analyze their results, and quickly realized that the *Literaturnaya Gazeta* poll was an anomaly. Russia's post-Soviet citizens held attitudes that resembled those of Soviet generations before them. "It was impossible to reach any conclusion other than that what we considered a typical Soviet person is a far more persistent structure than Soviet institutions," said Levinson. In one survey, half of respondents said the winners of Russian parliamentary elections in 1999 were not honest, but a majority said they were satisfied with the results of that election. That same year, the number of those surveyed who said they acted in opposition to what they considered correct was higher than it had been a decade earlier, in 1989. More people told pollsters that they were forced to bend their morals for the good of the cause than they had under Soviet rule. Levada noticed the old habits returning: "An absolute preponderance of patience over active protest; adaptation over resistance; and passive displeasure over a struggle for one's rights." The citizen was again making do, adjusting to the rules of the game rather than looking to effect change.

By the end of the decade, the data showed that the habits and pathologies of Soviet Man were reproducing, taking on new forms and worming their way into a wider set of social institutions and relationships. This left many at VTsIOM disheartened. "The people are leaving you, turning away from what remains of your ideal," said Levinson. The institute's director, an erudite, liberal, and widely loved sociologist named Tatyana Zaslavskaya, said in exasperation, "I don't understand anything," and retired. Levada was named the new head.

From the moment of the Soviet collapse, Levada worried that its fall was an outcome that came about too easily for the average citizen, an effective revolution that didn't require anything revolutionary at all from most people. It was an event that happened *to* individuals, not one made by them—and thus could be internalized as yet another imposition from above. "After the crash of the Soviet system," Levada wrote, "the person who rose to the surface was not a fabulously liberated hero, but someone inclined to adapt to what is required of him in order to survive. A person ready to declare allegiance to a democratic system out of disgust with the old system, not because of any deep or genuine belief in democratic values."

IN 2000, THE YEAR Vladimir Putin ascended to the presidency, Levada published a new essay, an attempt to work through what for him had become a frustrating mystery: the persistence of the Russian personality type he had spent so much time coming to understand. Who was this person, if he or she could no longer fairly be called Soviet? Levada titled the essay "The Wily Man," which identified a new species, not *Homo sovieticus,* but something more lasting and universal. The Russian wily man, Levada wrote, "not only tolerates deception, but is willing to be deceived, and even . . . requires self-deception for the sake of his own self-preservation." Levada saw him as ultimately a clever and resourceful creature. "He adapts to social reality, looking for oversights and gaps in the ruling system, looking to use the 'rules of the game' for his own interest, but at the same time—and no less important—he is constantly trying to circumvent those very same rules."

For the wily man, interacting with the state is a game of half-truths and deceptions, served up as offerings to the bureaucratic machine, and told to one another as justification for squelching ambition and a sense of morality. Given weak levels of social bonds and under-developed institutions, the wily man is ultimately alone, which leads to a paradox of Russian life that goes back generations: "If a person is forced to carry himself like everyone else, and to demonstrate this publicly, he frees himself from responsibility for those shared positions—but that doesn't mean he has gotten rid of this basic lone-liness in relation to everyone else." Freedom from responsibility provides the illusion of freedom itself. Ultimately, the wily man and woman harbor no illusions about the true nature of the state; it is just that they don't see an alternative to it, and thus make a calculation to swim with the current rather than against it. "It seems that the Russian people need the protection of the state but they do not want to serve it," Levada observed.

For Levada, the concept of the wily man was a way out of what he saw as a false choice between what he had come to believe were two equally unconvincing myths. The first was that propagated by official propaganda, which portrayed the Soviet citizen as happy and satisfied, dedicated to building Communism. The second was its reverse image, popular among the liberal intelligentsia and many in the West—that the Soviet people are dissatisfied and harbor animosity against the state, and are primed to act against it. Levada understood the truth as somewhere in the middle, in contemporary Russia as in Soviet times. True sadists and torturers are few, and yet the life of a dissident is lonely, unglamorous, and oftentimes plain miserable. Most people are neither Stalin nor Solzhenitsyn, but, in their own way, wily.

The wily man is not merely a Soviet phenomenon, but a character type with much deeper historical roots. In Russia's pre-revolutionary past, when some 80 percent or more of the population were peasants, the folklore of the time—further exaggerated after the fact by Soviet propagandists—held that the peasants, especially serfs, were the keep-ers of a greater truth that their masters could not access or understand. The masters may have had the power, but virtue and authenticity were on the side of those without it. Some years before Levada pub-

lished his essay, Zaslavskaya, the first director of VTsIOM, had spoken of the "wily serf" mentioned in Pushkin verses, who, while
remaining in bondage, is constantly able to undermine and outsmart
his baron. It was a frequent theme in nineteenth-century Russian literature, with popular tales presenting such figures as everyman folk
heroes. The Soviet state, distant and opaque yet meddlesomely omnipresent, provided a natural backdrop for the genre. Outwitting the
clumsy bureaucratic machine became a kind of national sport. And
what came next—the many deprivations and cruelties of life in Russia in the 1990s—was no less ideal an environment for such a character, making his attempts at self-preservation noble, even brave.

The final years of Levada's life were Vladimir Putin's early ones in
power. Then in his seventies, Levada watched as Putin restored the
authority of the Russian state the only way he knew how: by bringing the many arms of government administration under his direct
control, creating a "vertical of power" that was responsive to his whims
and orders. Nearly every part of Russia's political and economic life
would become subservient to this overarching system, from television channels and oil companies to the court system and the Russian
Orthodox Church. In 2003, VTsIOM was itself subsumed into the
vertical of power: it was nominally privatized, with the ultimate effect of delivering it into loyal hands, who, when necessary, would
soften polling results and their implications to avoid unduly upsetting the Kremlin. Levada and the band of like-minded colleagues that
had been with him since the sixties left and formed a new, independent research institution: the Levada Center.

After successive waves of disappointment and hardship in the
nineties, the Russian public largely welcomed the arrival of a leader,
and a system, that promised to restore basic competency to the state
and stability to their lives. Over the years, polls conducted by the
Levada Center showed Putin's approval rating reaching well above 80
percent. This was in no small measure a product of the state's mo-
nopolistic control over television, the media with the widest reach,
and its squelching of those who would represent an alternative, but it
was also an expression of buried historical grievances—Putin was less
the country's captor than a manifestation of its collective subcon-

scious. "For Putin, the complexes of Soviet man are very understandable, and he uses them like a resource," said Gudkov. "The traits of a person who is dependent, envious, strangled, aggressive—in this sense, wily."

It was Putin's great luck that his assemblage of power coincided with a rise in global oil prices, fueling a consumer boom unprecedented in Russia's history. In Putin's first two terms in office, a period stretching over eight years, real wages tripled. Now wiliness could also be paid for in cash—or at least nicer food on the shelves and higher-quality household items, and, for the urban middle class, IKEA furniture, vacations on European beaches, and meals at Moscow's ever-increasing number of nice restaurants. Levada understood the Putin-era wily man, and while he was discouraged by Putin's staying power, he did not judge or curse him. The wily man was persistent, maybe even eternal—an instructive avatar for making sense of the unspoken compact between the ruler and the ruled.

Levada died in 2006 at the age of seventy-six. Toward the end of his life, his mood had turned dour and pessimistic. "He was gloomy," said Gudkov. He lamented to friends that the wily man had not perished along with the Soviet Union, but managed to outlive the laboratory that had nurtured him for so many years. Wiliness keeps Russia in a historical loop, and, as Levada once wrote, "Transcending its limits has so far proved impossible."

THE RUSSIAN LANGUAGE HAS an especially rich word for a person skilled in the act of compromise and adaptation, who intuitively understands what is expected of him and adjusts his beliefs and conduct accordingly: *prisposoblenets*. Perhaps the most skilled chronicler of this form of survival and advancement—a process that could appear absurd and repulsive, if totally understandable—was Sergei Dovlatov, a prison guard, Soviet newspaper reporter, and, after he exhausted the patience of Soviet authorities, political émigré in New York City. In his quasi-autobiographical essays and novels, Dovlatov portrayed his loosely masked narrator as a kind of unrealized *prisposoblenets*, a person who might well have traded his principles for material comfort if not for a bumbling, ironic, and booze-soaked sense of individuality that always got in the way. His cynicism was outflanked by his fundamental decency. In the context of the late Soviet Union, Dovlatov's failure even in the act of being a moral sellout made him both a loser and an oracle of truth.

Dovlatov's 1981 book *The Compromise* deals with this combination of pitifulness and dignity in the twilight years of Soviet power. "There are no angels or villains. There are no sinners and saints," Dovlatov writes—just people trying to come to terms with what they can't control, and to carve out some small space for the private and the humane. He describes a world populated by people like his newspaper editor, a "timid manipulator" who was both insecure and imperious; a young woman from the provinces for whom "lying without hope of gain is not lying, it's poetry"; and a colleague who speaks in wooden-tongued metaphors, which prompts Dovlatov to observe, "A metaphor: there are dozens of euphemisms like that for lies."

The question of the lie—what it meant to tell one, and how not to—was a central concern of the intellectuals who came of age during the relative openness of Khrushchev's thaw, which lasted up until the violent denouement of the Prague Spring. This was Levada's generation. They were called the *shestidesyatniki,* the people of the sixties. One of the touchstone events in their lives was the publication, in 1962, of Solzhenitsyn's *One Day in the Life of Ivan Denisovich,* the tale of an ordinary day in a Stalin-era prison camp. Its power came from its unspoken exponentiality: multiply the life of Ivan Denisovich by a few million, and one got a feel for the scale of the state's treatment of its own people.

In *One Day* and other works, Solzhenitsyn's subject was the cruelty of the Soviet system, but he also documented the ways people sought to survive that system, cheating it and outsmarting it wherever possible. The horrors of the Gulag illuminated a choice that lay just beneath the surface of ordinary Soviet life: Is it not morally correct to act unjustly toward a system that is itself deeply unjust? Ivan Denisovich gains small advantages for himself, unnoticed. "Better to growl and submit. If you were stubborn they broke you," he explains early on. But he retains vestiges of his humanity. His insistence on taking off his cap while eating his meager, unappealing meals is his way of asserting his individual dignity. To expect more from a person is to misunderstand the circumstances in which he finds him- or herself. "How can you expect a man who's warm to understand a man who's cold?" Ivan Denisovich asks, in perhaps the book's most famous line.

After the publication and success of *One Day,* a momentary relaxation of Soviet censorship not to be repeated for twenty-five years, Solzhenitsyn wrote an essay that was typed out one copy at a time and circulated among Moscow intellectuals. It was called "Live Not by Lies," a cri de coeur to refuse to contort oneself to the system's demands of a person's basic understanding of the truth. He begins by recounting the seeming omnipotence of the state: "They put on trial anybody they want and they put sane people in asylums—always they, and we are powerless." There are no benefits in resistance, and too many in conformity; as Solzhenitsyn writes, it feels as if "we take a step alone—and suddenly find ourselves without white bread, without heating gas, and without Moscow registration." Solzhenitsyn chose to focus his gaze not on the rulers in the Kremlin, but on those whom he saw as keeping them there: "We lie to ourselves for assurance. And it is not only they who are to blame for everything—we ourselves, only we."

Levada, like many in his circle, was also a close reader of George Orwell and was particularly influenced by Orwell's notion of doublethink, made famous in *1984.* As Orwell describes it, the citizen trapped in an omnipotent system "knows in which direction his memories must be altered; he therefore knows that he is playing tricks with reality; but by the exercise of doublethink he also satisfies himself that reality is not violated." For Orwell, the telling of "deliberate lies while genuinely believing in them" is a way of staying sane, an effort at retaining a sense of individual will—in short, "indispensably necessary."

But Levada felt that Orwell exaggerated the distinction between the ruling elite and those without political influence. Orwell saw the elite as cynical and knowing producers of doublethink, whereas their victims are essentially forced by circumstance and their own powerlessness to go along with it. For Levada, both the rulers and the ruled were responsible for their arrangement, with each side finding something calming and familiar in its existence. Average citizens had grown to depend on the paternalistic aspect of the state, even as they feared or actively disliked it. And those "on top," as Levada put it, were no more coherent or rational in their actions than those on the bottom. The country's political rulers, Levada wrote, "live by the same rules of wily doublethink" and "if from time to time they feel compelled to declare their determination to get out of this vicious circle, they actually only become more entangled in it."

I FIRST SET FOOT in Russia in the summer of 2001, a year after Levada published his essay on the wily man. I had been taking Russian-language classes throughout my first two years in college, and this would be my introduction to the land I had thus far known only from textbooks, flash cards, and practice dialogues ("Where is your suitcase?" "Here it is." "It's so big!"). My choice to study Russian had been whimsical, almost accidental: one of those pursuits best suited for a teenager and his glorious surpluses of time and curiosity. Now, at nineteen, I had ended up in a dark and unrenovated—but inviting and endlessly charming—apartment on the Petrograd side of St. Petersburg, where I would spend the next months living with a host family on a street named for Liza Chaikina, a member of the underground resistance during World War II who, at the age of twenty-three, was captured and killed by the Germans. During the day, I studied Russian on the grounds of the Smolny Institute, a college built in the early nineteenth century that became Lenin's headquarters during the Bolshevik Revolution. Not that I was yet fully capable of imbibing the history that surrounded me.

Those months passed in a happy blur of my host mother's fried bliny with jam in the mornings, a creeping grasp of noun declensions, evenings in the upper rafters at the Mariinsky Theatre, even later evenings at a bare-bones nightclub fashioned out of a one-room concrete bomb shelter, and the nightly sprint back to Liza Chaikina Street. During the summer months, St. Petersburg's many drawbridges go up around one in the morning to let ships pass along the Neva River, and only come down again long after dawn. If I missed the moment to get across to the Petrograd side, I was trapped until morning—but then again, wandering for hours along St. Petersburg's canals, lit by the spectral light of the summertime White Nights, often felt the luckier outcome than making it home. In hindsight, I would understand that I caught St. Petersburg in a moment between the abject chaos and hardship of the nineties and the routinized, top-down strictures of the vertical of power that would descend in the years to come. Russia felt alive precisely because it was so undetermined: in those years, life was hard and a bit madcap, but felt like it could go in any number of directions, and its people had yet to pick one. Or have one picked for them.

Over the next decade, I returned to Russia a number of times, mainly staying in Moscow, the capital city that, on my first visits, felt every part the imposing megalopolis compared to St. Petersburg's dilapidated charm, a place that reminded me of a would-be Venice left in the hands of Soviet party bosses and work brigades, and then in no one's hands at all. (St. Petersburg's romantic shabbiness began to recede, in ways both good and bad, in 2003, when the government pumped millions into renovation works in advance of the city's tricentennial celebration.) In Moscow, it's an often-repeated cliché that the streets were designed not for people but for tanks, and that's indeed how it feels: to cross an underground tunnel on foot beneath a six-lane highway that cuts through the center of town is to imagine yourself an extra in a film meant to showcase grandeur and might, with your particular human form needed only for purposes of scale.

But Moscow, too, quickly won me over. It vibrated with the energy of wholesale reinvention: the people I met were hungry, curious, adventurous, unbound by rules and expectations, whether other people's or their own. The mood was rambunctious and unapologetic. But there was also a sorrow and a weight to the place; the city had been the epicenter of a terrible failed experiment, one that had resulted in great tragedy for so many, and even if the particulars rarely came up in conversation, this feeling led to what felt like a collective inability to indulge in small talk or the trifling banalities that often lubricate social interactions everywhere else. You show up for tea in Moscow—or anywhere in Russia, really—and within minutes you're diving into questions of history, love, fate, power, art. That's not to say life couldn't be fun, or hilarious, but it was fundamentally treated with consequence.

It was this mixture of sorrow and hilarity that drew me to Dovlatov, a writer whose work can be read as a pained ode to inner freedom, though one that purposefully never takes any sort of brave or clearly demarcated political stance. He participates in society's obligations while also gently mocking them. In *The Compromise*, the narrator manages to defy and subvert the demands of the system by, say, escaping for vodka-soaked jaunts with young women from the provincial party office instead of writing plodding columns extolling the wisdom of Brezhnev's agricultural policy. Though he does write the column in the end: he steals five minutes from his hangover to write a letter in the voice of a milkmaid whom he was supposed to have interviewed but only saw in passing. Dovlatov's antihero nominally follows orders and carries out the will of his higher-ups, who themselves have their own bosses to please, even as he does so in such a louche and half-assed way that it registers as a kind of quiet protest. Over a lunch of booze and sandwiches, he convinces the initially hesitant father of the 400,000th baby to be born in Tallinn—an entirely manufactured statistic—to give his newborn son the rather strange-sounding name "Lembit," after an Estonian folk hero, just as Dovlatov's editors had demanded. At a funeral for a local television luminary, he gives a faux-heartfelt eulogy for a man he has never met, and then realizes it wasn't even the right person anyway: the coffins had been accidentally mixed up at the morgue.

In *The Suitcase*, a series of essays cataloging the jumbled experience of emigration, Dovlatov describes how he once played the juvenile but satisfying prank of hiding the leather shoes of the mayor of Leningrad. Late into an official lunch, fueled with plenty of cognac and champagne, the mayor took off his shoes under the table—Dovlatov then grabbed them with his own feet and maneuvered them into his briefcase. When the mayor was told it was time to go sit on the tribune for the public dedication of a new metro station, he huffed in bewildered terror, then feigned illness and missed the ceremony entirely. It is not exactly a political démarche or a deed worthy of Solzhenitsyn, but it is an act of resistance all the same, the kind that's much more common and recognizable.

My friend Natasha introduced me to her father, Igor Yefimov, a writer and editor who was close to Dovlatov in Leningrad. Yefimov published Dovlatov at his émigré press, Hermitage, after they both arrived in the United States in the late seventies. "In our understanding, dissidents were people who pronounced they knew better than the authorities how things should be, how to rule the country," Yefimov told me. "We didn't believe we knew that. We were simply concerned with speaking and writing how we thought and felt." Dovlatov had an acute eye for tragicomedy, an awareness of human weakness and self-delusion. His prose was the most revelatory guide I could find to the Russia I experienced every day: a place where people were clear-eyed about the state's inefficiency and corruption, but also had no illusions about their own survival mechanisms, the ways in which they were bound up and implicated in the system.

In the 1960s, Dovlatov, a conscript just out of university, was sent to work as a prison-camp guard in the Komi Republic, in the country's remote north. He later described his three years there in a series of letters to Yefimov, which were gathered together in a book called *Zona*, or *The Zone*, Russian slang for the parallel universe of prison life. Dovlatov's overarching impression was that he was sure his position in the Komi camps was no more than an accident of fate: "I just got my doors mixed up, and instead of ending up in the prisoners' barracks, I landed in the army ones." In *The Zone*, Dovlatov writes of how he and the prisoners under his watch "spoke the same criminal slang, sang exactly the same sentimental songs, endured exactly the same privations." In fact, he goes on, emphasizing the point, "we were very similar to each other, and even interchangeable. Almost any prisoner would have been suited to the role of a guard. Almost any guard deserved a prison term." This struck me as the great plea of Dovlatov's writing: to complicate the pose of easy moralizing and to recognize all the incredible and tragicomic ways people make do in whatever system they're stuck with. These compromises and adaptations make us all a little bit complicit, but, for that, entirely human. And this humanity offers a refuge of freedom, however limited or imperfect, in a world that may offer little of it.

At the start of 2012, I moved back to Moscow to work as a journalist, covering Russia for foreign audiences at *The Economist,* and, with time, for *The New Yorker.* In the Western imagination, Russia is a nation held captive by a dictator interested only in his own power and profit—as the story goes, Putin lords over a population of 145 million people, trapping them in a cage welded shut by propaganda and repression. Yet over the course of several years, as I reported on a period of major historical turmoil and change for Russia—street protests the winter I arrived, extravagant preparations for the 2014 Winter Olympics in Sochi, the annexation of Crimea, a standoff with the West over the war in Ukraine, fallout from allegations of meddling and collusion in the 2016 U.S. presidential election, and the combined toll of sanctions and economic crisis—I met ordinary Russians who showed no sign of being somehow held against their will. These were not necessarily enthusiastic Putin supporters, or even people who voted for him. Instead, they treated the Putin state as a given—neither good nor bad, but simply there, like an element in the earth's atmosphere—and then went about constructing their lives around it. Sam Greene, head of the Russia Institute at King's College London, once described the strange balance of "the people's preparedness to see the state as simultaneously dysfunctional and yet legitimate, unjust and yet worthy."

Governments, of course, exist in America and Europe, as do all manner of external structures and constraints that people—myself included—must constantly navigate. The pressure of conformism is universal and ever present, a feature of existing in the world no matter where you find yourself. But the presence of the state and the aura of inevitability of its demands struck me as particularly acute in Russia. One could not live in ignorance or indifference to the urges and caprices of the state; in fact, it was to your advantage to guess what it wanted from you, and to deliver that while also being clever enough to extract some benefit for yourself. This, roughly speaking, is the predicament of Levada's wily man, for whom the state contains both the threat of great hardship and the promise of incomparable opportunity. I came to understand that in Russia, the two forces—state and citizen—speak in dialogue, a conversational timbre often missed by the foreign ear. Gudkov—Levada's onetime student who became a respected sociologist and pollster in his own right—wrote that for many Russians, "the state is not simply a technical apparatus of large-scale administration, but a symbolic institution, embodying and reproducing the basic understandings of human nature." The state takes on almost pantheistic importance: though made by man in his image, it is also an omnipresent force whose power exceeds that of its creator.

In Moscow and in my travels around the country, I met fiercely proud and brilliant men and women—activists, economists, journalists, business owners—who believed the best, if not the only, way to realize their vision was in concord with the state. It was hard to believe they were wrong; nor was I confident I would choose any differently. There was my friend with a graduate degree from Oxford who came back to Moscow to take a job in a state-run think tank, a place where smart young professionals thought up good ideas—half of which were implemented, and the other half of which, those with more worrying political implications, were discarded. I would periodically have lunch with a youth activist who had been unable to resist the offer to take a seat in parliament—where he was quickly told to vote along party lines, as the Kremlin dictated, or risk losing the funding for his youth programs.

For a while, the most fashionable job in Moscow was working on state-funded urban-beautification projects: expanding pedestrian zones, renovating city parks, launching bike-sharing programs, rethinking public transport routes. Such initiatives made the city undeniably more pleasant and humane; with time, similar efforts expanded to other cities around the country. Even in the absence of larger democratic reforms—if anything, Russia's politics tacked in an opposite, unmistakably regressive direction—its cities became more desirable, attractive, and enjoyable places to live. A debate emerged among my friends in Moscow: Is it laudable to lend one's talents and expertise to the state so as to achieve real change on a local level, or does this only help perpetuate an unjust and inefficient system? The question was never really settled, but surfaced time and again, a referendum on the permissibility of compromise that repeated at regular intervals. Does harnessing the resources and power of institutions you ultimately consider malevolent to achieve something good mean the joke is on them, or you? Although the Gulag is a mostly unhelpful metaphor for understanding Putin's Russia, I found myself returning to one thing Ivan Denisovich learned in the camps: if you're stuck inside an unjust system, isn't cheating it a bit here and there for your own purposes an entirely rational, even virtuous, response? Maybe there are no good answers to these questions, an impossibility captured in a Russian saying: *mezhdu dvukh ognyei*—"between two fires"—the condition of being stuck in the middle of two opposing forces bigger than yourself. Making it out the other side is just about the best outcome available.

The more I thought and wrote about the ways people actually live and work in Putin's Russia, the more I realized it was largely impossible to separate them into two camps: the oppressed and the oppressors. Yes, there were obvious victims and those whose resolute, unyielding positions brought them great frustration and hardship; just as there were the unambiguously corrupt and sadistic who used the state's authority merely to line their pockets or who got off on enacting all manner of petty cruelties. But most of the people I encountered were neither. They were strivers, nimble and resourceful, who usually set out with virtuous and thoroughly understandable motives. What fascinated me were the compromises and prevarications required in bringing those initial motives to life, and how, over time, those concessions can change a person and the very rationale that motivated one's actions in the first place.

After Levada's death, Gudkov was named head of the Levada Center. He and I met a number of times in his office on Nikolsky Lane, a bustling pedestrian thoroughfare that runs between Lubyanka Square, home to the iconic edifice made of yellow brick that was the headquarters of the KGB—now the FSB—and the fancy, jewel-box boutiques of a GUM department store. Gudkov is in his early seventies, and exudes an inviting professorial warmth and intelligence; he is unfailingly generous in narrating the ideas of his mentor, Levada, and the conclusions of his own research. As we spoke, he would often leaf through bound notebooks on his desk, pointing at various bits of polling data the center had received over the years. In 2014, for example, after the annexation of Crimea, Gudkov and his colleagues saw a huge spike in the number of Russians who would like to see a full-scale invasion of Ukraine: as many as 75 percent of those surveyed. But almost no one—just 5 or 8 percent—expressed a willingness to bear any real costs for such military adventurism, whether in the form of tightening spending at home on pensions or medicine, or having their sons and husbands sent to fight in Ukraine as soldiers. Gudkov paraphrased the prevailing attitude: "I may support this—but let the bosses take responsibility and pick up the tab." What emerged from the numbers was a portrait of Russian society with a deeply contradictory attitude toward its rulers, and a rather scrambled understanding of its own role and responsibilities—a form of modern-day doublethink that Gudkov chalked up to a "wily" ability to be all things at once. Loyal and disobedient. Aggressive and pitiable. Proud and insecure. "It's been twenty-five years since the collapse of the USSR," Gudkov said, "but the personality type born in that period has proved remarkably stable—a system of consciousness that is easy to manipulate, yet difficult to change."

Levada's idea of the wily man gave a name, and a conceptual framework, to people I saw all around me. I started to recognize such men and women everywhere: the onetime liberal television host who, sensing a change in the political winds, became the country's most bombastic and vile propagator of homophobic and anti-American diatribes; the pitiable yet heroic philanthropist who allows herself to be used in pro-Putin political advertisements, so as to bring in more resources for her children's charity; the human rights activist who learns to become less an antagonist to the state than an ally, in a hope that she can use her proximity to power to help those who have nowhere else to turn. At one point, an acquaintance who had long been a vocal and unshrinking opposition activist took a job with the state television network RT—they promised her a public platform and sizable resources to highlight particular cases of suffering and injustice.

Many of the Russians I began to observe and take note of were driven by an understandable fear of the consequences if they rejected the compromises on offer; others felt the pull of success and recognition and the chance to realize something of genuine personal significance. All those motives felt understandable, and it would be false for me to suggest that in those circumstances, I would never fall under their sway. Of course, the act of compromise could often look unambiguously venal and contemptible, its rewards measured in your *migalka,* a flashing blue siren for your car that indicates official privilege; a free pass from investigators, who close their eyes to corrupt practices at your business while shaking down other entrepreneurs far less corrupt; or the expensive British education for your children, even as you rail in public against the evils of the decadent West. (This is an updated list of the kind cited by Dovlatov, who described the "standard assortment of Central Committee allocations: expensive cold-cuts, caviar, tuna, chocolate-covered marshmallows.") But that was the kind that interested me the least. I was more drawn to those people whose choices seemed understandable and human—efforts rooted in admirable, even noble, ambition, but realizable only by means of Levada's wiliness.

The more I applied this prism to those around me, the less sure I became of how to judge them. Was this blend of guile and nimbleness to be admired or resisted? The end result was far from uniform. Some people muster the cunning and cynicism to extract all manner of benefits and privileges from the state; others are left broken and demoralized. Understanding the impulses behind these compromises, and how they function in practice, promised to unlock the condition and lived experience of Russia in the Putin age. I became convinced that the most edifying, and important, character for journalistic study in Russia is not Putin, but those people whose habits, inclinations, and internal moral calculations elevated Putin to his Kremlin throne and who now perform the small, daily work that, in aggregate, keeps him there.

CHAPTER 1

MASTER OF
CEREMONIES

—

I N THE FINAL DAYS OF 1999, JUST AS HE HAD EACH DECEMBER FOR
several years, Konstantin Ernst prepared to film the presidential
New Year's address. Ernst, then thirty-eight, with a face of cheerful,
perpetual bemusement and a floppy mane of brown hair that nearly
covered his shoulders, is the head of Channel One, the network with
the country's largest reach, a position that grants him the stature of an
unofficial government minister. He is not only the chief producer of
his channel, but also, by extension, the director of the visual style and
aesthetics of the country's political life—at least the part its rulers
wish to transmit to the public. The New Year's address, delivered at
the stroke of midnight, is a way to do exactly that: a way for a Russian leader to impart a sense of narrative to the year past and offer
some guiding clues and symbols for the year to come. The tradition
took shape in the seventies, under Leonid Brezhnev, whose rule
stretched on for so long that his droning, puffy-faced New Year's ad-
dresses all blended together. Gorbachev tried to instill a sense of discipline and purpose in his New Year's appearances, even as, with each
passing year, the country was in a state of slow-motion disintegration.

Boris Yeltsin, who took power in 1991, continued the tradition.
And so, on December 27, 1999, five days before the new millennium, Ernst and a crew from Channel One made their way to the

Kremlin to film Yeltsin's address ahead of time, to have everything ready in advance per long-standing practice. By the late nineties, Yeltsin, once a feisty, charismatic advocate of democratic reform, had entered a spiral of decay of both body and spirit, becoming an enervated shell of his former self. He was still capable of episodic vitality, but was largely weakened and chiefly concerned with leaving office in a way that would keep him and his family safe and immune from prosecution. The country was only a year removed from a devastating financial crash that had led the government to default on its debt and saw the ruble lose 75 percent of its value; at the same time, Russian troops were fighting their second costly war in a decade in Chechnya, a would-be breakaway republic in the Caucasus. Ernst watched as Yeltsin sat in front of a decorated tree in the Kremlin reception hall and spoke a few saccharine words into the camera, the standard appeal to unity and patriotism and the opportunities of the new year—including, as Yeltsin mentioned, the upcoming presidential election in the spring that would determine his successor.

After he finished, as the Channel One crew was packing up, Yeltsin told Ernst that he wasn't satisfied with his address. He said he didn't like the way his words had come out, and he was also feeling hoarse—could they rerecord a new version sometime in the coming days? Ernst said yes, of course, but they should hurry, since there wasn't much time left before the new year. Yeltsin proposed the thirty-first of December; Ernst pleaded for an earlier appointment, reminding him that given Russia's massive size and eleven time zones, the clock strikes midnight in Chukotka—the first place the president's address is aired—when it is still the early afternoon in Moscow. Fine, Yeltsin said, come on New Year's Eve at five in the morning.

Ernst and his crew set up their equipment the night before, and returned before dawn on the morning of the thirty-first. Valentin Yumashev, Yeltsin's son-in-law and confidant, quietly handed Ernst the text of Yeltsin's new address. Ernst tried to contain his shock: Yeltsin was about to announce his resignation, departing the presidency in sync with the close of one millennium and the dawn of another. His successor would be Vladimir Putin, a politician whom most Russians were just getting to know: Putin had risen from bureaucratic obscurity to become head of the FSB, the post-Soviet successor to the KGB, and had been named Yeltsin's prime minister four months earlier. Even as Yeltsin's administration sputtered to a close, he was still capable of the dramatic, unexpected flourish—no one in his government, let alone the country at large, expected him to leave office before the end of his term. Ernst told a production assistant to enter the text into the teleprompter without letting anyone else in on the news. It should come as a surprise to everyone. At ten in the morning, Yeltsin entered the reception hall, took a seat, and began to speak.

"I have taken a decision, one which I pondered long and painfully. I am resigning today, the last day of the departing century," Yeltsin began. He spoke with the labored cadence of a tired man. "Russia should enter the new millennium with new politicians, new faces, new people who are intelligent, strong, and energetic," he said. His speech turned reflective, intimate even, spoken in a language of fallibility that Russians had not seen from their leaders before, and have not seen again. "I want to ask your forgiveness—for the dreams that have not come true, and for the things that seemed easy but turned out to be so excruciatingly difficult. I am asking your forgiveness for failing to justify the hopes of those who believed me when I said that we would leap from the gray, stagnating totalitarian past into a bright, prosperous, and civilized future. I believed in that dream, I believed that we would cover the distance in one leap. We didn't," he said. His physiognomy matched his words: his eyes were narrow and tired, his breathing heavy and full of pained effort. "I am leaving now. I have done everything I could."

Yeltsin finished by rubbing a visible tear from his eye. The air in the room was heavy with emotion. Someone from the Channel One crew started to clap, then another, and soon they had all risen to give Yeltsin a standing ovation. They swarmed around him. The most experienced member of the team was a woman named Kaleria Kislova, a veteran producer, then seventy-three, who had filmed every New Year's address going back to Brezhnev. She walked up to Yeltsin, her face ashen and uncertain, and asked him, "Boris Nikolayevich, how can it be?" He gave her a reassuring hug and said, chuckling, "Here it is, babushka, Saint George's Day." It was a moment of wry humor: Saint George's Day, a holiday in late fall, entered Russian lore during serfdom, as the one time each year when an otherwise indentured peasant was free to move from one baron to another. Yeltsin and the Channel One crew drank champagne, toasting the new year and the import of the scene they had all just shared. Ernst was impressed by the gravity of Yeltsin's decision: he had voluntarily given up power, an essentially unprecedented move in Russia's political history—and, in so doing, had restored in Ernst's mind the image of Yeltsin as a decisive and courageous politician. All the equivocating and sloppiness of the past few years seemed instantly swallowed up by this one moment.

The next order of business was for the Channel One crew to film a New Year's address by Putin, which would air at midnight, after Yeltsin's. Putin's face looked young and taut on camera, a picture of vitality compared to the obviously unwell Yeltsin. "The powers of the head of state have been turned over to me today," Putin said. His tone was serious, reassuring, businesslike. "I assure you that there will be no vacuum of power, not for a minute. I promise you that any attempts to act contrary to the Russian law and constitution will be cut short."

Ernst got into a waiting car and set off with copies of both speeches, Yeltsin's and Putin's. He sped from the Borovitsky Gate, a commanding tower of red brick on the Kremlin's western edge, and rode through the capital with a police escort, blue sirens flashing. He headed toward Ostankino, the sprawling complex of television studios and a 2,000-foot-high broadcast tower that beams out the country's main stations, including Channel One. Once he arrived, Ernst handed over the cassettes and, exactly at noon, gave the order to broadcast Yeltsin's address.

Ernst watched from his perch in the channel's control room. Yeltsin hosted a lunch reception with ministers and generals in the Kremlin's presidential quarters. "The chandeliers, the crystal, the windows—everything glittered with a New Year's glow," Yeltsin remembered later. A television was brought in, and his guests, some of the toughest men in the country, watched the announcement in total silence. Putin's then wife, Lyudmila, was at home and hadn't watched Yeltsin's midday address, which meant she was confused when a friend called her five minutes after it ended to congratulate her. She presumed her friend was offering her a standard New Year's greeting—until the friend explained that Lyudmila's husband had become the acting president of Russia. A news segment on Channel One showed Yeltsin and Putin standing side by side in the Kremlin's presidential office, a ceremonial passing of authority more persuasive than any election campaign event. On their way out, Yeltsin told Putin, "Take care of Russia."

The following morning on Channel One, after Putin's address and the hours-long, heavily kitschy New Year's variety show—as much an annual tradition as a holiday table laden with sweet Sovetskoye Shampanskoye and salads heavy on the mayonnaise—the network cut to news breaking from Chechnya. Overnight, Putin had gone on a surprise trip to visit Russian troop positions. Wearing a fur-trimmed parka, surrounded by military officers, he handed out medals and hunting knives to the assembled soldiers, telling them the war they were fighting was "not just about defending the honor and dignity of the country" but also "about putting an end to the disintegration of Russia."

Ernst found the message compelling, and was happy to broadcast it on his channel. He was worried about separatism in Chechnya spreading elsewhere, that Russia risked falling apart, its institutions of power atrophied and vulnerable. "Surgical intervention was needed," he thought. Ernst had a fatalistic, if imperial, view of history: the fate of all large countries is preordained, and some are doomed to collapse. Yet others may remain whole: "In moments when everything has gone to hell, a person shows up, who might not have known of his mission ahead of time, but who grabs the architecture of the state and holds it together." That was Putin, Ernst felt.

Ernst is a known workaholic, and stayed late into the night at Channel One, overseeing New Year's coverage, an important evening of programming for the network in an ordinary year, all the more so given the extraordinary events of the day. Ernst felt that the symbolism of the moment belied something real, that one era had actually given way to another. The country would have to adjust, to accustom itself to a new set of challenges and rules, and, he hoped, a new horizon of opportunity. What was true for Russia was also true for Channel One. "We would find a new intonation together," Ernst believed.

ERNST WAS BORN IN 1961, the scion of a notable family within the Soviet scientific establishment. His father was a biologist who specialized in animal husbandry, and his father's post atop a research institute afforded young Ernst the best of what late socialism could offer: a roomy Moscow apartment, the best schools, summers at the dacha and camps for other privileged children. Ernst was bright and ambitious, and by the time he was in his twenties, in the mid-1980s, he bristled at the restrictions imposed by the country's decaying gerontocracy. But he also thrived in that system, receiving a doctorate in genetic engineering and his own state laboratory, where he was in charge of a dozen researchers. It was a common story for many in his generation: the sons and daughters of the nomenklatura elite resented and pushed against the constraints imposed by a musty state apparatus, even as it afforded them sterling educations and careers.

From a young age, Ernst was obsessed with film, and he dreamed of becoming a director but, at his father's urging, pursued a scientific career. In 1986, when Ernst was twenty-five, he was offered the rarest of opportunities: a two-year research fellowship at Cambridge University. He turned it down and left his post at a state biology institute. (The institute's director was stunned, and found only one possible explanation: "So, you're marrying an American woman?" he asked Ernst in disbelief.) Turned loose, Ernst floated among the circles of quasi-underground directors and filmmakers that began to appear during perestroika. The big Soviet studios wouldn't give a major project to someone who wasn't part of the officially sanctioned cultural establishment, but new, more marginal forms were available to anyone who could get his hands on an 8mm camera. Ernst shot a music video for a friend, an ironic mash-up of angsty punk concerts in Moscow and footage from Stalin-era choreographed athletic parades. His next assignment was to shoot a concert by Akvarium, the godfathers of perestroika-era rock, who, in 1988, performed together with Dave Stewart from the British pop band Eurythmics in Leningrad.

When Ernst and I met, in a voluminous conference room at Channel One—the space doubles as a screening room, with a large projection screen and a professional sound system—he described those days with vibrating enthusiasm. It's clear that an important part of his self-image is grounded in that period, when he was not an all-powerful television demigod but a scrappy outsider trying to outmaneuver a lumbering system and do something interesting in its cracks—and who couldn't believe his luck in pulling it all off. "I felt like a person who was deceiving everyone," he told me. "The Soviet Union was still in full force—and yet there I was, with no formal education as a director, filming some Western musicians, not to mention my rocker friends, who themselves were banned only two or three years before."

Ernst found work as a director at *Vzglyad,* or *Viewpoint,* a pioneering newsmagazine program that gained a huge following among young and urbane audiences in the late eighties. The show was earnest and curious, talking in matter-of-fact language about topics that, given their lack of coverage elsewhere, seemingly did not exist in Soviet society: corruption within the Communist Party, the new class of perestroika-era millionaires, the failing Soviet war in Afghanistan, the famed dissident Andrei Sakharov. By addressing such topics, *Viewpoint* was performing not merely a journalistic function but also a civic one, leading its viewers to think over questions they hadn't considered before and expanding society's zone of responsibility. Ernst was thrilled to be a part of it. "A small crevice had appeared, and we spent our time trying to expand it further, to discuss what concerned us, and, as it turned out, what concerned everyone," he said.

Viewpoint seemed all the more important for what it was not: everything else on late-Soviet television, a world of ossified ritual, cumbersome and dully predictable. News anchors spoke in what was often called "oak language," a heavy lexicon of bureaucratese and outmoded boosterism that fooled no one. Before *Viewpoint* and simi-

lar programs that followed, the Soviet television viewer was left confused and unmoored: she did not believe the hollow propaganda
shown to her, but she was presented with no alternative way of understanding her life and the world around her.

Alexei Yurchak, a Russian American anthropologist at Berkeley,
in his book on the paradoxes of the era, *Everything Was Forever, Until
It Was No More,* explains how, seeing that Soviet news consumers did
not receive an accurate description of reality from the state and could
not easily access any competing description, "one could conclude
that the late Soviet world became a kind of postmodern universe
where grounding in the real world was no longer possible." Yurchak
relays a telling moment from the sixties, when a number of prominent Russian linguists appealed to the Central Committee to update
a rote phrase repeated during the televised funerals of Soviet digni-
taries. For years, announcers would repeat the same formulation: an
important party figure was always "buried on Red Square by the
Kremlin wall." But, with time, as space in the Kremlin wall became
scarce, high-ranking functionaries were cremated, their urns placed
in crevices inside the wall itself. Soviet viewers could see for themselves that the action shown to them on television did not correspond
with the voice-over. The linguists wanted to fix this incongruity, and
proposed a new standard phrase: "The urn with ashes was placed in
the Kremlin wall." Amazingly, this appeal was rejected; the Central
Committee insisted on keeping the original formulation. So for decades more, Soviet viewers watched one thing happen onscreen while
an anchor described to them another. For the party bosses, the stubborn continuity of ritual was more important than reality itself, even
when viewers could see for themselves the gap between the two.
How could a person not develop a distrust toward just about everything? "Since nothing about the representation of the world was
verifiably true or false, the whole of reality became ungrounded,"
Yurchak writes.

Ernst and the rest of the producers and journalists at *Viewpoint*
wanted to speak about reality as people observed it in their everyday
lives. Making the show was also, quite simply, fun. Ernst saw it as a
way to realize his creative, directorial impulses, while also taking on

the stale "old grandpas" who were running the country into the ground. Ernst told me that he and his colleagues pushed the country to "verbalize things that were impossible to say before, and the fact that such things were being talked about forced people to think about who was to blame." In August 1991, he went to Crimea for summer vacation; he felt a premonition that something was afoot, and came back to Moscow on the eighteenth. The next day, he woke up to see that the regular morning television show had been replaced by *Swan Lake:* a coup was under way, a last-ditch attempt by a cabal of reactionaries to put an end to Gorbachev's perestroika. The crew of *Viewpoint* hid equipment in their apartments and went on air with emergency programming. The coup failed, Gorbachev was reinstated, but the end was near. On December 25, in a televised speech, Gorbachev addressed 290 million Soviet citizens for the last time. The country was no more. "The old system fell apart even before the new system began to work," Gorbachev said. Cameras filmed the Soviet flag being lowered from inside the Kremlin. Years later, Ernst told an interviewer that, compared to *Viewpoint,* perhaps "only Boris Yeltsin himself played a larger role in bringing down the Soviet state."

But when we spoke at Channel One, Ernst was less eager to take credit. He told me that the collapse of the Soviet Union was a serious personal blow, not at all what he wanted or intended. At the time, as a brash *Viewpoint* producer, he was full of disdain for the Communist Party and the out-of-touch mummies who led it, but he had faith in the country itself, and thought that with smarter leaders, it just might manage to survive. The *Viewpoint* team didn't see themselves as political revolutionaries, even if, after the fact, history ended up pushing them in that direction. "When you're taking part in a big historical process, you don't always understand how it will develop down the line," Ernst told me.

Ernst's professional interests were more aesthetic than narrowly political, but in moments of profound transition, the two interests converge. In January 1991, eleven months before the Soviet breakup, he had begun to produce a new show that gave him a chance to indulge his niche, art-house impulses and curiosities. It was called *Matador*—Ernst simply liked the sound of the word—and was unlike anything on television, covering foreign films and cultural oddities with a rough, do-it-yourself quality. Ernst appeared with his long hair and black leather jacket, and ambled around the frame with a wireless microphone—until then, correspondents had either remained behind a desk or locked in place for choreographed stand-up shots. He aired segments on the avant-garde German filmmaker Rainer Werner Fassbinder and the festival of San Fermín in Pamplona. In one episode, he put on a sixties-era American military uniform and narrated the scene from Francis Ford Coppola's *Apocalypse Now* in which U.S. helicopters fire on a Vietcong-held village to the music of Richard Wagner's "Ride of the Valkyries." The show was weird, rough, and captivating—a distillation of Ernst's idiosyncrasies and obsessions. "As always, during any great rupture, cracks and openings appear in the system, which allow just about anyone to enter," he told me. Ernst had slipped in just as the country was in a state of mass bewilderment, in search of new models and points of orientation. They would come, above all, from television.

ERNST WAS AMONG A handful of young television producers and journalists experimenting with new styles and techniques, devising a visual identity for a traumatized and disoriented country. It wasn't just a question of style, but of helping people make sense of unfamiliar surroundings. "The world had changed, values had changed—and people needed signposts," he told me.

In 1995, Ernst produced a series of public service advertisements called "Russian Project," the first attempt to use television to propagate a shared sense of values in post-Soviet Russia. Famous actors appeared in folksy scenes that conveyed elementary lessons: look after your mother, have confidence in yourself. In one, an elderly man walks into a crowded Moscow metro station, where a group of buskers are playing an old-time military march. He stops to listen; the melody brings back the memory of a wartime love affair from long ago. As the music swells, a short tagline appears: "We remember." Ernst produced dozens of minute-long spots. They seemed simple, and they were, but their effect was profound. "People felt lost, like they had been discarded," Ernst told me. "It was important to let them know that not everything in the past was bad, that we still share something in common."

His most beloved project from that time was a show called *Old Songs About Important Things,* a winking, faux-retro musical set on a Soviet collective farm. Popular actors crooned the most beloved tunes from the Soviet songbook. Ernst made the show with a like-minded young director named Leonid Parfyonov. *Old Songs* was postmodernism with a mission: rather than throwing out a century's worth of music and film because the political context in which it was produced had been discredited, Ernst and Parfyonov wanted to reclaim the part of the cultural repertoire that retained its quality and relevance. One plotline borrowed the motifs of *Cossacks of the Kuban,* a popular 1950 film that was initially praised as a high form of socialist realism, and later, when the mood shifted, was discredited for the same reason. Ernst and Parfyonov liberated the film from the baggage of the past, saving and repurposing the bits that still resonated, or were simply a joyful good time. "It's about admitting that there were things that were good, that there is nothing to be ashamed of, and that we don't have any other history," Parfyonov told an interviewer at the time. "What else can we reflect? Why should we struggle with ourselves?"

The series cost a lot to produce—the premiere had a budget of $3 million, an unheard-of sum for a Russian television program—and was hugely popular, cementing the reputations of Ernst and Parfyonov, both then in their early thirties. They became close friends. "We really resembled each other back then, we had a similar understanding of what we wanted to do," Parfyonov told me. They were united by a shared sense that, as he put it, "post-Soviet television needed to do everything differently, to start all over at the beginning. We had to learn again to celebrate New Year's, to talk about history, to figure out which holidays and anniversaries mattered and how to relate to them." They salvaged the best of the Soviet century while unabashedly celebrating the pleasures of the capitalist world that had replaced it.

Ernst had been put in charge of coming up with a plan for new programming at Channel One—then known by the acronym ORT, for Russian Public Television—by its then director, Vlad Listyev, a beloved television host who had been one of the driving forces behind *Viewpoint* in the late eighties. In March 1995, Listyev, who had been running the channel for only five weeks, was shot and killed in the stairwell of his apartment building in Moscow. His murder, never solved, was rumored to be connected to his decision to reevaluate how ads on the network would be bought and sold, potentially depriving a number of gray-market middlemen of a lucrative revenue stream.

In Moscow, Channel One's main shareholder, Boris Berezovsky, a rapacious and power-hungry oligarch with interests in everything from oil to automobiles, proposed that Ernst take over. Ernst resisted; he found Berezovsky distasteful and untrustworthy but agreed to become the channel's chief producer, in charge of its creative output. For Berezovsky, the channel was not a commercial project—at the time, advertising revenue did not cover the costs of running the network—but a political one, a way to make himself indispensable, a kingmaker in waiting.

The opportunity came in 1996, when Channel One joined a united propaganda campaign waged by the country's main television networks in advance of that year's presidential election. The network's news and information programs did everything they could to propel Yeltsin to victory and disparage his revanchist Communist challenger. It was the most unambiguous and sustained information offensive since Soviet days; even if Yeltsin's supporters were guided by the virtuous aim of staving off a Communist revival, they implanted a paternalistic tone into the Russian media landscape, one that would only metastasize with time: We know best, trust us, take your medicine. On the eve of the election, the channel aired an ominous and fear-inducing television spot that ended with a timer counting down to the end of voting. Anna Kachkaeva, a television critic and professor of media studies, saw Ernst a few days after and asked him about the advertisement, which she found rather heavy-handed and manipulative, even if she, too, was rooting for a Yeltsin victory. "From the brainwashers, hoping for your understanding," Ernst answered with a mischievous smile. When I spoke with Kachkaeva about this moment years later, she told me that even as Ernst "retained a sense of hooliganism," he came "to understand what kind of instrument he holds in his hands, that he is a person of the state. He feels this mission as his own."

In October 1999, Ernst agreed to take on the role of general director at Channel One. His relations with Berezovsky, for whom Channel One very much remained a personal plaything, were complicated and often tense. Yet Berezovsky thought of Ernst as a "very sensible, well-educated person," and one with great potential as an administrator. "That all turned out to be true," Berezovsky remembered years later. "But, as subsequent events showed, he has no real political position. That would be well and good in a stable democracy, but absolutely dangerous in a transition to a totalitarian regime."

Parfyonov told me that, as he saw it, Ernst's own impulses —his "drive"—stayed the same, but the surrounding environment changed, and would change again several times over in the years to come. Parfyonov prized his independence, which left him with ever-fewer opportunities on federal airwaves; Ernst's instincts pushed him in the opposite direction. "Kostya wanted to be both an artist and a creative director," Parfyonov said. "But it would prove impossible to be a creative director without serving the state in one way or another."

As the Yeltsin era came to a close, Channel One boosted the image of Putin and built him up as an inevitable successor, while relentlessly attacking others from the political elite who sought the presidency. Putin was shown as a de facto commander in chief, overseeing military operations in Chechnya; his rivals were presented as infirm, corrupt, even murderous. Putin's poll numbers rose by four or five points a week. He went from an unknown entity to the most popular political figure in the country. In a sign of the fluidity between the two spheres of power, a recently departed director general of Channel One became the deputy manager of Putin's election campaign, privately dubbed "Project Putin" by its organizers. In a way, it was a repeat of 1996, when television spurred on Yeltsin's reelection and, in so doing, became aware of its own power. But this in fact was something new: the invention of a candidate from thin air, a television phenomenon from the very start. Fears of terrorism and the renewed outbreak of fighting in Chechnya consolidated support around Putin. The culminating episode was Yeltsin's New Year's speech.

Channel One was a dutiful cheerleader in the months that followed, as Putin easily won his first presidential election. Ernst began the project of inventing a visual language for the Putin era from the moment of Putin's inauguration that May. He proposed the ceremony be moved from the State Kremlin Palace, a modernist, glass-and-concrete box built in the fifties to host party congresses, to St. Andrew Hall, an ornate Tsarist throne room that provided a grand and imperial spectacle.

Perhaps the most decisive single episode in Channel One's modern history came three months later, when the Russian nuclear submarine *Kursk* disappeared on a training exercise in the Barents Sea. A torpedo exploded in its hatch, sending the vessel and its crew of 118 men to the seafloor. Most were killed instantly, but twenty-three survived, and barricaded themselves in a rear compartment to wait for rescue. It never came. Russia initially refused foreign help. The Russian navy issued an ever-changing stream of misinformation; Putin himself remained on vacation on the Black Sea. Nine days later, Norwegian deep-sea divers finally opened the hatch and found the crew dead.

By then, Berezovsky, who had backed Putin and even claimed credit for engineering his ascent to the presidency, had fallen out with him. He unleashed his network. Channel One hammered away at the Kremlin's incompetence and compared its handling of the *Kursk* disaster to the fumbling response to Chernobyl in 1986. (The country's other main networks were equally scathing and critical in their coverage of the Kremlin's response to the *Kursk*.) One evening, a segment on Channel One's flagship news program broadcast a moving scene. Journalists were barred from visiting the *Kursk* launching site and interviewing family members, but a *VESTI* reporter managed to track down two young widows of men on the submarine. The women were crying, desperate with anger and fear, and subjected the government to scathing criticism. Putin was livid—not so much at the incident itself but at its appearance on television, that coverage was guided by something other than loyalty to state interests. He and his advisors in the Kremlin believed such newsreels were manufactured, or at least grossly manipulated, as part of an information war being waged by Berezovsky. When Putin himself finally traveled to the closed military city where the *Kursk* was based to address the bereaved relatives, he lashed out at the media. "Television? They're lying! Lying! Lying!"

Ernst, undercutting his own boss, encouraged this view, signaling to Kremlin officials that Berezovsky was manipulating coverage for his own political reasons. What's more, according to reports in the Russian press, Ernst confirmed one of the more noxious conspiracy theories raised by Putin in private: that a number of the grieving women shown on television were fakes, just a bunch of cheap actresses, or even prostitutes, paid to cry and shout. Ernst adamantly denies he ever told his interlocutors in the Kremlin any such thing. The entire *Kursk* episode—the accident itself, and the state's response—remains murky, shrouded by a cover-up at the time and extensive mythmaking in the years since. If anything, Ernst's role was reactive. "He followed events, he didn't make them," said Sergey Dorenko, a Channel One host who was particularly savage in his treatment of the Kremlin's handling of the *Kursk* disaster. Ernst eventually fired Dorenko. "But he was very collegial," Dorenko told me. As he remembers, Ernst took him to a quiet corner of his office and said, "Sorry, it's a forced situation, nothing personal."

The Kremlin was intent on ridding itself of Berezovsky's influence. "The concert is over," Putin's chief of staff, Alexander Voloshin, told Berezovsky, ordering him to unload his shares in the channel. Berezovsky tried lobbying Putin directly, but heard the same thing: a channel with the capacity to reach up to 98 percent of Russian households would not be allowed to remain under Berezovsky's control. If he didn't sell, he would meet the same fate as another media titan who tried to take on the Kremlin, Vladimir Gusinsky, who faced criminal prosecutions and was forced to hand over his channel, NTV, and flee the country. Even as those around Putin treated Berezovsky with growing scorn and impatience, they held Ernst in great esteem. "He is a very talented person," Voloshin said of Ernst at a court hearing, years later. "All we had to do was save him from Berezovsky's influence." When I spoke to Ernst, he seemed to echo that version. Berezovsky used the *Kursk* disaster to try to pressure Putin, he told me. On Berezovsky's command, the channel's news staff were "waging some kind of political battle rather than doing reporting work," he said. Ernst fired a number of Channel One managers—on his own initiative, or at the winking suggestion of the Kremlin, or a combination of the two—and ended up in direct conflict with Berezovsky.

Ernst, of course, had picked the winning side. Under duress, Berezovsky sold his stake in Channel One; before long, he wound up in London, where he hardened into a strident, emotive, and not always reliable critic of Putin. (He died, apparently of suicide, at his mansion outside London in 2013.) Ernst seemed glad to be rid of him, and became spiteful of the man who promoted him to the top of the Russian television universe. Once, a Channel One correspondent sent footage from a press conference Berezovsky held in the West. Ernst declined to air it, saying, "Don't send me any more of his shit." He had always bridled under Berezovsky, and now that Berezovsky was the Kremlin's open enemy, Ernst could indulge his distaste as much as he liked.

Berezovsky, for all his increasingly curdled animus toward Putin, never managed to develop a sharp hatred of Ernst. From his exile, Berezovsky reflected on their time together at Channel One, and its pained denouement. "Ernst could not exist without relying on the state," he told the weekly magazine of *Kommersant,* a Moscow paper. "He made a choice not so much against me personally but *for* Putin. It was a choice in favor of power."

ERNST NOW CONTROLLED the largest platform in the country. He could realize his creative vision, a worldview that aspires to a certain cosmopolitan savviness while ultimately remaining subservient to the state and its needs. In speaking with me, Ernst called himself a "liberal-minded patriot," and said that over the political system's

many fluctuations, "my attitude toward the state has never changed."
As Ernst understands it, he has always felt part of his country, rooting for it and wanting it to be the best version of itself. He proudly
calls himself a *gosudarstvennik*—a statist—a term used by many in
Russia's ruling class, including Putin, to describe themselves. A *gosudarstvennik* finds virtue and inherent legitimacy in the state itself; it is
a timeless and self-evidently righteous entity, and its interests come
first. "It would be strange," Ernst once told me, "if a channel that
belonged to the state were to express an anti-government point of
view."

As the Putin age took shape, Ernst grew into the role of the era's
premier visual stylist. With his guidance, Putin's subsequent inaugu-
rations became even more highly produced affairs, involving several
hundred cameramen and producers, and more than twenty-five cameras, several of them mounted on helicopters and overhead tracking
cranes—the sort of technical complexity a channel might deploy for
the Super Bowl. Another Ernst innovation was reimagining the annual Victory Day parade, on May 9, a celebration of the defeat of
Nazi Germany. The parade had long functioned as a display of imperial might, but for many years had remained staid and formulaic;
Ernst gave it a soaring and decidedly modern cast, a spectacle of
power filmed with the camera angles and production values of an action movie. Sweeping shots captured the pageantry on Red Square
from above; Ernst put cameras in the cockpits of bomber planes and
broadcast scenes reminiscent of *Top Gun*.

"For Ernst, a sense of immense visual scale was always important,"
said Andrei Boltenko, a producer and director who worked with him
at Channel One. Boltenko explained that in the early 2000s, he and
Ernst, along with the rest of the channel's leadership, felt that Russia
was full of hope, a hope the population saw manifest in the state.
Viewers wanted a story of resurgence—both their own and the
country's—fed back to them on the air. "It was synchronous," Boltenko told me. "The scale of the television form matched the scale of
belief in the state."

The first Putin call-in show aired in December 2001, and has appeared nearly every year since. The format resembles a televised mar-

athon. Putin fields questions from factory workers in the Urals and concerned mothers in the Far East, often for more than four hours. Inevitably, he comes off as sagacious and omnipotent, a mortal raised to divine rank. Ernst told me that when he first introduced the idea to Putin, "He listened and said, 'That's interesting.'" In one moment, Putin can promise a new children's playground; in the next, he might conjure up months of withheld salaries for laborers building a new cosmodrome. Ernst acknowledged that the show is a particularly Russian phenomenon: "The Russian mentality stipulates that the leader of the country, no matter how this person is called—president or tsar, prime minister or general secretary of the Communist Party—is seen to answer for everything, that there is one person who symbolizes the entire state."

Throughout the early 2000s, stage-managed programs like the call-in show blurred with ostensibly factual news and information programming. It was all of a piece: building the myth of Putin as a quasi-sacred figure, in a realm above politics, and shunning any unwelcome developments that complicate that narrative. A news segment on Channel One from January 2004, two months before that year's presidential election, was typical. The occasion for the report was Orthodox Christmas. It opens with a fairy-tale scene: fields of pristine, crisp snow surround a small church, which is lit by soft, artfully placed offscreen spotlights. From the distance, a silhouette appears: Putin. He walks through the white snow, toward the church, where he is greeted by an Orthodox priest with a long beard. The two go inside, welcomed by a crowd of believers, their faces glowing with the joy of true faith. It is an emotive scene, far more compelling than a news anchor reading into the camera, or, for that matter, a televised debate—a form Putin avoids every election cycle. Who needs the usual campaign coverage when the country's main television network is airing such composed and beautiful gems?

Ernst's Channel One took pains to avoid the sins, as the Kremlin understood them, of Berezovsky and the *Kursk* disaster. It aired little breaking news, lest something uncomfortable happen, and was supremely careful in how it presented tragedy, and in what doses. In September 2004, less than a year after the scene of Putin at Christmas services, Chechen terrorists seized an entire school in the city of Beslan, in the North Caucasus. Officials deliberately misstated the number of hostages, claiming there were just 354 people held at the school, when in fact there were more than a thousand. Channel One, along with other state channels, cited the lower number. The terrorists, watching news coverage on a television in the teachers' room, became even more enraged by this falsehood.

On the third day of the standoff, a series of blasts were heard at the school, followed by a frenzy of shooting and mayhem. Foreign networks covered events live. Channel One interrupted its programming for ten minutes to cut to Beslan, then quickly returned to a Brazilian soap opera called *Women in Love*. Fighting between terrorists and Russian special forces lasted for hours and left more than three hundred people dead, most of them children. That evening, as gunfire was still erupting inside the school, Channel One showed the American action movie *Die Hard*. Afterward, Ernst defended his coverage of the siege. "The main task of television is to mobilize the country. . . . Russia needs consolidation," he told the Russian British journalist Arkady Ostrovsky. "Our task number two is to inform the country about what is going on."

Even as Channel One faithfully transmits the Kremlin's line, it does so with a measure of professionalism and restraint, at least compared to its two main peers and competitors on Russian television: Rossiya, the country's second channel, wholly owned by the state; and NTV, now owned by Gazprom-Media, a holding company with ties to Yury Kovalchuk, a banker close to Putin. Although all three networks present Putin as a leader with no challenger or equal, the propaganda offerings on Rossiya and NTV tend to be cruder and more grotesque, often indulging in tragicomic excess. Rossiya, for example, is home to figures like Arkady Mamontov, who suggested that the protest-art collective Pussy Riot was an American plot to corrupt Russian young people, and that a meteor that struck central Russia in 2013 was punishment for the sins of homosexuals. Dmitry Kiselev, the most extravagantly foul personality on all of Russian television, hosts a weekly show on Rossiya, where he expounds on everything from homosexuality ("Banning gays from distributing propaganda to children is not enough. I think they should be banned from donating blood or sperm, and if they die in a car crash, their hearts should be burnt or buried in the ground as unsuitable for the continuation of life") to the arms race (Russia is the only country that can turn the United States into "radioactive dust") and the U.S. electoral process (the 2016 election campaign was so "revoltingly foul that there is real disgust at the fact" that they "still talk of democracy in America"). NTV, meanwhile, specializes in true-crime programs and breathless, darkly conspiratorial pseudo-documentaries—including several aimed at discrediting the country's opposition by linking it to vague foreign plots. The regular use of hidden-camera footage and ambush interviews suggests a degree of cooperation between NTV and the Russian security services.

Such offerings rarely appear on Channel One—not out of some deep ideological opposition felt by Ernst, but simply because they do not correspond to his artistic vision of what is beautiful and worthy. "I actually don't think he's a liberal," said Nikolay Kartozia, a television producer who has known Ernst for years and has made a number of documentaries for Channel One. "But for sure he is an intellectual and an aesthete." This reputation has allowed Ernst to remain friends with many figures from the ever-shrinking world of independent, liberal-minded Russian media, and, at the same time, has made him a target of envy and suspicion, disliked by his rivals at Rossiya and NTV. "People covered in mud don't like to see someone a little less dirty than themselves," said Vera Krichevskaya, an independent documentary filmmaker who has worked on television projects over the last two decades.

One day, I had lunch at a stylish Moscow café with Yulia Pankratova, who was a news anchor on Channel One from 2006 to 2013. She is in her early forties, with a warm smile and close-cropped hair. After leaving Channel One, she launched an online video series that covers museum exhibitions and cultural events. Pankratova told me that during her time at Channel One, its employees had prided themselves on operating with "taste and style," a collective sense that "you can do propaganda, but you can't let yourself fall below a certain level." Her news program had a measure of elegance and restraint—

even as it quite regularly spent thirty minutes out of forty showing Putin and his meetings with ministers, factory bosses, ambassadors, and whatever other supporting characters were serving as props that day. Pankratova would play little games of quiet rebellion, like stretching out the Putin segments to comic length, until they looked plainly satirical, and her producer would implore her to shorten them; the next day, ostensibly following orders, she would speed through the Putin-related news with great haste, prompting another, opposite complaint from the show's producer. It was childish, and ultimately ineffectual, but allowed Pankratova to feel as though she retained a degree of individuality, a sliver of herself.

Pankratova told me of the day, in October 2006, when Anna Politkovskaya, the famed investigative journalist, was shot dead in the stairwell of her Moscow apartment building. Pankratova wanted to lead the news with the killing. She understood the topic was "not necessarily forbidden—but I had to talk with someone first." It was a weekend, and none of the top bosses were around. She called her direct supervisor, the head of news, and asked whether she could mention the killing. He said he would call her back. A few minutes later, he did, and said yes. She presumed he had consulted with Ernst. But other times she asked and was told no, like in 2010, when a series of terrorist bombings hit the Moscow metro, leaving forty people dead during morning rush hour. She was forbidden to talk about the attacks in her morning news bulletin; Channel One addressed them only later in the day, presumably once the major networks had had a chance to coordinate their coverage and tone with the Kremlin. But she also knew when not to even try. Pankratova told me that later in her tenure, she didn't even think to inquire whether she could mention protests organized by Alexei Navalny, an anti-corruption activist who emerged as the country's leading opposition politician. "Let's say I'm driving to work, and hear on the radio that Navalny organized a protest the day before—I know we are not going to air this news, and that's that," she told me. "I don't go to my editors to ask. I have no desire to talk with them about this. What would be the point?"

Pankratova was meant to intuit the rules rather than have them spelled out. That would be impossible, anyway. The calculus is always changing, depending on the exact circumstances and the political mood of the day. People inside the system are supposed to make the right call on their own, relying on intuition and guesswork and, when in doubt, always erring on the side of caution.

That goes for Ernst even more so. Part of his job, and what makes him good at it, is that he is sensitive to those fluctuations, able to pick up on shifts in the official mood and pass them along to his staff at the channel, oftentimes so subtly that no one even notices that any messages are being transmitted at all. Ernst is in regular, daily contact with various officials in the Kremlin, but, as he told me, "No one ever tells you: 'Don't show Navalny, don't use his name.'" Instead, Ernst explained, "Such messages aren't conveyed with words. After all, federal television channels are run by people who aren't stupid."

THE PASSIONS OF A twentysomething aspiring filmmaker still live within Ernst, along with unabashed ambition, his desire for social reach on a mass scale. "The news is momentary and ephemeral," he told me. "But the artistic realm, this is something deeper; it can stay in people's minds forever." Ernst also told me that while his interlocutors in the Kremlin pay close attention to Channel One's news coverage, they leave him alone to make creative series and films with virtually no oversight. "We have some domains that the authorities consider important, but also have other domains they don't notice at all," he said.

Over the years, Ernst has brought a number of television genres to Russia, including the *American Idol*–style singing competition (*The Voice*), the *Jerry Springer*–like daytime chat show (*Let Them Talk*), and the late-night talk show (*Evening Urgant*). Ivan Urgant is forty-one years old, suave, and gently mischievous. On his nightly program, he interviews celebrities and cultural figures while sneaking in some of the more subtle and biting political satire found on state television— even if delivered in ultimately ineffectual form, like sarcastically calling a governor arrested for outsize corruption a Russian "Robin Hood." Urgant's episodic forays into political commentary may be harmless, but the fact that they exist at all requires Ernst's personal imprimatur. "Believe me," a person familiar with the channel told me, "each and every political joke on Urgant's show, no matter how toothless, must have Ernst's signature behind it."

In 2004, Ernst coproduced the science-fiction thriller *Night Watch*, the first big-budget, Hollywood-style production made in Russia after the implosion of the Soviet film industry. Based on a popular Russian fantasy novel, the film is set in a recognizable, modern-day version of Moscow—except that, after dark, some people lead parallel lives as vampires and shape-shifters and witches who practice black magic. This nighttime underworld is populated by "dark" and "light" forces, who do gruesome battle with one another. (An American critic who saw the film described its aesthetic as "Dostoevsky, Roger Corman, and a Trent Reznor video all walk into a bar.") *Night Watch* set box office records in Russia, earning $16 million in movie theaters, a sum made more impressive by the fact that the film outperformed the latest Lord of the Rings movie showing in Russia at the same time. *Night Watch* proved that Russian studios could wrest back domestic audiences from Hollywood, and, what's more, compete on the global market: Fox Searchlight acquired *Night Watch* and showed it in over forty countries.

When the film was released in New York and London, Ernst spent a lot of time in interviews clarifying that the "light" and "dark" forces in the film don't neatly correspond to good and bad, as most Western critics and viewers assumed. The "dark" characters, Ernst explained, are in fact free: "Free from obligation, free in the sense of personal fulfillment. They do what they want." The "light" ones, however, are squelched and frustrated, "held back by a huge amount of responsibility and ideas about how they should behave in regard to others." Ernst was clearly sympathetic to the honesty and forthrightness of the "dark" side. In the film, a little boy chooses to join the "dark" side and tells his father, who is one of the "light" ones, "You are no better than the dark. You are even worse. You lie and pretend to be good." If *Night Watch* is a loud, headache-inducing special-effects thriller, it is also a morality play for Russia's post-Soviet transition, when the country moved from the constraints of the ersatz and suffocating "light" side to the unconstrained "dark" world. The dark world may be scary, but it's real and honest in a kind of Hobbesian way. People think they are going to the movies to be entertained, Ernst said after *Night Watch*'s release, but "under the guise of entertainment, they are sold certain codes of conduct, which allow them to position themselves in reality more precisely."

Over the years, as Ernst shepherded along mainstream successes like *Night Watch*, he also championed shows far edgier than had previously appeared on Russian state airwaves. In 2010, a controversy erupted over *The School*, a Channel One series on teenage life made by Valeriya Gai Germanika, a young female director with a punk, counterculture style. She filmed the series in a real Moscow school, giving it a documentary edge; its characters drink beer, smoke cigarettes, insult their teachers, and terrorize one another. It was simultaneously hailed as a raw, uncomfortable portal into the lives of Russian young people, and decried as a morally subversive provocation. In 2013, during a particularly acute moment of conservative revanche in Russia's politics—the country's parliament had just passed a bill outlawing so-called homosexual propaganda—Channel One aired a twelve-part series called *Ottepel*, or *Thaw*. It was set in the Khrushchev years of the early sixties, when the Soviet Union was going through a short-lived social and political opening. The show found a large audience and was well received as an exploration of the questions of compromise, individual responsibility, and the stifling of artistic talent in an authoritarian system. In the penultimate episode, one of the main characters, a thoughtful man with whom viewers are meant to sympathize, is revealed to be gay.

Ernst has also commissioned documentaries on subjects that would be otherwise ignored on Russia's federal airwaves, or at least not treated with the bracing directness Channel One gives them. There was one on Yevgeny Yevtushenko, the famed poet of the 1960s generation, who gave lyrical voice to the crimes of Stalinism while managing to coexist with the Soviet system; another told the story of Babi Yar, the Nazi-led massacre of thirty thousand Jews outside Kyiv in 1941, a horror the Soviet leadership paid little attention to for decades. Nearly everyone I spoke to in the Moscow media scene, even those with liberal sympathies who otherwise hold their noses at Channel One, praised a film shown on the network in 2012 called *Anton's Right Here*, about an autistic teenager living in a dreary provincial town. Autism is given little attention in Russian society—stigma and discomfort from the Soviet era remain—but the film treats Anton with a degree of humanity and dignity seen nowhere else on Russian television.

Ernst has retained his *Matador*-period taste for the cultish, buying the rights to American programs like *Californication, House of Cards,* and *Mad Men.* Four days before Ernst turned fifty, in 2011, Putin came to the channel's headquarters to congratulate him. They had tea and dessert with two dozen Channel One staffers; Putin offered some words of praise and congratulations. "I want to thank you all," he said. "You are a truly potent factory for making this very interesting intellectual product—a very necessary and beneficial one." Ernst may well have prepared a sly present for himself. The night of his birthday, Channel One aired the first Russian showing of *Gonzo,* Alex Gibney's documentary about Hunter S. Thompson. It must have been an odd experience for most of the network's viewers—a strange swerve from the channel's middlebrow programming—but a typical gesture for Ernst, the hybrid auteur and bureaucrat. Arina Borodina, a media critic in Moscow, tried to sum up Ernst's worldview. "He's daring by nature, he likes to take risks," she told me. "He doesn't grovel to power—but, at the same time, he's a Putinist, he's sincerely very loyal to him." (What's more, Borodina added, only Ernst can give the Kremlin the kind of beauty—sumptuous and regal—that it wants reflected on the country's television screens.)

Perhaps no episode speaks as clearly to the duality in Ernst's personality as the decision, in 2017, to air the third season of *Fargo,* the quirky, black-comedy American miniseries, in a late-night slot on Channel One. What other Russian television boss would ever think to buy the rights to the show, or even know of its existence? However, a character's musings that "Putin's done some great things with Russia. You just have to know which palms to grease" was dubbed on Channel One to refer to North Korea. Another character in the original version speaks of Putin in the context of "untruth" as a weapon:

"The truth is whatever he says it is." Channel One kept the short monologue on truth and untruth while omitting any mention of Putin. The whole story struck me as containing the entirety of Ernst: he had the requisite eye and sophistication to enjoy a show like *Fargo* and want to air it on his channel, but the wherewithal and smarts to know he should do so without allowing a critical word against Putin to slip in.

ERNST CAN SEEM A lonely figure in the world of Russian television. He is too loyal, too implicated in all manner of Kremlin intrigues to be fully accepted by the country's liberal intelligentsia, who are skeptical, if not hostile, to the Putin state, and certainly wary of such proximity to it. Yet the Russian political class, for its part, does not quite see Ernst as one of its own; his tastes are too esoteric and idiosyncratic. Those in the Kremlin's orbit do not doubt his fundamental loyalty, but they can be dumbfounded by his fascination with German art-house cinema or underground samizdat literature from the seventies and eighties. Some years ago, Oleg Kashin, an independent political columnist, wrote a fanciful memoir in Ernst's voice for the weekly magazine of *Kommersant*. Looking back from some point in the distant future, Kashin's Ernst writes, "This is what no one ever wanted to understand, that I, controlling my empire, always remained on my own. I made all decisions alone and always carried my responsibilities alone: political, artistic, financial."

Ernst masks this solitude well. It may be his greatest skill: seeming natural and comfortable in every setting, able to talk with equal fluency in the languages of an obsessive cinephile or imperious state minister. "He knows how to seem one of the gang everywhere," said Kartozia, the producer who is friendly with Ernst. I met Kartozia at the Moscow offices of Friday, a midsize entertainment channel that he launched and now heads. It became impossible long ago to do real political journalism on television, he told me, so he decided to focus on projects he enjoys—namely lifestyle and comedy and reality programming. Of Ernst, he said, "You can spend three hours talking with him, and you'll see you have so much in common, you'll be sure you're from the same circle. I have the sense it works quite the same in the Kremlin."

Ernst is a regular visitor to the Kremlin's weekly planning meetings for media bosses. The meetings are closed, and what happens at them is the subject of much speculation and mythmaking. Presumably, Putin's advisors explain the agenda of the moment and how it should be covered on state airwaves, and television heads have a chance to gauge how well their programming matches the official mood. Kachkaeva, the critic and media studies professor, who keeps in periodic touch with Ernst, told me that in their chats the subject of Ernst's dealings with people at the top remains taboo: "He hints at such conversations, but never tells details, never talks about what is asked of him."

When I asked Ernst himself about his relations with Kremlin officials, he similarly demurred, and tried to depict the weekly planning meetings as a perfunctory measure, a question of logistics and administration. "It's a chance for people to talk," he said. "They might tell us: 'Here is the president's schedule,' or some other upcoming events. Or maybe the government is planning to impose a new tax, or raise the pension age, and it's necessary to explain this, why it is happening. They can suggest experts who can go on television for this or that topic. It's informative for me, for the channel."

Ernst's presence at the Kremlin is obviously about much more than that. As Borodina, the media critic, told me, "It's a ritual, a formality—and one that's probably more important for them than him." It's expected that he will show up and demonstrate that he belongs, that he will till the plot entrusted to him, as Borodina put it. But, she went on, "it's useful for everyone to compare clocks, as it were. For Ernst, visits to the Kremlin are as much an essential part of the job as running the channel itself."

Among the producers and correspondents at Channel One, the Kremlin meetings are known as going "behind the ramparts"—a reference to the spiky peaks atop the Kremlin walls—where everything is at once opaque and deeply significant. It is evident to the channel's staff that Ernst and other top television bosses are given loose instructions, perhaps only vague hints and signals. "Nobody comes back from those meetings and says, 'Now we have to do this or that,'" Pankratova, the former news anchor, explained. The Kremlin's wishes for the channel are manifest in much subtler ways. "Maybe later that afternoon you see the top editor for a particular show call over one of the hosts to say something, to give some instructions," she told me. "Or maybe you notice that a certain Russian region suddenly gets more coverage, that out of nowhere there are news pieces about this place, or that topic."

Vladimir Pozner, a storied figure in Russian media—he got his start as the singular, go-to television spokesman for the Soviet Union in the United States in the seventies and eighties—has hosted a weekly Channel One interview show for the last decade. Guests have ranged from Gorbachev to Hillary Clinton. Pozner speaks fluent English and is a kind of throwback Americanophile, in thrall to cigars and baseball and Carnegie Hall. His sensibilities lean liberal, or at least erudite and cosmopolitan, and he freely transmits his own worldview on air while carefully observing the overall rules and limits of the system. When he and Ernst were initially discussing the format of Pozner's show, Pozner asked Ernst to clarify who could be interviewed and who couldn't, to settle the question once and for all and to avoid repeated fighting over individual guests. "I'm a grown-up, I understand there are probably some people I can't invite," Pozner once explained. They came up with a list, around ten people in all, according to Pozner. (In interviews, Pozner regularly says that he agreed to keep the individuals' names secret, but he speaks openly about the fact of the list itself.)

Ernst was no more forthcoming with me. "There is simply an understanding that some people are not worth putting on air, whether it's because they are too radical, or, in the view of the channel, don't merit the attention," he said. That position is born out of protective loyalty to the state, but also out of personal self-interest. "If a person stages a provocation on a live broadcast, it's you, not them, who is going to answer for it," he explained.

One touchy subject that is rarely mentioned in the Russian press is the lives of Putin's daughters. In 2015, it was revealed that Katerina, at the age of twenty-nine, was quietly appointed to head a $1.7 billion science and technology hub connected to Moscow State University. She was also married to the son of one of Putin's oldest confidants (the two have since divorced). Shortly after the wedding, Katerina's husband got a billion-dollar loan from another member of Putin's inner circle to buy shares in a large petrochemical company, a stake now worth several billion dollars. But none of this would ever be discussed on Channel One. "Holding back information that, say, a water main had broken somewhere and people risked drinking unclean water—this would be a crime," Ernst told me. "But not discussing Putin's daughters, that's totally fine, society is in no way put in danger by this." Ernst acknowledged that viewers of Channel One may get less than a full picture of the world—but the omissions are essentially irrelevant. "People will always find out what is genuinely important," he said. "And about what is not so important, well, maybe not." The border between the two is determined, of course, by Ernst. He may receive some episodic hints and nods from above, but on the whole he can navigate those questions just fine on his own.

Channel One's historical legacy, and continued profile, means that nearly every Kremlin official, government minister, and security service chief thinks of the channel as somehow his or her own; each considers Ernst obligated to broadcast whatever schlock, spin, or clumsily staged footage is given to him. Some of it he rejects, some he puts on air. Channel One shows a lot of what Ernst calls "parquet"—after the wooden floors in government offices—which shows seated meetings in which some minister or governor reads out a report to Putin or another top official. It's an entirely uninteresting format, but it appears nearly every day on Ernst's channel. "You know, there is an expression," he told me. "Sometimes it's easier to give in than explain why you don't want to." The saying is most often used in regard to women and unwelcome sexual advances.

Even as the demands of the position pulled him ever closer to the rigidity and uniformity of the state, Ernst tried, at least in his own head, to retain his own sense of impudence and daring. His friendship with Parfyonov continued. In the early 2000s, after the state took over NTV, where Parfyonov was among the most beloved hosts, he was fired from the channel and ended up on the margins of federal television. Parfyonov was not an opposition figure, but his stubborn insistence on a certain freethinking approach to his work made him seem a threat, or at least an unwelcome presence, to those in power.

Channel One, thanks to Ernst alone, was the only place on state airwaves that would commission anything at all from Parfyonov. "It took a lot of strength, and nerves, to keep him on the air," Ernst told me. At one point, Ernst thought he could arrange a regular job for Parfyonov at Channel One, as the cohost of a talk show with Pozner. They had Putin's approval, but then Ernst's rivals at Rossiya and NTV intervened and got Putin to change his mind. Word came down from on high that the show wasn't going to happen, and that was that.

Still, Parfyonov continued to produce the odd program here and there for Channel One. They were studiously apolitical, historical documentaries on subjects ranging from the Russo-Turkish War of 1877 to a stolen Rubens painting. One film unearthed the life of Vladimir Zworykin, a scientist and inventor born in the Russian Empire in 1889 who emigrated to America after the revolution; in the 1920s, as a researcher at the Westinghouse laboratories in Pittsburgh, Zworykin came up with the cathode-ray technology that made modern television possible. (With great effort and persistence, Ernst was able to track down and import Zworykin's first prototype color television, made in the fifties; when it arrived, he and Parfyonov unwrapped the large package like giddy children on Christmas. It is now displayed in the conference room outside Ernst's office at Channel One.)

For the 200th birthday of Nikolai Gogol, who forged a new style of Russian literature in the 1840s, Parfyonov made a two-part documentary for Channel One, rich in computer effects and phantasmagoric surrealism. But as Parfyonov knew, even when working on anodyne subjects like nineteenth-century authors, he remained suspect in the eyes of the Kremlin, and getting him on air was bound to be a delicate operation for Ernst. "I surmise, though I never discussed this with him, that when I told him, say, 'I want to do a film about Gogol,' he warned whomever he needs to in the Kremlin ahead of time, just so there wouldn't be any problems later," Parfyonov told me. As he imagines it, Ernst didn't exactly ask for approval, but "maybe had a word or two."

In 2010, Ernst helped put together a new television prize named after Vlad Listyev, whose short-lived tenure as head of Channel One had ended with his murder a decade before. Ernst arranged for Parfyonov to be its inaugural recipient. Dozens of guests, television luminaries and powerful cultural figures in dark suits and evening dresses, sat at tables spread out in a vast hall. Ernst himself was sitting ten feet from the stage. Parfyonov was visibly nervous when he started to read his acceptance speech from the podium. He took an awkward sip of water and unfolded a sheet of paper. In today's Russia, he said, mournfully, a correspondent on state television ultimately serves "his boss's bosses." He continued, "Such a correspondent is no longer a journalist but, rather, a state official following the logic of service and subordination." He declared that it had become impossible for a television reporter to say anything unscripted or unwelcome about the country's political leaders, Putin especially. The ruling elite, like the politburo of old, were "treated like the dearly departed." He quoted a Russian axiom: "Speak well of them or do not speak of them at all." The audience sat mute and stone-faced.

Near the end of his address, Parfyonov said, "Not being a hero myself, I cannot demand heroic deeds from others. But the least we can do is call things by their names." Russian television was deeply sick, corrupted by its servile relationship to power. It had become skilled at "providing thrills, fascination, entertainment and at making us laugh," Parfyonov said. "It hardly deserves the title of a civic, social, and political institution." Many in attendance saw the speech as a direct salvo at Ernst, his old friend and colleague.

That evening, after the ceremony, Parfyonov went up to see Ernst in his office. Each of them remembers this encounter somewhat differently, but both agree that it was short. Parfyonov didn't apologize, and Ernst wasn't angry, at least not outwardly. In the days to come, Ernst repeated the same cryptic answer when asked about the ceremony: "You can't edit a Nobel Prize speech." What's said is said. Parfyonov told me he gave the speech with no particular expectation: "I simply said what I thought necessary." Ernst was skeptical of Parfyonov's motives, and was clearly wounded. "He knew perfectly well that what he did would undercut me, that it would create problems for me, for the only person in this whole industry who had consistently supported him," Ernst told me. He said that he kept up his relations with Parfyonov, but, he added, "I can't call them friendly, because in that moment, as a friend, he betrayed me."

Even so, what little work Parfyonov did for state television continued to air on Channel One. He could sense that something was "hovering between us," but he and Ernst still felt a mutual respect, even as their allegiances placed them in inevitable opposition. In December 2011, the year after Parfyonov's speech, protests broke out in Moscow in response to fraudulent parliamentary elections. The protests quickly took on a broader series of moral demands, directed at the cynicism and corruption of the Putin system. At one of the demonstrations, Parfyonov addressed a crowd of tens of thousands of people, the first time he had done something so openly political. The appearance earned him his own spot on the unspoken blacklist. A new, harder, and more inflexible era was taking shape, and Parfyonov was on the wrong side of the barricades. Channel One showed the protests—they had become too large to ignore completely—but in a muted, restrained form, and its coverage of Putin in the run-up to the presidential election that spring was predictably hagiographic. Parfyonov and Ernst saw less and less of one another. "We had fewer and fewer common activities," Parfyonov said. "And then we had none at all."

Sometime later, I asked Parfyonov to describe what he continued to see in his old friend: "When I see Kostya consumed by producing something beautiful, he is, on the whole, the same person I've known from an early age," he told me. "But now he has almost unlimited possibilities, about which he's always dreamed. He is the best television producer of his time, and the current authoritarian system, in need of him, granted him his powers."

IN THE SUMMER OF 2007, Putin traveled to Guatemala City to give a rare speech in English, with a touch of French, to the assembled delegates of the International Olympic Committee, making a personal appeal to award the 2014 Winter Games to Sochi, a resort town on the Black Sea. He promised to spend billions to show off a "new Russia" to the rest of the world. The bid was successful. It was immediately clear that the Sochi Games would be an event of great pride and importance to Putin, who saw them as a capstone to Russia's economic and geopolitical revival under his leadership.

The opening ceremony would demonstrate Russia's might and prowess before billions of viewers. The job for pulling it off went to Ernst. "Putin is no fool—he knows who is who in his own circle," a longtime Russian television producer told me. "In terms of creating a show, he is number one—there is no other Ernst."

Ernst began work on the ceremony in 2011, a little more than two years before the opening of the games. The guiding principle would be to position Russia as a country with a rich and open history, very much part of the world, not separate from it. "We wanted to show that Russia is part of the global cultural village," said Andrei Boltenko, Ernst's Channel One colleague, who became creative director and screenwriter of the opening. He told me of a number of stylistic clues embedded in the show's aesthetic: the design of Russian medieval boyar costumes was inflected with the style of both Russian folk toys and the Japanese artist Yayoi Kusama; the Soviet Union's postwar reconstruction was modeled on the aesthetics of the Constructivist artist Yakov Chernikhov, with an echo of Frank Miller, the cultish American comic book artist, who himself borrowed from film noir and manga influences. "It was a harmony in which each culture has a little reflection of Russia in it, and Russian culture contains a reflection of the whole world," Boltenko explained.

As time went on, the ambitions of Ernst and his team grew enormously. The show's increasing technical complexity meant that the main stadium in Sochi, which had been planned as an open structure, had to be redesigned with a closed roof. Even in the final days of rehearsals, a number of details were tricky to nail down; a set change that should have taken a minute instead stopped the show for forty-five. Other Russian officials involved in the games wanted to simplify things and strip out the more extravagant and challenging elements of the show. "In certain moments, Ernst had to convince Putin personally," Boltenko told me.

On the night of the opening ceremony, in February 2014, Ernst watched the show from a control center high above the stadium in Sochi, following along with a wireless headset clipped to his ear and a bank of television screens in front of him. The action unfolded not only on the ground, but up above, with heavy set pieces gliding through the sky, held in place by invisible rail tracks hung from the stadium's roof. The show opened with a troika of horses lit up in white neon galloping across the night sky. Playful balloons in bright colors stood in for the onion domes of Saint Basil's Cathedral; the navy ships of Peter the Great sailed across a dark and wavy ocean seemingly cast from an inky woodcut. Natasha and Prince Andrei danced a stirring pas de deux among the pageantry of the ball scene from *War and Peace*—a romantic idyll broken by the icy clanging of the revolution bearing down on the country. A steam locomotive bathed in red light barreled down on the stadium, chugging along the invisible tracks, a stylized reference to Stalin's industrialization drive. The Second World War was represented with dark stillness and the distant rumble of approaching airplanes. From there, the show bathed in an extended finale of good cheer, rendering the postwar years as a time of athletes, cosmonauts, students, and *stilyagi*—Soviet proto-hipsters who liked jazz and dressed in Western fashions. As the show concluded and chants of "Ro-ssi-ya!" echoed through the stadium, Ernst leapt from his chair in the command center. "We've done it!" he yelled.

It was the most significant moment of Ernst's professional life. He had summoned the Russia of his own dreams, willing into being the country he wanted to live in: a place of folk tradition, avant-garde culture, feats of engineering, towering writers and artists, and monumental achievements in science and industry. Even many of those hostile to anything connected to the state were won over; Alexei Navalny called the immediate afterglow of the opening ceremony "nice and unifying—excellent." Yet Ernst's fantasy was just that: present-day Russia bore only glancing similarity to the one Ernst had conjured up. For one thing, the show was grounded in the past, ending in the 1960s, as if all that followed—stagnation, Gorbachev's perestroika, the Soviet collapse, the hardship of the nineties—didn't fit in the narrative Ernst wanted to share with his fellow Russians. "Few are given the chance to declare their love of homeland before the eyes of three billion citizens of the earth and, what is perhaps more important for me, to unite their fellow countrymen for two hours in a single emotion—even though it should be virtually impossible to unite many of them in a single emotion at all," he said later. "I have the audacity to believe I was lucky enough to pull it off."

ERNST DID NOT HAVE LONG to savor the fantasy he had brought to life—of an open, cosmopolitan, confident, and welcoming Russia. Two and a half weeks later, the stadium in Sochi hosted the closing ceremony of the games, also produced by Ernst. But by then, weeks of street protests in Kyiv had overthrown the government of Viktor Yanukovych, a crude, unpolished, and thoroughly corrupt politician from Ukraine's Russian-speaking east. Clashes between demonstrators and police turned violent. Those watching Channel One the following day saw the pageantry of the closing ceremony alongside news that Yanukovych had fled Kyiv and effectively vanished. Putin was incensed—he saw the question of Yanukovych's fate as a zero-sum proxy struggle with the West—and was intent on extracting a measure of geopolitical revenge.

Within days, incognito Russian special forces soldiers appeared in Crimea, the Ukrainian peninsula on the Black Sea with long-standing pro-Russian sympathies. By the end of the month, Russia had annexed the territory. Western opprobrium, sanctions, and attempts at isolation followed—a process that only deepened after the outbreak of fighting in the Donbass, the industrial region in eastern Ukraine from which Yanukovych originally hailed. Russia spurred on a separatist insurgency there, supplying funds, weapons, and diplomatic cover. Back home, the Russian media adopted a hysterical and bellicose tone. The events in Ukraine marked a break in the country's Putin-era history—a moment when citizens were no longer allowed to be passive and inert, but instead were primed to be jumpy, mobilized, and ready to defend the state at any cost. The need for enemies became obvious: to rally the patriotic masses for the struggles that lay ahead.

Channel One was by no means immune to the new mood. Its news programs and talk shows became consumed with talk of a coup in Kyiv, NATO's dark intentions, and the so-called Fascists who supposedly took over after Yanukovych. Ernst was a loyal foot soldier in this battle, but was quietly devastated. He had the lingering hope that his Olympics show would mark a bright new era for Russia. Instead, an entirely different one began. Boltenko, the creative director of the opening ceremony, said the whole Olympics team was leveled by a "clear and ringing collapse of all of our hopes." (Though, he added, Ernst is a hard figure to read: "To put it in military language, Ernst would never allow himself to lose face in front of his troops. There's lots about him we'll never know.") Another acquaintance said Ernst lived through a moment of "inhuman drama." In public, however, Ernst gave off an air of placidity, allowing only the stray, altogether muted comment about the way his Olympic glory was subsumed by Crimea and the events that followed. "Of course it was a shame there weren't a few more months to enjoy the pleasant aftertaste of the Olympics," he told the Russian edition of GQ, which named him "Man of the Year" in 2014.

Fundamentally, no matter how Westernized his artistic tastes might be, Ernst's own feelings were not so at odds with the lurching turn in the country's political mood. "He has never felt any sort of internal rebellion, there should be no illusions about that," said Arina Borodina, the television critic. "His desire to protect the state's interests is entirely genuine." Moreover, Ernst shared Putin's grievances about how Russia had been treated—by America especially—in the years since the end of the Cold War, and believed in the virtuous necessity of Russia's revanchist campaign. It was a moment of geopolitical score-settling, of upending a post–Cold War order that Ernst—like Putin, the rest of the Kremlin elite, and millions of Russians—felt had treated Russia unfairly.

The tone on Channel One shifted accordingly, even as it remained a notch more restrained and less fire-breathing than its rival networks. Its patriotic messages became more overt and less accommodating, whether in relation to the West or to those inside Russia who did not share in the officially sanctioned mood of righteous euphoria. "The channel should speak about the times from the perspective of citizens of the Russian Federation," Ernst told me. This task came easy because the newsmakers shared their audience's sentiments. "We—us at Channel One, as the citizens of the country—felt deeply offended, and we didn't need any additional motivation," he said. The network transmitted a soaring, deeply emotional set of messages aimed at showing how Russia had reclaimed its historical destiny and its natural birthright as a world superpower.

Once again, the country and the channel changed together. The experience of Katerina Gordeeva, a director who originally worked at NTV but left over disagreements with the channel's political direction, is telling. In early 2014, just ahead of the Olympics and a couple of months before Crimea, Channel One aired a documentary Gordeeva had made about the Siege of Leningrad, timed to the seventieth anniversary of the end of the blockade. (Between 1941 and 1944, the German army had the city encircled; more than a million people are estimated to have died during the siege, many from starvation.) When Ernst called her to propose she direct something for the channel, she hadn't worked in television for nearly two years. "I was grateful to him for the chance to make this film, to work in my profession again," she told me. The result was an honest and complicated picture of the Leningrad siege, a historical tragedy that has a very contentious history to this day. For years, Soviet propaganda highlighted the stoic heroism of the city's population, while burying the many discomfiting truths about what the city endured—a sanitized view of history that resurfaced in Putin-era Russia. "It's forbidden to talk about many of the horrors of the blockade, like people eating cats or stealing ration cards," Gordeeva said. Her film addressed that ugliness head-on. Although she would not have been shocked if Ernst had made her change or cut some material, he never did. "Not for a second did he suggest that 'this is impossible' or 'this won't make it onto the screen,'" she told me.

A year later, in the spring of 2015—that is, a year after Crimea and with the war in the Donbass ongoing—Ernst commissioned another film from Gordeeva. She was to make a documentary about the legacy of Joseph Brodsky, the acclaimed poet who was run out of the

Soviet Union and awarded the Nobel Prize for Literature in 1987. Gordeeva's film featured interviews with people who did not know Brodsky, but were influenced by him. Ernst didn't like the film and, two weeks before the premiere, told Gordeeva that Channel One would not be airing it. He wanted a straight biopic, not something so moody and atmospheric. "It was interesting work, but absolutely did not correspond to the plans of the channel," Ernst said. As Gordeeva remembers, he said her film "evokes feelings of suffocation and anguish that do not correspond to the present times." He added that anyone who didn't like it in Russia could always hit the road. (Gordeeva indeed moved to Latvia that year, not because of anything Ernst said, but because of her own growing discomfort at home.) Yet they remain cordial, and when Gordeeva became involved in a sports competition for children with cancer, Ernst agreed to cover the games widely on Channel One—even if, as Gordeeva put it, "he and I are, most likely, ideological opponents." When we spoke, Gordeeva reflected on how one year, Ernst felt it was natural and just to air a potentially edgy historical project on Channel One, and the next, considered it entirely impossible. "I think of it as the door to Narnia, always opening and closing," she said. "I got in thanks to the last crack that you could slip through, and then the door closed again. Maybe for good."

IN JULY 2014, at the height of the Kremlin-led information war against Ukraine, the West, and any forces seen to be aligned with them, a Channel One correspondent reporting on the war in the Donbass relayed a gruesome tale. A woman who had fled the city of Slavyansk, which had been under separatist control for several months and had been recaptured by Ukrainian forces, told of a scene that happened, she claimed, when the Ukrainian military reentered the town. She said that Ukrainian troops gathered everyone in the central square and publicly executed a three-year-old boy and his mother, whose husband had joined a pro-Russian rebel militia. The boy, she said, had been crucified, nailed to a wooden board and tortured to death. He cried out as he bled; people in the crowd fainted.

The segment was of a piece with Russian state news reports at the time, which portrayed the Ukrainian authorities as cruel and bloodthirsty Fascists. But even among the regular cavalcade of horrors on state television, the story of the crucified boy stuck out for its shocking barbarity. More important, it quickly became clear that the story wasn't true. Independent journalists in Slavyansk could find no confirmation; no one in the small town where the execution supposedly occurred had heard anything about it. The woman had apparently made the whole thing up, either as a result of her own trauma or at the prompting of the channel's producers. The incident was a stain on the network, and a blow to Ernst personally. "The only thing more terrible than a dead boy is the shame when it turns out the boy is fictional," wrote Oleg Kashin, the journalist and columnist.

The day the segment appeared, Ernst was away on vacation in Bilbao. He is evasive in telling the story of how the interview made it on air, but the fact of his absence suggests a momentary lapse in the quality control of Channel One's propaganda output, or that someone wanted to set him up, broadcasting something egregiously false with the knowledge that Ernst would have to answer for it later. (As a person at Channel One explained it to me, if a news segment veers even slightly toward criticism of the authorities, a million different editors will review it again and again before it goes on air, just to be safe; if a segment buttresses the state line, no one really thinks to check: it can go straight to broadcast without much oversight.) In any case, seeing as Ernst is both "tsar and god" of Channel One, as one former member of the news team put it, ultimate responsibility falls to him. He agrees: "I answer for my channel one hundred percent," he told me.

When I asked Ernst about the fake story, he tried to deflect, calling it a "meme created by liberal journalists." Then he insisted that the Channel One anchor had told the audience that the information hadn't been verified and the channel couldn't vouch for its authenticity. That wasn't true; even when, in continuing to play the woman's interview, Channel One announcers began adding that "the heart refuses to believe" such a tale, the phrase was clearly meant to strengthen the dramatic effect, not undermine it. Ernst finally suggested that the woman was "psychologically unwell," and given that Slavyansk had fallen under Ukrainian control, Channel One journalists couldn't check her story themselves. Five months after the original segment aired, a news anchor acknowledged that the channel "was not able to confirm or refute the information" it had shown viewers but insisted that the tale was the "real story of a real woman who escaped from hell in Slavyansk." Beyond that, the network never carried out an investigation into the false story or disciplined those involved. How could it? Those who put the story on air were behaving in the spirit of the times, enacting the wishes and needs of the state as they understood them. Ernst was clearly uncomfortable talking about the episode—he realized it was a shameful moment for the channel and for him—but he couldn't wholly separate himself from it. These are the rules of being a Russian television boss.

The Slavyansk story may have gotten an outsize degree of attention, but it was just one incident in what would prove a long season of politically driven fraud on Channel One. On July 17, 2014, Malaysia Airlines Flight 17, headed from Amsterdam to Kuala Lumpur, was shot out of the sky as it passed over the battlefields of eastern Ukraine. All 298 people on board died, their bodies scattered among the wildflowers and tall grass. Suspicion immediately fell on the Russian-backed separatist forces—it appeared the rebels had used a BUK anti-aircraft missile system, covertly provided by Russia, aiming at what they thought was a Ukrainian military aircraft. (With time, open-source researchers, as well as Dutch state investigators, traced the particular BUK launch system to a Russian anti-aircraft missile unit based in western Russia.)

From the first hours after the catastrophe, Russian state media, including Channel One, went into a prolonged fury, giving voice to just about every far-fetched alternative version of events possible: that the Malaysian airliner had been targeted by a Ukrainian anti-aircraft missile on purpose, either as a provocation or in the mistaken belief that it was Putin's plane; that it had been attacked accidentally as part of an air defense training mission gone wrong; or that it was shot down by a Ukrainian fighter jet. The explanations were contradictory and absurd. The aim of each theory was not to persuade viewers but simply to confuse and wear them down. In November 2014, as the Dutch Safety Board began recovery of the wreckage, the host of a Channel One evening news program aired what he called "sensational" footage. A satellite image, supposedly taken by Western intelligence services and passed to Russia by an American scientist, purported to show the Malaysia Airlines Boeing 777 being attacked in midair by a Su-25 fighter plane, presumably belonging to the Ukrainian air force. "The image supports a version of events which has hardly been heard in the West," the Channel One host said.

The image was quickly outed as a fake. The time stamp from the supposed satellite didn't match when the plane was actually shot down, the Boeing aircraft shown on Channel One had identifying markings that clearly distinguished it from the one actually downed over Ukraine, and the terrain underneath was partially taken from an overhead photograph of eastern Ukraine posted online two years before. When I asked Ernst why his channel gave voice to such an easily provable falsehood, he acted as if the segment was the result of a simple, accidental error. "Yes, we're human, we made a mistake, but not on purpose," he told me.

The truth is that baldly fake stories aren't much of a strategic disaster for Channel One, at least in the right doses. The reason comes down to the difference between the clumsy propaganda of the late Soviet period and the postmodern approach of the Putin age. The propaganda of today's Russia is skilled at playing into preconceived notions, telling people what they are already inclined to believe, rather than trying to convince them of what they don't, as Soviet television did. Widespread internet access has made it all the more impossible for Channel One, or any state information resource, to assert one single truth and presume no one will have access to alternative ones. At the same time, information programming has the effect of nudging the viewer toward believing nothing at all, to becoming so overwhelmed and exhausted by the information onslaught that she simply throws her hands up. Truth becomes a matter of theories and guesses over "Who benefits?" The assertions that MH17 was shot down by a Ukrainian fighter jet or a Russian-made missile system jostle next to one another in the same frothy information soup. The facts feel equally confusing and difficult to make sense of. It's all just noise. What matters is the overall narrative: Russia is just and powerful, and the West is seeking to weaken it. On the question of MH17, especially, the Russian state's approach seems to have worked: a year out, a poll showed that only 5 percent of Russians blamed their government or the separatists for the disaster.

Ernst, perhaps unsurprisingly, denied that his aim is to overwhelm and dispirit his viewers into adopting a pose of cynical disbelief toward everything. He fell back on the argument, by no means particular to Russia, that truth is a subjective concept, a matter of one's allegiances and biases and parochial interests. Once, when we were arguing about the merits of an official Dutch report that is based on a years-long investigation and presents a great deal of evidence suggesting Russian culpability, Ernst told me our disagreement came down to a question of belief: "You believe the Dutch report is true, and I believe the Dutch report is unprofessional." It was as if we were arguing about religion or aesthetics rather than a set of facts.

Nowhere is this relativist prism more present than in Ernst's understanding of Channel One in comparison to television networks in the West. His intellectual path over the last several decades is typical of many in his generation, people with talent and ambition who resented the idiotic and stifling controls of the Soviet system—all while imagining that everything must be the polar opposite in the West, and in America most of all. When the barriers between the two worlds collapsed, the West that Ernst and his like-minded peers discovered frustrated, confused, and disappointed them. Ernst saw for himself the failings and blind spots of the outlets he once worshipped—CNN and the BBC, above all—and concluded not only that these institutions had their own deficiencies, but that they were no better than or different from what Ernst had thought he was trying to transcend all those years.

In the eighties, Ernst came across a copy of *All the President's Men,* the 1976 film about Bob Woodward and Carl Bernstein's investigation of Watergate for *The Washington Post.* He was enraptured by the film's portrayal of journalism's civic power, the moral force that comes from its critical distance and independence. "But now," he told me, ruefully, "of course we know it's not like that at all." Someone always has a personal interest, a stake in the game, with higher forces standing just offscreen, guiding and manipulating events for their benefit. Ernst, like many in his generation in Russia, wears his cynicism as a sign of enlightenment—he is alive to how the world really works, aware of its true rules and logic, not like those idealists who remain blinded by their naïveté. "I grew up and traveled all over," he told me, "and, especially in recent years, it's become increasingly clear to me that justice, democracy, the complete truth, they don't exist anywhere in the world." It would be impossible to convince him that today's CNN or BBC doesn't translate its respective state's fundamental positions and interests to the same degree that Channel One does. Western networks do have their own biases and ingrained narratives, but those are of a different degree and, most important, serve a varied and contradictory set of interests, not merely the state's alone. Like so much of what can loosely be called propaganda, it is a notion grounded in an element of truth, but stretched to an exaggerated degree, purposefully ignoring any complicating nuance. "People who make television are citizens of a specific country, from a certain nationality, with particular cultural codes," Ernst told me. And so Channel One must play the game the way everyone else does.

IN SEPTEMBER 2014, half a year after the annexation of Crimea, at a moment of pronounced tensions with the West and a climate of aggression and fear fostered by state television, a new program appeared on Channel One. It was called *Vremya Pokazhet,* or *Time Will Tell,* and was essentially a political shoutfest: a loud, often crass debate show covering the issues of the day, which without fail revolve around how the West is trying to keep Russia down or otherwise treat it unfairly. Since then, on an almost daily basis, the program has followed a set format: a few token liberals and a foreigner or two appear alongside pro-Kremlin journalists or politicians in front of a live audience, led in an animated discussion by a pair of hosts who don't hide their skepticism of the liberals and foreigners and always give the last word to the pro-Kremlin cheerleaders. It makes for dizzying, exhausting television, but is successful, at least according to its own rules: *Time*

Will Tell is entertaining in a carnival-sideshow sort of way, and if you relied on it for your only sense of the world, you'd be certain that Russia is the subject of a nefarious geopolitical conspiracy led by the United States and Europe, and is duty-bound to defend itself.

When a producer called me to ask if I would appear as a guest—it turns out it's hard to find Russian-speaking Americans in Moscow willing to get yelled at for an hour on live television—I agreed, curious about how the program is actually put together, what it feels like on the factory floor, as it were, of the state propaganda enterprise. On the day I was set to appear, I was met by a minder at the entrance to Channel One's studios, and led through a vast warren of long hallways. I took a chair in the makeup room and endured a heavy dusting of face powder, emerging with skin the pinkish color of a supermarket peach. The studio audience numbered about a hundred people, who were given the signal to clap when the show returned from commercial break or one of the pro-Kremlin guests made a particularly acerbic point at the expense of one of the show's villains—which today meant me. Once the live show started, it became clear I was meant to play the role of the pitiable imbecile and birthday party piñata: everyone would get a chance to step up and have a whack. We discussed everything from Russian Olympic athletes facing bans for doping allegations to Syria, where both Moscow and Washington had forces deployed. The questions were, to put it mildly, rather leading. The United States carries itself with an air of impunity, one of the show's hosts told me—"Isn't that disastrous?" Another turned to me and posited, "Obama referred to Russia as a 'regional power.' Can't we say that's when all our problems between the two countries began?" I felt bruised, but more annoyed that between my stammering Russian and interruptions by the hosts and the other guests, I didn't get a chance to say more than a couple of sentences.

I returned to *Time Will Tell* every now and then over the next months, each time certain, as I sat in the makeup chair, that this would be the day I would manage to say something subversive and devastatingly convincing on Russian state television, the day I would break or otherwise disrupt the choreographed rules of the genre. Of course, that never happened: not only was I outnumbered, but I could interject for only a few seconds at most, and to make any points at all I inevitably had to huff and puff and raise my voice. In the end, I came across as just another agitated, screaming talking head, an interchangeable member of the choir in a symphony of noise. It was like Channel One's approach to MH17: I was not dangerous, even when I raised points that challenged the Kremlin narrative of events, but in fact useful, doing my part to make issues of fact seem muddy and unknowable, proving that everything is a question of perspective and allegiance. I once traded impressions with another American living in Moscow who regularly goes on the show. He admitted the obvious: "I don't know exactly how I'm helping them, but I wouldn't be there if I wasn't." In fact, Channel One was so eager to have him appear on the show, they gave him a contract worth $2,500 a month. (I declined any suggestion of compensation for my appearances.)

Time Will Tell, like much of the Russian news, has an outsize obsession with the United States and the minutiae of its every political hiccup, a consequence of the Russian ruling class's simultaneous fascination with and revulsion for the U.S. political system. This became all the more true in 2016, during the presidential contest between Hillary Clinton and Donald Trump. The evening news on Channel One took to the character of Trump: antiestablishment, instinctual, and attracted to raw power. Ernst told me, "Of course everyone here was pleased with Trump. He seemed to represent a change in the American political trend." Trump openly favored a transactional style of politics, with little appetite for things like values or norms—here was a person Putin could sit down with and divide up the world as Soviet and American leaders did at Yalta in 1945. Clinton, Ernst thought, came across as a "nasty and wicked old woman," full of haughty and outmoded ideas of how other countries should conduct themselves.

On *Time Will Tell,* Clinton and Trump were frequent topics of discussion, with rather clearly defined roles for each. Clinton was the chief representative of American hegemony and imperialism. If she was elected, Russia could expect more sanctions and attempts at isolation, maybe even war. Trump, meanwhile, was attractive precisely because he represented a break from the status quo, a showman with nice things to say about Putin and bad things about Obama, who, by the end of his second term, had become the Kremlin's chief geopolitical nemesis.

Time Will Tell reflected the Russian state media's overall narrative on Trump: excitement bordering on euphoria after his surprise victory; mocking hostility toward the notion that Russia, whether through hacking or trolls, might have had anything to do with that result; and a creeping sense of confusion and disappointment as Trump proved unable to single-handedly cancel sanctions and reconfigure U.S.-Russian relations on the terms the Kremlin had been hoping for. During one broadcast, when we were discussing an address Trump had made to the United Nations the day before—Channel One's news program had called the speech "lengthy and rather pompous"—I asked the hosts if they felt any regret for how Russian state media, their show included, so clearly favored Trump during the campaign and transmitted to viewers the idea that he was the preferable candidate for Russia. Were they sorry now? One of them, Anatoly Kuzichev, forty-eight, bald, and with a permanent wry smirk, turned the question back to me: "Imagine there are two candidates. The first says, 'I hate Russia and will do all I can to destroy it.' The second, however, says, 'I will do everything possible to be friends with Russia.' So, who would you root for in Russia's place?" I pushed again. Does Kuzichev have any regrets? "Yes, we are sorry," he said, his voice rising. "We're sorry that everything was just words. Yes, we were rooting for Trump. I can confirm that. We acted like fools who naively believed a bunch of words."

The last time I went on the show, the topic of the day was a report released by Russia's Federation Council, the upper chamber of parliament, on all the ways the United States had interfered in elections around the world. It was a classic flourish of whataboutism, a frequently employed technique that dates to Soviet times—"Over there, they lynch Negroes" was a habitual, even hackneyed refrain of Soviet officials—meant to turn the tables, to deflect any accusation by throwing it back at the accuser, even if the counttercharge has little to do with the topic at hand. Like all good whataboutisms, the report on election meddling was not entirely without merit: just as the American record on race relations was frequently appalling during the Cold War (and remains so today), the sense of unprecedented violation among the American public over Russia's interference in the 2016 election can indeed veer toward naïveté and hypocrisy. But to argue that, say, former vice president Joe Biden's suggestion that Russia would be better off if Putin refrained from running for a third term was as egregious as the charge that Russian intelligence officers hacked the email accounts of U.S. political figures was absurd. The viewer at home was meant to be convinced not of Russia's innocence, only of everyone's shared guilt.

In the studio, the Russian senator who wrote the report spoke of how the U.S. State Department had declared that unless "a certain Russian citizen" was registered as a presidential candidate to face Putin in the country's 2018 election, Washington would consider the contest illegitimate. How's that for interference! The senator was, of course, referring to Navalny, the opposition politician whom presenters and guests on Russian state television avoid as much as possible, and, if absolutely necessary, invoke by all manner of vague euphemisms: Putin has called him "this gentleman" and "the aforementioned person." ("Why should I contribute to Navalny's political rise?" Ernst once asked me, genuinely confused at the suggestion that Channel One could stand to give him, and other opposition figures, more airtime—or any at all, for that matter. "History shows that no ruling system ever helps its opposition; if that opposition has real support from a significant portion of the population, then it takes power on its own.") In any case, the whole example had been twisted and overblown; after Navalny's candidacy was rejected by Russia's electoral commission, a U.S. State Department spokesperson expressed concern over "restrictions on independent voices in Russia." It was a routine, milquetoast diplomatic statement. But that distinction was flattened into oblivion by the senator and the show's hosts, one of whom turned to me and asked, with the alarm and incredulity of a talking head on U.S. cable news denouncing Russian electoral interference: "Joshua, honestly, do you consider such a thing acceptable?"

Most noxiously, the Federation Council report, and the discussion of it on *Time Will Tell,* gave voice to a familiar trope: that anti-Kremlin protests in Russia are somehow the work of foreign forces, the U.S. State Department above all. I suggested that it was a sign of the political elite's fear of their own people—dissatisfaction and protest are presented as phenomena with exclusively foreign origins, not the result of genuine, homegrown sentiment. I was shouted down before I could finish the thought. "Fantasy!" "Russophobia!" "What does this have to do with anything?"

One of the regular hosts, a man in his early fifties named Artem Sheinin, was the most ribald, unrestrained, and obstreperous performer. Sheinin is squat and muscular, a former paratrooper who fought in the Soviet war in Afghanistan in the eighties and retains the gruff, no-nonsense pose of a military man. Once he brought out onstage with mocking ceremony a bucket labeled "shit," claiming that one of the guests that day, a Ukrainian blogger, had some months before said in jest that he would eat a bucket of shit if the territory of Crimea wasn't returned to Ukraine. Sheinin decided to test his word on live television. (The blogger declined; the bucket was revealed to be full of chocolate.) Another time, he grabbed by the neck an American guest who taunted him by saying that Russians are all talk and no action. The show's other host had to separate them. On air, Sheinin's questions to me were often quite openly antagonistic, but lightened with irony and a mocking smile; he seemed delighted at the thought of catching me—and, by extension, the U.S. government—in some gotcha contradiction. Here was clear-cut proof, he said, gesturing at a huge projection of the Federation Council report, that America had interfered in Russian politics. "If we didn't ask for America's opinion and UN laws give it no right to meddle in our election, then why is it doing so? Can you explain this?" His questions were grounded in exaggeration and willful misinterpretation, but tinged with a faint whiff of truth. U.S. foreign policy certainly can be naive, hypocritical, and self-referential. There was no point in denying that. I tried to resist the role of spokesperson for a century of U.S. foreign policy, but it was a hard position to avoid. Any attempt at injecting nuance—clarifying, for example, that many in the American press criticize the use of U.S. military abroad—was taken by Sheinin and the other hosts as a cue for attack or interruption, firmly placing me back on enemy soil in the viewer's mind, a hostile figure not to be trusted.

One evening, I went to visit Sheinin in his office at Channel One, curious to see what kind of conversation we could have outside a live broadcast, whose form straitjackets us both into our particular roles. *Time Will Tell* is now on four hours a day, taking up a sizable chunk of the channel's daytime programming. The show is clearly deemed a success. Sheinin walked in from a long stretch of hosting duties, having changed into a pair of camouflage pants and a T-shirt emblazoned with the crest of the Russian Airborne Troops. "I feel more comfortable this way," he told me.

Sheinin was forthright in describing the show, and his role on it, as instruments in a larger information war between Russia and the West. He spoke in the language of battle, saying he saw no difference between himself and those Russians who went to fight in the Donbass. "Whatever the particular topic and event of the day might be, or how they unfold, we discuss it from the perspective of 'us' and 'them,' or, let's say, 'my country' and the 'enemies of my country.'" Those enemies, whether Western governments or the foreign media, want to "impose on the minds of our citizens a false idea of themselves and of their nation. My task is to debunk these myths and these misconceptions," he said. *Time Will Tell* does that not by hiding uncomfortable news or accusations of Russian misbehavior, but by making those charges seem ridiculous and shallow. Continuing the metaphor of battle, Sheinin said, "I destroy the information enemies of my country by revealing their weakness and dubiousness."

In prosecuting the current information war, Sheinin is guided by what he sees as the results of the last one. In his understanding, the Soviet Union collapsed because its citizens found themselves overwhelmed—assaulted, even—by a sudden wave of new information about their country and its past. After decades of enforced silence, they were not equipped to make sense of all they encountered once perestroika removed the barriers to knowledge. Sheinin said he was often among those who stood in line for the *Moskovskiye Novosti,* the famed paper of the late eighties that published historical exposés on the Gulag and less flattering sides of the Second World War. The people "simply lost their minds. They believed everything," Sheinin told me. "They were told that our history is a series of continuous mistakes: it's all black, all terrible, we lost everything, repressed and killed everyone." The problem wasn't that these accusations were false, but that the state was pathetically ill-equipped to manage this powerful stream of new and shocking facts. "Yes, much of it was true," Sheinin said. "But really, it was only half true, because it negated the truth that people had known up until then." Now, on *Time Will Tell,* he has taken up a position on the "information front lines," as he put it, where he has a chance to rerun the battle for the country's consciousness of a generation ago. "I don't want to occupy any sort of neutral position," he said. "I did that once—and my country was broken, torn apart, trampled."

As we spoke, our conversation stretching into its third hour, I was struck by how measured and thoughtful Sheinin was off camera; he never shouted over me or interrupted me midsentence. We had an extended and substantive discussion, even if we agreed on little. I told him he barely resembled his on-air evil twin. "It's strange," he said, "people don't come up to a boxer on the street and ask why he's not attacking them with his fists." He knows that when he's on set at *Time Will Tell,* his viewers are expecting a bare-knuckle fight—that's what they've turned on Channel One to watch. (Viewers want "intelligible drama, understandable emotions and conflicts," he told me.) And so, he said, "my job is to make sure they get their boxing fix." But after the match, as it were, he doesn't have to throw punches anymore.

I asked him if Ernst, with his particular vision of artistic standards, ever gave him a hard time for his more rough-and-tumble antics. (During one of our conversations, Ernst told me of the crisis of the day at the channel: dealing with the fallout from an on-air outburst by Sheinin, who had used the word "dumbfuckery" in telling a ribald story to the studio audience. "After all those hours on live TV, sometimes a person can say stupid things," Ernst said.) Sheinin said he imagines that when, say, he tries to choke a studio guest on live television, Ernst might want to rein him in, but knows there's likely no point. "Ernst can't help but understand that when you have a program like this, whose whole format is built around that sort of thing, you are either ready for certain risks, or you shouldn't air this show at all." Ernst is a television demigod, a figure of unparalleled stature and influence, but in some key ways he is also a captive of his position. If he wants Putin's license to spend millions on flying troikas, he sometimes has to tolerate Sheinin and his buckets of shit.

JUDGING ERNST'S LEGACY IS DIFFICULT—or at least requires a heightened degree of compartmentalization, an acknowledgment of his powers for both white and black magic, his sizable talent for art and propaganda, or, most honestly, an admission that determining the precise border between the two is often impossible. Ernst did not have the choice between becoming a great and influential auteur, speaking to millions of his countrymen and offering them a guiding hand, or ascending to a position of political reach and power, with all the obligations and compromises contained therein. The deal on offer was both or neither. He's proved exceptionally gifted at pulling off that combination; to some extent, his skills and abilities are universal, but he is ultimately very much a creature of modern Russia.

One of the more frequent parlor games within the insular world of Russian media is predicting Ernst's imminent downfall: the opening ceremonies will be his last great show; he can't survive the conservative turn after Crimea; the hostility and aggression expected from Channel One will push him away. Ernst is always rumored to be on the verge of being fired, or quitting, his empire taken from him. Yet he has survived, and remains at the height of his powers. The great seduction of television—the ability to turn your vision into a concrete image and to see that image reflected onscreen—continues to animate him to the point of obsession, just as it has for more than three decades. He is no less consumed with the minutiae of the picture on Channel One than ever before. One former member of the channel's news staff told me of how once, at five in the morning, Ernst called the station from home to say he didn't like the tie the anchor was wearing and that he should change it.

I once asked Ernst why he has stuck around for so long, what still motivates and drives him, especially since the space for freewheeling and irreverent programming on Channel One has shrunk, while the intensity of its propaganda offerings has grown. To him the answer feels obvious. "I can make an impact on the place where I was born, on the people with whom I speak the same language, with whom I have a shared history and understanding, share the same smells and songs and movie quotes. I know these people and can understand them. I love them."

An influential businessman in Moscow told me he once asked Ernst the same question: Aren't you tired, you must find the requirements of the job exhausting and distasteful. According to the businessman, Ernst answered, "You have no idea what a high it is, to be able to influence that many millions of people." Leonid Parfyonov, Ernst's old friend and collaborator, told me that this seduction is what attracted Ernst to television in the first place, and continues to keep him there today. "He always wanted to be a trendsetter, with the power to create a whole fashion, a style, to show people something that changes them, gives them a way to make sense of their time, to understand themselves," he told me. "This is a great power and, for Kostya, I'm sure a great joy."

CHAPTER 2

BEWARE OF
DRAGONS

—

WHEN THE BOMBS STARTED FALLING, HEDA SARATOVA WAS ALONE with her four-year-old son in their Grozny apartment. She watched Russian planes scream overhead and, a few seconds later, heard a rumbling boom and saw a cloud of dust, smoke, and obliterated concrete swirl toward the sky. In between the bombing runs, artillery shells thwacked into apartment blocks with seemingly random logic. Saratova could hear the tinny pitter-patter of Kalashnikov fire. The noise was unrelenting, morning until night; it felt like someone was holding a bucket to your ear and banging on it without pause, for days on end. *Bang bang bang.* She prayed for just a minute of silence; it never came.

It was the fall of 1999, and Russian federal forces had just re-entered Chechnya, restarting a conflict that had ended, inconclusively, three years before. Saratova had known there would be trouble after a band of Chechen rebel fighters invaded the neighboring Russian republic of Dagestan, with the ostensible aim of establishing a pan-Caucasus Islamic emirate. The incursion gave Moscow a ready pretext for a new military campaign. At the same time, a number of apartment bombings blamed on Chechen terrorists hit several Russian cities, alarming the public and giving the final casus belli to the Kremlin. (To this day, the bombings remain unsolved, with ominous but unproven links to the Russian security services.) The Chechen campaign was overseen by Putin—first as prime minister, then president. He cemented his political authority on the basis of tough talk against those whom he labeled terrorists. If necessary, he said, "we'll waste them in the outhouse."

Saratova was thirty-three, with a vivid smile and a flowing cascade of dark brown hair that she kept tucked under an unobtrusive cotton headscarf. She spent the years of the first war, from 1994 to 1996, up in the mountains, in her family's home village. After the war ended, during what would turn out to be a short-lived interregnum between the fighting, she came to Grozny to escape an unhappy marriage: ten years earlier, her family had reluctantly given her as a second wife to a local traffic policeman. The first wife had treated her poorly, and Saratova was happy to be rid of them both. In Grozny, she and her son, Shamil, lived in a cramped first-floor apartment. When the bombing started anew, their neighbors fled to the mountains or refugee camps in Ingushetia, the Russian republic to the west of Chechnya. Those with the means went to Moscow, or even abroad. One day, Saratova's brother-in-law arrived to pick up Shamil and bring him back to the relative safety of their village. She hadn't heard anything from home, and wasn't even sure if the two of them had made it.

Saratova was the only one left in her stairwell of the building, living below five floors of empty apartments. She would look out one window and see militants scurrying about, on the hunt for protected fighting positions; through the other she would see Russian tanks rumbling past, stopping every now and then to fire their cannons at the militants on the other side of the building.

Grozny, once a bustling Soviet provincial capital, had become a haunted shell of a city, a place of oil-drum fires and wild dogs, where buildings, missing entire walls, stood like ghostly dollhouses, their mangled interiors visible from the street. The grim brutality of the war rarely made it to federal airwaves. One of the few honest, unblinking chroniclers of the war was Anna Politkovskaya, the reporter for *Novaya Gazeta,* who made countless trips to Chechnya. She wrote with horror, yet with no small amount of empathy for the Russian soldiers sent to fight a war they didn't understand: "exhausted men with unbalanced minds," she called them. Some were indeed outright sadists and murderers; many more were simply cannon fodder used without thought or care by inept and cynical generals. Politkovskaya described the reality faced by Saratova and Shamil, and the thousands of others trapped in Grozny, dodging sniper fire in the few minutes a day they left the house, and at home, praying that the jets overhead would haphazardly strafe some other building. "Going out into the streets of Grozny increasingly resembles a step towards the abyss. Going back to your apartment can be like a trip to the next world," Politkovskaya wrote.

With time, Saratova realized that the only people left in the other stairwells were frail and elderly *babushki*. She gathered them all in her apartment so they wouldn't have to fend for themselves, fetch water from the one well on the block, or lie alone on the cold floor during intense bouts of fighting. She cooked for them and had them sleep wherever there was space: in her bed, on the couch, on a pile of blankets in the entryway. As Politkovskaya described, the daily quest for provisions made for a terrifying expedition. Each morning, Saratova darted across the courtyard to the well, praying she could make it back with a bucket of drinking water without attracting a fusillade of shelling or sniper fire. One day, she saw a sixteen-year-old Chechen boy struck down as he was dashing back from a supply run, a bag of flour stuffed into his backpack. The bullet pierced the backpack before it entered his torso; he kept running for several paces, flour spilling out behind him, leaving a trail of chalky white powder on the ground, before he collapsed and died. Saratova recognized him by his boots—he lived across the street. She and the *babushki* buried him in the courtyard.

The daily horrors of the war led her to sympathize with the rebel side. Chechnya's separatist militants were not without their own cruelty and use of wanton violence, but at least they were doing battle with the Russian federal forces, whom she saw inflicting a real and unambiguous campaign of terror on the Chechen people. Guerrilla fighters started coming by the building; Saratova would bake them fluffy rounds of *lepyoshka* bread and hand over keys to one of the many abandoned apartments where they could rest for a night or two. She would chat with one, "Black Wolf," whose kind and noble bearing struck her as incongruous with his role as a rebel field commander.

Not long after, Black Wolf stopped by to warn her that the fighting was getting ever closer and she should leave now. If she stayed put, she might not get another lucky break. She decided to depart for the relative safety of Ingushetia. As she was packing, a Chechen journalist gave her a videocassette to pass on to the foreign press when she arrived. Saratova agreed. She had been wondering why Western governments were not intervening to try to stop the fighting; relaying documentary footage to them felt like her chance to prod them into action. She hid the tape in a shopping bag. At a checkpoint manned by Russian soldiers, she shook with fear, reciting in her head the ninety-nine names for Allah over and over to calm her nerves. The soldiers let her pass. In Nazran, Ingushetia's largest city, she went straight to the one hotel where Western reporters and aid workers tended to live—it had become too dangerous to stay overnight in Chechnya—and offered up the tapes. She sat with a researcher from Amnesty International and watched what she had brought. The images were horrific but by this point familiar: dead bodies frozen in ghoulish poses, buildings with huge holes where their roofs or walls had been.

From that moment, Saratova discovered a new mission for herself. She became a kind of one-woman documentarian, bringing evidence of atrocities and human rights violations committed by Russian soldiers out of Chechnya and into Ingushetia, where she would share it with aid workers and journalists. She earned money as a fixer, gathering information for foreign correspondents. It wasn't long before she fell in with the local field office of Memorial, a Russian NGO that had been founded to research and commemorate the history of Stalin-era repressions but, with the outbreak of the First Chechen War, had become one of the country's premier human rights advocacy organizations. Memorial's researchers worked out of Nazran and passed in and out of Chechnya on reporting assignments, collecting news of the latest raid on a village or evidence of torture and summary executions.

"It was a terrible, fearful time," said Eliza Musaeva, who ran the Memorial office in Nazran. "Heda had a serpentine ability to get to the toughest, most no-go areas, places where anyone else would find it simply impossible to pass any further. But she somehow always figured out a way." Saratova herself remembers how, in order to cross otherwise closed checkpoints, she invented sick relatives who must be visited. Three months into her stay in Nazran, she went back to her village to retrieve Shamil—he and his uncle had managed to get there unharmed—and brought him to live with her. She sometimes took him on her reporting trips, hiding videocassettes in his small backpack.

Saratova became close with Natalia Estemirova, another researcher at Memorial. Estemirova was in her early forties, born to a Russian mother and Chechen father; she grew up in Grozny, where she taught history at a local school and, with the onset of the violence of the Second Chechen War, began gathering evidence of abuses perpetrated by Russian troops. Early each morning, Saratova and Estemirova would set out from Nazran, crossing the border into Chechnya and passing columns of refugees headed in the opposite direction, bringing their extended families and life's possessions out of the hellscape Chechnya had become. As the two women neared the fighting, smoke would obscure the road like a thick fog.

Estemirova and Saratova documented the aftermath of Russian military operations: the missing husbands and sons, the victims of torture, the bodies unceremoniously buried in the village cemetery. There was little they could do in terms of advocacy or aid work; they were there to record the evidence of atrocities and to hope, with decreasing faith, that this might put pressure on Moscow to temper its prosecution of "anti-terrorist operations." It was a dangerous pursuit. They were harassed and intimidated by surly and pitiless Russian officers, and regularly ended up caught in shelling or machine-gun fire. To others, perhaps, it seemed that Saratova was fearlessly indifferent to the danger she faced, but the truth is, she was constantly aware of all the ways she could be killed. One time back in Grozny, on her walk home, she was caught in an attack by an assault helicopter. She ran to the nearest apartment building and cowered in the entryway. Small pieces of shrapnel slammed into the concrete wall all around her. She made sure to cover her face with her hands. If I am going to die, she thought, at least let me die with a beautiful face.

IN THE RUSSIAN IMAGINATION, Chechnya, a thousand miles south of Moscow on the edge of the Caucasus, is a place of violence, home to a people who are to be feared and ultimately subjugated, yet accorded the respect one gives to a valiant enemy. Throughout the nineteenth century, the tsar's army waged a prolonged campaign against guerrilla fighters in the mountains. In 1818, the Russian general Alexei Yermolov—an irascible sadist who led Russian forces in the Caucasus for more than a decade—erected a fortress in the Chechen flatlands and called it Groznaya, quite literally, "Fort Terrifying." Leo Tolstoy and Mikhail Lermontov served in the Caucasus as young military officers, and in their novels and short stories, they created the image of the Chechen as a fierce and proud warrior locked in a perpetual, almost preordained, struggle with the Russians. In *The Cossacks*, Tolstoy has a Chechen fighter tell a Russian adversary, "Your men slaughter ours, ours butcher yours."

After the Bolshevik Revolution, Soviet power held the promise of modernization, and with time, a sizable number of Chechens joined the Communist system as professors, doctors, and state functionaries. But many remained hostile to Moscow, and were at best distant believers in the Soviet colonizing project. The collectivization of agriculture was particularly foreign and unwelcome in Chechen society, which continued to value family and clan above class loyalties. Thousands of Chechens were shot during the repressions of the thirties. During the Second World War, countless Chechens fought on the Soviet side against the Nazi invaders; others seized the moment to try to overthrow Moscow's rule.

In 1944, as the close of war approached, Stalin ordered the deportation of nearly the entire Chechen population—half a million people—along with the Ingush and the people of several other Caucasus nations. It was a decision driven by Stalin's mix of paranoia and cruelty; he used the pretext of perceived collaboration with the Germans to justify the massive forced resettlement campaign. "Operation Lentil," as the NKVD, the Stalin-era precursor to the KGB, called it, was launched in the predawn hours of February 23. Chechen families were rounded up in open-bed trucks and crammed into freight wagons, which took weeks to chug their way to the outer reaches of the empire, eventually dumping their human cargo in the distant steppes of Kazakhstan and Kyrgyzstan. The ground was frozen and unforgiving. Disease and starvation were rampant. According to the NKVD's official reporting—meaning the real numbers were surely much higher—a quarter of those deported died in the first four years of exile.

Saratova's mother, Sovdat, was eleven at the time of the deportation. The day before the raid, she went to visit her aunt in a nearby village and decided to spend the night. The next morning, the NKVD showed up, taking Sovdat and her aunt into custody and shipping them off to Kazakhstan. Sovdat was separated from her mother, who was deported separately—her father had died when she was an infant—and never saw her again. For a long while after Sovdat got to the Central Asian steppe, she would linger under the wide-open night sky and imagine that her mother was somewhere not far away, looking up at the same starry tableau. After five years, she learned her mother had died during the journey. Sovdat was regularly hungry, sick, and cold, as winters stretched on for nine months and temperatures regularly dipped more than fifty degrees below zero. The family of Saratova's father, Bagai, had it slightly easier: They had been able to grab a bag of watermelon seeds before being taken from home. They planted the seeds upon their arrival in Kazakhstan and managed to feed themselves from their modest backyard garden.

The crucible of deportation and exile exacted a horrible toll on the Chechen people, leading not just to the deaths of many thousands, but also scattering family clans and interrupting the transmission of customs and beliefs. Chechens pride themselves on their dignity and toughness—the noble stoicism of the mountain highlander—and, even in Central Asia, they somehow managed to keep many of their traditions alive. Hospitality is awarded near sacred importance, with almost nothing more crucial than how you welcome a guest into your home. Bagai would later pass along the legend of how, while his family was in exile, one of his younger brothers died not long after birth. That same day, another Chechen family stopped by unannounced. Bagai's parents felt so compelled not to spoil the mood of their guests that they hid their child's body under a bed and kept putting out food and pot after pot of tea deep into the night. The guests left the next morning, and only then did the family mourn their infant son and give him a proper burial.

Solzhenitsyn encountered Chechen communities in Central Asia, where he, too, was exiled by the Soviet authorities. (He was sent to remote Kazakhstan after his release from the camps.) He was struck by how the Chechens, unlike any other group or nationality he had encountered, were not tempted by the benefits of compromise, and never allowed themselves to become fully Sovietized. "There was one nation which would not give in, would not acquire the mental habits of submission," Solzhenitsyn wrote in *The Gulag Archipelago*. The Chechens, he went on, "never sought to please, to ingratiate themselves with the bosses. Their attitude was always haughty and indeed openly hostile." Solzhenitsyn tells the story of an interfamilial Chechen blood feud that erupted in a small Kazakh village, which the local Soviet police were too terrified to try to resolve, but which was eventually extinguished by a council of respected Chechen elders. "Here is an extraordinary thing—everyone was afraid of them," Solzhenitsyn wrote of the exiled Chechens. "No one could stop them from living as they did. The regime which had ruled the land for thirty years could not force them to respect its laws."

In 1957, four years after Stalin's death, Khrushchev allowed the Chechens to return home. "Chechens remember everything," Khassan Baiev, a widely respected Chechen surgeon, told me. "We know who is who—when Stalin died, the whole country was weeping, but we were dancing the *lezginka*." The wound of the deportations and years in forced exile did not heal quickly. Saratova's parents returned in 1957 and settled in her father's village in the mountains. In 1965, her mother gave birth to baby Heda, the second of five children and the only girl. Her parents rarely spoke of the time they spent living in Central Asia, evoking it only when, as children, Heda or her brothers would misbehave or act selfishly, and they would hint at the hardship they endured during their own childhoods. Saratova's father kept a wooden frame used for knitting and two heavy wool shawls that his mother had worn in exile, and Saratova could see that he guarded them like cherished heirlooms.

When the Soviet empire crumbled in 1991, Saratova was twenty-six, studying to become a schoolteacher. Chechnya's history of pained relations with Moscow and distrust of its rulers immediately rose to the surface. A former general in the Soviet air force named Dzhokhar Dudayev, a flamboyant character with a trim mustache and a taste for fedoras, returned home and seized power. Taking advantage of a moment of chaos and weakness in Moscow, Dudayev declared Chechnya's independence. Saratova watched the announcement on television. Part of her was proud, and hopeful: Maybe it would really work out, and finally the Chechen people would rule themselves, unencumbered by Moscow. But she was also scared, her mood weighed down by a nervous premonition that none of this would end well.

BACK IN MOSCOW, YELTSIN—distracted by countless other priorities and crises—didn't pay much attention to what was happening in Chechnya. But by 1994, his military advisors convinced him that Chechnya could be retaken in what one called a "small victorious war." The path to that war was clumsy and improvised—both sides were slapdash in their preparations for armed conflict, and negligent in their efforts to avoid it. Russian tanks rolled into Grozny on New Year's Eve in 1994, but the soldiers were given foggy orders and little information about the city they were storming. The promised easy victory turned into a bloodbath. Russian forces quickly became encircled. More than a thousand were killed in the failed assault, presaging the mayhem to come.

Saratova spent the war with her family in their home village high up in the mountains of the Shatovsky district, a two-hour drive from Grozny. When Russian jets screamed overhead, her mother gathered Heda and her brothers and ushered them into a dark cellar. Her mother endured the hardship and fright of the war without complaint or displays of emotion. Her father was a different story. Heda had always thought of him as a formidable, even menacing, figure—a tough man of few words who, if you disobeyed him, was liable to take off his leather belt and give you a couple of sharp smacks to the behind. But the ever-present bombing, the constant need to hide, to fear for his children's lives, left him greatly diminished, a shell of a man consumed with dreadful anticipation. The belt Heda had once so feared was now pulled tight on his ever-shrinking frame, holding up billowing pants that, with every passing week, threatened more and more to slide off his waist entirely. He paced across the yard, plugging his ears with his fingers, reciting Islamic prayers over and over.

The conflict turned into a grinding and bloody stalemate. Over two years of fighting, approximately a hundred thousand Chechens and more than five thousand Russian soldiers were killed. Dudayev himself was killed by a Russian guided missile when his satellite phone betrayed his location. Finally, the war became politically untenable for Yeltsin, and he dispatched emissaries to negotiate a political settlement. In 1996, a cease-fire led to a pause in the fighting. The next year, the Kremlin and Chechnya's self-proclaimed leaders reached an agreement that prolonged the fragile peace but stopped short of deciding the republic's status; it gave Chechnya a form of autonomy that allowed many of the trappings of statehood without formally granting it. A period of instability and outright banditry ensued. Kidnapping for ransom became an industry. The more nationalist figures who had led Chechnya during the war were pushed aside by those under the sway of violent Islamism, especially Shamil Basayev, a seasoned militant who allied himself with foreign fighters, who flocked to Chechnya from across the Middle East, bringing cash and extremist ideology. In Moscow, Putin watched these events with mounting fury. One of his first moves as prime minister was to declare the Chechen government illegitimate.

With both sides—Basayev and his men, and Putin and his—itching for another fight, it was only a matter of time before one broke out. To Saratova, if the First Chechen War seemed to pass relatively quickly—"as if I ran a couple times here and there, and then it was all finished"—the second felt much tougher and nastier, a drawn-out, barbarous campaign of violence for its own sake. Federal forces took advantage of near total impunity to indulge in all manner of atrocities: killing children as sport, raping women in front of their families, throwing grenades into cellars packed with terrified civilians and waiting for the boom. "By the time of the second war, the Russian military understood our psyche, how to speak with us, really cause injury," Saratova said. "For a Chechen, death isn't nearly as terrifying as humiliation."

The hallmark of the second war was what became known as "cleansing operations." Russian forces in masks showed up in the middle of the night and took away the sons and brothers and husbands of whichever unfortunate family they chose. The unlucky ones ended up at "filtration points" set up outside villages, little more than mobile camps for torture and murder. Politkovskaya described what awaited a Chechen village after the arrival of Russian troops: "Federal raids, night purges, marauding, morning discussions of who was taken away this time and what was stolen along with them, regular burials, stories about the ways those survived were tortured, and whose corpses looked like what."

After Saratova's move to Ingushetia, where she linked up with Memorial and other human rights researchers, she began to offer up her services to foreign journalists and aid workers. They were among the only people interested in documenting Russian war crimes, and Chechens were, on the whole, eager to share information to be broadcast to the outside world. Journalism, fact-finding, and advocacy all merged: what mattered was getting the raw truth of the war to people who cared, even if they were unable to stop the carnage. Timur Akiev, another researcher at Memorial, often ran into Saratova at the Kavkaz checkpoint, the sole crossing between Chechnya and Ingushetia, which became a hub for exchanging information about which road was closed or what village was under bombardment—the Rick's Café Américain of the Chechen war. "Heda never sat in place," Akiev told me. "She was always full of ideas: where to go, what to do, how to do it."

It was no accident that many of the human rights workers in

Chechnya were women. It was tricky, and quite dangerous, for a man to travel around Chechnya, given the default suspicion toward all military-aged men and the patchwork of checkpoints where a person could be detained and subsequently vanish. A woman had a better chance of avoiding scrutiny by projecting an air of Caucasian modesty while hiding a camera in her bag and taking testimony from relatives of victims. It was also considered safer to work in tandem. Of all her female colleagues at Memorial, Saratova preferred to partner with Estemirova, the former history teacher. On their fact-finding missions, Estemirova struck Saratova as not only fearless but tireless; she could keep going long after Saratova decided she needed a nap or a break for a cup of tea. They both had young children, whom they would bring to Memorial's office in Nazran. For a while, they even shared an apartment, a large single room, free of decoration except for stacks of papers and the odd children's toy. Lana, Estemirova's daughter, was six years old at the time. "I think my mom had genuine respect for Heda," Lana told me recently. "They didn't always agree, and certainly weren't best friends, but they lived through some real horrors, which gave them a sense of solidarity toward one another."

Of all their joint missions, Saratova was most shaken by an expedition to the village of Komsomolskoe, in the lower foothills outside Grozny. The surrounding countryside had been the site of some of the most intense clashes of the second war, and the two women entered the village just hours after Russian forces finished carrying out a "cleansing operation." They found scores of corpses, including several that had been mutilated. Some bodies were missing their ears; others, their heads. Villagers had gathered 250 bodies to bury at the local cemetery. Saratova noted the silence: no one cried, not a whimper or moan of anguish, just total stillness and quiet. A woman had just buried one son and was waiting by the body of another. At least the bodies had been found and identified, the woman said. That was what passed for good news in Chechnya.

For the tight-knit community of human rights researchers and advocates working in Chechnya, Saratova was one of their own. She came off as tenacious and brave, and, like nearly everyone in the field, she was driven by an acute humanistic impulse. "I always knew her to be an honest and decent person," recalled Igor Kalyapin, the head of the Committee Against Torture, a Russian legal-aid NGO. "When she talked with someone who had endured suffering or tragedy, she felt real concern for them—it wasn't just for show." I heard something similar from Tanya Lokshina, an associate director at Human Rights Watch with deep experience in Chechnya. "Heda can establish contact with people very easily," she told me. "She is good at demonstrating that she really cares," she went on. "I got the sense that in that moment, she really feels it. She can call up a kind of instant empathy. When Heda sobs, she sobs genuinely. It's sincere."

But Saratova's colleagues also had reason to be wary. A number of times she led foreign journalists into situations that proved dangerous or uncertain, and others were forced to come to her aid. She could also appear a little too flexible in her sense of professional ethics, ready to bend the rules if the payoff seemed worth it, and always on the lookout for personal benefit. Svetlana Gannushkina, an esteemed human rights activist who often works on cases related to Chechnya, told me of a time she and Saratova were helping a Chechen family apply for asylum in Europe. Saratova wrote up a draft of the family's application, adding a number of exaggerations and falsehoods to make their story seem more dramatic and grave, Gannushkina said. She refused to confirm that version of events. Saratova got upset. "Why won't you help these people?" she asked. "I'm not going to lie," Gannushkina answered. "Why should I make things up when Chechnya is home to more than enough terrible stories?" Gannushkina also heard from colleagues that Saratova solicited money from some of the Chechen families she helped, a kind of consultant's fee for bringing their personal plight to the world's attention—an arrangement of mutual benefit, perhaps, but a practice considered anathema by Gannushkina and most other human rights advocates.

Saratova told me she could not recall the incident with the Chechen family's asylum application; she and Gannushkina had worked together on dozens of such applications without much disagreement, she said. As for the notion of her taking money, she called the persistence of such stories "a fabrication and an attempt to tarnish my name." The most she ever accepted from asylum seekers were tokens of gratitude for her help, she insisted. She still has deep admiration and respect for Gannushkina—though, as she put it to me, "I have plenty of things to criticize about her own work, and her own approach to some individual cases." All the same, she added, "I keep arguing that we should not stand on different sides of the barricades."

Regardless of the particulars, it seems clear she and Memorial made for an increasingly awkward fit, and eventually she left the organization. "She was not capable of being managed," Akiev said. "She refused to obey any rules or regulations. And this could create problems not just for Heda but for any organization she might be associated with." Saratova herself wanted more freedom in her work, the ability to pick up different assignments and combine human rights research with reporting tasks for foreign journalists and advocacy organizations. Even so, after she and Memorial formally parted, Akiev told me, "warm and collegial relations remained. We all stayed in touch for a long while afterward." Yet questions, too, persisted. Ekaterina Sokirianskaia, who worked as a researcher for Memorial in the North Caucasus, once asked Estemirova why she continued to go on joint fact-finding missions with Saratova. "Oh, that's Hedka, that's just the way she is," Estemirova said, using the affectionate form of Saratova's first name. As Sokirianskaia put it to me, "Natasha understood her shortcomings and forgave them, because she believed Heda had other merits."

Saratova continued to ferry journalists in and out of the conflict zone, and kept sharing information with her acquaintances at Memorial on the latest siege or cleansing operation. After a year or two, the scale of the fighting subsided, but the conflict remained on a low-scale simmer, erupting in periodic flashes of violence. Although Russian soldiers had quickly captured Grozny and other main cities, they kept dying in high numbers in guerrilla warfare in the mountains. Even more politically dangerous for Putin, Chechen militants carried out terrorist attacks in Moscow and other Russian cities. In 2002, after Chechen terrorists took more than seven hundred hostages at a Moscow theater, it was obvious that the Kremlin's strategy must change. The solution was "Chechenization," a policy under which the Kremlin ceded much of the political and military responsibility to its proxies in Grozny. If there was to be a war, let it be among Chechens.

The face for this policy was Akhmad-Hadji Kadyrov, a former chief mufti of separatist Chechnya. He had supported the call for jihad against the Russians during the first war—only to switch sides and declare allegiance to Moscow in the second. "He sincerely believed that he was saving the Chechen people from certain death," Ilyas Akhmadov, who served as the foreign minister of Chechnya's short-lived separatist government, told me. The elder Kadyrov, steeped in Chechnya's long-standing Sufi tradition, considered fundamentalist Islam, in the form of the Wahhabi practice that was seeping into the republic, as urgent an enemy as Russia. He was ready to make a tactical alliance with Moscow to destroy it. Despite Akhmad Kadyrov's defection, Akhmadov remembers him as "an energetic and brave man, with a great deal of personal courage."

Saratova had long held Kadyrov in great esteem, and his public break with the rebel movement and willingness to work with the Kremlin came as an unpleasant surprise. She thought it was not only ill-advised but treacherous—and quite foreboding for Chechnya. She was dismayed to see Kadyrov and Putin together at a staged event on television. For her, Putin was the personal embodiment of a policy aimed at the destruction of the Chechen people. She rued the turn toward extremist Islam in the rebel cause and had no patience for the creep of Wahhabi practice into Chechen society, but those evils paled in comparison to the horrors the Kremlin had inflicted on her land over the decade. And here was Kadyrov, sharing a stage with Putin, shaking his hand, smiling in his presence. What can this man really accomplish, Saratova wondered, if he is standing next to the killers of our people?

But Kadyrov had Moscow's backing, which also meant he had its military strength and financial resources. In 2003, with Chechnya once again incorporated into the Russian state, Kadyrov was elected president of the republic, in a vote held under military occupation. Seven months later, he was dead, killed by a bomb blast at a Grozny stadium as he watched Russian soldiers on parade. Later that day, his younger son, Ramzan, then twenty-seven, was summoned to meet with Putin. Until then, Ramzan's main interests had been boxing and weight lifting. He was also in charge of his father's personal militia, the so-called Kadyrovtsy, no less feared for their cruelty than the Russian troops that had tried to pacify the republic for years. In the meeting with Putin, which was televised nationally, the younger Kadyrov's blue nylon tracksuit set him apart amid the Kremlin's pompous formality. With Putin's blessing, Ramzan Kadyrov claimed the throne that had been granted to his father.

Just after the assassination, Politkovskaya went to interview Ramzan in the family's home village of Tsentoroy, a place she described as "one of the unsightliest of Chechen villages, unfriendly, ugly, and swarming with murderous-looking armed men." The two had a frosty meeting, and it ended with Ramzan calling Politkovskaya "an enemy of the Chechen people" and declaring that she "should have to answer for this." In an article about the encounter, Politkovskaya called the situation in Chechnya "an old story, repeated many times in our history: the Kremlin fosters a baby dragon, which it then has to keep feeding to stop him from setting everything on fire."

IN THE YEARS AFTER succeeding his father, Ramzan's authority in Chechnya became absolute and far-reaching. He wrested power not just from the Russian generals and intelligence officers who once oversaw Chechnya, but also from internal rivals hailing from other prominent Chechen clans. With time, he emerged as Chechnya's version of a feudal lord, nominally subordinate to the imperial center but with wide leeway to rule over his own kingdom as he pleased. The streets of Grozny filled up with billboards and huge, building-size posters of him and his father. "Ramzan Kadyrov is a Patriot of Russia," one read. "Happiness is Serving the People!" read another.

Russian federal troops became less visible, confined to a shrinking number of checkpoints and mountain outposts. The uniformed men with automatic rifles in the capital and in smaller towns were Chechen forces, not Russian, and although in theory most reported to Moscow, their ultimate loyalties lay with Kadyrov. Between twenty and thirty thousand men came to serve in units under Kadyrov's unofficial control. Many were former rebel fighters who had waged war against Russia. Their oaths were to Kadyrov personally, not to the Kremlin.

Putin swallowed this arrangement, likely because Kadyrov's militias enabled him to crush Chechnya's Islamist insurgency. In 2008, 237 people were killed in violence related to the lingering guerrilla campaign; in 2010, the number stood at 127. By 2012, it had dropped to 82, and in 2015, 14. Kalyapin, the head of the legal-aid NGO, said that Putin and the security officials around him operate under the assumption that success in the war against Islamist terrorism in the Caucasus—one of the signal achievements of Putin's presidency and a pillar of his popular legitimacy—couldn't have been accomplished by strictly following the law. "They think that to keep the peace with legal methods is impossible. So that's why you have Kadyrovtsy, who terrorize the population, who kidnap, and, yes, torture people. But they think it can't be done any other way."

As Kadyrov accrued power, Moscow came to matter less and less in Chechnya. "Federal law does not work at all," Gannushkina, the human rights activist, told me. "So what is there, then? One thing, just one law, which can be formulated in two words: Ramzan's order." The republic is governed by diktats inspired by Sharia jurisprudence and Kadyrov's personal interpretation of *adat*, a traditional Chechen code of behavior. Headscarves for women are mandatory in government buildings. It is nearly impossible to buy alcohol anywhere in the republic, at least legally. Kadyrov has praised the practice of polygamy, given his approval to vigilantes who drove around Grozny firing paintballs at women deemed to be dressed immodestly, and displayed an ambivalent attitude toward so-called honor killings—the murder of family members believed to have brought dishonor on their clan—condemning the practice while placing it within Chechen tradition.

Human rights work became more difficult and exceedingly dangerous. With Chechen forces in control, the authorities could easily track people village by village, determine who is related to whom, and decide what levers of pressure to apply. If Russian federal troops lashed out with crude force, blind to the many communal bonds that undergird life in Chechnya, their Chechen counterparts have the local knowledge and informant networks to pick their targets, and use family ties and Chechen custom to go after them with brutal efficacy. Many Chechen human rights activists who tracked abuses during the wars have now taken up more neutral and anodyne issues, like education and women's health; others have left the profession entirely. One of the few people who have continued to monitor human rights violations told me that victims of state abuses became less likely to appeal for help and often wanted no attention brought to their cases at all. Now it can make things worse. "The misfortune of one person becomes the misfortune of a whole family," the activist said.

In February 2008, people close to Kadyrov passed along that he was unhappy with Memorial's activities in Chechnya and would like to speak to representatives of the organization. Oleg Orlov, the group's board chair, who was based in Moscow, immediately got on a plane, along with Gannushkina. He thought the trip would perhaps allow them to gain a measure of protection for staff members in the organization's Grozny office. On the day of their appointment, he and Gannushkina, together with several local colleagues, waited for hours. Just before midnight, two cars came to pick them up and deliver them to one of Kadyrov's residences. Sirens blaring, they drove along an empty road that had been cleared of traffic and passed through a wrought-iron gate flanked by a pair of bronze lions. "It was like some kind of Babylon," Orlov said.

They walked into an enormous foyer, bare except for a billiard table and a display case with a collection of rare weapons: antique sabers, ornate pistols, an engraved machine gun. When Orlov sat down with Kadyrov, he tried to raise some of the issues Memorial was working on in Chechnya—forced disappearances, torture, extrajudicial executions—while avoiding outright confrontation. That proved difficult. Kadyrov presented himself as Chechnya's "chief human rights defender"; he didn't seem to understand the purpose of independent bodies like Memorial. "If there is an issue, tell me—I can solve anything," he said to Orlov. "He wanted to give the impression of a person who gets joy from helping Chechnya, who truly thinks about Chechnya, and who lives a difficult life," Orlov said.

The next day, Kadyrov again met with the representatives from Memorial. This meeting was broadcast on Chechen television. Kadyrov proposed the creation of a municipal human rights council for Grozny and named as its head Natalia Estemirova, Saratova's old partner, who had become one of the most high-profile and respected activists still working in Chechnya. "Just like that, like a tsar and a god, he decided and made it happen," Orlov said. As Orlov came to understand, Kadyrov thought that the move would bring Estemirova's activities under his control. The arrangement didn't last long. Estemirova continued to investigate abuses carried out by Chechen security forces. A month later, she gave an interview on federal television in which she criticized Kadyrov's policy of requiring women to wear headscarves in public buildings. She was called in to see Grozny's mayor, and then Kadyrov showed up and announced that he was dissolving the Grozny human rights council. As Estemirova later told Orlov, Kadyrov warned her, "Think about the consequences— think about yourself, about your daughter."

In July 2009, Estemirova traveled to the village of Akhkinchu-Borzoi. She spoke with locals about a killing in which armed police officers had dragged a man suspected of being involved in the militant underground to the center of the village and shot him dead. By then, Saratova had become cautious and less willing to overtly challenge Kadyrov and his ever-increasing number of acolytes and enforcers. "I saw how much she was risking," Saratova said of Estemirova. "I had started to risk less." The two friends were drifting in different directions: Saratova now shied away from direct confrontation, looking for a path of coexistence for herself and her two children: Shamil, now a teenager, and the younger Sharip, age five. Meanwhile, Estemirova continued her fearless work, meticulously tracking and publicizing rights abuses committed by Kadyrov's forces, just as she had the crimes of the Russian military. After her trip to Akhkinchu-Borzoi, Estemirova gave an interview on the assassination. Orlov told me that the human rights ombudsman in the Kadyrov administration, a thoroughly loyal figure, summoned the head of Memorial's Grozny office, Estemirova's boss. "Do you understand what you are printing—do you remember what happened with Anna Stepanovna?" the official said, referring to Politkovskaya. He went on: "Keep in mind the exact same thing could happen with Natasha Estemirova."

Around eight thirty in the morning on July 15, 2009, Estemirova left her apartment in the center of Grozny and headed toward the Memorial office. She was met in the street by a number of armed men, who bundled her into a waiting car. Neighbors would later say that she managed to scream out that she was being kidnapped. Saratova had gone for a picnic that day at Lake Kezenoyam, a mountain lake known for its temperate waters the rich blue color of a tropical sea. While there, she got a call from a journalist in Moscow: Natasha has gone missing. Saratova, like everyone in Estemirova's network of friends and colleagues, was immediately riven by fear. Such disappearances rarely ended well. Journalists and activists raised the alarm, calling every state office and police station in Chechnya they could think of, hoping that Estemirova would show up—detained, maybe, but at least unscathed. At a little after six that evening, Saratova got the news: Estemirova's body had been found, riddled with bullets, dumped in a field off a highway.

At an emotional press conference the next day, Orlov declared, "I know, I am sure, who is guilty of the murder of Natasha Estemirova. We all know this person. His name is Ramzan Kadyrov, the president of the Chechen republic." Even for Chechnya, the audacity and cynicism of the killing seemed shocking. Saratova vibrated with anger and desperation, the sense that no one was safe, that if the powerful turned on you, there was no refuge or protector. She joined a spontaneous march of a few dozen people in Grozny, carrying a hand-drawn sign reading "Who's next?" She began to look at the omnipresent police and security forces in Chechnya and saw only killers wherever she went: on every street corner, in the entryway of every building. She worried for herself and her large familial clan, not just her two sons and four brothers, but the dozens, even hundreds, of relatives who could face difficulty or real danger because of her work. Who could realistically protect them? And what about me, she thought, under whose wing am I going to hide? Ten months after Estemirova's murder, she got an anonymous text message. The point was clear: Stop—or you'll be stopped. The sender made sure to remind Saratova that he knew her children's ages and where they studied. She bought three tickets to Moscow that same night.

FOR NEARLY A YEAR, Saratova stayed in Moscow. She also traveled to Switzerland for a few weeks on a fellowship program. She thought of relocating permanently, but the idea of life in exile, even if only in Moscow, seemed fitful and unsatisfying. She missed her elderly mother, and felt the Chechen pull for home, for having a position and role in her own society, a person of some utility—and status— not just another displaced Chechen looking to survive in someone else's land. She returned to Grozny.

"When I came back for good, I knew I would have to change the style of my work, maybe even change myself," she told me. "The old way could not exist any longer." She would have to adapt to the reality around her: Kadyrov's power was nearly absolute, and to challenge it was pointless, even suicidal. A less antagonistic and more cooperative relationship with the authorities might allow her to help more people. "Yes, that means I will have to close my eyes to some things," she knew, "but these are problems where even if I wanted to, I wouldn't be able to do anything." But there remained a whole realm of cases in which the Kadyrov state's interests weren't so central, and perhaps a certain proximity to the authorities might aid her work.

The potential of working within the system became clear when a number of former militants came to her and complained of the Chechen state's unwillingness to allow them to reintegrate into civilian life. They wanted to get a formal pardon, to find jobs and live openly, but they were being followed and detained wherever they went. Saratova went to see an acquaintance who was a deputy minister in Kadyrov's government and explained the problem. He said he would meet with the young men. Fifteen showed up. Over the next days, Saratova shuttled between the police and the state-appointed

Islamic leaders and helped arrange amnesty for the group. She did the same for a cousin, a militant who went by the nickname "Gimpy Fox," who returned to civilian life and set up a small farming business. She felt that she was able to actually help people—not, as she put it, "just count bodies," as she had for so many years.

At first, Saratova was measured in her support for Kadyrov. She was not a person of categorical declarations and strongly held positions; she had a sensitive gauge for always locating the permissible and the advantageous. "Heda always acted in accordance with the spirit of the times, and found ways to benefit from it herself," Gannushkina said. "Heda did not change. Only the circumstances did." Where abuses continued in Chechnya, Saratova would suggest, they were the fault of some bad apples, police officers and commanders among the Kadyrovtsy whose actions were contemptible but isolated, not reflective of the system as a whole.

After Estemirova's murder, Kalyapin, the head of the legal-aid NGO, decided to set up a new human rights body composed of volunteer lawyers from around Russia who would rotate in and out of Chechnya every one or two months. None would have family ties to Chechnya, and the fixed terms of their assignments made them less vulnerable. Kalyapin asked Saratova to join as a local coordinator. She agreed. A few months later, she was called in for a meeting with Chechnya's human rights ombudsman, the same man who had hinted at the danger Estemirova was in. The ombudsman railed against the members of Kalyapin's group, calling them a bunch of spies, up to all sorts of nefarious schemes meant to undermine Chechnya and its leaders. Afterward, Saratova released a public statement announcing that she was leaving Kalyapin's organization because she disagreed with its methods. She was bitter recalling this moment to me years later, saying that the words published in her name had actually been written by the ombudsman's staff.

Kalyapin was disappointed, but not shocked—by then he had observed Saratova's gradual drift, a kind of magnetic pull toward the one unquestionable source of power in Chechnya. He heard from a mutual friend that Saratova was in tears when she relayed how she was pressured to withdraw her participation in Kalyapin's new group.

There were threats to one of her sons. Kalyapin was somewhat sympathetic, or at least understanding of what Saratova was going through. He had seen it with other Chechen friends and contacts who had morphed from Kadyrov skeptics, even open critics, into resigned supporters. "Many of them never made a conscious decision," he told me. "It was more of a psychological process—they simply got tired of being afraid." You encounter the specter of Kadyrov everywhere you go in Chechnya, he explained, and after a while, you make the choice—maybe not even fully clear to yourself—that it's easier to love him than to constantly live in fear. It helps that the Kadyrov regime welcomes and celebrates all the converts it can get. Winning over onetime doubters and antagonists is a way of proving the regime's fundamental virtue and shrinking the public space for dissent. "In Chechnya, if you are a notable person, you always have the opportunity to sell yourself to the state," Kalyapin said.

Saratova is coy about the array of threats and enticements dangled in front of her, but those who know her can imagine the likely contours of what happened. Sokirianskaia, an old colleague of Saratova's at Memorial, said the choice facing her and other Chechen activists was always quite clear: "You can leave and immigrate somewhere as a refugee, but you will show up as a nobody; you clearly won't be the person you were at home." Or, she went on, "You stay and become a person of the state, which gives you all manner of resources and possibilities." She imagined that this implicit offer—"status and influence and money"—proved convincing. Saratova's rhetoric evolved. She began to not only offer up positive propaganda, putting a flattering spin on Kadyrov's rule, but also sought to undermine those with whom she had once cooperated. She gave interviews to Chechen television reporters that cast doubt on the motives and practices of the human rights crowd in Moscow, including the staff at Memorial.

She made the sharpest break with her old circle in December 2014, in the days after a terror attack carried out in Grozny by a group of jihadist militants—an exceedingly rare event by then—left fourteen police officers dead and an office building in the city center in flames. The militants struck a police checkpoint and then barricaded themselves inside the high-rise that housed Chechen state press agencies. The battle went on for the better part of a day. Kadyrov was enraged: such a brazen attack was an affront to his claim of having brought peace and stability to Chechnya. In the fury of the moment, all critics of his regime, including journalists and human rights activists, were considered equally nefarious and hostile. Saratova went on a political talk show on Chechen state television and, at the urging of the host, singled out Kalyapin and his work for criticism. Kalyapin had mercantile interests, she said: "He is one of those people who came to the war so he could earn grant money." Unlike Kalyapin, she went on, she doesn't appeal to Western organizations for resources—with the obvious implication that he danced to the tune of his foreign sponsors. Afterward, she again called onetime friends and colleagues in Moscow, upset and crying, explaining that she had been pressured to say those things against her will—she didn't really mean it, can't they understand the impossible dead end she's in?

Some former associates pitied Saratova and her position. But just as many, especially those at Memorial, thought she had crossed a moral line that was difficult to forgive. "At first I tried to understand: okay, she did not behave correctly, but she is a hostage of the situation, she has a family to worry about, I can imagine the pressure she was under," said Akiev, who had, in 2009, become the director of Memorial's Nazran office. "I was not ready to accept her position, but at least I was able to make sense of it." Yet going on the offensive against those who had once accepted her as a colleague was another thing entirely. "There are situations when you can't say the truth," Akiev said. "But you can at least stay quiet, so as not to say an outright untruth—and Heda has not done that."

When I mentioned this sense of disappointment among those who had known her for two decades, Saratova was clearly pained. "It's hurtful," she said. "Why don't they try and understand, instead of cursing me?" She was certain that many of them were naive and too readily judgmental. "They are demanding of me what I can't give," she said, paraphrasing the critique, as she understood it, of those in Moscow: "Are you going to criticize Kadyrov? No? Then close down your organization and stop calling yourself a human rights worker." She had done neither. But that didn't make her oblivious of the reality of life in Chechnya today. "Trust me, I close my eyes to a lot," she told me. When I asked what, exactly, she had closed her eyes to, she demurred. "That is known only by myself and almighty Allah." But, she went on, "how can you say that everything in the republic is bad? The city has been rebuilt from ruins. We receive pensions on time. Salaries. Things work. This was never the case during the wars." Perhaps it is a false dichotomy—war or Kadyrov—but it is one that Kadyrov has succeeded in selling both to the Kremlin and to many Chechens. Not that those in Chechnya have much of a choice. Saratova, as ever, made the best of the moment and took a seat on the human rights council that reports to Kadyrov.

THESE DAYS, THE CENTER of Grozny is unrecognizable to anyone who saw it during the wars, when it suffered Europe's heaviest bombing campaign since Dresden in 1945. The rubble is gone, the streets repaved and well manicured—the central thoroughfare was given the name Putin Prospect, in honor of the man who is said to have brought peace, through warplanes and "cleansing operations," to the republic. The city's skyline is punctuated by the glass towers of Grozny-City, a collection of skyscrapers that house offices, luxury apartments, and a five-star hotel. Grozny is quiet and bland, with empty squares and grassy promenades. There is still a faint air of menace—men in black uniforms stand with automatic rifles on street corners—but the city's flashier attractions, including a man-made lake with a light show, seem whimsical and family-friendly. The sky-scrapers loom over the Akhmad Kadyrov Mosque, named for the elder Kadyrov. Known as "the Heart of Chechnya," it was built by Turkish artisans, and opened in 2008. It is ringed by manicured gardens and fountains decorated with colored lights. A vast hall, lit by Swarovski crystal chandeliers, can hold ten thousand worshippers.

One crisp fall morning, just after the day's second call to prayer, I walked through the gardens and past the mosque, making my way to a café off the main square, where I shared a pot of tea with Timur Aliyev, an advisor to Kadyrov. For years, Aliyev was one of Chechnya's most well-known independent journalists, the editor of a weekly newspaper called *Chechen Society,* which published investigations into human rights abuses and corruption. In 2008, in a moment of acute pressure from the authorities, he gave up his reporting work and took a job in Kadyrov's administration. "I once believed in this image of him as a brutal guy," Aliyev told me. "But then I got a chance to meet him." In their conversations, he found himself impressed by Kadyrov. "I was struck by his high ethical qualities," he said, "his high religiosity." Aliyev went on, "He thinks of himself not just as the head of the Chechen republic but as a person who looks after the well-being of each individual."

I asked Aliyev about Kadyrov's cult of personality. News broadcasts often lead with visits he's made to local schools and gyms; in Grozny, I heard plenty of stories of citizens appealing to the leader through messages on social media, and in many cases Kadyrov himself showed up the next day to fix some small problem or cajole an incompetent official into action. This was all positive, Aliyev said. "If we take the personal aspect out of this system, it stops being effective." As for a day when Kadyrov no longer rules, Aliyev told me, "I hope this time never comes." As far as I could tell, the logic of his about-face was not entirely unlike the choice faced by Saratova: on one path lies danger and hardship for you and your family; the other beguiles with a measure of comfort and access—and maybe, you tell yourself, even a measure of influence, a small lever to make life in Chechnya a bit better here and there. If Aliyev felt any lingering unease about his decision, it wasn't apparent to me. His support for Kadyrov seemed genuine.

During my time in Chechnya, I came to understand that Kadyrov's government, however illiberal, and however far from purely faithful to Islamic or even Chechen tradition, has much to offer a population recovering from twenty years of trauma and dislocation. Hardly a day passes in Grozny without a dance performance by a local troupe or an athletic competition featuring Chechen sportsmen. One night, I spoke to a woman who typifies what is left of Grozny's intelligentsia, a once thriving social class that was largely lost when the city was destroyed. "We were in a difficult position after two wars," she said. "Spiritually and morally dead. And while we should keep in mind all the negative parts of his character, in terms of the spiritual aspect, Kadyrov has put an end to our decline." She went on, though, to say that the state could do only so much, and that it would be up to the Chechens themselves to rebuild their culture— a tall order, given the state's degree of intrusion into everyday lives. "Ramzan on his own isn't culture. It's just a forced choice—to require this, ban that, build something here, and then declare this culture," she said. Some traditions were returning, others were being lost—often both at the same time. "When I was a young girl, my grandfather made me wear a headscarf," she said. "I was afraid of him. He explained to me, 'You are a Chechen girl, and so you will wear a headscarf.' But today we don't have such grandfathers, and instead their role is played by the Department of Spiritual and Moral Education."

The ascendancy of Kadyrov, and the de facto autonomy he enjoys from Moscow, is welcome and persuasive to many Chechens. Even if they don't care for him and the nature of his rule, he is at least one of them, not another interloper sent by Moscow. Kalyapin said that many who have suffered abuses at the hands of Chechen officials and security forces decline to seek restitution, telling him, "We'll figure it out, we don't need your Russian laws or courts." Many times in Chechnya, I was struck by the irony that in a desperate bargain to fend off the separatists of the nineties, the Kremlin effectively allowed Chechnya to become a kind of internal abroad, a self-ruled territory about which the original separatists could only have dreamed.

OVER TIME, THE RULES and logic of Saratova's work became clearer: on matters that concerned Kadyrov and his inner circle, she was powerless to do anything other than enthusiastically echo the official position. But in more peripheral, less consequential cases, she could be of some help. She could make a few calls and, for example, get the police to release a couple of teenage boys suspected of belonging to the extremist underground, who were ultimately deemed innocent. There was a twenty-five-year-old who was detained because he had once let a militant who was friendly with his older brother spend the night at his family's home. Police officers put a bag over his head and nearly suffocated him, then beat him with clubs. When Saratova dragged him out of the station, he could barely walk, his body limp and covered with dark blue hematomas. Another guy disappeared into custody for eight months. By the time Saratova finally found him, she remembers, "he smelled rotten and damp—like someone had buried him in the wet earth and forgotten all about him."

Saratova feels compelled to praise officers for begrudgingly and unceremoniously releasing the prisoner, even if they illegally detained and tortured him for months. "Obviously, I close my eyes to the fact that the person was detained for a month or two, if I want to get him out of there," she said. "I have to flatter people who have violated the rights of some young guy, but then, on my request, let him go." I could never quite figure out how much of Saratova's ease with Chechen law enforcement and security officials, relations that are sugarcoated with deference and praise, is an otherwise unpleasant tactic she forces herself to swallow—or, rather, is an altogether comfortable, even preferable, mode of existence. "I tell them: 'Oh, thank you so much, you helped find this guy and return him to his mother.'"

Chechen politics are defined by intrigue and patronage, and Saratova always makes sure she has a protector one or two levels above. She has cultivated personal ties with high-ranking officers in the Chechen security forces. Her connections do give her a degree of access, which can produce information, if not always results. Even the human rights activists in Moscow who are suspicious, if not outright disdainful, of her closeness with the Chechen authorities admit that she can often get an update on a case or track down a missing person's whereabouts faster than they can. In turn, Saratova uses this fact as a way to justify her proximity to power. "While Moscow activists write letters to the prosecutor's office and wait for an answer, anything at all can happen to this person," she told me. "But I solve problems right away."

Her relations with those inside the Kadyrov power structure flow both ways. She is far more likely to get instructions on which cases to pursue and which to leave alone than to uncover some information the authorities don't want her to have. By now she has come to understand on her own where the limits lie, and how to stay within them. She told me of a man who was filmed stepping on a poster of Kadyrov and saying, "It would make a good rag." He posted the video online and was arrested. Saratova declined to get involved. (A judge later ordered him to perform road-maintenance work.) There have also been plenty of occasions when she has been approached by relatives of men who were detained by Chechen security forces and never heard from again. She would ask around and determine that it was possible they did have some connection to Islamic militancy. (At least that's how she presented these stories to me.) The official position held that these men had been killed in armed clashes, and Saratova decided to leave it at that. "You can't return the dead, and the fear that I might bring harm to the living stops me from going further." Once a Chechen is suspected of being a militant, just about any man or boy in his whole familial clan can find himself in danger. "There are moments when I feel genuinely powerless," she said.

Saratova's access to certain officials in the Kadyrov system has made her one of the few accessible contacts with knowledge of the workings of Chechen law enforcement: who has been detained, where they are being held, what they are suspected of having done. Tanya Lokshina, the researcher at Human Rights Watch, continues to call Saratova every now and then, and stops by her office when she is in Grozny. "Sources of information are necessary," Lokshina told me. "I used to think Heda was the one making a compromise. Now I realize I'm the one making a compromise, by keeping up a relationship with her." Their conversations follow a now familiar pattern, she said. A person disappears, presumably taken by forces loyal to Kadyrov, and a panicked search begins. Lokshina calls Saratova to hear what she knows. Saratova will typically say: "Tanya, what a terrible story. I'm talking with the mother right now. She is sobbing. I'm doing everything I can." Then, without fail, she will add: "Just understand one thing. Publicity is very bad. We need to stay quiet, at least for a few days. If we start to shout, it will only make things worse." Saratova then promises to try to get the person out of custody, or at least officially charged and given access to a lawyer—but please, no big announcements or official moves just yet. Sometimes that produces a result. Just as often, it doesn't, and all Saratova has achieved is to keep things hushed up and out of sight.

"If she has the chance to help you today, she will," Igor Kalyapin told me. "But if tomorrow she is forced to undermine you, she'll do that, too." He told me of the time in February 2014, when he learned of the arrest of an activist named Ruslan Kutaev. Two days before, Kutaev had been among the organizers of an unsanctioned conference in Grozny on the seventieth anniversary of the 1944 deportation. In the Kadyrov era, memory of the deportation has been monopolized by the authorities, deployed in ways Kadyrov finds advantageous to his own image and hold on power, and ignored in most others. (Some years earlier, in a telling move, Kadyrov swapped the official Chechen day of remembrance from the day of the deportation, February 23, to the day of his father's funeral, May 10.) Kadyrov was upset by the unsanctioned event, and summoned Kutaev for a dressing-down. Kutaev ignored the summons—and quickly turned up in police custody, charged with heroin possession.

Kalyapin flew to Chechnya and went straight to the police station where Kutaev was being held, in a town called Urus-Martan. After waiting for an hour, he saw a pair of luxury sport utility vehicles with blue sirens affixed to their roofs speed through the station's front gates. A notorious high-ranking Chechen interior ministry official stepped out of one SUV, accompanied by Saratova. Kalyapin could tell she enjoyed the respect and recognition their arrival elicited in others. "I saw that she got a kind of pleasure from this," he told me. "The way she showed up in an expensive car with a siren on top, in the company of this high-ranking general, the way she could talk with him, what an important person she was."

When Kalyapin was finally allowed to see Kutaev, he could see that Kutaev's body was covered in dark bruises, with large hematomas on his thigh and shoulder; he had clearly been beaten—and not at all lightly. Kutaev said he had not been ill-treated. But later, in private, he told his lawyer he had been beaten and subjected to electric shocks. His defenders lodged several complaints with the court that went nowhere. Kutaev was found guilty and sentenced to four years in prison. Saratova expressed shock at the verdict and said she didn't think Kutaev was guilty; his sentence, she said, was "meant to show Chechen society who is the master of the house."

By then, Saratova's conduct was nothing new for Kalyapin—he didn't get particularly offended or upset over what he saw as her prevarications and petty betrayals. She could still, however, make small gestures of magnanimity, which to him seemed like flickers of old collegiality—or perhaps just guilt. One came that December, not long after the terror attack in Grozny and Saratova's subsequent television appearance denouncing Kalyapin. She passed a warning through mutual friends: a large demonstration was planned for the next day, ostensibly to denounce Islamist extremism, and it might end in the courtyard of his legal-aid committee's offices. There could be a provocation, she said. Kalyapin told his Grozny staff to be on guard and to make sure the security cameras were working properly. The next day, Saratova addressed the crowd on Akhmad Kadyrov Square, speaking about how human rights activists were overly concerned with protecting terrorists and not the families of the police officers they killed. People held up signs that read "Stop the flagrant lies of human rights defenders" and "Kalyapin Go Home." Several hours later, things turned rowdy, seemingly by plan, and a number of people charged the office, breaking the door and throwing firebombs. The place was totally destroyed, but no one was seriously hurt. When Kalyapin told me the story, I found myself wondering which moment was more telling: Saratova's tip to Kalyapin beforehand, or her actual participation in the rally that precipitated the riot.

OVER TIME, THE IMMEDIATE threat of the militant underground receded, even as special operations continued to drag on in the craggy, wooded hills of the Caucasus. Attacks in Grozny and other urban centers petered off to a manageable number—deadly and embarrassing for Kadyrov, but not frequent enough to threaten his hold on power. Yet as the insurgency faded into the background, it was replaced by another security threat: Islamic State propaganda began to take root inside the republic, especially among the younger generation. Chechen law enforcement agencies estimate that as many as four thousand Chechens traveled to Iraq or Syria to join the group. Most had fled Chechnya for Europe sometime during the First and Second Chechen Wars, but around four to five hundred are believed to have gone directly from Chechnya to the Middle East. (This, in part, explains the falling levels of violence inside Chechnya: the more committed fighters left for distant battlefields.)

For Kadyrov, the rise of ISIS presented both opportunity and peril: the danger posed to Russia by ISIS again demonstrated his importance to the Kremlin, yet it also called into question his claim to having built an ideal Chechen state, one to which the Chechens scattered all over the world should return home. In speaking of those who might be tempted by ISIS propaganda, Kadyrov's tone could sound noble and avuncular. "Even one person for us is a loss," he said. He would regularly hold late-night meetings with groups of young people who were supposedly planning to pledge allegiance to ISIS, televised spectacles that were clearly public relations exercises. Yet even in these stage-managed settings, the threat of violence was never far removed. Kadyrov finished one television appearance by saying of those Chechens who joined ISIS, "As the Prophet says, 'Wherever they appear, there is always blood.' The Prophet calls on us to destroy them all—we have done so and will continue to do so."

One gray and rainy autumn day, I traveled to a village in Chechnya's central plains to talk with a woman whose only son had gone to Syria. He had left Chechnya some years earlier to study medicine in Moscow, and when he and his mother spoke on the phone, nearly every evening, he showed more interest in his studies than in religion. The last time they talked, he told her of an upcoming exam; she said she would pray for him, and that it was time to find him a wife. The next day, he disappeared. Two months later, he sent her a text message saying he was in Syria. "I am on the path of Allah," he told her. He got in touch again to tell her he was off for the front. Some weeks later, another Chechen wrote her to say her son had been killed by rocket fire in Ba'aj, in northwestern Iraq.

His mother told me that her husband, her son's father, had died when the boy was nine, and that the family had lived in refugee camps in Ingushetia during the two Chechen wars. "He never saw war. We did everything we could to keep him away from it," she said. "It turned out he needed to go to Syria to die." What drew him there, and how he could leave her and his four sisters without a man in the family, seemed beyond her comprehension. "It's an infection, and all our young people have gotten sick."

The stream of young people leaving for Syria became Kadyrov's chief concern—which meant, by extension, the chief concern for all the deputies and underlings who orbit around him. The Syrian question came to dominate Saratova's work: she regularly fielded calls from mothers whose sons, suspected of harboring ISIS sympathies, had been picked up by the police; or from those whose sons and brothers had already disappeared in Syria and who were desperate for some information; and, as time went on, from relatives of young people who had joined ISIS but were now desperate to come home, terrified and helpless.

Eventually, the stream of Chechen recruits became a mere trickle, and then stopped entirely. Successive counteroffensives retook virtually all the territory once controlled by ISIS. The group was on the run, and no longer held the same mythical pull on impressionable young people; what's more, enough time had passed for word to make its way back to Chechnya about the danger and ugliness of the self-proclaimed caliphate. Those Chechens who had gone to Syria were effectively trapped: in many cases their travel documents had been lost or destroyed, and they were viewed with suspicion by just about every country they would have to cross through to get home, from Iraq to Turkey and Russia itself. Many were women and children who had followed their husbands to former ISIS-held territory, oftentimes with only a foggy idea of where exactly they were traveling, and for what purpose. And when the men died in battle—the survival rates for ISIS foot soldiers were not high—their wives and children were stranded, with no way back home. Those who did manage to get out didn't get far, quickly ending up in detention facilities for suspected ISIS members in Iraq. Saratova told me of as many as four thousand Russian citizens, many of them Chechens, who wanted to find a way back.

Saratova became one of the coordinators of a Kadyrov-led program to bring Chechen women and children home. Kadyrov presents himself as a father of the nation, making the return of every Chechen—whether a refugee in Germany or an ISIS widow in an Iraqi prison—a signal priority and point of pride. (It is harder for men to return from ISIS-held lands, at least without facing criminal prosecution and a likely prison term.) Saratova shuttled between government offices in Grozny and Moscow, always with a number of sullen, desperate older women in tow—mothers whose daughters and grandchildren were stuck somewhere in the maelstrom ISIS had left in its wake. They had ended up everywhere, from the last ISIS-controlled strongholds in Syria to overcrowded prisons in Iraq; their children were taken from them and handed over to state-run orphanages. It was clear that Saratova was not the decision-maker and had little influence over determining who could come back and when. That was up to the diplomatic skills of a man named Ziyad Sabsabi, Kadyrov's emissary in Damascus, who tracked down the whereabouts of Russian citizens on the ground. It was also up to the Kremlin, guided by the Russian security services, who were suspicious, to put it mildly, of people returning home from a lawless terrorist stronghold. But Saratova was allowed a certain role as the public advocate for the ever-swelling ranks of mothers, corralling them into a single coherent bloc and presenting their interests to those to whom she has access in Moscow: the Kremlin's human rights commission, middle-ranking officials in the foreign ministry, and journalists eager for any story with an ISIS angle.

"She was given the job of dealing with all these anxious crying mothers," said Sokirianskaia, who once worked with Saratova at Memorial and now directs an independent conflict-analysis center. "And she does this well. She listens to them, speaks to them, hears them out." Whenever I met up with Saratova in either Moscow or Grozny, she had a number of such women floating around her, mothers in patterned headscarves and billowy dresses, who were quick to pull out photos of their missing daughters. In Grozny one day, I spent an afternoon with Saratova tooling around to various appointments and events in the company of a woman named Dzhanet. Her daughter Ziyarat had been twenty-six and a schoolteacher when, in 2015, she followed her husband to Turkey for the summer, their two young children in tow. He said he was there for medical treatment. Then Ziyarat disappeared; the next thing Dzhanet heard, she was in ISIS territory, where her husband had gone to fight. Soon he was dead and Ziyarat and the children were trapped. "I can't explain what a tragedy this news was, and for a long time, I had no one to tell," Dzhanet said when we spoke in 2018. Ziyarat ended up in an Iraqi prison, and her mother feverishly picked up on whatever rumor or hint of news she could find: the Chechen women in the prison would be sent back, the Iraqi government was blocking their release, they had been sentenced to death, the FSB would allow them to return next year, or next month, or never. She asked Saratova the same question over and over: When will my daughter come home? To me, it sounded less a question than an invocation. And Saratova didn't have a real answer.

Once, over lunch in Moscow, Saratova pulled out her phone and played me a series of voice messages from the previous night. Her number circulates among Chechens and other Russian-speaking recruits in Syria and their families. A young man named Gadzhimurad, who had traveled to Syria and soured on the ISIS project, had set off to escape through the desert with his wife and two young daughters. "Heda, please help us," he said in the first message. It was night, and Gadzhimurad and his family were lost, dodging a convoy of Iraqi troops and a battalion of Kurdish forces; warplanes streaked overhead. "Will they shoot us, I don't know," he said. His wife also left Saratova a series of plaintive messages, frightful sobs muddying her voice. "This day may be our last. Today, we will go to Allah," she said. Saratova asked Gadzhimurad to figure out the name of the village where he and his family had stopped to hide. Then she had passed the coordinates to Sabsabi, the Chechen emissary, who in turn gave the location to Kurdish militia commanders. Sometime just after dawn, Sabsabi told Saratova that Gadzhimurad and his wife and children were safe. "Two minutes ago, they came to the Kurds," he told her. "I hope you had a chance to sleep." She hadn't, and when we met for lunch that day, her voice suggested a disoriented exhaustion, but she was happy that Gadzhimurad had made it out alive. A few weeks later, a plane landed in Moscow: Gadzhimurad's father met his grand-daughters on the tarmac. (Gadzhimurad and his wife remain impris-oned by Iraqi authorities in Erbil, along with a son born in detention.)

Another time, Saratova told me about the case of a twenty-three-year-old man named Said Mazhaev. He had traveled to Syria to pledge allegiance to the caliphate and immediately regretted it, he claimed. He and Saratova were in touch while he was in Syria, sending voice messages back and forth. Mazhaev injured himself on purpose, which led ISIS commanders to allow him to travel to Turkey for treatment. From there, Saratova helped him plot a route back to Chechnya. He was detained upon arrival, and given a prison sentence of two and a half years. Saratova wrote an appeal to the court, describing their correspondence and asking for a reduced term. His sentence was shortened to eight months. She considered the outcome a great vic-tory: Mazhaev could have easily died in Syria; instead, he would be home with this family in less than a year. "Why don't all the human rights activists in Moscow appreciate that?" she asked. She seemed genuinely offended that her former colleagues could not bring them-selves to give her any credit. "I think they are purposefully set against the Chechen authorities, expressly trying not to notice all the posi-tive things happening in the republic."

Over half a year, more than ninety Chechen women and children returned from Iraq and Syria. They were flown to the Russian base in Latakia, Syria, and, from there, chartered flights brought them to the Grozny airport. Each time, Saratova was waiting on the tarmac. She stood with a beaming smile, as the mothers, clutching their babies, descended the steps onto the asphalt. It was always a big scene for Chechen television, a celebration of Kadyrov's fatherly care for the Chechen people and a show of his might. Not just any regional Rus-sian leader would have had the wherewithal to bring back hundreds of people from the clutches of ISIS. Saratova held a banner that read "We thank Putin for our children."

She considered this one of the more onerous compromises re-quired of her. "When I see his picture or hear him speak, I remember that he destroyed thousands of our people's lives," she said. She remembers Putin's promise to "waste them in the outhouse," and knows what that led to—the disfigured corpses, the mothers at the cemetery. Yet she feels compelled to be filmed holding up a sign praising his benevolence. "I imagine that if I didn't do this, there wouldn't be a next round of women and children coming home," she said.

All the same, after nine such flights, the FSB managed to intervene and convince Putin that bringing such people back to Russia was a dangerous folly. The program was frozen. Yet more and more mothers kept writing and calling Saratova, hoping she could offer some measure of hope. All she could do was wait. She kept up the appeals to Moscow and the meetings with various midlevel officials and the press conferences for Russian journalists, but the flurry of activity belied a fundamental impotence. She could try to keep the mothers calm and hopeful—though that would grow harder with time—but she couldn't bring their children back.

IN APRIL 2017, *Novaya Gazeta*, Politkovskaya's old paper, ran a pair of horrific and sensational stories: more than a hundred men had been detained in Chechnya on suspicion of homosexuality. They were being held in a network of secret prisons, where they were tortured and forced to give up the names of other gay men. At least three had been killed. The story grew even darker as it unfolded, with accounts of beatings and electroshocks, and of men murdered by their own family members. Even for Chechnya, with its regular tales of brutality and rampant human rights violations, this cycle of repression felt especially heinous. The news spread quickly among the Moscow press corps, and the foreign media picked it up with an interest and urgency it hadn't displayed toward Chechnya in years.

A reporter from a radio station in Moscow reached Saratova at her office in Grozny. Had she heard the allegations? She hadn't heard any reports of these abuses or received a single appeal for help—but, she added, "I wouldn't even consider one even if I did." As for the position of homosexuality in Chechen society, she said, "I think that even if these people were to face the highest penalty, the society in which we live would not condemn such a thing." Her words, transparent in their callous indifference—perhaps even holding a coded incitement to violence—echoed comments from Kadyrov himself. "We don't have those kinds of people here," Kadyrov told an American television crew, adding, "Praise be to God." He went on: "If there are any, take them far from us, to Canada, so we don't have them. To purify our blood, if there are any here, take them." For Saratova, her own, similar response was something far beyond trying to play both sides—a human rights activist maneuvering to shield the authorities from oversight. She had become an outright public relations mouthpiece for the Chechen leadership.

As attention to the story grew, Saratova persuaded her contacts in Kadyrov's inner circle to let her arrange for a *Vice News* crew to visit the site of one of the alleged secret prisons, in Argun, a short drive from Grozny. "She believed that it was in the advantage of the Chechen authorities to show their point of view," said Veronika Silchenko, a producer for *Vice*. At the same time, Silchenko added, "it was clear she had an incredibly tormented conscience. All these humanitarian organizations are making so much noise about this story, and Heda wanted to show that she personally is not guilty, that she has nothing to do with it. It was as if she was trying to clear her name." Saratova cajoled reluctant officials into appearing on camera. In Argun, the local police chief led the journalists around some abandoned buildings, which was supposed to prove that the whole notion of anti-gay repressions was fabricated: Can't you see we're not torturing anybody here? When the same chief lined up the troops under his command on the base's parade grounds, the scene proved no more convincing. "Was there a single case where I told you to arrest some kind of gays?" he asked them. "No," they fired back. The chief turned to the camera and shrugged: Nothing to see here. Saratova's plan to undermine the allegations with a gesture of transparency backfired when the news crew showed footage of the Argun base to a Chechen man who said he had been held and tortured there. Yes, that's the place, he said—he had been electrocuted in a now abandoned wing of the building, and the police chief was among the people who had beaten him. When the *Vice* crew brought this evidence to Saratova, she was unmoved, and played naive. "If I have never seen a single gay person and none have ever brought me a statement, or even a verbal complaint, how can I confirm they exist?" she said.

Perhaps the most macabre detail in the whole story was how the authorities, knowing how to manipulate Chechen social codes, enlisted families as murderers of their own relatives. Homosexuality has long been judged harshly in Chechen society, but more as a taboo than the object of a crusade. It was something families tried to keep quiet, and that local security forces would use as a pretext for extortion and blackmail. "There were never killings, let alone on a mass scale," explained Elena Milashina, a *Novaya Gazeta* reporter with years of experience in Chechnya who led coverage of the anti-gay crackdown. "This became possible only after the signal came from above, from the Chechen authorities." Milashina heard of at least half a dozen cases in which families were told by the authorities to kill male relatives who were said to be gay.

"From the very beginning, when we realized this was a campaign against gays, we knew it would be very difficult, that no relatives would want to verify anything," Milashina told me. For many Chechen families, an accusation of homosexuality is worse than a charge of supporting terrorism. "That accusation— sympathy for terrorists, involvement in extremism, having ties to Wahhabi cells or even ISIS—is a familiar one," she explained. "It is, in a way, routine. It is considered a kind of norm." But a charge of homosexuality is something else in Chechen society. "No relatives will want to confirm this," she said, all the more if they participated in an honor killing, whether forced or not. "They don't want to testify against themselves or implicate their family further." When I asked Saratova about the question of anti-gay repressions, and how she conducted herself during the resulting outcry, she started by returning to her initial comments to the Moscow radio station. She had been flustered— it was all a big misunderstanding, she said. "I started rambling and somehow misspoke, never imagining that such a thing could be true," she told me. "I was caught off guard." It was hard to see what exactly had gotten so garbled: in the interview, the radio correspondent, clearly taken aback, had asked a second time if Saratova really meant that the killing of gay people would be accepted in Chechnya. "You understood me absolutely correctly," she answered.

As we spoke, more than a year after *Novaya Gazeta* first broke the story, it seemed to me that Saratova just wanted the whole topic to go away, to not have to answer any more questions from people like *Vice* reporters or me about the rights of a community whose very existence clearly makes her uncomfortable. She retreated to a position of detached indifference, rather than an outright call to violence. "If such people exist, it's their life, their problem," she told me. Of course torture and abuse are bad, she went on, but what can she do? The question of homosexuality is so toxic in Chechnya that she couldn't investigate even if she wanted—which, again, she didn't. "I didn't look into this too deeply because, taking into account our customs and traditions, I wouldn't have produced any results," she said. "I would be powerless to go up against a topic like this." She dismissed the notion that the Chechen state could have anything to do with such repression, but allowed that perhaps "their immediate relatives could have solved the question." Ultimately, she cloaked her indifference in a pose of good-natured concern: gay people should leave Chechnya for their own good. "I don't know if such people exist, but what's for sure is that they will never be welcome in Chechnya. This will never be considered acceptable," she said. "If there are people with such an orientation, they shouldn't publicize it, but leave and go to where this is welcomed."

When I spoke to Milashina about Saratova, she was dismissive and contemptuous. She considers Saratova unworthy of consideration, "a nonsense person with no influence whatsoever." Saratova just repeats the messages passed down from Kadyrov, doing no less than what she is told—and certainly no more, Milashina said. "She's just one more voice in Chechnya whose purpose is to justify the actions of Kadyrov."

More significant, Milashina told me, was what the story of the repression—and the reaction to it—demonstrated about Kadyrov himself. At first, the Kremlin promised to investigate the claims. Kadyrov has no shortage of enemies in Moscow, especially among federal law enforcement and the security services. They would be happy to use any pretext to weaken him in Putin's eyes. But the inquiry went nowhere and was quietly closed down. "So it turns out he really is independent," Milashina said. "And not only from Russian law, but from the Investigative Committee, from the FSB, from high-ranking officers who would like to put him in his place. He is subordinate to only one person: Putin."

IN THE YEARS FOLLOWING Estemirova's murder, in 2009, Memorial's office in Grozny remained open, but few victims of abuse came to ask for help, and those who did file claims often withdrew them once their families came under pressure. "People tell us, quite frankly, 'You can't even defend your own people,'" Oleg Orlov said. "What can we say, really? They are right." Even with all the difficulties, the head of the office, Oyub Titiev, a respected and stoic figure, a man with a palpable consciousness of his own dignity, did as much as circumstances allowed, and never more than he thought safe for the families involved. But every now and then, there was the chance to pursue a real investigation.

One morning in January 2018, when Titiev was driving from his home village of Kurchaloi to Grozny, traffic police waved over his car. A few moments later, he was taken into custody: police officers had allegedly found a bag with a couple hundred grams of marijuana on the passenger seat. The news of his detention immediately found its way to Moscow, where Titiev's colleagues at Memorial and friends in human rights circles had no doubt that he had fallen victim to a cynical and brazen setup. His arrest was reminiscent of the fabricated case against Ruslan Kutaev—they didn't even try to come up with a better scheme, his colleagues at Memorial thought.

Titiev's friends and supporters asked Saratova to rush to the police station in Kurchaloi. She was only happy to oblige; she is always eager to be the first on the scene, the hub of information through which all other spokes flow. Whatever slivers of news she learned, she passed on to those waiting with nervous anticipation in Moscow. After hours of refusing to admit they even had Titiev in custody, officers allowed his lawyer in to see him. Saratova also joined the meeting.

"It's terrible," she later told Tanya Lokshina, the lead researcher at Human Rights Watch. "But what can I do?" In the coming days, Saratova suggested that anyone could have walked by and thrown a bag of god knows what on the front seat after Titiev had been pulled over. In other words, the drugs weren't his—a rather honest acknowledgment of reality—but neither had they been planted by the cops. She was searching for a face-saving way out, a version of events that would allow the state to drop its charges while not having to fess up to the fact that it had framed an innocent man. But when it became clear that the Chechen authorities weren't interested in that outcome, Saratova went quiet. She was quite forthright, though, in acknowledging that she took Titiev's arrest as a kind of retrospective proof of the wisdom, or at least necessity, of her modus operandi. "If I didn't start to take into account where I live when I do my work, it's quite possible that something would have happened to me, too," she told me. Saratova sometimes attended hearings during Titiev's trial, and I asked her what she thought when she saw him inside the metal cage where defendants sit in Russian courtrooms. She answered, "That I could be in his place."

For what was putatively a simple drug possession case, Titiev's trial stretched on for months. Every now and then, Saratova would bump into Memorial staff members from Moscow and other former colleagues. They would fly to Chechnya to attend a hearing or two and give Titiev a wave and smile from the visitors' bench. Alexander Cherkasov, a longtime specialist on Chechnya at Memorial, told me of the time he ran into Saratova outside the courtroom. He looked at her dismissively. Sensing the mood, Saratova blurted out, "It's not us who are broken, it's our life," an aphorism made popular by a well-known Russian gangster film from the early 2000s about a crew of otherwise upstanding guys who are pushed to crime by their bleak circumstances.

Another time, when Gannushkina had come for the day, she and Saratova ended up in line next to each other while waiting to pass through the court's metal detector. "Oh, Svetlana Alekseevna, I'm so happy to see you," Saratova told her, as if they had last seen each other at the Kavkaz checkpoint during the war and would now reminisce about all the close shaves they had survived together so many years ago. Gannushkina could manage only to let out a laugh in response: just a few months before, in Grozny, Saratova had addressed a gathering of bussed-in protestors who were supposedly aggrieved by the work of Russian journalists and activists accused of making up all sorts of devious untruths about Kadyrov's Chechnya. Saratova had held a sign that read "Between two evils, does Gannushkina choose gossip?" She offered up commentary to Chechen state television. The slanderous criticism by Gannushkina and her ilk, she said, "denigrates the image of those who work hard here to defend their people, to defend Russia as a whole. . . . We won't allow them to do this." Gannushkina had seen the segment, and thus found Saratova's attempt at a breezy hello amusing— but not really a surprise, and certainly not confusing in its intent. "She thinks it's still beneficial to hold in reserve some kind of relations with me," Gannushkina said.

In March 2019, Titiev was found guilty, and sentenced to four years in a low-security penal colony. The verdict was actually softer than expected: Titiev would serve his time in the loosest form of incarceration, and would be eligible to apply for parole after only two months. (He was released in June 2019.) Perhaps the Kremlin had realized the absurdity of the case and went for the only concession it could allow itself. But the message was no less clear: human rights activists, especially in Chechnya, can expect repercussions if their work threatens state interests. Saratova's response was of a piece with her attitude throughout the trial. "I don't consider Titiev's sentence to have been politicized," she said. "But nor do I consider him to have taken part in what he was accused of."

ONE AFTERNOON, SARATOVA AND I set off from the center of Grozny, driving the length of Putin Prospect out of the city and onto a narrower road that snaked its way up through the mountains. The sun dropped behind the peaks, turning the air cool and casting a bluish-gray hue on our journey. A couple of hours later, we entered Urd-Yukhoi, Saratova's family village, the site of her parents' home, where she spent the first war and sent her son to wait out the second.

In the years since, her family had rebuilt the place, putting up a new house made of red brick, set in a courtyard behind a tall iron gate, in the traditional Chechen manner. We drank black tea and ate bowls of chicken soup flecked with fresh herbs. The house was large but empty, seemingly waiting to host a whole clan, all the siblings and cousins and grandchildren. I slept upstairs in one of the many spare bedrooms.

The next morning, we went for a walk around the property. Saratova showed me the wobbly, largely crumbled foundation of her family's original house, where, amid the dry earth and overgrown brush, we could see the door to the cellar where her mother would gather the whole family during heavy bouts of fighting. Across the valley were the towering green peaks over which the first Russian fighter jets would streak just after six o'clock every morning. She showed me the bench where she was sitting the day she last saw her twenty-year-old cousin Magomed drive past, before he was killed in an explosion up the road minutes later. Russian federal troops came by and told the family he had fallen victim to a rebel ambush, but Saratova had her doubts.

We headed up a sloping incline, coming to a clearing in the trees. Not long before, one of her brothers had built a soccer field for the children in the village. Now, she told me, she understood the choice the elder Kadyrov had made. "It took me a while, but I thought about it, and realized we should thank him," she said. In both Akhmad-Hadji and Ramzan, she sees necessary and welcome force, the strength to hold Chechen society together and to keep the Russians at a distance. She has no illusions about the relative balance of power, either between the Chechens and the Russians or between herself and Kadyrov. What her onetime colleagues and peers back in Moscow think of as surrender, she sees as a simple acknowledgment of reality. You may not like it, but those are the rules of survival— circumstances that became all the more clear after Estemirova's murder. I thought back to my time with Konstantin Ernst, who faces far less explicit and sharply defined pressures; his situation atop Channel One allows for a winking cleverness that eludes Saratova. Her circumstances are much cruder, as is her response to them. "No matter how much we shouted, how much we scolded those in power, how much we fought them, like a fish thrashing on a frozen pond, there was no point," she said. "On the contrary—it only made things worse."

The view from the clearing was beautiful, peaceful, even, with a grove of apple trees on one side and a wall of mountains on the other—a pastoral scene that was interrupted only by Saratova's recollections of violence and destruction in this very same place. She makes the trip to Urd-Yukhoi every couple of months, and each time remembers the bitter and terrifying moments she spent here—a reminder, she told me, that if she is going to live and work in Chechnya, there's no other course than the one she's settled on. "Any other way just can't work," she said. "I've tried everything else."

CHAPTER 3

THE LAST FREE PRIEST

—

THE WINTER OF 2012 WAS A TENSE, THOUGH VIBRANT, TIME IN Moscow. A series of large-scale protest demonstrations had erupted in response to widespread falsifications during the previous fall's parliamentary elections, but the deeper cause was a feeling of exhaustion and distaste for the Putin system among the capital's up-wardly mobile professional classes. Putin had announced that instead of giving Dmitry Medvedev a chance at a second term as president, he would run himself. The move confirmed that Medvedev's entire tenure had been a hollow and cynical joke; it destroyed even the pre-tense of a civic voice in the country's politics. Putin delivered the announcement, and that was that—the role of the Russian electorate, he made clear, is simply to ratify the will of the sovereign. A demon-stration in December on Sakharov Avenue drew tens of thousands of people—this was the occasion where Leonid Parfyonov, the televi-sion personality and onetime friend of Konstantin Ernst's, took the stage. Another protest, in February, on Bolotnaya Square, across the river from the Kremlin, attracted an even larger crowd, reaching a hundred thousand people.

The presidential election was scheduled for March. Putin was sure to win—he remained broadly popular, and had the power of the state apparatus to boost his candidacy—but the old, unspoken consensus that had governed his rule for the past decade had run its course. Previously, the state had walled off political matters from society at large, declaring politics its own dominion, in which the involvement or opinion of the citizenry wasn't necessary or welcome. In exchange, Russia's citizens—especially the burgeoning middle class—benefited from a modernizing country and the spoils of a booming oil economy, enjoying a degree of personal and consumer freedom unprecedented in Russian history. The editor and political analyst Masha Lipman dubbed it a "no-participation pact." That era had clearly sputtered to a close. But what would replace it?

The answer came, in part, one afternoon that February, when Putin went to a public meeting with the country's religious leaders at the Danilov Monastery, which dates to the thirteenth century. The oldest building remaining today is the Church of the Holy Fathers, built in 1565, a warren of chapels under bright green onion domes topped with shimmering gold cupolas. The grounds of the monastery, set on the right bank of the Moskva River, have served several functions over the centuries, from a place of prayer and reflection to a defensive structure against the invading Mongol army to, under the Bolsheviks, the site of a detention center run by the Soviet secret police. The property was returned to the Russian Orthodox Church in the 1980s, and since then has been the theological and administrative headquarters of the patriarchate, the Orthodox equivalent of the Vatican. Its symbolic fusion of the overlapping pillars of power in modern Russia was made complete in 2008, when an oligarch, with the Kremlin's encouragement, bought the monastery's eighteen prized bells back from Harvard University, where they had ended up after the revolution, and returned them to their original home.

That afternoon, Putin was greeted by leaders of Russia's officially recognized faiths: Orthodox Christianity, Islam, Judaism, and Buddhism. The obvious and ceremonial head of the proceedings—after all, everyone was on his home turf—was Patriarch Kirill, the leader of the church, then sixty-five, with a stern face, a silver beard that hung from his chin, frozen in place like a stalactite, and a tall clerical headdress in starched white. Matters of politics and faith in Russia have never been contained in separate dominions, whether under the tsars, who subordinated God's authority to their own, or in Soviet times, when the Orthodox Church was initially quashed, only to be artificially resuscitated and made to serve the Soviet political agenda. In the early years after the Soviet collapse, that history made the church leadership wary of the Kremlin. For a while, it seemed the church and the Kremlin were willing to make a series of situational alliances, without ever fully trusting or understanding each other. Kirill, who was named patriarch in 2009, moved the church closer to the state, enjoying its largesse and patronage while staying out of the earthly nitty-gritty of politics. Until now.

Kirill began by speaking of the nineties, hitting many of the same themes frequently raised by Putin and his proxies: the decade was a period of chaos and deprivation, a modern-day Time of Troubles—the historical period of famine, civil unrest, and impostors posing as kings, before the establishment of the Romanov dynasty in 1613. Similarly, Kirill argued, modern Russia was saved by a measure of divine intervention, and he left little doubt as to its author. "Through a miracle of God, with the active involvement of the country's leadership, we managed to leave this horrible, systemic crisis." He turned to face Putin directly. "I should say openly as a patriarch, who is obligated to tell the truth, without paying attention to politics or propaganda, that you, Vladimir Vladimirovich, personally played a massive role in righting this crooked twist in our history." Alluding to the upcoming presidential election, he said that Putin, of all those who might seek power, had "the best chances of parlaying his candidacy into the actual job." It was as direct a political endorsement as a Russian patriarch had uttered in the country's modern history.

Putin, desperate for a new political formula to explain and justify his continued hold on power, seized on the seemingly holy imprimatur and applied it to a new, hodgepodge ideology then in the making. His campaign that winter—and his presidential term to follow—came to be based on a mixture of a surface adherence to Orthodoxy, social conservatism, distrust of urban elites, and anti-Americanism, offered up as a kind of balm for the country's post-imperial confusion and disorientation. Liberalism would be cast as something perniciously un-Russian. "The voice of the church," Putin told Kirill at their meeting at the Danilov Monastery, "should be heard in full force."

The Russian Orthodox Church is an exceedingly hierarchical organization, and a largely conservative one. Most priests were unbothered by Kirill's foray into politics—Putin was broadly popular inside the church—and certainly did not feel emboldened to question him publicly. Under Kirill, the church had been edging toward a more open embrace of the state and its interests for some time, and his comments at the Danilov Monastery were the logical culmination of a policy set in motion years before.

Still, some inside the church were dismayed. The murmurs of concern from priests and other church figures were largely limited to Moscow and St. Petersburg, home to more liberal congregations—many of whose members had attended the large anti-Putin demonstrations that winter—and a small contingent of outspoken dissident priests.

One of the few opposing voices in the provinces came from a parish priest in Pskov, a city of two hundred thousand people in the forests of northwestern Russia, near the border with Estonia. Father Pavel Adelgeim was seventy-three, and looked the part of a jolly, welcoming pastor: kind and knowing blue eyes, a flowing white beard, and a flickering, tilted smirk. He had suffered repressions from the Soviet regime for his service as an Orthodox priest. As a result of that experience, and his deep study of the Gospels and centuries of church history, he was hostile to what is traditionally referred to in Russia as the "symphony" of Orthodox religion and state power. Adelgeim called it a "wily alliance," and wrote, "The Church participates in state affairs, and the state uses its ideological potential. The danger of a loss in quality appears for both sides."

Adelgeim was notable not just for openly questioning the church's direction under Kirill, but for his acrimonious and long-running feud with his own immediate superior, the archbishop of the Pskov diocese. It was unthinkable for a priest to challenge his archbishop, but the dispute animated Adelgeim much more than anything that was happening in Moscow. He wanted the church to stay out of the political sphere entirely, a tenet he followed in his own life. The chants of the crowds on Sakharov Avenue and Bolotnaya Square—and the actions of Putin himself—were as foreign to him as disco music. "I don't care whether this person is in the world or not," he said of Putin. "He has nothing to do with my fate; he is part of a machine, which sometimes works idly, other times with repressions."

At the time Kirill threw the church's implicit blessing behind Putin, Adelgeim was in the middle of a more immediate conflict. A change in internal church law under Kirill had shifted control over the affairs of an individual parish from the parish congregation to the bishop of the particular diocese to which it belonged. Adelgeim and his parishioners had resisted the reform, and fought it within the church's internal justice system and even in regular state courts in Pskov. Hearings had dragged on for years. "People want to come together, to participate in church life, but the desire of the diocese to rule all on its own, robbing people of all activity and initiative, destroys the unity of the congregation," Adelgeim said. The patriarch functioned like the Communist Party's general secretary during Soviet days, with archbishops in the role of his local party bosses. By 2011, the head of the Pskov diocese, Archbishop Evsevii, had forcibly reorganized the parish council at Adelgeim's church, removing eleven members and appointing a dozen others in their place.

Over the Putin years, and particularly under Kirill's leadership, the church had restructured itself in ways that mirrored the changes in Russia's overall political architecture. Just as Putin centralized politics under his personal vertical of power, Kirill sought to restore authority to the affairs of the church through a process of bureaucratic centralization. The free-form anarchy of the nineties, with its messy inefficiencies, gave way to a clearly delineated hierarchy, in which bishops—and ultimately Kirill himself—would be in charge of just about every aspect of church life and practice. Adelgeim mourned the disappearance of the humane and private space in his pastoral work. He feared the church risked losing sight of its mission, becoming part of the "bureaucratic apparatus of the Russian Federation."

Adelgeim's skepticism made him an outcast in Pskov, a disobedient annoyance to the diocese, yet deeply popular among his parishioners and a larger number of followers around Russia. Evsevii did little to hide his disdain, and sought to marginalize, even humiliate, Adelgeim whenever he could. Adelgeim took refuge in the Gospels, in which Christ tells his disciples: "You shall have suffering in the world, but take heart, I have overcome the world." His erudition was not limited to religious texts; he read history and literature widely, from Thomas Mann to C. S. Lewis. He liked to recall a line from Vladimir Vysotsky, the Russian singer-songwriter and bard of the sixties and seventies: "All through the ages, prophets, just like eyewitnesses, have been burned at the stake."

PAVEL ADELGEIM CAME TO his faith at the age of thirteen. His grandfather, a prominent industrialist in Ukraine, was executed during the Stalinist repressions of the thirties. In 1942, when Pavel was four, his father, a theater actor, was arrested and shot as a supposed wartime spy. His mother was sent to a labor camp, and Pavel was shipped off to an orphanage for children of "enemies of the people." When his mother was released, she, like many former prisoners, was ordered to live in the Soviet empire's outer reaches. She moved with Pavel to a settlement in the northern steppes of Kazakhstan. It was there, as an adolescent, that Pavel fell into a quietly religious circle; services were held in the deep of night in private homes, a secret society of the faithful. He decided he would devote his life to God, even as he had no illusions about what that would mean. "We knew we could be arrested, shot, sent to the camps, anything at all—that we should be ready," he recalled afterward.

In 1956, Adelgeim enrolled in the Kyiv seminary, an institution the Soviet authorities tolerated but kept under close watch. As he readied himself to join the priesthood, he traveled to the countryside to find a bride. Soviet cities were full of proletariat workers and intelligentsia engineers and professors; the provinces were where religion managed to stay alive. Adelgeim and a priest he knew traveled by train, bus, and horse-drawn carriage to Gaivoron, a village in the Ukrainian heartland whose residents weren't given internal passports, which effectively meant they were stuck in the countryside—you couldn't travel anywhere in the Soviet Union, let alone resettle, if you didn't have documents. The priest introduced Pavel, then twenty-one, to a young woman named Vera, a name that means "faith" in Russian. She was seventeen years old, with a shy smile and two thick braids. At the moment Adelgeim showed up at her family's modest wooden farmhouse, she was preparing for her school exams. He returned a few days later and spent hours reading the Bible to her as she listened and snacked on green apricots from the garden. They took a walk, coming to a stop under the shade of a cherry tree. He proposed.

Adelgeim returned to Gaivoron for the wedding, bringing along a few seminary friends. The local authorities refused to allow a church ceremony: everyone in the village was married according to standard-issue Soviet procedure. As one stern provincial official told them, a religious service would "cast a shadow on the conduct of scientific-atheistic work in our village." Pavel and Vera hopped in the back of a delivery truck and rode to a nearby village, where a priest married them at the local church in great haste, but with the full liturgical trappings of an Orthodox ceremony. When the authorities gave chase, they took off again, traveling through the night in a scene Adelgeim would remember years later: the gardens of the village abutted by a thick bog, lit under a huge moon that hung low in the sky; the warm air scented by the perfume of wildflowers.

Pavel was sent as a priest to Kagan, a small city just outside Bukhara, in the Uzbek Soviet republic. At the time, in the early sixties, the officially atheist Soviet state allowed the Orthodox Church a modest existence, while doing everything it could to make religious observance difficult and unpleasant. Priests could lead services and guide believers through the most basic traditional rites: baptism, Easter, eulogies, and the like. (Putin, for example, has said he was baptized in secret by his mother, who didn't tell his father, a faithful party member.) The church was sometimes jokingly referred to as the "Ministry of Ritual Services"—another obedient and personality-free Soviet bureaucracy. Any activity beyond the walls of the parish church was forbidden. Priests could not explain or encourage religious faith in their communities, nor carry out charity work or hold social events. Most important, they could not build new places of worship—that was the domain of the state, which was more inclined to shutter churches than open them. On the eve of the revolution,

Russia had fifty thousand church parishes; by the fifties, there was just a quarter of that number across the whole of the Soviet Union. Moscow, the epicenter of the sprawling empire, home to five million people, had only a hundred priests.

In Kagan, Adelgeim was assigned to the Church of Saint Nicholas, on the outskirts of town; it had been around since the nineteenth century, but after the revolution had been shuttered, then used as an infirmary for tuberculosis patients. It was made of red brick and, by the time Adelgeim showed up, was in a shabby way, cramped and dilapidated. One of the nastier tricks the Soviet state was fond of at the time was strong-arming priests into publicly rejecting their faith. The KGB threatened their families—a wife could lose her job, a child might lose his place in university—until a priest renounced God and the church. The most famous, and demoralizing, case was that of Alexander Osipov, a distinguished professor of Old Testament theology at the Leningrad seminary, whose renunciation appeared in the pages of *Pravda* under the headline "Abandoning Religion Is the Only Correct Path." In 1962, a similar article appeared in the paper in Tashkent, the Uzbek capital, featuring Vasily Pogorelov, an archdeacon whom Adelgeim knew and respected. For a while he and Vera had even shared an apartment in Tashkent with him. "I Renounce!" the headline declared, followed by all sorts of slander and criticism of his fellow clergy in the Uzbek diocese. For a long while after, Adelgeim would see Pogorelov in the Holy Assumption Cathedral in Tashkent, late at night, long after the evening service had ended, kneeling before the iconostasis and weeping. "Young, energetic, not even forty, crying such heavy tears," Adelgeim remembered. For him, the scene was a lesson in how succumbing to the state's demands could be a trap, a spiral that inevitably sucks you further and further from your conscience.

When Adelgeim got to his new church, he set out to repair the building. Members of the congregation helped him, and so did local Muslims from the neighborhood, who affectionately called him their "Russian mullah." Within a month, they had rebuilt three walls, laid a new floor, and installed a 200-year-old iconostasis brought from Moscow, effectively constructing a new church from a heap of ruins.

That would prove Adelgeim's downfall: he had breached the unwritten prohibition on building new houses of worship. The authorities looked for a convenient pretext, and formally charged Adelgeim with Article 190 of the Soviet criminal code, "Dissemination of knowingly false fabrications that defame the Soviet state and social system." The indictment read like a compilation of rather fantastical allegations: in addition to keeping a collection of banned literature at home, Adelgeim was supposedly the secret author of "Requiem," a series of elegiac poems by Anna Akhmatova about the agony of waiting for her son to return from the Gulag. He was sentenced to three years in a prison colony in the Central Asian steppe.

Years later, Adelgeim gained access to a number of sealed documents in his case. He came across testimony from Leonid Svistun, a friend from the Kyiv seminary who was among those who came along to witness his and Vera's furtive wedding ceremony. Svistun had told investigators that Adelgeim "demonstrated anti-Soviet attitudes" and spoke out against the church's official, Soviet-friendly leadership. "He refused to sing the Soviet anthem," Svistun had testified, even though in those days, no one sang the words—starting from 1956, the music was performed without lyrics, seeing as how they had been a paean to Stalin, whose memory had by then fallen out of favor. "Adelgeim belongs to the most reactionary wing of the clergy," Svistun had alleged. Adelgeim wrote that learning of the betrayal felt like "thunder from a clear sky." It also explained his friend Leonid's rapid ascent in the church: with time, he became Archimandrite Makary, a bishop sent on missions to Canada, Switzerland, and the United States. These were the sorts of positions that required the nodding approval of the state—the KGB, in particular. "The competent organs did not doubt him," Adelgeim knew.

In the labor camp, Adelgeim worked as a welder. He also studied law in the prison library, helping other inmates write appeals. His faith only deepened, along with his ability to anger the camp's administration. One day, the bosses sent Adelgeim on a welding job; he was struck by an overheard crane, which nearly crushed him. His right leg was amputated. Perhaps it was an accident, though Pavel and Vera would forever have their doubts. He served out the rest of his sentence, and was freed in 1972. Adelgeim was by no means serene about the years he lost, let alone his disablement, but he never expected anything else from the path of Christ. "He felt he was bearing a cross, and so he accepted all this evil, all this sorrow, with humility, even love, a feeling that this was the way it should be," Vera said. Adelgeim, a gifted poet, wrote a few lines on his return from prison life: "I am going home, farewell, guard towers / For three years you have watched over me / Better than any books / You helped me figure out life."

The state wielded influence over even the most minute of the church's activities through a body called the Council on Religious Affairs, which was, in turn, close to the KGB. The council's regional representatives, not the diocese, ultimately decided which priest would serve where—and if he could serve at all. Within each parish, local KGB cadres and Komsomol activists harassed churchgoers. On Easter Sunday, gangs of young men rode noisy motorbikes back and forth in front of churches, disrupting services and scaring off the old women who came to have a priest bless the eggs they'd painted. A person spotted at church a bit too often might have problems at work or university.

In search of a place to serve, Adelgeim and his family went to the Fergana Valley, a green chasm of fertile land fed by two Central Asian rivers, then to Latvia, and from there, in 1976, to Pskov. The city is set on the Velikaya River, which runs along the outer wall of the Pskov kremlin, an expansive medieval citadel made of white brick. Seventeenth-century merchant houses commingle with colonnaded, neoclassical administrative buildings built in the Soviet era. Pskov lived under German occupation for three years during the Second World War and was the site of heavy fighting, exacting a psychic and physical toll on the city. The resident head of the Council on Religious Affairs was opposed to Adelgeim's arrival—"over my dead body," he told Adelgeim of his chances of being given a parish in Pskov—but another local priest, Vladimir Popov, went to the KGB office to vouch for him. "They looked at him with suspicion," Popov told me. "For them, he was a quite resolute person, very determined." But Popov managed to convince them. "Don't worry, he has already served his time, he won't cause you any problems."

Pskov is home to more than thirty churches, of which, at the time, just four functioned as houses of worship. The rest, like churches all across the Soviet Union, had been turned into museums of atheism, or storehouses for grain, or were simply shuttered and left to slowly decay. Adelgeim bounced around between various congregations, and in 1980 got one of his own: Saint Matthew the Apostle, in Piskovichi, a village just outside town. It had been badly damaged in a fire, and was left with rotten walls and a dirt floor. As in Kagan, Adelgeim set out to fix up the place (by this time, nearly twenty years later, one could do so without being sent to a prison camp). He also contributed articles on various canonical questions to a small journal devoted to Orthodoxy. Despite the arcane subject matter, the articles greatly spooked the local party functionaries in Pskov. Adelgeim proposed that he show them the texts, steeped in biblical references and church law, ahead of time. "He didn't consider this a compromise," Vera said. "He had nothing against the government—he was interested in religious questions."

IN 1988, THE COUNTRY'S Orthodox believers prepared to commemorate the thousand-year anniversary of Russia's adoption of Christianity. According to legend, Prince Vladimir converted from paganism to Orthodoxy in 988, having sent emissaries to examine the religious practices of surrounding nations. Islam, the story goes, was ruled out because of the Russian people's fondness for drink. Those who returned from Constantinople, where they witnessed an Orthodox service at the Hagia Sophia, reported that they were so taken with the beauty of the liturgy that "we no longer knew whether we were on earth or in heaven."

The anniversary represented a decisive moment in the Russian Orthodox Church's modern history. Gorbachev's perestroika was in full swing, and he decided to allow the church to mark the anniversary with large-scale public celebrations. Soviet television for the first time showed Orthodox services in all their grandeur and mystery, with choral prayers and priests swinging incense in chapels hung with glimmering icons. The new attitude was a recognition of reality: interest in Orthodoxy had grown throughout the eighties, for it was one of the few corners of life relatively unspoiled by decades of Soviet dogma. But it was also a signal for the faithful, and their leaders, to push further. Priests went out into the public, preaching the Gospels to the uninitiated. They were allowed to reopen long-shuttered churches.

In Pskov, as elsewhere around the country, churches began attracting the curious and spiritually hungry. "Young people appeared in church," Popov recalled. "Society became interested in religion. At the same time, we had an opportunity to take the floor, to speak, to converse with people." Adelgeim was used to being hounded for his faith; he grew up practicing it in secret as a boy, and eventually lost three years of his life and his right leg on its behalf. "At first, he didn't understand," Vera remembered. "He couldn't believe it, everyone took it as a shock." Many priests had forgotten how to speak in a human and compelling language of faith, or had never learned at all. They were just as sick with the Soviet ailment as everyone else. The new environment of relative openness, and the sudden expectation foisted on them, froze many in place. "A lot of other priests weren't ready, they didn't know what to say," Vera said. "But Father Pavel had the mind-set of a pastor." His sermons drew ever-larger crowds. Vera worked at the House of Pioneers in town, and he began to come by in the evenings, answering young people's questions about Orthodoxy and the Gospels and the lessons they held for the suddenly unfamiliar times.

Adelgeim had developed a sizable following in Piskovichi. Now he turned his attention to a disused cathedral in the center of Pskov: Zhen-Mironosits, or Holy Women Myrrhbearers Church, a boxy white sixteenth-century chapel with a lone cupola topped by a gold cross. It was closed by the Bolsheviks in the 1930s, and by the later years of the Soviet Union was being used as a warehouse by Pskov's postal service. It sat on the grounds of a green, tree-covered cemetery, and, when Adelgeim got the go-ahead to reopen it, was in terrible condition. Within half a year, Adelgeim and a handful of congregants had put up a new roof. He led the first service one day in May 1989; so many people came that several hundred people stood

on the pathway in front of the church, spilling out across the cemetery.

By default, many in the Orthodox clergy resembled late-Soviet
dissidents. Like those with narrowly political grievances against the
Soviet state, the more active and visible members of the priesthood
wanted to forge a new ethics outside of the stifling tenets of Marxism-
Leninism—a way of understanding one's existence, and the responsibilities that come with it. To think in terms beyond the official
ideology was itself a political act. The first great Soviet-era preacher
was Alexander Mein, whose beloved explanatory sermons brought
thousands to Christianity in the later years of Soviet rule. He was
murdered in 1990, just before the system's collapse, struck in the head
with an ax as he walked to lead a Sunday service. That same year,
Gleb Yakunin, a priest from a parish outside Moscow, was elected to
the Supreme Soviet, a late, short-lived Soviet attempt at representative democracy. Yakunin, too, had a large following; in the seventies
and eighties, he had been a high-profile defender of religious freedom, and had spent seven years in prison camps and internal exile.

Adelgeim put aside his aversion to politics and decided to run for
a seat on the Supreme Soviet, too. "His stump speeches were like sermons," remembered Lev Schlosberg, an early pro-democracy activist
in Pskov. They served as fables for a new morality, blending biblical
lessons with calls for freedom of conscience and speech. One rally in
support of Adelgeim's candidacy grew so large that the authorities in
Pskov wanted to postpone it by a day so they could find a larger
venue. The crowd bristled at the idea and began to shout its disap-
proval. Adelgeim quieted them. "Let's carry ourselves with dignity,
in the image of God," he said. (In the end, Adelgeim's campaign was
blocked by local party officials, who refused to register his candidacy.)

The Soviet collapse removed the last formal barriers for the Orthodox Church—it was free to proselytize and expand its religious
mission without any oversight or limitation from the state. The
church was implicitly on the side of the new democrats; in the tense
days of August 1991, when, in a last, desperate attempt to keep the
Soviet Union intact, a group of hard-liners staged a coup, Patriarch
Alexy came out in defense of those agitating for change. As tanks

rolled toward demonstrators in the streets of Moscow, he made a radio address directed to his Russian "brothers and sisters": "Every person who raises arms against his neighbor, against unarmed civilians, will be taking upon his soul the most profound sin which will excommunicate him from the Church and from God."

A great deal of expectation fell on the church—who else was capable of making sense of this new reality? But just because it was one of the few institutions that could claim a non-Soviet, or pre-Soviet, source of legitimacy, it wasn't always the most certain or reliable guide. "When the Church was in exile it became a decorative instrument," said Valentin Kurbatov, a Soviet-era essayist and literary critic in Pskov who had been a practicing believer since the sixties and was among Adelgeim's earlier congregants. "It tried to pretend it was old, strong, healthy—but it wasn't." One priest who joined the clergy in 1991, the year the Soviet Union fell, told me that as the church sought to reinvent itself for new times, it was "eager for all comers, like a draft of new recruits." The quality of the priesthood varied, as did the seriousness and commitment of those who came to priests for spiritual renewal. On the whole, Orthodoxy is not known for its great preachers; it has not produced a charismatic speaker in the mold of Billy Graham or Martin Luther King, Jr. Adelgeim was among those few who injected his own personality and authority into his sermons. He was deeply knowledgeable in the Gospels, but always probing, vulnerable, searching along with the listener, in a constant state of study and reflection. "His philosophy was that genuine, intelligent faith requires labor," Kurbatov told me.

Freedom of expression and self-determination allowed for a flourishing of noisy, messy, independent thought, but also for a lot of bile to float to the surface. Congregations organized themselves as they pleased, which let Adelgeim open a children's home in Piskovichi and build a chapel for patients of the city's psychiatric hospital; but it also meant that other parishes were inundated with anti-Semitic tracts and intolerant, obscurantist literature. Many priests, eager to boast of their buzzing activity, were happy not only to baptize those without deep or genuine belief, but also to bless all manner of inanimate objects: banks, sports cars, military aircraft.

Patriarch Alexy's main project in the nineties was reacquiring and rebuilding physical churches, and filling them with a new wave of congregants. By the end of Alexy's reign as patriarch in 2008, the church had added twenty thousand parishes and a similar number of priests. The share of Russians who identified as Orthodox had grown to more than 70 percent. Alexy welcomed proximity to the state when it could provide tactical advantage, but on the whole he remained aloof and distant. Svetlana Solodovnik, a columnist at *Yezhednevny Zhurnal* who follows the church, explained that Alexy was "cautious with the state, he didn't want too close a contact with it—he knew that no matter how well the government related to him and the Church, it would only cause harm."

Even if Alexy avoided an outright alliance with the Kremlin, he got what he needed from it time and again. In 1997, the Duma, while reaffirming the secular nature of the Russian state, ratified the country's "traditional" faiths: Buddhism, Islam, Judaism, and Orthodox Christianity. The list pointedly left out all Western Christians, from Catholics to Evangelicals to Mormons, meaning that representatives from those faiths would have a much harder time operating in Russia. The Russian Orthodox Church had lobbied for such a bill for years as a legislative means of keeping out the competition. Alexy presented it to the Duma as a guarantee of societal, and thus political, unity. "Sects and pseudo-missionaries," he declared, posed a danger "not only for the church but also for the state."

That same year, Alexy oversaw the reopening of the Cathedral of Christ the Savior, perhaps Moscow's largest church, a regal structure in white and gold, first built in the late 1800s to commemorate the Russian Empire's defeat of Napoleon. Stalin ordered it blown up in 1931 to make way for the ultimate bureaucratic building, the Palace of the Soviets. But the enormous project was put on hold during the Second World War and was eventually abandoned by Khrushchev, who turned the construction pit into the world's largest outdoor swimming pool. Throughout the nineties, Alexy navigated a campaign involving the Moscow mayor and the oligarchs to build an exact copy of the original cathedral. From the moment it opened, it became the symbolic seat—even more than the Danilov Monastery—

of the post-Soviet church, a totem to its ease and favor with political power.

Meanwhile, Orthodox priests had gained the right to serve as chaplains within the army, and could soon preach not only to soldiers but to officers in the police and security services. Orthodox faith, once an impediment to a government career, was now in vogue, even advantageous. Orthodoxy allowed for a nationalist ideology that venerated the Russian state without the mothballed, inopeiable rhetoric of Communism. The FSB, the successor to the KGB, which spent decades hounding the Orthodox clergy, took it upon itself to restore and reopen a seventeenth-century chapel near its Lubyanka headquarters. Alexy came to sanctify the church, saying he hoped it would help FSB agents "carry out their difficult work" and "ensure the country's security in the face of external and internal ill-wishers, if not enemies."

As more power and resources flowed to the church, its formerly laissez-faire attitude toward the clergy began to tighten. Things for Adelgeim had changed even earlier, in 1993, with the appointment of a new head of the Pskov diocese, Archbishop Evsevii. As Adelgeim recounted years later, their first meeting did not go well. "From now on, life will be very different for you," Evsevii warned. Adelgeim could never be quite sure why Evsevii had such an immediate negative opinion of him. Evsevii hinted that an archbishop he knew had "explained everything" about Adelgeim. Evsevii had been warned, in other words. But of what, and by whom? Adelgeim wondered whether Makary—that is, Leonid Svistun—who by then had become archbishop of the Vinnitsa diocese in Ukraine, had passed along a spiteful review, fueled by the particularly curdled form of hatred that grows from a guilty conscience.

Sergey Bychkov, a noted historian of the church who grew close to Adelgeim in the eighties, had a simpler explanation: Evsevii, he told me, was a person of "Soviet formation," who, by his very nature—his authority in Pskov rested on hierarchy alone, not charisma or knowledge—was destined to feel "revulsion and loathing" toward Adelgeim. Viktor Yakovlev, an actor at Pskov's drama theater who had regularly attended Adelgeim's services since his arrival in

Piskovichi, said Evsevii never fully articulated or explained his animus. "If the archbishop had just said, 'You are doing this or that wrong,' everything that came later could have been avoided," he said. "But their conflict was about something else," Yakovlev continued, searching for the right word, before settling on one: jealousy. "But to think an archbishop is jealous of a common priest is, well, strange."

Some years before, Adelgeim had opened a small candle factory at the orphanage in Piskovichi as a way to support the home and for the teenagers living there to make a bit of money. Evsevii ordered him to hand it over to the diocese. At the same time, Evsevii removed Adelgeim as priest from the Piskovichi church and named a replacement, leaving him with no attachment to the parish he had served for more than twenty years and no direct oversight of the children's home. Once construction work was finished on the chapel connected to the psychiatric hospital, Evsevii said that Adelgeim would be forbidden to hold services there, too. Evsevii also moved to take over the choir school Adelgeim had opened in Pskov and converted it to a religious school run by the diocese.

As he carried out Evsevii's orders, Adelgeim stewed in a mounting sense of grievance and frustration. He recognized the archbishop's authority and did not "idolize equality," as he put it. It would be one thing if the hierarchy he saw in the modern church was rooted in Orthodox canon—this he would happily abide by—but it seemed to him that it was a question of autocracy for its own sake, a way to make life comfortable and controllable for the patriarch and his archbishops. He began to think more seriously about church teachings and law, and places where those codes differed from what he saw in the real practice of Orthodoxy, and set out to write a philosophical tract on the subject. *The Dogma of the Church in Canons and in Practice* came out in 2002. It is a dense, in parts impenetrable, work, a textual exegesis of church law and a dissection of the wording of the Gospels. He lays out a theory of power that flows from love—in particular, the love demonstrated by Christ. This brings "not formal power, which exalts the large over the small, but genuine power, which humbly and self-sacrificially serves those who are smaller than it, with love and responsibility."

Adelgeim devotes a great deal of attention to *sobornost,* a notion at the heart of Orthodoxy that speaks to a communal unity, a horizontal togetherness bound by faith and purpose. *Sobornost* comes when Orthodox believers are joined by "tasks and problems that require joint discussion, participation and common prayer, repentance, thanksgiving and love at the Holy Eucharist, shared understanding and decision-making." This church is not quite democratic, but it isn't rigidly hierarchic, either.

Dogma was an unmistakable critique of the church in its current form—a self-interested corporate structure that has forgotten the principles of *sobornost* and instead "expresses the triumph of individualism, caring only about its own rights." Without *sobornost,* the church becomes just another earthly hierarchy; its leaders, "generals and godfathers." Adelgeim does not hide his displeasure with Evsevii—in fact, he devotes an entire chapter to documenting their conflict, how one parish after another was taken from him. "For ten years the Archbishop has been ripping out my roots and slowly uprooting me from the Church." Later in the book, Adelgeim invents a fictional archbishop to expand the point, but it is clear whom he has in mind: "He is upset by any kind of initiative. It prevents the bishop from asserting himself. His interests revolve around his own prestige. He admires himself and adores flattery. Time and again he demands recognition, worship and admiration of his virtues."

Dogma was an immediate sensation in the Pskov diocese, and even in broader church circles, among those who were concerned by the drift toward rigid, top-down bureaucracy. For others, the fact that a parish priest had dared write such a thing was a scandal. Evsevii was furious. During a sermon at Pskov's Trinity Cathedral, he declared that Adelgeim, a "servant of Satan," had defamed him and the church. He called for a formal meeting of the diocese's governing council, to serve as a ritual of public denunciation. Adelgeim was not invited. Over the course of seven hours, priest after priest from the Pskov diocese stood to criticize Adelgeim and his book. Their speeches grew more colorful and grotesque as the proceedings wore on. Adelgeim had displayed "great boorishness." His work was "sacrilege," filled with "slander of the ruling archbishop, mockery of our belief, of its holy canons." Adelgeim was a "traitor," "spiritually sick," "a plaything in the hand of the devil." A number of priests called for him to be defrocked.

Adelgeim felt his book had been misunderstood. His concern, which came from a place of love, had been misconstrued as something venomous. He was also saddened: the church, he feared, increasingly resembled a "totalitarian sect, closing in on itself." He went on: "This is terrible, because the laws of history show that such a closed system is guaranteed to fall apart." A couple of priests dared to veer from the party line at the meeting of the diocese council. Popov, who had helped Adelgeim find his way in Pskov in the eighties, stood to warn of a creeping "spiritual Stalinism." But such voices were few. Some clergymen had come to Adelgeim before the meeting and admitted that his criticisms were not without merit, and that he was right in much of his diagnosis of what ailed the church. But they couldn't support him, lest they, too, face Evsevii's wrath. Adelgeim forgave them. For a Christian, what other choice could there be? "I cannot demand martyrdom from them," he said. "That is a step that everyone must decide for himself."

A SENSE OF INJURY gnawed at Adelgeim, an intrusion and counterweight to the force of Christian humility that he preached to others and expected of himself. In moments of anguish, he felt apart from the modern church, above it, even. "He was sure he was in the right, that he had earned this position over the course of his life, and all these other priests had just shown up yesterday," Valentin Kurbatov said. These junior clergymen had still been Pioneers and Komsomol youth activists at the time he labored in a prison camp and ducked the KGB.

Evsevii was not done with Adelgeim. In February 2008, he demoted him from the position of parish head at Zhen-Mironosits, appointing another priest over him. That newcomer was Father Sergei Ivanov, a twenty-eight-year-old clergyman not long out of seminary. The physical contrast alone was striking: Adelgeim was a generation or more older, with a face creased by experience and struggle; Father

Sergei's beard was still a rich brown, and he walked with a gait that was at once faster and nimbler but less deliberate. A Russian journalist visiting Pskov described encountering him outside Zhen-Mironosits: "When Sergei Ivanov walked out of the church, dressed in a leather jacket and jeans, and got into his white Mazda, no one would have thought that he had a priestly ordination."

Adelgeim was wounded by his demotion and, at first, had difficulty accommodating himself to the presence of Ivanov, his nominal superior, who was given to a certain carelessness, like leaving his shopping bags on the church's altar. Viktor Yakovlev, Adelgeim's longtime parishioner, observed the two at a service at Zhen-Mironosits not long after the reshuffle. Standing side by side, they looked like a "schoolboy and an academician," Yakovlev said; Adelgeim was "deeply offended, and shocked; he was clearly suffering." But he stayed quiet and did not protest to the diocese. Deep down, Adelgeim believed that "the Church has the right to treat him like a father can treat his son," Kurbatov said. That included, when it was deemed necessary, doling out punishment, if for no other reason than "ecclesiastical expediency," as the archbishop explained in this case. With time, Adelgeim developed patience, even a kind of pastor's empathy, for Ivanov. He is "not a bad person," he thought, "just weak, easy to manipulate, and the diocese takes advantage of him."

Not long after Adelgeim lost his place at Zhen-Mironosits, Patriarch Alexy died, at the age of seventy-nine. He had guided the church from when it had been a marginalized institution, under constant pressure, through the period of its fits-and-starts revival under Gorbachev, and into the modern era of regrowth and expansion. It was now nearly a decade into Putin's rule (although, at the time, Medvedev was formally president), and the church, like the state, had found its confidence, and had both the resources and the mechanisms to carry out its will.

In February 2009, Metropolitan Kirill was named His Holiness Patriarch of Moscow and All Russia. In the waning years of the Soviet Union, he had served as archbishop of Smolensk and head of the church's external relations department. Kirill's biography has no small measure of duality. Both his grandfather and his father were priests who faced repression in Soviet times, and in the eighties, Kirill's own career briefly stalled when he spoke out against the Soviet invasion of Afghanistan. But he was also the subject of whispers about ties to the KGB: it seems impossible that he would have been put in charge of Russian Orthodoxy's relations with the outside world without the approval of the security organs. A cache of Soviet-era secret-police files, briefly opened in the nineties, hinted at what could have been his onetime KGB code name: "Mikhailov." Kirill seemed more than comfortable with the notion of the symphony of church and state, and outlined his thoughts on its ideal form in an early speech as patriarch: "Symphony implies a harmonious combination of interests and distribution of responsibility."

Kirill set about formalizing church practice and operations, and creating his own vertical of power. Just as Putin had restored central authority to the Kremlin by making sure most local revenue flows first to the federal budget and then back out to the regions, Kirill ordered that the dioceses send a greater share of the monies they collect to the patriarchate in Moscow, which would then disburse them as it saw fit. Kirill also reorganized the geographic structure of the dioceses, creating new ones and combining others, installing a new layer of archbishops and metropolitans loyal to him alone. The system of education inside church seminaries was also standardized. Kirill faced a dilemma that was not entirely dissimilar to Putin's in the early 2000s: how to govern a sprawling, messy system that varied widely in quality. Both chose the path of top-down micromanagement. "Kirill wanted to turn the Church into a well-functioning mechanism," said Solodovnik, the columnist who writes about the church. "He did that not by motivating or inspiring people, but by instituting terribly bureaucratic methods."

Much of the spiritual mission of the church was routinized. Seven thousand new churches were built; more than ten thousand men joined the clergy. Priests were expected to send photographic proof of baptisms and count the number of participants in Easter processions. Each parish was ordered to employ a social worker and a person in charge of youth outreach, who had to report back every month: how many people were brought to the faith, how many alcoholics were saved. When I spoke with a priest from a parish just outside Moscow whose sympathies skew liberal, he said that while he and Patriarch Kirill have "different reflexes, different habits," he was ultimately sanguine about Kirill's rule. "The tough reaction of Kirill is a reaction to chaos," he said. "It's not my style, but I understand its logic: problems and deficiencies are up to the ceiling. We can't fix all of them—we will simply drown." The priest explained that although centralization under Kirill means that a priest has less say in how to lead his congregation, he's glad that the more unsavory, renegade wings of the church have also been tamed. "I don't like that my freedoms have been restricted, but I do like that the *Protocols of the Elders of Zion* are no longer being distributed in front of churches, or that the Black Hundred movement"—a militant and paranoid anti-Semitic sect with roots in the late Tsarist period—"has been purged," he said. "Any rational, thinking person should consider this great."

One of the legalistic changes instituted by Kirill was the adoption of a new organizing charter. It clarified who is in charge of a particular parish. Before, the formal head was the parish council, a body made up of local congregants and chaired by the parish's lead priest. This council had final say over their particular church's property and finances. New language made the archbishop head of every congregation in his diocese, giving him formal power to vet decisions made by the council and to remove its members at will.

Adelgeim feared the rules "consolidated dictatorship" within the church. At Zhen-Mironosits, Father Sergei Ivanov pushed through the charter without telling members of the parish council, on which Adelgeim and many who were sympathetic to him sat. Adelgeim lodged a complaint with the Pskov city court; in one of the few legal battles Adelgeim ever won, a judge ruled that Father Sergei had acted incorrectly. For a long while, no one at Zhen-Mironosits heard again of the new statute—until 2011, when Archbishop Evsevii called for a special session of the parish's governing council. He wanted it to adopt the measure once and for all. Adelgeim said they should delay the vote until all thirty-five members could read the document. The next he heard was that eleven of his supporters had been removed from the parish council on the order of the Pskov diocese. The official reason was that they had refused to vote as the archbishop desired. Shortly after, thirteen more council members were expelled, until the remaining few people finally ratified the charter.

The dispute kicked off a long-running legal campaign, as Adelgeim took his case from church courts to secular ones. Decisions were put off, or bounced from one part of the chain of command to another. Adelgeim's stubbornness was not appreciated among the clergy in Pskov. When I spoke with Popov, who had helped him find a parish in the eighties, he told me the most important thing for a priest should not be protecting "civic rights" but "comprehending one's purpose before God." He added, with some regret, "I was a supporter of not politicizing the situation, of limiting it to deeper questions, keeping it within the Gospels."

The rector of Pskov's Trinity Cathedral, a priest named Ioann Mukhanov who functioned as Archbishop Evsevii's de facto deputy, was put in charge of handling the conflict, questioning Adelgeim and other parish members who opposed the new charter. On one of my trips to Pskov, I went to see Mukhanov at his office next to Trinity Cathedral, which occupies a central place inside the city's kremlin. Whereas Zhen-Mironosits is idiosyncratic and charmingly rough around the edges, Trinity Cathedral is airy and imposing, with towering walls of polished icons. Mukhanov had been among the priests who gathered to criticize Adelgeim after the publication of *Dogma*. "How can Father Pavel go with the cup of Christ and in the image of God pronounce the name of the archbishop whom he had slandered?" he said at the hearing. "I raise the question of removing the priest Adelgeim from service." Fifteen years later, in our conversation, Mukhanov stood by his words, but with what struck me as a tone of cool dismissiveness more than burning passion. "How could you not be critical in the face of genuine lies, and, it goes without saying, rudeness and personal attacks?" he said. When I asked about Adelgeim's disagreements with Archbishop Evsevii, and with the diocese as a whole, Mukhanov waved the whole thing off as "embellished." Father Pavel "simply had a personal grudge against the archbishop, which spoiled their relations, nothing more," he said. As for the particulars of the dispute over who should be the legal head of the parish, Mukhanov seemed genuinely confused by Adelgeim's position. "He wanted to prevent the archbishop from becoming the immediate head of his parish. How can you do that? Is such a thing even possible? Well, only if your parish won't be part of the Russian Orthodox Church."

For Mukhanov, too, the conflict hinged on the matter of *sobornost,* but he saw the question differently: the unity of church life meant that all its congregations must submit to the same laws, recognize the same authority. Father Pavel and others at Zhen-Mironosits, he went on, took *sobornost* to mean that "any parishioner can do whatever he wants, amend the charter however he likes." But what kind of society, political or faith-based, could allow that? The church is fundamentally hierarchical, and no amount of good intent can make it otherwise. As I listened to Mukhanov, it struck me that the disagreement between Adelgeim and the diocese was indeed one of deeper symbolic importance. Does the strength of the Russian Orthodox Church, its claim to a single truth, derive from the submission of its members to the larger institution? Or does the sublime, ineffable magic of faith lie in the willful choice, made with trust and love, of each of its followers—a path that, by definition, is personal and idiosyncratic?

One snowy evening, I paid a visit to the Moscow apartment of Andrey Kuraev, an outspoken theologian and deacon, one of the few remaining internal critics of Patriarch Kirill and the direction of the church under his rule. "I must say, to my chagrin, in today's church I do not see asceticism in any sense of the word, including political," Kuraev told me. Over the years, Kuraev has been hounded out of various teaching positions, and now lives the unsettled life of an ordained Orthodox priest without a permanent ecclesiastical home. "None of our bishops, church writers, and thinkers—no one, really—is able to say, 'That's enough, we don't need any more.' You see, the patriarchate is like a form of gas that enters a room and takes up all the volume available to it. The patriarchate seeps everywhere and into everything it can."

Not only had the church under Kirill not found the will to refuse political influence, it also had come to be associated with wealth and material comforts. The patriarch had been spotted wearing a $30,000 watch, which he denied owning until his media advisors tried to clumsily and obviously edit it out of a photograph, causing the scandal to erupt anew just as Kirill had thrown his support behind Putin. Around the same time, it became known that the patriarch owned a luxury apartment in a prime Moscow location—a fact revealed when his upstairs neighbor was forced to pay nearly a million dollars in compensation for the supposed damage the patriarch's rare-book collection suffered when the neighbor's apartment renovation unleashed clouds of dust. None of this seemed to fit Kirill's monastic vows, nor the principles of Christian asceticism and modesty.

In private, some members of the clergy, and certainly a great number of parishioners, fretted over Kirill's foray into the political arena, his backing of Putin, and his use of the church's authority to weigh in on political matters. The church's abundance of comfort with money was also distasteful for many. But the debate was muffled.

That all changed on February 21, 2012, when five women wearing neon-colored balaclavas burst into the Cathedral of Christ the Savior and ran toward the altar. They thrashed about, kicking up their legs and shaking their fists in the air, shouting out a mock prayer: "Virgin birth-giver of God, drive away Putin!" They mocked the church's ties to the country's security services ("Black frock, golden epaulettes"), its corruption ("The march of the cross consists of black limousines"), and Kirill's entry into politics (the patriarch "believes in Putin," they sang, "Would be better, the bastard, if he believed in God!").

They called themselves Pussy Riot. Guards escorted the women out of the cathedral rather quickly and, at first, the incident didn't attract much attention; but the music video they released on the internet—"Punk Prayer: Mother of God, Chase Putin Away!"— went viral a month later, when three of the activists were arrested and charged with "hooliganism motivated by religious hatred." Pussy Riot's performance was further evidence of the fusion of church and state in Putin's Russia—they sang of how the authorities "lead a convoy of protestors to jail, so as not to insult the Holiest One"—and the church, in its reaction, confirmed their warning. Church officials demanded the women face punishment. Very quickly, the language of religious leaders and bureaucratic officials started to overlap. Kirill said that during Pussy Riot's church performance, "the devil laughed at us"; any calls for leniency for the women were an attempt to "justify and downplay this sacrilege." His spokesman called the action "a sin that will be punished in this life and the next." When prosecutors filed charges, the official text of the indictment spoke of "blasphemous acts" that inflicted "weighty suffering on those persons who find their spiritual home in the service of Orthodox ideals." The symphony had become a closed loop: the church was calling for earthly justice, and the state was citing heavenly motives in delivering it.

In Pskov, Father Pavel was not pleased with the manner of Pussy Riot's action—a cathedral is a sacred place, meant for reflection and communion with the eternal, not disruptive protest—but he couldn't deny that they had hit on a point in need of examination and discussion. As he understood it, they had enacted a *moleben,* a prayer of supplication, against the union of "the state machine with the organism of the Church, freedom with force, love with greed." He thought of them as reminiscent of holy fools, peculiar figures in Orthodoxy who are known to commit grotesque and provocative acts and are first judged as hooligans or madmen, but after their deaths are revealed to have been saints all along. Adelgeim believed church officials should agitate for Pussy Riot's release. By getting involved in such a petty, un-Christian way, the Orthodox Church risked losing influence in society, he feared. Even if that process started out slow and barely noticeable, it wouldn't stay that way for long. "A fire is lit with a single match, and then it blazes out of control," he said. As was his habit, he returned to scripture: "It is like the apostle Paul warns: 'Be very careful, then, how you live—not as unwise but as wise, making the most of every opportunity, because the days are evil.'"

Adelgeim was among only a small handful of Orthodox priests who spoke out in defense of Pussy Riot, or rather, who spoke against the un-Christian nature of openly seeking the women's punishment. Church officials in Moscow used the moment to isolate or purge dissenting voices, and to align the church with the growing conservative vector in politics. The church sought to position itself as the Putin system's moral compass and ideological bulwark. Andrey Kuraev, who also opposed Pussy Riot's prosecution, explained how Kirill's political calculation mirrored that of Putin: "The patriarch, realizing he had lost the intelligentsia, made a bet on the so-called Cossacks— that is, far-right, ultra-Orthodox patriots, desirably armed."

For Putin, Pussy Riot was a godsend: an opportunity to paint those opposed to his rule as a bunch of godless freaks and punks who make a mockery of Russia's most sacred traditions. This was certainly the message the church propagated to its flock. Several weeks after Pussy Riot's action, the patriarchate organized a mass prayer service at the Cathedral of Christ the Savior. A flyer advertising the service warned of how "anti-Church forces fear the growing power of Orthodoxy in the country" and how they were joined by those who "promote the false values of aggressive liberalism." More than sixty thousand people were bussed in for the event.

"This is the terrible sin of Patriarch Kirill," Kuraev explained. "He legalized the right to hate. That is to say, if previously one felt embarrassed by manifestations of hostility, the language of enmity, then after Pussy Riot that changed. From then on, it is considered that no, this is sacred hatred—in fact necessary. We are being insulted. We must defend ourselves, fight back, be good with our fists." In August, five months after their performance, the three defendants were found guilty and sentenced to two years in prison. The message was clear: to act out against Putin is to act against the church, and vice versa. Each institution will defend the interests of the other.

The first, and most immediate, benefit for the church is material. State support for Orthodox institutions came to reach more than 2.5 billion rubles a year, almost $40 million. Orthodox organizations also became the leading beneficiaries of a range of state grants, funneling millions more to church activities. Meanwhile, in Russia's system of informal relations, in which unspoken signals are as important as official decrees, it is welcome and desirable to support church initiatives; governors make it known to business leaders and investors that they would be wise to fund local church projects if they want to stay in the administration's good graces. Russia's top officials, from Putin and Medvedev to the defense minister and mayor of Moscow, are sure to be filmed at religious services, lending their authority and image of power to the church, just as the church offers it to them. The church has also been able to directly and openly intervene in civic life. After Pussy Riot, with the church's urging, parliament voted for a law that made it a crime to offend the "religious feelings of believers." A religious-education bloc was introduced to the public school curriculum. Adelgeim saw the effects in Pskov, where the archbishop forced the cancellation of *Jesus Christ Superstar,* the Andrew Lloyd Webber musical, at a state-run theater in town. As with Pussy Riot, Adelgeim was less concerned with the particular question than the precedent it set: "I'm not speaking to whether it's good to perform plays about Christ, but about the danger in the clericalization of government."

Adelgeim grew ever more pessimistic, afraid that faith itself, even God, was becoming superfluous in the church's quest for advantage in the here and now. He saw that church leaders were demanding ever-less spiritual effort from parishioners, that they had lost the voice of clarity and truth, and instead spoke in terms of rituals and obedience. Orthodoxy became the realm of formal keywords and symbolic gestures. Check this box, the implicit bargain held, and receive a guarantee of salvation and spiritual wholeness. But Adelgeim feared that the church's true authority, that of Christian love and practice, was running empty—an emptiness masked, at least temporarily, by the church's ascendance in public life. In an essay on the dangers of Patriarch Kirill's "romance" with the state's imperial power, he warned of how "when the confession of faith is crowded out by ideology, when sovereigns cross themselves and lavish their imperial church with gifts, the Church becomes rich in wealth but impoverished in spirit. Secular and spiritual power are united by violence."

To his parishioners in Pskov, these manifestos and philosophical debates felt far away, and, outside of a small circle, were the subject of only glancing attention. For most of them, Father Pavel was the warm, patient, avuncular pastor you knew and depended on when, say, your mother was sick or you were having problems keeping your kids in line. He rose at seven most days and headed to Zhen-Mironosits for the morning service. There were baptisms and funerals to attend to. Once a week, he held an evening Bible study for a few dozen regulars. He answered questions both quotidian ("As a man, I am not ready to give up the sin of sex; can I be saved?") and profound ("How does one separate the meaningful from the superficial during confession? What really concerns God?"). The trunk of his old Volga was always stuffed with donated coats and toys that he would distribute to those in need.

Adelgeim and Vera kept their home open to anyone looking for a kind word, guidance on some biblical question, or simply a bowl of hot soup. If he was rushing off to a court hearing when a local alcoholic stopped by looking for a meal, he would tell the man to make sure to come back later. Most evenings, he and Vera would be called upon by all manner of visitors: a young man who had spent some years at the Piskovichi children's home, a parishioner worried about her unmarried daughter, a group of well-wishers from Moscow or St. Petersburg who wanted an audience with Father Pavel.

It was a full life, frustrating and difficult, but such is the path of Christ, Adelgeim believed. Although he was effectively persona non grata in the Pskov diocese, he had attracted a wide following around Russia. Many thousands read his public online journal and passed around recordings of his sermons. A popular one spoke to the synergy of word and deed. How a person spends his or her life is a "choice of freedom, of one's conscience," Adelgeim said, explaining that one's actions, including the act of faith, are choices made of free will. Yet simply proclaiming faith does not offer a pass to the eternal—this comes from carrying out God's commandments in the here and now. This is the task of a Christian life. "You must hear the word of Christ, accept it and understand it," he said. "But moreover, it is necessary to be faithful to this word, to carry out this word in your life and to serve it in your actions."

THE NOTION OF A SYMPHONY between the Orthodox Church and the Russian state dates back to the fourth century and the ideas of *sym-*

phonia developed by the Roman emperor Constantine. Later, the dynasty of Russian tsars linked their legitimacy to God's will and enjoyed a supremacy over religious matters not matched by Western European monarchs, who were subject to rulings from the pope. State power and religious authority were often one and the same, a governing philosophy most clearly articulated in Tsar Nicholas I's policy of "Orthodoxy, Autocracy, and Nationality" in the 1830s. A portrait with the tsar's image was hung in churches, where it was the subject of flowery prayer; at the same time, the state enforced Orthodox belief through the law, punishing heretics and skeptics with criminal charges.

The particular contours of that symphony were nearly wiped out by the Bolsheviks—though it's worth noting how readily and enthusiastically much of the Russian peasantry denied their faith and set about destroying churches after the revolution, raising the question of how deep their belief was in the first place. What's clear is that the country's new rulers were militantly and aggressively atheistic. Lenin oversaw a bloody anticlerical campaign. In 1922, Patriarch Tikhon was placed under house arrest at Donskoy Monastery. Persecution continued under Stalin, who would eventually imprison 85 percent of the country's Orthodox priests and monks. Few of them survived the camps; many more were killed before they got there.

The most decisive events occurred in 1927, with the dilemma faced by Metropolitan Sergius. Patriarch Tikhon had died three years earlier. Before his death, sensing the growing pressure on the church, Tikhon named three bishops as his successors. But two had fled into exile, and the third, Metropolitan Peter, was under arrest. That left Peter's deputy, Sergius. When Peter was executed, Sergius became acting patriarch by default. Stalin and others in the politburo saw something useful in Sergius, a church figure who could recognize and sanctify Soviet power while also serving as a presentable face to the outside world. They would allow Sergius his position, and the church a chance at survival, if he would agree to such a deal. (Metropolitan Kirill—no relation to the current patriarch—another potential candidate, had refused the offer, telling a Soviet secret policeman, "You are not a cannon, and I am not a cannonball, with which you could hope to destroy the Church." He was sent into internal exile, and later shot.)

On July 29, 1927, the main Soviet newspapers carried a declaration from Metropolitan Sergius on their front pages: "We wish to be Orthodox believers and at the same time recognize the Soviet Union as our earthly home, whose joys and successes are our joys and successes, and whose misfortunes are our misfortunes." It was an unmistakable gesture of loyalty and subordination. The faithful, Sergius implored, should be thankful to the Soviet state for attending to their "spiritual needs." This at a time when churches were being closed by the dozens and priests were being shot and sent off to the Gulag in large numbers. Sergius's wager was that his public capitulation would protect Orthodoxy as a cohesive body, that if he didn't sacrifice himself, the church would be destroyed completely, atomized into thousands of tiny, disconnected, underground chapels. *Sobornost* would die.

The experience of the Second World War recalibrated the symphony once more. Stalin appealed to Orthodoxy, more than to socialism, to mobilize the country for a costly military campaign, presenting the Soviet Union as a defender not only of Marxism but of Christian civilization. Sergius played his part, calling on "Orthodox warriors" to come to the Soviet Union's defense, joining "country," "faith," and "fatherland" as one whole. It was time to "humbly sacrifice everything, even life itself." As the war came to a close, and in the years to follow, Soviet authorities allowed some churches to reopen. The state had little choice: it had used Orthodoxy as a means to rally the population and, having awoken this force, could not immediately suppress it. What's more, Nazi forces had reopened many Orthodox churches in Soviet territory they had captured. It would be awkward and politically untenable for Soviet authorities, having liberated these towns, to close the churches once again. In 1943, Stalin needed a religious figurehead to show off to a visiting British delegation; he ordered the country's surviving bishops to be flown on Red Army airplanes to Moscow, where they duly elected Sergius as official patriarch.

After the war, mass repressions against religion largely ceased. The Orthodox Church carried out orders and assignments passed to it from the Kremlin. It came to play an active role in the so-called Peace Offensive, a Cold War–era initiative backed by the Soviet Union that criticized Western imperialism and military action. Adelgeim remembered Metropolitan Filaret in Kyiv, who, during services in the city's Saint Vladimir's Cathedral, dissuaded parents from baptizing their children—quite the suggestion from a priest. Even though large-scale arrests and killings had ended, the state continued to target clergymen it considered unreliable or disloyal—such as Adelgeim himself. On the whole, it was nearly impossible to remain an actively serving priest and not bend, where necessary, to the demands of the state. Some, especially those with greater ambitions, did more than bend: the top echelons of Orthodoxy were thoroughly infiltrated by the security organs, and those who weren't undercover agents still had to navigate relations with the KGB if they wanted to ascend the church hierarchy. In their book *Russian Orthodoxy Resurgent*, John and Carol Garrard describe the form those contacts often took: "Co-operation ranged from passive acquiescence in party decisions, to serving as a mouthpiece for KGB propaganda . . . up to and including active collaboration by 'false brothers' . . . who denounced their own flock."

The modern Orthodox Church has never fully come to terms with this history. It has done much to celebrate the memory of those it calls "new martyrs"—people who suffered, and often died, for their faith at the hands of Communist authorities—but does not touch the question of who, exactly, was inflicting that suffering, let alone whether church leaders themselves bore responsibility for it. After the Soviet collapse, Patriarch Alexy issued a declaration acknowledging that, during the Soviet period, not "all servants of the Church were equal to the task of their vocation." But he never went into detail, and did not return to the subject. Shortly afterward, Gleb Yakunin, the Soviet-era dissident priest, outed three Orthodox leaders who had signed their names under Alexy's missive as having been onetime KGB officers. The church retaliated by defrocking and excommunicating him. Yakunin joined a breakaway wing of the Orthodox Church, an alternative and officially unrecognized structure that had been established in newly independent Ukraine.

For Patriarch Kirill, who was implicated in his own dealings with the KGB, the question of collaboration is indeed a thorny one. Neither he nor the patriarchate have ever acknowledged the rumors. When I spoke with Andrey Kuraev, he told me of a different, and more confounding, type of cooperation with the state. The Soviet authorities, he explained, preferred weak, morally corrupt priests, lacking charisma and genuine belief; if the state had to tolerate the existence of the Orthodox clergy, let them be as unappealing as possible. That meant an archbishop who wanted to get rid of such a priest could never get the Council on Religious Affairs to agree; after all, this was exactly whom they wanted. As a kind of workaround, some archbishops might whisper something to the KGB about the priest being politically unreliable, thus disposing of him in a roundabout way and hopefully getting a more competent replacement. "And so, in such a case, it turns out I'm acting like an informer, a rat," Kuraev said. "But as a result the Church benefits, parishioners, too. Is that ethical?" As in Soviet society as a whole, the compromises inside the church were so knotted and contradictory that they defy easy reflection or judgment, all the more so a generation or two removed. It may not be the path of enlightenment, or healing, but after speaking with Kuraev, I began to understand the church's all-too-human impulse not to deal with this messy and unpleasant history.

The role of Sergius is left equally unresolved. "It is impossible to measure the full scale of His Holiness Patriarch Sergius," Kirill once said, before adding, with implicit approval, "He did not provide the godless regime a pretext to destroy the church and wipe it from the face of the earth." One of the lengthier expositions from a high-ranking church figure on his legacy comes from Tikhon Shevkunov, a prominent bishop and head of the Sretensky Monastery, in Moscow. Shevkunov also oversaw the construction of a huge cathedral on the monastery's grounds dedicated to the memory of the "new martyrs." His status is far greater than his position alone suggests: he is rumored to be Putin's "confessor," guiding Putin through Orthodox practice and imparting a note of religious faith in his rule. In 2017, Shevkunov gave a long and revealing interview to a respected Russian journalist, Zoia Svetova, who pressed him on the church's influence over matters of state and his ties to Putin. (He largely dodged the Putin question, saying only, "I have the happiness of being a little familiar with him.") Is today's church still ailing from Sergius's choice? Shevkunov began his answer by weighing Sergius's options: preserve the church's survival at the cost of "the most diffi-cult compromises," or "die heroically along with his companions." Shevkunov couldn't quite bring himself to say whether Sergius's choice—opting for compromise—was a good thing or bad: "All that I can say, God forbid we end up in his position." Shevkunov ac-knowledged that having made his bargain, Sergius could only watch powerless as repressions against the church continued apace. Did that make his compromise pointless? Shevkunov didn't quite say. "The most abominable thing we can do from our position of safety today is to begin judging specific people on one side and the other," he said. "The Church has not canonized Metropolitan Sergius. But I have no intention to judge him from the vantage point of our era, much less throw stones at him."

Adelgeim could be forgiving of those priests who collaborated with the repressive machine: he wrote a letter to his old friend Leonid Svistun, by then Metropolitan Makary, suggesting a willingness to move past the unpleasantness of so many years ago. "I do not justify your action, but I understand it," he wrote. "In our country, thou-sands of people, by their own will and the will of others, became ac-cidental cogs in a giant meat grinder that worked to pulverize human fates." Makary never answered.

Adelgeim was more categorical when it came to the history of Metropolitan Sergius. For him, Sergius's declaration represented "the first step in the convergence of the Orthodox Church and the Soviet, and then post-Soviet, state. Compromise came to life and increasingly went beyond the limits of the permissible." In a way, Adelgeim was warning against the church's own wiliness, how it engaged in a clever dance with power, growing close to it when advantageous, subtly ma-nipulating it when it wasn't looking. He saw the church as fueled by the same cocktail of fear and self-interest as Yuri Levada's wily man.

Yet Adelgeim was not without his own compromises. He endured Evsevii's humiliations, and what he saw as the archbishop's violation of Orthodox canon, and always obeyed the ultimate decision of church courts and higher-ranking officials. After he was demoted from his position at Zhen-Mironosits, he was forced to bite his tongue at nearly every service. He could have joined Yakunin's alternative church, for example, which followed Orthodox canon even if it was not officially recognized. But abandoning the church, especially when it was ailing, as Adelgeim believed, was impossible. Leaving even for something like Yakunin's version of Orthodoxy would have severed him from his congregation. God, Adelgeim knew from scripture, opposes the proud but favors the humble.

NOTHING WAS PARTICULARLY STRANGE about the request Adelgeim got in the summer of 2013. He helped out young people and those who were lost, in need of direction and a spiritual foundation, all the time. From his years at the children's home in Piskovichi, Father Pavel had an easy way with children and young adults, including troubled ones, and enjoyed guiding them through their dilemmas. An acquaintance called him to ask if he might talk with a twenty-seven-year-old man named Sergei Pchelintsev, who seemed to be in the throes of a mental breakdown. A couple of days later, Seryozha showed up at the wooden gate outside the Adelgeim home in Pskov.

Seryozha was in a jittery, nervous state. He said he hadn't eaten or slept in three days. Vera had him lie down for a while. Adelgeim took him to meet some other young people who had come to visit him from Moscow, but Seryozha ran away and rolled around in the grass. Adelgeim and Vera brought him home to rest, but he took off again. Finally Seryozha's father arrived to check on him and announced that he would take him back to Moscow on the train that evening. Before leaving, Seryozha told Adelgeim he "understood everything," without saying what; he then asked Adelgeim to take him in or, barring that, find him a place in a monastery. Let's first talk about Orthodoxy a bit, Adelgeim said. We can do that next time. Go home for now and we'll think about monasteries later.

The next day Adelgeim and Vera got a call that Seryozha had run away from his father and was still in Pskov, at the city's hospital, with no money or phone. Adelgeim went to pick him up. Back at the Adelgeim home, Seryozha ate a bowl of soup, then disappeared once again, this time returning after an hour or two. He seemed to Vera "uncollected, anxious, unnatural, twitchy. He couldn't decide if he wanted to sit down, stand up, run away, come back." That evening, Vera started to make dinner, and handed her husband a knife so he could peel a squash from the backyard garden. He and Seryozha sat on a mustard-colored couch in the corner of the kitchen and started to talk about Saint Luke of Crimea, an Orthodox bishop and surgeon who defied the Bolsheviks in the years after the revolution. Vera could hear their conversation as she walked to the stove.

A minute later, Vera heard a terrible scream. She ran back to the couch. Her husband sat in a pool of dark blood, frozen and quiet, bent over toward the table. Seryozha yelled, "Demon! Demon! Demon!" dropped the knife, and ran out onto the street. Vera called an ambulance; as she waited, she could hear Seryozha pacing up and down the road in front of the house, still in a dark trance, screaming out: "I have sinned! I have killed a holy man!" A police car chased after him and a number of officers threw him to the ground. Paramedics showed up and made their way to the kitchen. One bent down to look at Adelgeim, then turned to Vera: "A direct strike to the heart. That's it. He died right away."

Father Pavel Adelgeim left this life four days after his seventy-fifth birthday. He was buried in the cemetery at Zhen-Mironosits, on a sloping hillside under the shade of an alder tree. Several hundred mourners came from all over Russia for the funeral. The crowd resembled the one that had gathered on the day of Adelgeim's first service after reopening the church, nearly thirty years before, but it was even larger. People squeezed onto the patches of grass between the graves, taking up every bit of free space, lining up all the way to the church's parking lot. Evsevii didn't come, blaming ill health. Sergei Ivanov was among those who held Adelgeim's casket aloft and lowered it into the ground, an image that stuck with Vera: the two had clashed in life, and somehow made peace with each other in death. A number of sympathetic priests from Moscow and St. Petersburg gave eulogies; Father Pavel died a martyr's death, they said, which could only have been God's intention. One, who had known Adelgeim for three decades, spoke of his "difficult, even unbearable, life path."

In the days after, Kuraev, the critical Moscow priest, declared, "The last free priest of the Moscow patriarchate has been killed." I later asked him what he meant. Adelgeim, he told me, was the only remaining priest not in schism with the church who was able to "say something critical about the patriarchate, a person still with something to lose who spoke his mind, even after the Orthodox clergy was told 'Go forward and stay silent.' Such people are not left at all." Kuraev told me that the very circumstances of Adelgeim's death proved that he was a genuine pastor, true to his faith and mission. "He opened his home, and his life, as the Gospels instruct. He did not run away or look for easy conversations. His death was that of a pastor on duty."

Seryozha was found psychologically unfit to stand trial. In court, Vera stood and said she forgave him out of Christian love. But she, like others in Father Pavel's congregation, was not quite sure that all was as it seemed. How was it that this young man had shown up out of nowhere and killed Adelgeim with one blow? Whispers of a setup circulated; after all, Adelgeim had no shortage of enemies in the diocese. As Vera recalled, a police investigator told her that the story of her husband's murder was indeed not so simple, but she never heard more. In a way, it didn't matter, or at least wouldn't change things: Adelgeim had the instincts and reactions of a pastor, and would have welcomed anyone into his home, even a man who would turn out to be his murderer. He died, as Kuraev put it, on his post. After the court hearings finished, Seryozha was shipped off to a psychiatric ward, and no one heard more of his fate.

VERA MET ME AT THE GATE, holding back a large golden-haired dog who was bouncing around in overeager excitement. We were joined in the yard by her elder daughter, Masha, who had survived meningitis as an infant and has been mentally handicapped since. She is now in her fifties, wholly dependent on Vera, though, as Vera would say, she herself has come to be no less dependent on Masha's company. Vera once described her life as "difficult but happy," and that's reflected in how she carries herself: with grace and humor, but with the kind of seriousness of purpose that comes only through hardship. Her stories are often funny, but never trivial. We walked through the backyard, where she keeps an impressive garden of tomatoes and eggplants and herbs, and into the kitchen. A new wraparound couch took up much of the space in the room; she had moved the old one, still bloodstained, up to the second floor. Upstairs, Masha pointed to it: "That's where Dad was killed." Adelgeim's study is preserved the way it was the day he died: painted icons hung in the corner, a thin, spartan mattress lay on a wire bed frame, his wooden prosthesis leaned against the wall.

Their home still remains open to friends and parishioners. Though, Vera pointed out, in all these years not one person has visited from the clergy of the Pskov diocese—even in death, Father Pavel remains a taboo and unwelcome subject for the archbishop. But lots of others pass through. I spent hours talking with Viktor Yakovlev, the actor, who has become something of a posthumous factotum for Father Pavel, narrating his life's work and explaining his positions on everything from the Local Council of the Orthodox Church of 1917 (the last time a patriarch was elected in an open contest) to the use of modern Russian instead of Old Church Slavonic in the liturgy (Father Pavel favored the change, arguing that prayers should be understandable and more than a kind of musical accompaniment for worshippers). One day, we were visited by Petr Gusev, a chatty and congenial man in his seventies. It turned out he was once a lieutenant colonel in the KGB, and was put in charge of watching over Adelgeim upon his arrival in Pskov. "I heard a lot about this person," Gusev said. "He and the authorities had a certain misunderstanding, but he was also said to be well-read, intelligent. I was interested, I wanted to see for myself." Gusev stopped by to talk with Adelgeim, and then started to come often, sometimes bringing his wife. Their conversations would veer from the Gospels to Adelgeim's prison term. In the 2000s, Gusev became a member of the congregation at Zhen-Mironosits.

In late 2016, three years after Adelgeim's killing, FSB agents raided the apartment of Ivanov, the parish head at Zhen-Mironosits, and found a couple dozen grams of methamphetamine hidden in his refrigerator and a pistol with a silencer in the closet. It seemed the whispered talk in Pskov of his ties to local criminals was true. The trial was quick and kept out of public view; Ivanov was sentenced to three years of probation. The diocese at first tried to act as if nothing had happened; Evsevii said not to believe slanderous rumors, that "the enemy Satan acts through people." He then quietly named a new priest to head Zhen-Mironosits, and Father Sergei was never heard from again. It struck me as a sad coda to Adelgeim's legacy, pathetic and ridiculous, that the priest who had displaced him ended up the subject of a narcotics bust.

When I spoke with Ioann Mukhanov, the priest who was effectively Evsevii's deputy, he avoided making any particular judgments on Adelgeim's legacy or the church's treatment of him. It was clearly an uncomfortable subject: he had not cared for Adelgeim when he was alive, disparaging him in quite colorful language, but was less comfortable doing so now. "He was a good preacher, literate and eloquent," Mukhanov told me. "It is a great misfortune that he was struck by tragedy." He went on: "The Lord will figure out why this happened. Was it punishment, or glorification, a martyr's death? Can it be that it was punishment? That is not for us to judge." As for the church's role in society, and its relationship to the state, "we can only be happy," Mukhanov told me. The Russian state in its current form "understands that Orthodox faith brings nothing but good to any community, any organization or structure," he said. "We provide the state with ethical citizens," patriotic and faithful.

Less than a year after Adelgeim's death, Russia annexed Crimea. The war in the Donbass began the next summer. The official rhetoric of the state, and the Orthodox Church, became even more bellicose and self-isolating. Russia was on a virtuous path, and attempts by the United States and others to isolate it were only further proof of the moral rightness in the country's drift toward conflict, direct or metaphorical, with the West. In 2015, Russia entered the war in Syria, backing the Assad regime with airstrikes and special forces operations. State television was filled with action shots of Russian fighter jets taking off and releasing bombs on targets uniformly presented as "terrorist" bases. Kirill, who had, in the eighties, signed a resolution condemning the Soviet war in Afghanistan, backed Russia's military intervention in Syria. The Syria campaign "has a defensive character" and is therefore "justified," he declared. His spokesman went further: "The fight with terrorism is a holy battle."

In a widely circulated essay, Sergei Chapnin, editor of the official journal of the patriarchate, lamented that the Russian Orthodox Church has become a "Church of Empire," a "post-Soviet civil religion providing ideological support for the Russian state." As the Kremlin sought to deliver a kind of nationwide self-realization through the flexing of Russia's neo-imperial muscles, the church provided the necessary spiritual and ideological language, while also growing its own appetite. Chapnin spoke of "Orthodoxy without Christ," in which the official rhetoric of the church emphasizes "Russian saints and Russian greatness; we care about being a patriot." At the same time, Chapnin said, "we somehow forget the Gospel, and Christ himself isn't quite so necessary." Weeks later, Chapnin was fired from his position.

Orthodoxy has reached a curious position in Russian society: 70 to 80 percent of the population claim to be believers, and surveys show that the church as an institution is trusted nearly as much as Putin, and certainly trusted more than the rest of the Russian government, which regularly polls significantly lower. Russia is among the only countries in Europe where the outward manifestation of Christian faith is growing, rather than retreating. Together, the Kremlin and the patriarchate have given voice to a narrative in which the West is not only a geopolitical foe, but a spiritual one, home to a decadent and insidious culture of tolerance that must be resisted. In one of the more bizarre examples of this tendency, the patriarch's spokesman, under a pen name, released a dystopian novel that warns of the horrors of liberalism, portraying Moscow in the year 2043 as overrun by Ukrainians, Islamists, and homosexuals. Standing up to Western capitals on political disputes like Crimea or sanctions is seen, in part, as a defiant moral gesture—first NATO shows up, followed by gay-pride parades.

Russian society is, in fact, conservative on questions like homosexuality, but, tellingly, was not aggressively or vocally so until told
to be. The 2012 law banning so-called homosexual propaganda reflected not the demand of the electorate, but an attempt to manipulate it. Sadly, it worked: once the law was passed and the dangers of
homosexuality were discussed on state television, attacks on gays and
lesbians followed. But conservative rhetoric from the church, echoed
by the population, is often discordant with reality. Divorce rates in
Russia are double those in most countries in Western Europe; the
same holds true for per capita abortions. For many, Orthodoxy is
merely a label of self-categorization, interchangeable with calling
oneself ethnically Russian, and a way of making clear what one is *not*:
a cosmopolitan and liberal Western individualist, the bogeyman of
the moment. But it has become less clear what Orthodoxy stands *for*,
what vision of the human condition it offers. As Adelgeim warned,
"Faith in the strong"—whether in the Kremlin or the church—"has
replaced divine providence."

The church has borne a cost for its proximity to the Kremlin, especially as a result of Russian policies in Ukraine: it lost thousands of
Orthodox believers in Ukraine, who rejected the authority of a religious institution seen to be so close to a state they consider an aggres-
sor. Kirill has tried to maneuver relations on all sides, and even
distanced himself at certain moments from Putin—he declined, for
example, to absorb parishes in Crimea after annexation—but nonetheless, he is viewed, at home and abroad, as a figure who has unambiguously entered the political realm. The reverberations were most
sharply felt in October 2018, when Patriarch Bartholomew of Constantinople, the ultimate authority over the world's Orthodox
churches, granted the Ukrainian church *tomos,* or formal independence from the Russian church led by Kirill. It was a painful blow and
an embarrassment for Kirill, who had spent great effort positioning
the Russian church as the spiritual authority for all the world's
Orthodox believers, or at least those in the former Soviet Union
and Eastern Europe. He disavowed the authority of Patriarch Bartholomew, leading to a dramatic rift inside Christianity—perhaps

THE LAST FREE PRIEST | 163

the most acute schism since the split of the Catholic and Orthodox churches in the eleventh century.

EVERY FIFTH OF AUGUST, the day of Adelgeim's death, friends, supporters, and old parishioners gather in Pskov for a memorial service, a day of reminiscence and celebration. At nine in the morning, five years to the day since Adelgeim was stabbed to death, I crammed myself into the lower chapel at Zhen-Mironosits. I stood pressed against other worshippers, listening to the hypnotic and mystical tones of the Orthodox prayer service. Afterward, we filtered out into the cemetery; the warm light of late summer broke through the trees in bands of yellow and green. A chorus of bells echoed through the grounds. Even more people joined the crowd, and we walked uphill, toward Adelgeim's grave site. It is marked with a carved wooden cross, a heavy gray stone, and a portrait of Adelgeim, bearded and smiling. There are always a few bouquets at the grave, but on this day they were overflowing, a cascade of tulips and carnations and daisies spilling out onto the grass.

A priest named Viktor Grigorenko addressed the crowd; Grigorenko is the nephew of Alexander Mein, the charismatic preacher murdered in 1990, and now serves in a church outside Moscow built on the site where his uncle died. "How is it that priests are killed?" Grigorenko asked. "Evil takes up arms against the truth. It opposes those who bring the word of God to this world, who speak of Christ and his Gospels." His voice carried down the slope of the cemetery; I stood on a patch of dirt partially shaded by the same alder tree that stands over Adelgeim's grave. "Today is the day when we remember Father Pavel; the day when we not only grieve at his tombstone, but also rejoice that such a person, such a priest, lived among us," Grigorenko said. "Father Pavel is looking to us today, expecting that we will accept his torch, this torch of truth, and take the responsibility upon ourselves to preach, to make our lives a sermon. Let each of us here today feel this call, that we must testify in the same way as he did, for our Lord Jesus Christ."

CHAPTER 4

KING OF THE PRIDE

—

IN JANUARY 2014, DURING THE EXTENDED NEW YEAR'S HOLIDAY, a weeklong vacation that is a holdover from the Soviet calendar, Oleg Zubkov took his family skiing in Avoriaz, in the French Alps. Zubkov, who was forty-five years old, is the founder and director of two privately run zoos in Crimea. He has a bubbly, comic personality, and an almost familial affection for the hulking, 500-pound lions that wander his parks. He is known to bound into their enclosures the way a father might surprise his young children, pulling their ears or giving them a playful slap before wrapping them in a tight hug and offering up a peck on the forehead. Zubkov has no formal training in veterinary science or animal biology, but he carries himself with instinctual ease among the tigers and baboons and giraffes in his parks, and his love for the panoply of creatures in the animal kingdom is palpable and infectious.

At the time of his family's ski vacation, Zubkov had been running his parks for more than ten years and had become a successful and well-known figure in Crimea, a peninsula of verdant hillsides and rocky beaches that juts into the dark waters of the Black Sea. For hundreds of years, Crimea has occupied a magical place in the Russian psyche, as a land of military glory and languid, romantic seaside holidays. In the 1850s, it was the scene of the Crimean War, a bloody and drawn-out conflict between the Russian Empire and an allied force of British, French, and Ottoman troops. Russian defenders in the port city of Sevastopol, on Crimea's southern coast, held out under the nonstop cannon blasts longer than expected; the city eventually fell, but a heroic legend was born.

The region was a popular site for rest homes and health spas dating back to the tsars. Tolstoy passed through Sevastopol as an artillery officer, and Chekhov wrote *Three Sisters* and *The Cherry Orchard* in Yalta. After the Bolshevik Revolution, as the socialist state offered vacation privileges to chosen members of the proletariat, Crimea became a popular spot for mass tourism. In 1920, Lenin issued an edict, "On the Use of Crimea for the Medical Treatment of the Working People," which led to generations of Soviet factory workers and railway engineers and members of the intelligentsia coming to the peninsula for extended summer holidays. During World War II, Crimea saw heavy fighting; Sevastopol again came under siege, and again defended itself valiantly. Afterward, as the country rebuilt, long stretches of the shoreline were taken over by a new generation of sanitariums, blocky concrete towers with staircases leading down to the rocky beach. A stay at the Artek summer camp, in the hills overlooking the southern coast, was the dream of every Soviet child.

In 1954, Khrushchev ordered the transfer of Crimea from the Russian Socialist Republic of the Soviet Union to the Ukrainian one—a legalistic formality that meant little until 1991, when the Soviet collapse left Crimea part of the newly independent Ukrainian state. More than half the population was ethnically Russian—the highest ratio in Ukraine—and many, if they thought about such things at all, carried a residual affection for Russia, largely because it was the main inheritor of the Soviet Union's historical legacy. The memory of the Great Patriotic War, the constellation of sanitariums, the songs of beachside campfires—all these Soviet vestiges felt as if they belonged in Moscow's dominion.

Zubkov, born in a rural town in central Russia, first arrived in Crimea in 1983. He, too, thought of himself as Russian, but made a nice life for himself in Ukrainian Crimea. He didn't pay much attention to questions of borders, history, and language; those issues seemed remote. Then came the turbulent autumn of 2013.

At the time, Ukraine's president was Viktor Yanukovych, the old-school political roughneck from the Donbass, the Russian-speaking industrial region in the country's southeast. He had emerged on the political scene in 2004 as the primary antagonist in what came to be known as the Orange Revolution: his victory in a presidential election that was immediately deemed fraudulent had kicked off weeks of protests. His challenger, Viktor Yushchenko, was ultimately named president. Yanukovych slinked off to obscurity, only to reappear some years later when he reinvented himself as a businesslike manager—not necessarily likable, but an antidote to the disastrous political circus that Yushchenko presided over after the Orange Revolution. Yanukovych also seized on Ukraine's geographic and linguistic divides, and played to the grievances of the Donbass. By 2010, Yushchenko's presidency had become so ineffective and mired in scandal that Yanukovych ran for president again and, this time, won.

Zubkov disdained Yanukovych, largely because as a young man, Yanukovych had been convicted of theft and assault. According to Zubkov's moral code, forged in the do-gooder spirit of Soviet youth organizations, these transgressions disqualified him from running the country. But Zubkov made his peace with Yanukovych, or at least was ready to wait until the next presidential election. In the meantime, with Yanukovych in office, the siphoning of wealth that long defined Ukrainian politics reached grotesque levels. The country's customs and tax services were transformed into agents of feudal tribute, and Yanukovych used inflated state-procurement contracts to enrich his circle of relatives and friends. He constructed a corrupt machine that answered only to himself and his two sons, a network known as the Family; his older son, Oleksandr, a former dentist, was soon running a $500 million business empire. Zubkov found all this loathsome but tolerable. His parks were flourishing: there was the original zoo, in Yalta, on the coast; and a large safari park in Belogorsk, on the inland steppe. Beyond that, he had plans to open five more parks all around Crimea. He bought a four-seat helicopter so he could fly among his many future projects.

In the fall of 2013, after years of false starts and protracted negotiations, nearly all observers in Ukraine—journalists, politicians, even members of Yanukovych's immediate entourage—presumed that he would sign a long-awaited association agreement with the European Union. It was a technical document that granted certain trade preferences to Ukraine with EU member states, and for EU officials in Brussels, it was the sort of formality that seemed boringly routine and self-evident. But in Ukraine, the agreement carried more symbolic meaning, taking on the significance of a referendum on the country's future. Most decisively, the agreement was anathema to Russia—and in particular, to Putin. If Yanukovych signed it, Putin's vision of assembling the states of the former Soviet Union under Russia's own trade union would be crushed. Just as previous Ukrainian presidents had been, Yanukovych was skillful at playing the West and Russia off one another, buying time and extracting favors from each side. Even though the United States and the EU insisted they were not waging a bidding war with Putin, that's exactly what negotiations had become. For its part, Russia offered Ukraine $15 billion in aid and natural gas discounts, and its bid appeared successful. On November 21, Yanukovych announced that he would not sign the association agreement.

The decision led to street protests in Kyiv. At first, the Maidan—the city's central square that lent the protest its name—was occupied by students and young people who were angry that Yanukovych, as they saw it, had denied them the European future they had envisioned. The protest encampment wasn't very large, but one night in late November, Yanukovych ordered riot police to clear the square. They did so, roughly and violently. The next day, hundreds of thousands of people came out to the Maidan. Demonstrations went on for weeks, with tensions mounting on all sides. The clash began to feel existential. The issue was no longer just Yanukovych's canceling of the EU agreement—protestors also rallied against runaway corruption and the crude authoritarianism of his rule. They saw Putin and the Kremlin as pernicious forces, and a nationalist, anti-Russian note crept into the speeches and protest signs on the Maidan. "Ukraine above all" read one poster; "Putin, get out of our home" read another. There was also the more blunt slogan, scrawled in graffiti: "Fuck the Russians."

In Crimea, as Zubkov saw it, the situation felt exactly the reverse: the EU agreement threatened to cut Ukraine off from Russia, trading hundreds of years of shared history and cultural values for no clear benefit. What were closer ties with Brussels worth if that meant forsaking deeper, more emotive concerns? And for many in Crimea, the Russian market was the immediate and necessary one; the benefits of trade with Europe were distant and theoretical. Zubkov's parks attracted more Russian tourists than Europeans. He considered Yanukovych a crook and an outright idiot, but that didn't mean he shared the grievances of demonstrators gathered to oppose him.

Zubkov watched television broadcasts from the Maidan and grew ever more anxious, especially as he observed creeping hostility toward all things Russian: not just toward the state but the language, the cultural inheritance, the recognized cast of heroes. It felt as if the leaders on the Maidan and their supporters looked at people like Zubkov with suspicion and judgment, merely because of their residual affection for Russia and their fear that a victory for the Maidan protestors would, by definition, mean a loss for the Russian population in Crimea.

On the way to his family vacation in the Alps, Zubkov had a stopover in Kyiv between flights. He made his way to the center of town with his wife, Oksana, and their thirteen-year-old son, Yaroslav. The Maidan resembled a guerrilla encampment, with tents dotted around the central square and huge cauldrons of soup and porridge bubbling over open flames. Protestors shielded themselves from riot police with barricades made from spare iron and wood. Oily black smoke rose from fires burning inside metal barrels. When I asked Zubkov to recall his time on the Maidan, he told me of the aggressive people on the square, the "bums" and "people brought in from villages" roaming around. Oksana remembered a "warlike hatred in the air." They came across a life-size mannequin of Yanukovych locked in a cage, sitting on a golden toilet. Whatever animus Zubkov felt toward Yanukovych, such a grotesque display seemed too much: he was the elected president; if you don't like him, vote him out of office next time; those are the rules.

The three of them made their way to Kyiv's Bessarabska Square, where they came across a toppled eleven-foot granite statue of Lenin, which protestors had pulled down and beaten with sledgehammers some weeks before. Lenin lay on the ground, battered and defenseless. For those on the Maidan, especially supporters of various Ukrainian nationalist movements, Lenin represented a history of colonial oppression, a foreign system and ideology imposed on Ukraine by Russia. The parallels with the current moment were obvious to those inclined to see them; the coming months would see a wave of what was called Leninopad, or "Leninfall," the toppling and destruction of hundreds of Lenin statues all over Ukraine.

Zubkov and Oksana were deeply saddened by the scene, not because they had any particular attachment to this figure of long-ago history but because, as Zubkov put it, the image of Lenin "embodied an entire epoch." Zubkov and Oksana weren't Communists, but that wasn't what Lenin stood for to them: he represented a mythologized past, a time of brotherhood and equality that, even if it never really existed, nonetheless occupied a place of nostalgic affection in their minds. The rupture caused by the Maidan threatened their memories and understanding of their own history—a personal and subjective fear, but that didn't make it any less real. They stood by the statue, cracked and sprawled out on the frozen pavement, and began weeping. Zubkov hugged his wife and son. "We cried for the legacy of the Soviet Union, for veterans, the elderly, for people who endured so much and are still alive," he said. "We were not ready to accept what was happening."

ZUBKOV WAS BORN IN 1968 and grew up poor in a small village near Kursk, in western Russia. During the war, it was the site of the largest tank battle in history. One of his grandfathers went off to the front and never came back. Young Oleg was raised by his mother, Maria, and never knew his father. Across the Soviet Union, it was a time of gradually expanding, if minimal, comfort, but not for the Zubkov family. Their house was a wooden hut, its walls made from old and rotted logs, patched up with branches and muddy clay. When the place flooded, as it did often, they would rush to stack their few possessions on top of the only table in the house. Yet the surround-ings were beautiful: dense forests of pine and birch, which opened up to meadows the color of finely buffed emeralds. Each morning, Zub-kov walked two miles to school, along the river and through a grove of oak trees, passing a long-abandoned pre-revolutionary manor.

His modest idyll came to an end in the fifth grade, when his mother remarried. His stepfather had a weakness for drink, and fre-quently moved the family from town to town in search of work. Zubkov knew he wanted to leave behind this life of poverty and booze and bad luck. When he was fifteen, he enrolled in a naval voca-tional school in Kerch, a port city on Crimea's eastern tip. He became a model Soviet student of the time: he was elected his grade's student representative, joined the local Komsomol committee, and took part in various student olympiads. His report on the results of the Com-munist Party's Twenty-seventh Congress—held in 1986, the first to be presided over by Gorbachev—was awarded a top prize in a com-petition held for young people across Ukraine.

With his good grades and promising Soviet résumé, Zubkov se-cured a place at a naval academy in Kyiv, where he studied to be an officer. In spring, he left for training missions, sailing through the English Channel on the *Khasan,* a patrol ship, and watching planes take off from the *Kiev,* the first Soviet aircraft carrier. He was training to be a political officer—that is, a military commissar, in charge of overseeing a unit's ideological fitness. Even as his instructors praised him, however, Zubkov began to doubt the system he was preparing to enter. He could see how nothing worked, that the country was falling apart, yet every day at the naval academy he was fed tales of Soviet greatness. He had begun to date Oksana, a medical student whose father worked at a museum in Kyiv. One night, they all gath-ered for dinner to mark the Soviet holiday commemorating the Bol-shevik Revolution. Oksana's father proposed a toast. "Comrades, let's drink to the mistake of seventy years ago." Zubkov had never heard someone say such things openly, let alone with the assumption that everyone at the table felt the same way.

The gap between observable reality and what was depicted on television and in classrooms grew wider. How could Zubkov do his job as a political officer? The choice, as he understood it, was either to "constantly tell your bosses how great Communism is, and have no authority with those under your command; or speak in your own voice and tell things like they are, and have no opportunities for career advancement." It was the spring of 1991, when Soviet power was on its last breaths, and the naval academy gave Zubkov a way out. Any student who wanted could take his diploma and be exempted from naval service. Zubkov, along with sixteen of his classmates, took the offer. "I was certain that, even with my enthusiasm, I wouldn't be able to break the military system," he said. "Most likely it would break me."

Zubkov ended up with a low-level position at the Ministry of Light Industry in Kyiv. His status quickly rose when, on one of his business trips abroad, he bought himself a Ford Granada; back in Kyiv, ministers were driving around in Soviet-made Volgas, and Zubkov's Ford made him a suddenly popular employee. But then came the upheaval of the nineties, and the need to hustle and reinvent oneself. Zubkov opened up a tourist agency and did fairly well. But he and Oksana, now his wife, wanted open, green space; Zubkov missed the saline crispness of the sea air in Kerch. They moved to Yalta, wedged on a picturesque bay, pinched between the Black Sea and green hillsides dotted with vineyards. It was hard not to love Yalta, its subtropical climate and bounty of grapes and peaches and bulging sweet onions, even the cafés along the promenade that specialized in gristly *shashlyk* kebabs and syrupy cognac. But Zubkov was dismayed at how the city was underfunded, left to slowly decay and be pilfered by the new crop of *biznesmeny* who left town as quickly as they came. In Crimea, newly independent Ukraine had been bequeathed a "beautiful pearl," as he put it. It just needed some polishing. But no one had the time or resources or attention for that.

In 1995, Zubkov took over a small zoo outside Yalta, down the hill from a popular forested park. It was called Skazka, or "Fairy Tale." The zoo had appeared only a few years before, when a film crew left behind some animals they brought to Yalta to film for a low-budget movie. Zubkov signed the contract and became the owner of an acre of land, along with four ferrets, three Cameroonian goats, a half dozen deer, who knows how many squirrels, and one yak. He acquired a handful of silver foxes and some emus, built new enclosures, and fixed up the pathways. There was no one to ask about how to build a modern zoo; the only information Zubkov could find was in a dusty Soviet tome he tracked down called *Guidelines for Basic Rules of Safety and Sanitation for Zoological Gardens of the USSR*.

He confronted the usual problems, like securing the necessary permits to renovate the grounds, not to mention corruption. When local tax inspectors showed up and threatened him with a fine that amounted to a month's worth of profits, he went to their offices the next day with a small army of macaques and baboons. Each of the monkeys held a sign Zubkov had painted for them. One read, "Down with the beastly tax administration." That démarche managed to simultaneously befuddle and charm the employees of the tax inspectorate. The fine was revoked. Later, he was visited by building inspectors, who said that a furnace he used to heat the primate enclosures in winter was illegal. One told him the problem could be solved for six hundred Ukrainian hryvnia, which soon turned into six hundred dollars, nearly twice as much. (The inspector explained that it wasn't all for him: he would get only fifty dollars; the rest would go to the head of his office, a judge in town, the local police precinct, and so on.) Zubkov recorded the conversation on a voice recorder tucked into his pocket. When he pulled it out, the inspector ran away screaming; he later sent an underling to ask if he could have the audio recording for safekeeping. "Bribe-takers were scared to step into my office for a decade," Zubkov said.

With time, as the zoo became more popular, and its running more routine, it also started to feel small—a patch of shady trees and a few animals in the hills above a resort town. Zubkov ran for a seat on the Yalta City Council and won. He then ran for mayor and lost, coming in second. "I needed to find a place for my energies," he told me. Zubkov looked around for a territory where he could build a new park, and found an old abandoned Soviet-era military base in Belogorsk, in central Crimea, away from the coasts—a flat, unremarkable patch of steppe dotted by former collective farms. He bought the huge plot, more than eighty acres, and began to work up plans for an open safari park: not a mere warren of cages and enclosures, but a swath of open savannah in the middle of Crimea. Lions and tigers arrived from all over: China, South Africa, the forests of Siberia, circuses all over Europe. Monkeys and giraffes and peacocks filled the enclosures. The base had an underground bomb shelter, which Zubkov turned into a karaoke room—no one could hear you sing behind the armored doors, meant to withstand a nuclear blast. Before Zubkov could open the park, local officials in Belogorsk launched a criminal investigation against him for illegal construction and hinted that all could be resolved for forty thousand dollars. He refused, the case eventually died out, and, in April 2012, six years after Zubkov acquired the land, Taigan opened its gates for the first time. Half a million people visited in its first year.

All the while, Zubkov chafed at what he viewed as the forced and unwelcome Ukrainian-ness around him. The food in the local shops was labeled in Ukrainian, not Russian (bread was *khlib,* not *khleb*), and much official government business, permit forms and applications and the like, had to be done in Ukrainian, a language that was familiar enough yet still unshakably foreign to Zubkov. The school textbooks approved by officials in Kyiv and sent to Crimea emphasized Ukrainian historical tragedies, such as the Holodomor, a man-made famine caused by Stalin's policies in the early thirties, and, as Zubkov saw it, downplayed Soviet valor and sacrifice in the Great Patriotic War. Despite his disillusionment with Soviet ideology, Zubkov remained a believer in the idea of the Soviet Union as a big, powerful, welcoming motherland. Victory in the war was a central element of that narrative, and Crimea, in particular, played a crucial role in that history. Crimea saw some of the bloodiest fighting in the whole of the Eastern Front as Nazi forces waged an eight-month campaign to capture the territory. Sevastopol held out the longest, facing constant shelling and bombing runs, with Soviet troops fighting from underground artillery batteries hidden in the cliffs. It was named a Hero City after the war, one of twelve across the Soviet Union.

The chaos and violence of the wartime years led to contentious notions of heroes and villains—one person's nationalist freedom fighter was another's Nazi collaborator. Perhaps the most divisive figure was Stepan Bandera, an impassioned believer in an independent Ukrainian state, who, in the thirties and forties, led a more radical and militant wing of the nationalist movement that had taken form inside the Ukrainian Soviet republic. He spent much of the war in German custody: as interested as the Nazi regime was in taking advantage of anti-Soviet nationalism, it had no intention of actually allowing it to flourish. But the language of his movement had an unmistakable Fascist tinge, and his followers took part in the murders of Jews in those parts of Ukraine that fell under Nazi control. Bandera was killed by a KGB assassin in 1959 and branded by the Soviet state as an unmistakable Fascist—not because of his positions toward Jews and other ethnic groups, but for his opposition to Soviet power.

Post-Soviet Ukraine had an unsettled relationship with Bandera. He was lionized in some quarters, cursed in others, and treated with foggy indifference by many. The country's politicians recalled his memory from time to time as a way of scoring easy political points, a cheap fob to nationalist sentiment and an attempt to retroactively create a sense of shared history and identity. In 2010, then president Yushchenko, fearing a political challenge from a nationalist flank, posthumously gave Bandera the Hero of Ukraine award for "defending national ideas and battling for an independent Ukrainian state." Zubkov, like many in Crimea, was uneasy with this sort of sacralization of Bandera, even if it never truly reached the degree he imagined or feared. His discomfort at being a citizen of independent Ukraine was always more emotional than objectively provable. In isolation, each of these small slights did not represent any particularly grave insult—who really cares about Ukrainian-language food labels?—but taken together, they were discomfiting. Zubkov felt left behind: Ukraine developed its modern national identity in part by rejecting the Soviet past, which could not help but entail an implicit differentiation from Russia, the natural successor of the Soviet Union and the keeper of its language and history. Like many in Crimea's ethnically Russian population, Zubkov feared he was not acknowledged or appreciated by successive governments in Kyiv. For a while, he was content to participate in various pro-Russian movements that tried to propagate Russian history and language in Crimea.

That changed with the Maidan. The protests caused not only a political rupture in Ukraine, but a cultural and civic one. Suddenly, cleavages between the Ukrainian-speaking western regions of the country, which once belonged to the Hapsburg Empire, and the Russian-speaking east, with its Soviet-built coal mines and metallurgical factories, took on new force. With its historical ties to Russia and a majority Russian-speaking population, Crimea seemed to fall into the anti-Maidan camp by default. Even if the assumption was unfounded, Maidan's leaders did little to dispel the notion, and did not address the fears of those in Crimea, like Zubkov, who were more worried than encouraged by the protests. "Once Maidan appeared, it felt like Ukraine forgot about us, as if the country was solving its own problems, which had nothing to do with us," Zubkov said. "We were just somewhere out on the periphery."

The day that Zubkov, Oksana, and Yaroslav happened to pass through the Maidan was actually a relatively quiet one, a lull in the ebb and flow of clashes between protestors and riot police. Things got nasty later that month, as the emergency passage of draconian anti-protest laws led to violent counterdemonstrations and the deaths of several protestors. In late February, the Maidan Revolution reached its denouement, with several days of sniper fire and rolling street battles. More than seventy people were killed. Much about the climactic finish of the protests, and of the Yanukovych government, remains unclear. The Maidan was a storm that gathered force over time, sweeping up those who tried to control it—Yanukovych, Putin, Western leaders. The story of the revolution contains facts that are uncomfortable for all sides: from the role of far-right elements in battling Yanukovych's police to efforts by Putin to bribe Yanukovych in the hope that he could restore order. Western officials were more circumspect than Putin. Though they disliked Yanukovych and sympathized with the liberal opposition that had become the Maidan's public face, they did not anticipate what would happen if, in fact, their side won.

On the morning of February 22, just hours after agreeing to hold an early presidential election in a deal brokered by three European foreign ministers, Yanukovych fled the capital. Protestors headed to

Mezhyhirya, the sprawling residence Yanukovych had built for himself on illegally privatized land outside Kyiv. Hundreds of people gathered to amuse themselves with the assortment of gilded kitsch they found on the property: monogrammed golf clubs, Yanukovych-branded bottles of vodka, a block of gold shaped like a loaf of bread. Activists used the sauna to dry out documents that Yanukovych's guards had thrown into the river before fleeing. In Kyiv, disbelief quickly gave way to euphoria. Just like that, Yanukovych was gone, a turn of events understood on the Maidan as a victory over corruption and autocracy—and over Russia.

In Crimea, Zubkov and Oksana watched with trepidation. They feared that aggressive gangs of nationalists would come to instill terror in Crimea's Russian-majority population. Zubkov was convinced, for example, that a train full of Banderovtsy—the preferred slur for would-be Fascists, supposedly motivated by the example of Bandera—was barreling toward Crimea to incite violence and exact revenge. Oksana later told me, "It seemed impossible to imagine that such a transfer of power could happen in Kyiv and for there not to be consequences here in Crimea." She and Zubkov became more convinced when the interim government in Kyiv proposed rescinding a law that gave the Russian language special status in majority Russian-speaking regions in the east, including Crimea. Ukraine's acting president quickly rejected the idea, but the damage had been done: from that moment on, residents of Crimea and the Donbass felt certain that the victors of the Maidan were driven by inherently anti-Russian aims.

The collapse of Yanukovych's rule presented Putin with a potential geopolitical catastrophe, as he saw Russia losing nearly all its influence over its neighbor. Putin was never fond of Yanukovych, but at least he was a pliable client, who could be bought off and manipulated. Now Putin saw dark visions of the Maidan leaders coming to power and leading Ukraine into NATO, kicking Russian submarines and destroyers out of their port in Sevastopol and replacing them with American vessels. Putin never believed in spontaneous and genuine street protests—such demonstrations must always be the work of higher forces, of the United States above all—and for him, the

Maidan was no different. He was certain Washington had unseated Yanukovych and, if left unchallenged, could set in motion a chain of events that could threaten his own hold on power. Within days, "little green men"—Russian soldiers in camouflage uniforms with no insignia—began popping up in Crimea, surrounding the airport and regional parliament. Zubkov saw them by the Supreme Council building in the center of Simferopol. They seemed disciplined and polite.

The show of force effectively hemmed in Ukrainian military units in Crimea before they, or the West, could make sense of the situation, but just as important was the simultaneous information campaign. Local Crimean television was shut off and replaced with Russian broadcasts, which delivered a nonstop feed simultaneously discrediting the new government in Kyiv and the West while building up Moscow as a savior and protector. A vicious feedback loop was set in motion, with the exaggerations and falsehoods of the Russian-led propaganda campaign sloshing around with the fearful gossip circulating among the population. For Zubkov, it was a potent cocktail: "We saw what happened in Kyiv not as a victory of the people, but as an armed coup," he told me. "The truth is, we really didn't know much. It was impossible to judge the situation soberly. But what we did know is that we needed a guarantor of security."

That guarantor was Russia. To help it execute its strategy, the Kremlin quickly settled on an obscure forty-one-year-old politician named Sergey Aksyonov, who had previously led a marginal pro-Russian party in Crimea and had rumored ties to nineties-era gangsters. His supposed mafia nickname was "the Goblin." Aksyonov was instated as the republic's head. Once in power, he acted as if he were responding to the will of the people—and, in part, he was in tune with the heady zeitgeist of the time—but it was clear his real orders came from Moscow. He forced through a vote in Crimea's parliament calling for a referendum, in which the people of Crimea would vote on whether to separate from Ukraine and join Russia. By the time it was announced, the referendum seemed a mere formality: Moscow would have little problem getting the result it wanted. Not that the referendum's organizers left any room for subtlety. A billboard popped up along the main road between Simferopol and Sevastopol asking which country you'd rather be part of: Russia, identified by its tricolor flag, or Ukraine, marked by a big, black swastika.

Zubkov welcomed the idea of the referendum. Joining Russia seemed a magic solution that promised to fix a number of collected frustrations and threats—both long-standing ones, like grumblings over language, and more immediate concerns, like the supposed Banderovtsy on the march from Kyiv. He thought of Crimea's potholed roads, its closed and decaying factories, and all the government officials who, instead of helping him develop his parks, had only stuck their hands out for bribes. Modern Ukraine had become a country where "bureaucrats don't know how to create anything, only steal, and presidents think it's okay to build their personal dachas in national parks." He presumed, naively, that all this was somehow a particularly Ukrainian problem, that things must surely be different in Russia. After all, Russia was swimming in oil money, had just hosted the Winter Olympics, and was promising Crimea not just its protection, but also economic investment and higher wages and pensions.

Zubkov was taken by a wave of emotion. He is a natural showman, a zookeeper with a carnival barker's sense of how to grab people's attention. Some years before, during his short-lived political career in Yalta, he had acquired a decommissioned Red Army armored personnel carrier. He had used it as a piece of campaign theater: he would drive around the streets of Yalta, blasting out announcements for his mayoral bid from the loudspeaker. Now he wheeled it out of storage. He mounted Crimean and Russian flags on the APC's frame and draped signs along its sides, urging "Everyone to the Referendum!" and declaring "Crimea Is with Russia!" If necessary, he promised, he would give the APC to one of the ragtag self-defense battalions that had cropped up all over Crimea. One afternoon, a few days before the announced referendum, a correspondent from a pro-Kremlin television channel came to Taigan. Zubkov was in a buoyant mood, and wanted to put on a good show. He posed in the grass with one of his lions. "We have fighting lions," he said, suggesting that the park's lions and tigers could form a reserve paramilitary force to ward off any aggressors from Kyiv. It was unclear if the whole thing was a joke or not; in Crimea those days, it seemed like anything could turn out to be true. "We will defend the choice of the Crimean people with all available forces and means," Zubkov said, wrestling playfully with a squirming lion as the television reporter retreated off camera. Zubkov petted the lion's bushy mane and grabbed it in an affectionate embrace. "If our motherland demands, everyone will go to defend the borders and interests of the people of Crimea," he said, motioning toward a pride of lions that had assembled in the grass. He pulled down the jaw of one, revealing four sharp fangs, each the size of an index finger. "Look at these teeth!"

Zubkov and Oksana spent the morning of the referendum in Yalta. They went to an impromptu polling station that had been set up at a local music school and, with great elation and satisfaction, voted in favor of joining Russia. By then, after several weeks of buildup, and the Kremlin's heavy hand, the announced results of the referendum came as little surprise. The self-declared Crimean authorities, led by Aksyonov, said that turnout was 83 percent, with 97 percent voting to join Russia. Given the general chaos in Crimea at the time, and the stage-managed nature of the whole process, it may be impossible to ever get an accurate measure of the results. A report issued a year later by the Kremlin's own human rights council gave an estimate of 30 to 50 percent voter turnout, with 50 to 60 percent voting in support of joining Russia. In Washington, President Obama declared the referendum "a clear violation of Ukrainian constitutions and international law," warning that "it will not be recognized by the international community." But for those who favored joining Russia, Zubkov and Oksana among them, the euphoria of the moment—an almost narcotic high—far superseded concerns over things like voting irregularities or the referendum's doubtful legality.

A few days later, Zubkov opened Taigan for a party, inviting local bureaucrats and letting in hundreds of people for free. They wandered around the park, hugging and congratulating one another, listening to classic Soviet songs over the park's loudspeakers. Zubkov got in the APC and sped through the grounds, riling up the crowd. The sounds of "The Sacred War," a World War II–era battle hymn, whose words are probably more well known in Russia than those of the country's national anthem, reverberated around the park. "Arise, vast country, arise for a fight to the death, against the dark Fascist forces, against the cursed hordes," the song begins. By the time of the chorus, the lyrics reach a martial froth: "Let noble wrath boil over like a wave! This is the people's war, a sacred war!" As he zigzagged around in his military vehicle, Zubkov was supremely happy, pleased that he, along with the rest of Crimea, was finally "going home." The party went on deep into the evening. As it turned out, those gathered at the park had another reason to celebrate: early on the morning of the vote, a new tiger cub had been born. In honor of the occasion, Zubkov gave it the name "Referendum."

TWO DAYS AFTER THE VOTE, Putin gathered Russia's political elite in the Kremlin's Saint George Hall to announce Crimea's formal annexation. He cited the peninsula's historic ties to Russia and Khrushchev's error in transferring it to Ukraine in the first place. "In people's hearts and minds, Crimea has always been an inseparable part of Russia," he declared, recalling its role as the baptismal site of Vladimir the Great, the first Russian tsar to adopt Orthodoxy. He was interrupted every few seconds by applause from an audience of rapturous supplicants: government ministers, parliamentary deputies, regional governors. He spoke to the fears of people in Crimea like Zubkov, who were convinced by the fog of propaganda and rumor that Fascists had been on the march to do them harm, until Russia came to protect them, saving them, as Putin said, from the "intentions of these ideological heirs of Bandera, Hitler's accomplice during World War Two."

Putin's speech, more a source document outlining the rules and motifs that would govern his presidency going forward than it was anything to do with Crimea, was laced with equal parts grievance and triumph. He was furious, but, in delivering Crimea, satisfied and proud at the spoils he had brought home: at long last he exacted a measure of historical revenge for the injustices suffered by Russia in the years since the Soviet collapse. "If you compress a spring all the way to its limit, it will snap back hard," he said. In the days that followed, Putin's public approval reached an all-time high of 86 percent. He had spoken to the confusion and frustrations of a whole country, for which Crimea functioned as a mass psychological remedy. Oleg and Oksana told each other how good it felt to sleep under peaceful skies, citizens once again of a great and mighty state.

Zubkov's enthusiasm continued even as Crimea became an international no-go zone, where no Western banks or firms would conduct business. Sanctions meant that even large Russian companies were afraid to maintain a presence in Crimea, lest their global operations come under threat. In those early days, it was impossible to withdraw cash from a bank machine or pay suppliers outside Crimea. Zubkov kept Taigan's funds in a Ukrainian bank, which, after annexation, blocked access for clients in Crimea. Zubkov could not buy the meat required to feed the park's animals: his lions and tigers consume a total of a thousand pounds of meat every day. With his funds frozen, and Taigan's animals beginning to go hungry, Zubkov slaughtered pigs and goats from the park's small farm. But the Kremlin was making big promises, earmarking $7 billion for Crimea in 2014 alone and forecasting that three million Russian tourists would visit Crimea that year. Zubkov felt part of a historic process. "We were trying to achieve something, we had big ambitions, and I was inspired by all the new possibilities," he told me.

Six months after Crimea's annexation, Zubkov decided to run for a seat as a deputy in Crimea's regional parliament. He met with Aksyonov, who promised him a place on the candidate list of United Russia, the pro-Kremlin party to which nearly all Crimea's functionaries and bureaucrats fled, knowing perfectly well where power now lay. But a few weeks later, Zubkov showed up at United Russia's party conference and learned that his name was not on the list. All he saw were some friends and relatives of Aksyonov's, but, as far as he was concerned, not a single person who was well known or respected in Crimea. Disappointed, Zubkov tried to run on another party's roster, but United Russia held up the necessary paperwork that would allow him to reregister. The election passed and he was left without a seat. It was the first signal that modern-day Russia was not the place Zubkov had imagined.

Zubkov's real troubles began at the end of 2015, when widespread blackouts hit Crimea. Groups of covert saboteurs, led by Crimean Tatars who had fled for Ukraine and by Ukrainian nationalists, blew up all four power lines that deliver electricity from mainland Ukraine to the peninsula. Crimea was still dependent on Ukraine for much of its basic functioning, including supplies of water and energy. The attacks on the electricity grid cut off power across the peninsula and plunged much of it into nighttime darkness at the onset of the first frosts. Zubkov had previously bought two generators from China, one for each of his parks, and turned them on as backups. They worked for a few days, then sputtered out. At Skazka, Oksana wheeled a small generator between enclosures, giving a few moments of heat to the zoo's tropical fish, iguanas, and alligators. Taigan was left without power completely.

A number of influential officials in Moscow intervened on Zubkov's behalf. One high-ranking politician hinted at Putin's own demonstrated warmth toward wild animals; over the years, Putin has tracked rare Amur tigers and led a flock of endangered Siberian cranes in an ultralight plane. Remember, the official told Zubkov with a wink, who else "loves tigers, lions, and other animals in need of protection." That made saving Taigan "a matter of state importance," the official said. Zubkov's high-placed friends in Moscow were able to get the Crimean authorities to deliver a diesel-powered generator to Taigan.

The next day, at an emergency meeting of his cabinet to address the blackout, Aksyonov singled out Zubkov for criticism. Everyone knows how much money Taigan brings in, so let Zubkov solve his own problems, he said. What about hospitals and schools? "If you ask me to choose between feeding lions and delivering power to children, I'll choose children," he said. He instructed Crimea's chief prosecutor, Natalia Poklonskaya, to look into whether Zubkov was violating the law. Poklonskaya said that if Zubkov did not return the generator, he could be charged with theft of state property. Thus began a game of absurd Ping-Pong: on Sunday night, officials sent by Aksyonov came to confiscate the generator, leaving Taigan and its two thousand animals in darkness. Zubkov again appealed to the Russian media and influential friends in Moscow. Ultimately, the country's minister of energy—an official whose usual duties involve looking after Russia's power grid and overseeing oil and gas production—got involved and ordered the generator brought back to Taigan. At ten in the evening, Crimean officials came again and plugged the machine back in. But, as would become clear ten days later, at Skazka, in Yalta, three rare Amur tiger cubs had died as a result of the blackout. They had a viral infection made worse by the cold. Poklonskaya charged Zubkov with neglect. He called her an idiot. Aksyonov warned that "Zubkov won't get anything from the state by relying on the language of blackmail."

From then on, Zubkov was almost constantly under investigation for one violation or another. He was fined for the alleged illegal import of a collection of monkeys, jaguars, and a kangaroo; in the days after annexation, but before Russian law came into force, Zubkov brought the animals to Crimea in accordance with Ukrainian customs regulations, still formally in effect at the time, but considered retroactively null a year later. The authorities declared that a large billboard Zubkov had installed on the main highway was an illegal construction and must be torn down. Crimea's tax inspectorate said that the entry tickets for Skazka were not marked with the proper stamp, and warned that the zoo might have to close for three months to print a new batch.

Zubkov's legal problems skirted between tragicomic and simply tragic. His slapdash wiliness in running his parks went up against the purposeful scheming of Poklonskaya and those urging her on. A five-year-old boy playing in Taigan knocked over a stone figurine, which fell on him; one toe had to be amputated. Poklonskaya filed charges against Zubkov. A part-time security guard at the park was found dead in the staff dormitory. Zubkov said the guard had an alcohol problem; Poklonskaya's office intimated that he had been attacked by a rogue tiger. I spent one afternoon in court watching as Zubkov tried to appeal a guilty verdict for allegedly assaulting another one of his employees at Taigan. What all sides seem to agree on is that, late one night, a maintenance worker got drunk, commandeered one of the park's vans, and crashed it en route to see some young women on

Crimea's southern coast. When police brought the worker and the crumpled van back to Taigan early the next morning, Zubkov smacked the guy upside the head—or, as the worker and Poklonskaya later alleged, delivered a severe beating that required hospitalization. Zubkov was sentenced to three years of probation. The incident was hard to render in black and white: Zubkov is the sort of hotheaded baron who might indeed give a thwack to those working for him, but Poklonskaya was clearly on a mission to cause as much trouble as she could for him and his parks. Their drawn-out feud quickly became personal. When Zubkov threatened to close down Skazka and Taigan in an act of protest, Poklonskaya said, "Yes, for God's sake, let him get into a cage himself."

Zubkov suspected the Crimean authorities had their own personal motive in going after him. He had heard whispers that Crimea's deputy prime minister, Nikolai Yanaki, had issued an informal directive for Crimea's various government agencies to find whatever they could on Zubkov. Yanaki owns a handful of parks that could be considered competitors to Skazka and Taigan, including a dolphinarium near Yalta. Contrary to local hopes, and promises from Moscow, profits from the tourist market went down after annexation. The much-heralded new wave of visitors from Russia was not enough to replace the missing tourists from Ukraine. Another way to drum up profits is to force your competition out of business, or take it over for yourself.

Zubkov was not the only animal park owner to suffer. A different operator of dolphinariums in Crimea, who ran four parks across the peninsula, saw his business run into the ground from two sides: first, the Crimean authorities found one violation after another, keeping the parks from operating for two years; then, when the owner wanted to stem his losses, to close down and take the dolphins out of Crimea, Poklonskaya's office blocked the move. The scheme pushed the dolphinariums toward insolvency, at which point they could be scooped up for a reduced price from a desperate owner, or simply nationalized. During Ukrainian times, greedy officials had plenty of opportunities to enrich themselves, but the state itself was weak and full of all sorts of inefficiencies and internal conflicts—the sorts of things that gave a businessman like Zubkov room to maneuver. Russia, meanwhile, is home to a much more coherent and inflexible bureaucratic machine, where officials and courts and the fines levied by various inspection bodies act in parasitic mutual benefit.

Every now and then, a well-meaning intermediary would tell Zubkov that Aksyonov was ready to make peace, but Zubkov could imagine what the terms would be: "If you come to him on your knees, ready to obey—and even better, with a suitcase full of cash—then you will be his comrade." All Zubkov's plans for expansion had vanished; success was now defined by managing to keep his two existing parks open. Crimea's regional veterinary service was always showing up for inspections, flagging some sanitary infraction or dangerous disease. One day, responding to an anonymous complaint of a suspected tuberculosis outbreak, they shot taser darts at a number of baboons, knocking them unconscious, and threatened to shutter the park for two months. As Zubkov saw it, the only thing Crimea's administration was capable of was "putting on the squeeze, taking away, dividing things up between themselves."

He began to fear that Crimea had made a mistake in joining Russia, and that the blame was his as well—he was among those who had acted rashly, even foolishly, caught up in the emotive swirl of the moment. He had been frightened, and naive, ready to believe the promises, shown on Russian television and passed around between neighbors, about all the ways life would improve once Crimea became part of Russia. "Four years later, I know the actual state of affairs—that the Russia shown on television and the Russia of real life are two different countries," he told me. He had voted for one, and ended up in the other.

THE TURNOFF TO TAIGAN is hard to find. After Zubkov's billboard was torn down, there were no markers indicating where you should make a right off the highway, onto a narrow country road that winds its way among fields of poppies and sagebrush. But then a self-contained kingdom of pastel buildings rises out of the Crimean steppe. I made my way to the park on a bright, warm spring morning, a short-lived and glorious annual window in Crimea's calendar when the wind already blows warm and is laced with the faint scent of the sea, but before the hordes of tourists and pensioners show up to invade the sanatoriums for their twenty-day stays.

My trip had not been easy. After annexation, Ukraine sealed off access to the peninsula, closing the single road to commercial traffic and shutting down the rail lines. Until 2018, when Russia completed a $4 billion bridge from the mainland, the only way for Russian tourists—these days, there aren't many other kinds—to travel to Crimea was by infrequent and overcrowded ferry over the Kerch Strait, or by plane. The flight from Moscow takes two hours, and after 2014, fares from Russian cities have been generously subsidized by the Kremlin as a way of boosting the tourist trade, given international sanctions and Crimea's general isolation. But seeing as how Ukraine formally considers Crimea its own land, merely under temporary occupation, the government in Kyiv made entry by sea or air a crime, because you don't first pass through Ukrainian territory. To comply with Ukrainian law, you must obtain special permission to enter Crimea from Ukraine's migration service and then drive in from mainland Ukraine.

I went to Kyiv first to get my pass. That evening, I caught an overnight train to a provincial hub in southern Ukraine, close to where the Ukrainian mainland meets the thin strip of land at the top of the Crimean Peninsula. A thirty-minute taxi ride took me to the crossing, where suspicious Ukrainian border guards asked about the purpose of my visit, wondering what business I had in an area they consider enemy-occupied territory. Once I got a Ukrainian exit stamp on my Crimea pass, I schlepped my duffel bag a mile or so through a no-man's-land comprising a single pockmarked road in a state of prolonged decay, lined with signs warning that the muddy fields on either side are dotted with land mines. I eventually got to the Russian-held crossing, a more fortified and technically sophisticated encampment. Pole-mounted cameras scanned the traffic below; border guards with German shepherds walked among those waiting in line to cross into Crimea. My passport made me an automatic curiosity for the Russian officers manning the post—they don't get many Americans crossing into Crimea from mainland Ukraine on foot. They gave me a quiz similar to that of their Ukrainian counterparts: What were my plans in Crimea, whom would I see, what was I going to write? I answered vaguely, but apparently satisfactorily, and was sent on my way. Out on the other side, another taxi, with Crimean plates—that is, Russian—was waiting for me. We drove three hours to Taigan.

When I showed up, Zubkov met me by the park's main gate in a golf cart he had outfitted like a comical miniature police car, with a spinning red siren on the roof. He was in a bubbly mood. There had been another court hearing that morning on the alleged beating of his former employee, but the judge seemed inclined to at least consider Zubkov's appeal. Zubkov had already changed out of the electric blue suit he had worn to court and into his regular camouflage getup. "I feel much safer here than among people, outside my park," he told me as I took a seat next to him. "Here there is no duplicity. The rules are clear: you just have to feed the animals, take care of them, and they answer you with love, devotion, respect." We sped off, heading to see the lions, the prize attraction in the park and the animal for which Zubkov feels the most affection, even fatherly warmth. It was late in the afternoon, and the first pride we came across was loafing in the shade of some tall grass. Zubkov stopped the cart and hopped out, smothering a 400-pound lion with the sort of hug you give a Labrador, rubbing his cheek against the lion's and giving its nose a soft poke with his finger. The lion rolled its head and yawningly opened its jaw. I found the exchange so alarming—I was waiting for the animal to bite off Zubkov's arm—that it somehow became reassuring; surely only a person supremely confident in pulling it off would dare slap a lion, even gently. We got back in the cart and darted around with lurching, childlike speed. Zubkov would leap out, wrestle with a lion, give it a kiss, and chase after another one with a fake roar. He'd ask a family of lions in baby voice if they were enjoying lunch as they crunched their teeth on a knot of sheep bones flecked with blood and fur.

We walked toward a pride of white lions resting near one of the park's perimeter fences. I remarked that the biggest of the group, a regal beast with a straw-colored coat, seemed to be looking at us with a bit of skepticism. "Of course," Zubkov said. "She's a real lioness. She wants to gobble us up. She's not friendly at all." The lion growled and stood up on her hind legs. I inched backward. Zubkov took off his rubber slipper and waved it at her. "I'll take off my slipper and you'll be sorry," he yelled. The lion gave him a look of resigned obedience and walked off. "Here it is," Zubkov said, showing off his slipper. "The secret nuclear weapon against lions: one slipper and you're fine." (Zubkov's magic slipper is an object of comedic fascination among the park's regular visitors, and has birthed its own memes on the internet.) We kept driving and found another pride nearby. With Zubkov's nudging, and against my initial will, I got out of the cart and made my way over to a lion with a shiny coat of golden fur sitting under an acacia tree. Zubkov insisted on taking a picture. "Give her a real hug, get right up close!" he yelled. I inched forward in microscopic steps, trying to appear as if I were actually closing the distance between myself and the lion without actually doing so. Zubkov nudged me closer, until I was kneeling at the lion's hind legs, forcing a grimaced smile. For the flash of a second, I gave the lion an awkward hug, my arms not quite closing around its neck. Zubkov snapped a photo.

We pulled up back by the entrance, near where Zubkov's APC, still draped in patriotic pro-Russian banners, sat parked on the asphalt. I asked what it made him think of now. "Mixed feelings," he told me. "It's a monument to my spasm of enthusiasm, the hope that with the return of Crimea to Russia, more of my projects are going to be realized, that new ideas will come to life." But it's also a reminder, he said, of how "all these rosy dreams and patriotic feelings were, over the course of several years, barbarically destroyed." He keeps the APC around for the tourists—the park still gets a few visitors who want to get a picture of themselves in front of this artifact of the "Crimean Spring"—but also because, as he put it, "it's a part of history, of my own, too." Just as he was pained to see the Lenin monument in Kyiv pulled down, he doesn't think it would be right to remove this historical relic. "After all, this luminous moment did, for a moment, really exist."

For all his disappointment, Zubkov's faith in the state—and in Putin most of all—remained tenacious. When his problems started, he wrote letter after letter to Putin, outlining his troubles with the new, Moscow-backed authorities. The appeal to the tsar is a long-standing Russian tradition. But the Kremlin redirected his letters to Aksyonov's administration, where they quickly disappeared. One year, during Putin's annual press conference on Channel One, a Crimean journalist asked Putin about the fate of Taigan. Zubkov was proud, and his hope was buoyed yet again. "If such a question snuck into the ear of the president, then if not him, someone on his orders should work out this issue and solve it," he said. Zubkov had seen the seemingly magic effect of such exchanges before. "If the question was, 'Please give me a puppy, Comrade President, my dream is to have a Chinese pug,' then the very next day a deputy in the city council would show up with a dog and say, 'Here's your gift from the president.'" But nothing happened; not the next day, or in the months that followed. Zubkov understood that for Putin to support him would be to implicitly criticize Aksyonov, his handpicked governor, making things complicated for Aksyonov in Crimea, potentially upsetting the local balance of power. Putin didn't need that, maybe couldn't even risk it, Zubkov knew. The appearance of placid, cheerful stability in Crimea, the showpiece of Putin's third presidential term, is more important than whether the owner of some safari park out in the middle of nowhere is being treated fairly. "I stopped hoping," he told me. (Hearing Zubkov talk, I was reminded of the implicit bargain Putin made with Kadyrov in Chechnya, where the need for surface calm has given Kadyrov carte blanche to rule as he pleases.)

Yet Zubkov couldn't fully shake his belief that, if only he could plead his case to the right person, someone might save things for him. Once I was driving with him when he got the news that Maria Zakharova, the spokesperson for the Russian foreign ministry, had visited Skazka in Yalta with her six-year-old daughter. Zakharova is an active user of social media—her frequent gym selfies, in particular, became a cult favorite among Russian political journalists—and had written a favorable review of Skazka. Zubkov couldn't resist indulging the notion that Zakharova would pass along her warm feelings toward his parks to her boss, Sergey Lavrov, the minister of foreign affairs, who might favorably mention Zubkov's name to Putin after some meeting in the Kremlin. It seemed silly, but in Putin-era Russia, such personality-driven serendipity is indeed how careers are launched, fortunes determined, business empires made and lost. Zubkov decided to call Zakharova to invite her and her daughter to Taigan. "You'll never forget it, you won't see anything like it anywhere in the world," he told her, his voice turning giddy. "Let Crimea recharge and inspire you!" He plotted out the details of her visit. But she never came. The next day, in Sevastopol, the naval port in Crimea's southwest, her daughter was bitten by a feral dog, and they flew back to Moscow.

I spent the night at the hotel Zubkov built on the grounds of the park, in a room that combined the mood of a safari camp in the African savannah with the finishes of a motel somewhere outside Reno. A portrait of a lion hung over my leopard-print sheets, tucked under leopard-print pillows. Outside, the distant roar of a lion provided the bass notes to a top melody of mellifluous birdsong. The next morning, I had breakfast in the park's White Lion restaurant, which, not long before, the Belogorsk prosecutor's office had declared to be an illegal construction, alleging that Zubkov had not filed the necessary paperwork correctly in 2012, when Crimea was still governed by Ukrainian law. The charges were filed in such a way that they barred Zubkov from leaving the country. He still managed to travel abroad, he told me, by first driving to Belarus—Russian citizens can enter without border checks—and flying out of Minsk.

Over the days I spent at Taigan, it became clear that it is not just Crimean officials who make Zubkov's life difficult. The general complications of running a sizable business in territory much of the world considers to be illegally occupied presents as much, if not more, of a challenge. On our tour of the park, when I saw a lion feasting on a sheep carcass, I asked Zubkov where he gets the whole animals he uses as food. Before 2014, he said, he brought them overland from Ukraine. With that supply route closed, he now brings them from a farm in the Caucasus, across the Kerch Strait in Russia—but in the winter the ferry sometimes doesn't run for two weeks in a row. All the park's furniture and statues and dishware come from China. Before, goods could be shipped from Guangzhou to the Ukrainian port in Odessa. Now they must go to Vladivostok, then to Moscow, down south by truck to the ferry, and across the strait. The cost of bringing in supplies has gone up by as much as five times.

If the referendum were held today, Zubkov would vote to remain in Ukraine. But it's too late for that now. "History does not allow for the subjunctive case, 'what I would have done if,'" he said. "This has happened, and it happened with my participation." He bears his personal measure of responsibility. Meanwhile, a nationalist group in Kyiv with links to the Ukrainian security services put him on an informal blacklist of people it considers enemies, citing his comical public threat to deploy his lions to defend the referendum's results. He may wish he never left Ukraine, but traveling there is now impossible. He said it was like being trapped in a bad marriage. "It can feel like a mistake, you're going to face the music, you might even fall out of love, but if you have a family, children, you feel obligated to stick around." Oksana offered up an old Russian saying: "You saw what you were buying, so eat up, even if you choke on it."

ONE MORNING, I WENT into the city of Belogorsk itself, a ten-minute taxi ride from Taigan. It is a quiet, unremarkable place, home to sixteen thousand people, the sort of provincial center, with a house of culture in the main square and rows of concrete apartment blocks, that you find all over the expanse of the former imperium. In Soviet times, the region was home to legions of communal farms, growing stone fruit and grapes and cereal grains. In recent years, locals have tried to keep agricultural production alive, half successfully, but the truth is, there isn't much going on in Belogorsk. A standard-issue Lenin statue, arm outstretched in a gesture of avuncular guidance, stood in a patch of shade by the local school. There had been no Leninopad in Belogorsk, or anywhere in Crimea. Preserving a reverence for the image of Lenin—entirely severed from any actual understanding of his ideas, let alone their disastrous implementation—was a way the residents of Crimea distinguished themselves from the revolutionaries on the Maidan. Lenin became an avatar for a particular reading of the past, which, after the events in Kyiv, carried unavoidable implications for the present: Lenin signified that the Soviet empire was mighty and just, and thus, so is Russia, its modern-day descendant.

Not only had Belogorsk's Lenin remained firmly in place, but, after Crimea became Russian, the city had added other statues. In front of the regional administration building now stood monuments to Alexander Suvorov, the eighteenth-century Russian military leader, the last to hold the title "Generalissimo" before Stalin; and a number of Soviet World War II heroes: bomber pilots and tank commanders and partisan fighters. I had an appointment to see Galina Perelovich, the head of the Belogorsk region and one of Zubkov's chief antagonists—she issued the order for the removal of the park's roadside billboard and regularly sent the regional tax and veterinary inspectors to sniff around for the smallest violations. Hers was a common tale for government functionaries in Crimea: she had a long history as a bureaucrat serving the Ukrainian state, but in 2014, she announced her support for Russia and took up a post under the new administration. She had previously been the head of Aromatnoye, a village whose name literally means "aromatic," where, in Soviet days, farmworkers crushed lavender and sage into fragrant oils. After annexation, Aksyonov offered her the job as head of the Belogorsk region, the equivalent of a small-town mayor being named head of a large rural county.

Perelovich, who is fifty-five, with a bob of fine blond hair and the manner of a go-getting collective-farm leader, welcomed me into her office, a spartan, boxy space with a row of green houseplants and the obligatory Putin portrait on the wall. She struck me as someone who is both easily convinced and enthusiastic to convince others. She started by telling me of her Ukrainian roots: both sides of her family originally hailed from western Ukraine, lands that shifted back and forth between Polish and Russian control and in recent years have been home to a resurgent Ukrainian nationalism. But Perelovich was wary of Maidan, and, like the Zubkovs, saw something frightening and ominous for Crimea in the protests. The revolutionary events in Kyiv reached their climax in the final days of the Sochi Olympics; Yanukovych fled Kyiv two days before the games finished. Perelovich watched the closing ceremony on television at home in Belogorsk and perked up as the camera panned to Putin, who was sitting in the audience. "I was watching, and, as a woman, wife, mother, grandmother, was directing my thoughts toward him: 'Vladimir Vladimirovich, protect us.'"

She supported joining Russia. "In my heart, I felt bad for Ukraine," she told me. "But with my mind, I knew that only Russia would be able to help." The referendum, and the annexation that followed, led to a series of pained phone calls with her relatives in western Ukraine. "We had a misunderstanding, of course," she said. "In their eyes, it didn't make sense. They couldn't understand: How can we just, all of a sudden, go for such a betrayal, pack our things and leave?" She understood that each side had its own truth, and had long ago stopped trying to persuade her family members of anything: "They saw it one way. We saw it differently, and made our choice."

In part, Perelovich's satisfaction at having joined Russia was rational and material. When Yanukovych's political party, the Party of Regions, was ascendant, Perelovich joined as a member. "A long time ago, I was taught that a blow from a palm is nothing like that from a fist," she told me. If you want to strike with decisive strength, you have to do so alongside others, as part of a group, a force larger than yourself. She valued the sense of security, the easy, prefab unity that comes from belonging to the ruling party. But the Ukrainian state could never provide for the Belogorsk region; with time, Perelovich felt ignored, left to fend for herself. She told me of how, before every election cycle, she promised her constituents that the Ukrainian authorities would lay a gas line, and each time, they never did. Belogorsk was the last place in Crimea without gas: for decades, people heated their apartments with basement furnaces powered by wood and coal. After the annexation, Belogorsk got its first gas connection, a major event in these parts. I pictured how Belogorsk residents could support joining Russia for that reason alone: Imagine you had lived without gas for as long as you could remember, and for the better part of two decades, the government that might do something about it never found the resources or the will to fix the problem; maybe it simply didn't have the money. So when someone who seemed like he might have the resources—Putin—suddenly appeared on the scene, it didn't take much to project onto him all the vigor and decisiveness that was missing in your previous rulers, who remained as distant as they seemed impotent. (That Crimea's new bosses had since fallen behind on their plan to lay new gas lines in the Belogorsk region was a detail on which Perelovich did not dwell.)

It was also clear that Perelovich was moved by what she felt as the pull of history. She wanted to see the version of events that was most comfortable and familiar reflected back at her. I found her explanations squishy and hard to understand in their particulars—she seemed driven more by a mood than an articulable list of desires. In Soviet days, the country "set one goal and one task, and we could sing one song in one language and not worry." It was under post-Soviet Ukraine that what gave her comfort and direction vanished, and what had been lost she would forever associate with Russia, the "one powerful rod" in her life. With the referendum, she said, "we returned to the place where life had been good for us." I understood that as less a physical or geographical space than a mental and emotional one.

A sense of psychic contentment made up for the logistical difficulties that came with the annexation. She told me about the winter of the blackouts, when Belogorsk sat in the darkness for weeks on end. As she explained, in the days before the new year, with the power flickering on and off across the peninsula, she asked everyone around town to lower their energy consumption to the absolute minimum. No one was to use heavy machinery or power-sucking appliances. She wanted there to be enough juice left so residents could watch Putin's New Year's address at midnight. The gambit worked: across Belogorsk, the blue light of hundreds of television screens filtered out of the concrete apartment blocks and into the black night of the steppe. Just after midnight, with Putin's speech over, the power went out again. "I remember, everyone said: 'Well, that's okay, at least we saw the president.' Everybody was patient, they knew the moment will come when things will look up." Her tale seemed apocryphal—

more a kind of moral fable than a factual recounting of events—but she clearly believed it.

Perelovich's conflict with Zubkov was partly structural—her bosses had declared him an enemy, and she was not the type to question the party line—but it was also about the virtues of patience. Zubkov was not willing to sit in the dark in order to watch Putin, metaphorically speaking: he had parks to run and was full of his own plans and ambitions; he wasn't going to limit himself as part of some collective sacrifice for goals he didn't recognize or share. Zubkov was certainly capable of wiliness—he was plenty wily in running his parks under Ukraine—but he didn't fit the particular contours of wiliness *à la russe,* at least the way the game is played in the Putin era. "He wants everything quickly, and all done for him alone," Perelovich said. She fell back on a would-be persuasive mode I could imagine having been employed by the head of the regional party committee of Aromatnoye a generation ago. "Taigan is a very nice park, with a lot to see—people are drawn there. But he needs to recognize that in order to develop, he can't neglect others. It can't just be the way he wants it. That's impossible." Why couldn't he be a bit more patient, willing to compromise with the state, which had only the best intentions for Belogorsk?

At a particularly tense moment in Zubkov's relations with the Crimean authorities, Aksyonov held a meeting of his council of ministers in Belogorsk. He suggested that what Zubkov really needed was a good psychiatrist. Perelovich, the ever-loyal functionary, outdid Aksyonov in her displeasure. "I think everyone has heard about the rather specific character of the park's director," she said. Taigan has given Crimea "nothing but tears," she went on. "This may sound rude, but I'll be very happy if it moves to Turkey." (At the time, Zubkov was periodically threatening to relocate the park to an area outside Istanbul if his problems in Crimea continued.) When I reminded her of those comments, she said she had misspoken, or been misunderstood. "I knew about Oleg Alexandrovich's plans, that this park won't go anywhere, that he'll open up a new one in Turkey. So that's what I said: 'Yes, I agree, let Oleg Alexandrovich go to Turkey.'" After the dismantling of the billboards, and her comments at the hearing, things got tense between her and Zubkov. Her office launched new cases: Zubkov was fined for the shadow one of the park's buildings casts on a neighboring property. In a fit of spite, Zubkov canceled the ticket discounts he offered residents of Belogorsk. When we spoke, Perelovich was eager to downplay the conflict. She said that once a new federal highway running across Crimea was finished, built by the Kremlin at a cost of $2.5 billion, Zubkov could put his billboard back up. "Let me speak like a woman, not just the head of regional administration," Perelovich told me. "Everyone has his or her wish list, things we'd like to see happen, but it's important to express yourself correctly, to weigh your actions, take other things into consideration."

ONE GROUP IN CRIMEA never had any illusions about Moscow's rule. On the eve of annexation, just over 10 percent of the population were Crimean Tatars, an ethnic group that traces its roots back to the Mongol horde that made its way to Crimea in the thirteenth century and to various indigenous peoples who lived on the peninsula. For centuries, the Crimean Tatars were ruled by a local khan, who was elected by the nobility, and followed a relatively loose, moderate form of Islam. If any nation could make far-reaching historical claims to the land in Crimea, it would be the Tatars, whose khans ruled for centuries from the ornate palace in Bakhchisaray, in the peninsula's inland center.

Relations with the Russian state were never easy. When Catherine the Great seized Crimea from the Ottoman Empire in 1783, she won over the last Tatar khan with jewels and goodwill. But relations between newly arriving Russians and the Crimean Tatars deteriorated, with fights erupting over who owned the land and whose interests took priority. Stories abounded of mistrust and disrespect; to fuel the Tsarist-era construction boom, Russian laborers took headstones from Crimean graveyards as building materials. That ill will pushed many Tatars to aid the opposing side—the British-French-Ottoman alliance—in the Crimean War. They suffered greatly in the war's aftermath. More than half the Crimean Tatar population, nearly two hundred thousand people, fled for Turkey. After 1917, the Soviet authorities initially promised a degree of autonomy, only to roll back these limited freedoms, closing down mosques and shooting much of the Tatar political leadership.

The memory of famine and terror led some Crimean Tatars to join the side of the Nazis during the Second World War. As in Chechnya, the true story of collaboration is murky, contradictory, and covered up by so many layers of myth and legend that no clear picture remains of the events of seventy years ago. But it is certain that some Tatars joined units directed by the Germans, though many had been captured and forced to fight against their will. At the same time, no small number of Tatars joined underground resistance units on the peninsula; even more had been enlisted in the Red Army and were waging war against the German military on the front. Stalin had no interest in this complexity; his real aim, as with the Chechens, was to use allegations of wartime collaboration to carry out a policy of ethnic cleansing. On May 18, 1944, NKVD agents woke up Tatar families in the middle of the night and told them to prepare for a long journey. Just about the entire Crimean Tatar population, estimated at around 240,000 people at the time, was rounded up, crammed into railway wagons, and shipped to the distant corners of Central Asia.

Abdureshit Dzhepparov was born in a small village in Uzbekistan. His family returned to Crimea in 1969, when he was nine. They settled in the plains surrounding Belogorsk, which had been known as Karasubazar before all place names were Russified after the deportation, a ten-minute drive from the plot of land that would become Taigan. A short taxi ride took me from my room of multiple leopard prints to Dzhepparov, who is now sixty, with a creased face and a silver beard. He told me of his youth, when he was a Crimean Tatar activist, which, in those days, meant writing appeals to officials in Moscow and sending articles abroad. He was hounded by Soviet authorities, who were constantly calling him in for questioning and opening criminal investigations against him. His case was finally closed in 1987, as a goodwill gesture by Gorbachev, who was beginning negotiations with Reagan. As was the case all over the crumbling empire, the slow-motion decay of Soviet authority created openings for the Crimean Tatars, who grabbed land that had been lost during the deportation, setting up new encampments and building homes. Dzhepparov was one of the organizers of the movement. The practice continued after the Soviet collapse; Ukrainian courts were largely sympathetic, or just impotent, and thousands of Tatar families were able to register plots they had effectively taken over by squatting. Dzhepparov and I spoke in a house he built in the early nineties, in what had been an open field. We sat on the carpeted floor, sipping coffee and nibbling on dates. Dzhepparov carries himself with an air of quiet refinement, a well of deep sadness undergirded by dignity and self-composure.

"If I talk about my sons, it destroys me, and after that I can't function," he said. But he felt compelled to tell me about them all the same. His older son, Abdullah, was always into sports, a wrestler, with an appetite for exploration and adventure. As a boy, he loved to play the role of stoic and noble soldier, even going so far as to take his plate of food and eat by himself in a trench he had dug on the family property. One day, in 2013, when Abdullah was twenty, he announced that he was leaving for Turkey, where he would continue his studies and work a bit on the side. (The Tatar and Turkish languages are similar, with the Tatars also sharing historical and religious links with Turkey, where there is a sizable Crimean Tatar diaspora.) After half a year, when Abdullah's Turkish visa would have expired, he still hadn't returned home, and Dzhepparov began to worry. He started to ask around, and then heard some news: Abdullah had died in Syria. As far as Dzhepparov could piece together later, though the information was spotty and secondhand, Abdullah had been moved by the call to fight in a holy struggle and joined a militant group battling forces loyal to Assad.

The next year, in the fall of 2014—six months after Crimea's annexation—a friend came to visit Dzhepparov. A wave of arrests and disappearances was spreading through the Crimean Tatar community. On the whole, the Tatars had been skeptical of the Russian takeover; many, in fact, had been openly and vocally opposed to it, and after annexation the space for such dissent shrank to almost nothing. The Kremlin-backed authorities moved to close the well-regarded

Tatar-language television network. Far more ominously, a number of young Tatar men had vanished and turned up dead with signs of torture on their bodies: one was found with a bag over his head; another had been left hanging in an abandoned building. Scores more had been arrested on vague "extremism" charges. The evening Dzhepparov hosted his friend, his younger son, Islyam, then eighteen, entered the living room to serve them coffee. Islyam was fastidious and precise in his mannerisms, cleaning the shoelaces of his sneakers with a toothbrush, for example. Dzhepparov remembers him pouring the coffee that day with "particular elegance." He got down on one knee in front of his father and their guest, and poured a stream of thick, dark coffee into small cups. Islyam then left the house to go visit cousins who lived nearby. "He left, and I haven't seen him since," Dzhepparov told me.

Later that evening, a neighbor came up to the house. He said that he had just seen Islyam and one of his cousins, Dzhevdet, who was twenty-three, bundled up and thrown into a blue minivan with tinted windows. The men who hustled them away wore black uniforms and acted "fast and professional," the neighbor told Dzhepparov. He presumed the boys must have been taken by the Russian security services or those with shadowy links to them, and guessed it must have something to do with Dzhepparov himself: Was it his past activism, or his attempts to find out his older son's fate in Syria? The next day, in a sign of solidarity, more than a hundred Tatars arrived at Dzhepparov's house to show the Crimean authorities that the case would not go unnoticed. On the third day, some four hundred came. Dzhepparov was visited by a Crimean Tatar official who had taken a high-ranking position in the post-annexation Russian administration. Dzhepparov had a message: "Tell Aksyonov that he should meet with me, hear me out, and respond to our problem." He meant not only the disappearance of his own son, but also the dozens of similar cases in the months since Russia's takeover. "If he doesn't react, then I will—and I won't come alone, but with thousands of people."

Aksyonov, frightened at the prospect of thousands of angry Tatars in the streets, agreed to a meeting. He received Dzhepparov at his office in the parliament building in Simferopol, a brutalist monument built in the eighties that suggests a hulking alien spacecraft landed in the center of town. He promised unlimited resources in the search for Islyam and Dzhevdet. "I didn't come just for my son," Dzhepparov told him. "The fact is, right now in Crimea, mosques, schools, people's homes are being subject to regular searches. Young men are being arrested, disappearing. The people are worried—and this can cause a storm." They agreed that Aksyonov would come to Belogorsk.

Three days later, he did. The streets were filled with thousands of Crimean Tatars who had come from all over the peninsula. Aksyonov's security detail put on a show of force, positioning armored personnel carriers along the road and lining the rooftops with snipers. Aksyonov started to make familiar promises—that he would put an end to the searches and arrests—when Dzhepparov made a proposal: "We have questions," he said. "We need a way to pose them to you, to get answers." He suggested they form a regular group of Crimean Tatar activists and leaders that would meet with Aksyonov. Many of Dzhepparov's allies and friends in the Tatar community were skeptical, seeing nothing good or hopeful in rulers installed by Moscow, whatever the century or context. But Dzhepparov thought it a necessary compromise, not only to help his son or learn more of his fate, but for the vitality and security of the Tatar population. "Negotiations are always needed, with everyone you encounter," Dzhepparov told me. If nothing else, they are a way of gaining time, learning more about your counterpart while keeping the most egregious violations in check. "Just don't give up your core principles."

The contact group met four times over the next year. Dzhepparov and its other members achieved some concrete successes. They convinced Aksyonov to throw out criminal charges against a number of imams who had been accused of extremism. It was a revealing window into what is known in Russia as "telephone justice." In front of Dzhepparov and the others, Aksyonov would pick up a phone and call the judge in the trial, telling him to close the case. A dozen Crimean Tatars walked out of jail. The group began to solve problems not directly connected to human rights: they managed to keep open a urological clinic, run by an esteemed Crimean Tatar doctor, that the authorities wanted to close, and to find new land for the expansion of a Tatar cemetery. I asked Dzhepparov if he found this proximity to Aksyonov and his circle distasteful, having to shake hands and act collegially with those who, in large measure, bore responsibility for the innumerable difficulties faced by the Crimean Tatars after annexation—not least, the disappearance of Dzhepparov's own son. "I have the choice of shaking hands with this person—without pleasure, of course—and maybe this will result, let's say, in more people released from prisons, life being somewhat easier for our population," he told me. "I am prepared to bear these costs if they will be of some use." He heard plenty of criticism from fellow Tatars that he was legitimizing an illegal occupation, trading a few piecemeal victories for tacit acquiescence of more serious and ongoing violations. But Dzhepparov thought the moral imperative was to help those he could: What's moral is that thanks to his group's involvement, this or that particular person walks free.

Dzhepparov never learned the fate of his son. And, as the months went on, Aksyonov became less interested in even pretending to take the issues raised by the contact group seriously. Its efficacy waned. Then one of its members was the victim of an attempted kidnapping. Not long after, local Crimean security forces carried out a search of that member's home, conspicuously roughing up the place in the process. Investigators claimed he belonged to a Muslim organization that was formally banned in Russia. Officials from Aksyonov's administration told the other members of the group that they should publicly declare they had nothing to do with him, to effectively disavow him and leave him to the authorities. They refused. "They told us there won't be any more meetings," Dzhepparov remembered. "Okay, if that's the way it is, then let there not be."

The contact group fell apart. Although the wave of disappearances came to an end, arrests of Crimean Tatars continue. This reflects a shift in tactics. Crimea emerged from the early, more chaotic days immediately after annexation, when ragtag self-proclaimed militias roamed the streets, to a routinized system of law enforcement, a steamroller with only one gear, long familiar to other regions in Russia. Tatar activists, or even those who support them, face arrest for charges of extremism or separatism—not only possessing certain religious texts, but merely questioning the annexation's legality, can end in trial. FSB officers and riot police regularly turn up at Tatar-run cafés, mosques, schools, and private homes to carry out raids and make arrests, usually taking a whole batch of young Tatar men at a time.

Dzhepparov continues to urge restraint. Now is not the time for open, direct resistance, he tells his fellow Tatars. Given the large size of Tatar family clans and the close-knit ties within the community, a localized standoff could quickly lead to a wider armed conflict, which would only end in disaster. "If the situation suddenly became truly confrontational, they would finish off all our people in a matter of weeks," he told me. Sometimes Dzhepparov shows up at the scene of an arrest or standoff with the police and tries to quiet emotions. "I have lost more than anyone," he tells people. That gives him a certain authority. He tells the brother or cousin or mother of an arrested Tatar that he understands their pain and anger, but if he hasn't gone over to using force or joining an underground militia, then they shouldn't, either. "You must also endure." Otherwise, he says, "it will be a disaster, a total catastrophe."

Through a friend in the security services, Dzhepparov gained access to telephone billing records showing that after Islyam's disappearance, his mobile phone connected to networks in mainland Russia. If he made it to Russia, Dzhepparov thinks, perhaps he's being held prisoner. "Maybe he's alive there. At least that's what I want to think." Recently, he researched to see how long it took after Stalin's death, in 1953, for political prisoners to walk free from the Gulag. The answer was sometimes months, though in many cases, years. All Dzhepparov could do was hope for the passing of the Putin system—not just the man, but the whole ruling edifice—so that the country's political prisoners, including Crimean Tatars, maybe even his own son, might be freed. In the meantime, he and his fellow Tatars needed to act carefully, to avoid giving the state the pretext or opportunity to destroy their people once and for all. The most important goal is surviving to better days, not just as individuals but as an intact nation. "We must live to see those times in a way that does not make us blush, so that we have nothing to be ashamed of in how we passed these years," Dzhepparov said.

ONE DAY, I ARRANGED to meet Zubkov on a street corner in Simferopol, Crimea's capital, a drab, boxy city of standard-issue socialist housing blocks and Soviet-built bureaucratic offices, retro-futuristic edifices of cement and glass left to chip and fade in the Crimean sunshine. It is a place most tourists merely pass through on their way to the resort towns of the southern coast. Zubkov had come for yet another court hearing: the Crimean veterinary service had confiscated one of his baby tigers, and he had lodged a complaint to get it back. As we walked toward the courthouse, Zubkov told me the background to the case.

Some months earlier, he had agreed to transfer a seven-week-old tiger to a circus owner in Krasnodar, a Russian city on the opposite shore of the Black Sea. The two had traded animals from time to time over the years. A courier took the tiger, named Altai, from Taigan and brought it on the ferry to the Russian mainland. Inspectors from the veterinary service stopped him, found the tiger, and determined that it was being transported without an electronic identification chip. Zubkov admitted he hadn't wanted to waste the time implanting the chip—it could take two months to get the necessary approvals and registration—but all the tiger's other papers were in order, and in any case, he was ready to pay the required fine. But instead of fining him and returning Altai, the Crimean veterinary service impounded the tiger, claiming they couldn't be certain whom it belonged to. A sympathetic employee of the veterinary service told Zubkov that Altai had been held in the basement of its headquarters, where officials and their friends would come down to have their picture taken with the animal—until it got bigger and apparently bit someone, after which they passed it off to the small municipal zoo in Simferopol. Zubkov was appealing to get Altai returned to him.

The judge, a no-nonsense woman in her forties, gave Zubkov a chance to speak. He cited a line in the Crimean veterinary service's letter to him, which claimed that all "fauna located within the territory of the Russian Federation is state property." Zubkov was incredulous. "So I'm to understand that all animals now belong to the state?" he said. Zubkov's lawyer asked the representative of the veterinary service how it had come into possession of the tiger. "I don't understand the question. I can't answer it," the representative replied. All he knew was that the state had it now. Zubkov erupted. "A tiger has been seized and no one can figure out what is going on?" he said. "The state says the tiger doesn't belong to me, but can't say whose it is—as if we have tiger cubs running around like baby chickens in Crimea." The judge, who seemed both amused and exhausted by the dispute, adjourned the hearing for the day. Such is Zubkov's life: one court appearance after another, 157 in one year alone.

After the hearing, Zubkov suggested we take a walk to the Simferopol zoo, where Altai was being held. We strolled through a leafy park and bought two entry tickets for a couple dollars each. The zoo was cramped and run-down, the sort of place that had probably been a cheerful day out for Soviet vacationers in the seventies and eighties but looked tired thirty years on. A handful of families walked from one enclosure to the next, pointing at the animals, which were without exception lying on the concrete in a seemingly perpetual state of listless inaction. The zoo was run by a man in his thirties named Alexander Shabanov, whom Zubkov liked and respected. Over the years, Shabanov had asked for Zubkov's advice on looking after the animals in the zoo—what to feed newborn cubs, that sort of thing. He tried to do the best he could with the zoo's less than ideal conditions. Now he was in charge of keeping Altai, who, when Zubkov and I showed up, was lying in a rectangular cage the size of a cargo elevator. "He's sad here, that's obvious," Zubkov said.

He wasn't upset with Shabanov. "He is a young guy who is very dependent on those in power in Crimea. He is forced to maneuver between our friendly relations and the preservation of his own position." The zoo is wholly run by the state, and so when a higher-ranking official showed up and said, "Take this tiger," he did. He is no revolutionary; anyway, Zubkov said, the situation isn't worth any categorical displays. Let Shabanov keep his job and his future at the Simferopol zoo. "I don't think you can trade a man's fate for him standing next to me and yelling out this and that."

A little while later, I returned to the zoo to talk with Shabanov, who seemed as much a municipal bureaucrat as a zookeeper. He was in his office, giving a small army of clerks and accountants a stream of instructions: give me this to sign, stamp that and send it to this city council deputy, tell that one we'll have the report by Monday. We walked over to a bench near Altai's cage. "We didn't plan to have him," he said. "We didn't ask to have him. They brought him to us." Zubkov's supporters had organized a small picket calling on the Crimean authorities to return Altai, and the case was the subject of heated discussion on various online Crimean political forums. (Once, a picketer in support of Zubkov was fined the equivalent of nearly a thousand dollars; another was given a misdemeanor charge and sat in jail for fifteen days.) Shabanov seemed bemused by the whole affair, uneasy at the position he found himself in but powerless to do anything about it. "I'm just a link in the chain, far off from the real center of things."

Shabanov had been in charge since 2011. I asked about the switchover from Ukraine to Russia. He acknowledged that it was easier to run the zoo when Crimea was part of Ukraine—but that was largely because the Ukrainian way of doing things allowed for slapdash, informal fixes. Everything could be agreed on with a wink, a slap on the back, or, for some—he was careful to say this was not his method—a fistful of cash. He pointed to a Ferris wheel, built in Soviet days, that teetered precariously in a corner of the park. When Crimea belonged to Ukraine, it was always open for rides, even when something went wrong. "A mechanic came, twisted his wrench a few times, and it was working again in a few minutes," he said. That didn't hold after annexation. Under Russian rule, the ride sat closed and unused for months. "We had to change the bars in the cabins, swap out metal parts that had rusted, install closed-circuit television on the perimeter, bring it up to fire code, follow anti-terrorist measures, test the load weights all over again—all of that took a lot of time and money and paperwork," he told me. He waved his arms around, motioning toward the rest of the zoo. "It's that way with everything."

Zubkov, he said, had a difficult time adjusting to the new reality. It didn't suit his personality or management style. He had a vision of how things should be, and didn't have the patience or mentality to bend that vision to fit an arbitrary list of government-imposed regulations. Zubkov was brave, Shabanov said. "One of the greatest daredevils I've seen." But he could be difficult. "It's not always easy to be friends with such a rebel," he told me. As for Altai, he said, Zubkov simply didn't understand why commonsense logic can't win out over an annoying thicket of rules and procedure. "He thinks he should be able to say, 'Come on, we all know it's my tiger, just give it back.'" But that's not how the Russian system works: For those with political connections, the most onerous measures in the law can be overlooked or nimbly avoided. For everybody else, they are applied without humanistic reason or sympathy, and often prove suffocating.

Shabanov and I were sitting on a bench across from the tiger cage. Altai paced in slow steps across the cement. Talking about Zubkov, Shabanov started to riff more broadly on the Russian system he had been forced to adapt to, its complex web of regulations and laws and fines. Why is the state like that? he wondered aloud. "Well, in part, it's because of us," he said. He meant the Russian people. "We are always looking for loopholes to get around the law." He compared the cycle of law evasion and enforcement to an arms race: "They tell us we can't do this, so we come up with a way to do it slightly differently, the state responds by making that illegal, we figure out yet another way, on and on." The citizen is constantly trying to fool and outsmart the state, which, in turn, creates an ever-thicker blanket of rules to keep him from doing exactly that. "We have only ourselves to blame that the law is so complicated."

WHEN ZUBKOV TURNED FIFTY, he decided to throw himself a huge birthday party at Taigan. His kitschy, zany tastes are undergirded by such genuine enthusiasm that the effect can be infectious. I wouldn't necessarily place oil paintings of lions everywhere or commission waist-high elephant statues carved from mahogany wood for myself, but at Taigan, with Zubkov's effervescent hospitality, it all feels somehow logical, faithful to the *terroir* and mood of the place. He and Oksana had spent months overseeing the construction of a new banquet hall, a vast space the size of an airplane hangar, in which every surface would be covered by trompe l'oeil wallpaper and lit by twinkling, fake-crystal chandeliers.

On the night of his party, several hundred guests gathered around the fountain on the small square in front of the hotel and the newly finished event space. The cutting *thwack* of helicopter blades echoed in the distance, growing to a bass-heavy rumble. The chopper landed, sending birthday cards and napkins and hairdos flying, and Zubkov stepped out, dressed in a white tuxedo. "I'm glad that everyone I've shared my life with is here tonight," he said. "Have a great time!" We filtered inside. A giant projection screen flashed the tagline for the evening: "Oleg Zubkov, King of the Pride, Fifty Years." I took a seat next to a middle-aged man named Viktor. He said that he, too, had favored Crimea becoming part of Russia, and after it did so, he was eager to get involved in politics. He was a former municipal official in Yalta; he got to know Zubkov on the city council there in Ukrainian days, and like Zubkov had after annexation, he wanted to run again in Russian elections. But nobody had much use for him. "After Crimea joined Russia, we thought it was our time," Viktor said. "The fact that we've ended up on the sidelines, with all our paths of influence blocked, is strange and wild, but that's the way it is."

Over the next six hours, we ate Crimean oysters and piles of shrimp and a side of roast lamb, washed down with saccharine-sweet Crimean champagne and cognac the consistency of maple syrup, interspersed with enough bottles of mineral water—I hoped—to allow me to survive until the next morning. The emcees for the evening were Edgard Zapashny, scion of a four-generation Russian dynasty of circus performers, and Elena Yurchenko, a former government minister in Crimea from Ukrainian days. In a telling exchange—in that, in today's Russia such a thing needs clarification—Zapashny began the evening by remarking on Zubkov's success, saying, "He didn't steal it, he earned it," to which Yurchenko replied, "That's quite right!" We watched a film showing the dilapidated wooden house where Zubkov grew up. An Orthodox priest with long hair pulled back in a ponytail stood to give a blessing that turned into a booming variety-show sing-along. Later, a magician in an evening dress took the stage to do a number involving a white pigeon that took flight inside the banquet hall. Some other former deputies from Yalta got up to talk about how they supported Zubkov when he was just launching Skazka, in the nineties. My neighbor Viktor laughed: These guys are "inventing legends," he told me, leaning over. They didn't want to give up any land for the zoo, he said. They could have pocketed $5 million a hectare for selling it on the side. I asked him how, then, he and Zubkov had convinced them to give the land to the zoo. Viktor pantomimed choking someone by the neck.

A little while later, the human rights ombudswoman for Crimea—a state position that formally reports to Aksyonov—stood to give a toast, in which she praised Zubkov and admitted he causes her no small amount of headaches. "With Oleg, it's always a war," she said. "But I respect him, and always try and help as much as I can—without making the bosses angry."

CHAPTER 5

NOTES ON CAMP

—

THE ANNEXATION OF CRIMEA AWOKE A BURIED LONGING FOR imperial grandeur—a sense of national purpose and destiny that had been shattered by the collapse of the Soviet Union. There was something immediately and tangibly physical in Crimea's return, but it also hit all the right notes for the Russian national psyche, a measure of revenge for all the slights and insults of the post-Soviet era. The spring had snapped back hard, as Putin said in his triumphant address. Russia was moving borders, restoring them to their historically just configuration, and there was nothing the West could do about it. The sanctions and opprobrium with which Western capitals reacted were seen as a sign of virtue: isolation was proof of Russia's valor and the merit of its political course.

The outbreak of conflict in eastern Ukraine a few months later strengthened the sentiment. Russian infiltrators and patriotic-minded volunteers, high off the easy success of the Crimea operation, stirred up the anti-Kyiv separatist movement in the Donbass, a region of coal mines and depressed industrial towns that had long-standing cultural and economic ties to Russia. The war that followed was just another front in a conflict that had gone dormant but never really ceased since the days of the Cold War: a grand contest with the United States, and, more broadly, the West.

It was no longer a question of trying to subtly disrupt and outmaneuver Western governments and institutions. Russia now confronted them directly, with no more illusions or pretend geniality. This turn carried inevitable implications at home, with the conservative, even aggressive, drift in political culture taking on new momentum. Russia's citizens should be mobilized and on guard, wary of hostile elements both without and within. In his speech marking Crimea's annexation, Putin raised the specter of "a fifth column"—a "disparate bunch of national traitors" sowing discord inside Russia. The idea had circulated among reactionary circles for years, but Putin gave it energy, or, as the television host Dmitry Kiselev put it, his speech "legalized that term in the political language of Russia." The mood of the country's politics darkened, giving rise to a newly vigorous hunt for internal enemies.

In June 2014, NTV, one of Russia's main state-controlled television networks, aired a pair of sulfurous and conspiratorial documentaries about Perm-36, a unique historical museum set on the grounds of a former prison camp. The museum had been created by a group of local historians and enthusiasts in Perm, an industrial city just east of the Ural Mountains, who turned it into a memorial complex and civic platform for discussing not only the history of the Gulag and political repressions, but the lessons and implications of those events for the present day.

The NTV film played to the passions of the moment: namely, that the Maidan protests in Kyiv represented a violent movement inspired by the nationalist figures from Ukraine's past who had aided the Nazis. Russian state media hoisted Stepan Bandera, the Ukrainian guerrilla fighter with checkered allegiances, as their figurehead, his name a catchall for the dark forces that had surfaced during the war and were again supposedly on the march. Under Stalin, Perm-36 had held dozens of people from Ukraine and the Baltic states who were accused of aiding the Nazis; the truth was naturally more complicated. Some had taken part in arrests and killings, others were nationalist ideologues who saw the Soviet Union as an imperial power, and many were simply caught up in the confused violence of those years. Russian propaganda ignored those distinctions. "Students are told on almost every tour at this camp that Nazi accomplices, executioners, and terrorists were heroes," the narrator of the NTV film said. Gruesome footage of current fighting in Ukraine played, with the narrator explaining how, while Ukrainian forces "are bombing hospitals and shooting civilians, schoolchildren in the Perm region learn about the origins of this movement." The film charged that the museum's founders accepted money from the U.S. State Department, which pro-Kremlin ideologues consider the fulcrum of regime change.

The museum was taken over by the state and its founders were forced out. It was a localized manifestation of what was becoming a nationwide trend. In one instance, the head of a library of Ukrainian literature in Moscow was charged with hoarding "extremist" materials. "Ukrainian nationalism went hand in hand with German Fascism, and it has again reared its head today," the prosecutor in the case told the court. "And the defendant is one of the mechanisms for disseminating their ideas." (The librarian received a suspended four-year sentence.) These events were reflections of the new mood, the result not necessarily of exact instructions issued by the Kremlin, but of underlings and functionaries around the country trying to overperform in their duties, or looking to use a convenient moment to achieve their own agendas.

The museum had faced pressure before and had constantly fought off attacks from retrograde Communists and hostile bureaucrats. But the post-Crimea moment forced a final reckoning. The current battles were too entwined with those from history to leave an institution like Perm-36 free to reach its own interpretations and conclusions. Liberal circles in Perm, as well as in Moscow and St. Petersburg, were dismayed: Would the museum close for good? Could it even become a Gulag museum in reverse, extolling the contributions of Stalin and his prison camps?

NOBODY TOLD SERGEI KOVALEV where he was heading—prisoners were not told such information—but he figured it out pretty quickly. It was the winter of 1976, and Kovalev had just been convicted of "anti-Soviet agitation and propaganda" and sentenced to seven years in a Soviet penal colony. Kovalev was forty-five; earlier in his career, he had been a promising researcher at an institute of biophysics in Moscow, the author of more than sixty scientific publications. But like the nuclear physicist Andrei Sakharov, who became the moral center of resistance to the Soviet system, Kovalev had rejected the relative comfort of the Soviet scientific establishment for the thankless world of human rights activism.

Kovalev was one of the chief editors of the *Chronicle of Current Events,* an underground samizdat publication compiled through a whisper network inside the Soviet Union and printed abroad. Its mission was to enumerate and describe the Soviet Union's repressions of dissidents and the conditions in its prison colonies. For the Soviet authorities, who maintained that they held no political prisoners, even such a dryly factual almanac was an unthinkable provocation. Kovalev was arrested and put on trial—an event dutifully featured in the pages of the *Chronicle,* which continued to publish after his arrest. Kovalev was a figure of such renown in human rights circles that Sakharov attended his trial the very day Sakharov himself was awarded, in absentia, the Nobel Peace Prize in Oslo.

Kovalev's work on the *Chronicle*—assembling details on the humiliations and deprivations faced by prisoners—prepared him for the minutiae of camp life. As he rode in a locked train car, on his way to begin his sentence, he could imagine the world he was about to enter. He was ready for the lies, the constant pressure, the threat of punishment—the unending attempt to break you, to make you obey. It was as if a writer of dystopian fiction suddenly found himself in the cruel, topsy-turvy realm he had previously known only on the page. The train moved east, crossing toward the Ural Mountains, and even though the station stops were not announced aloud, Kovalev could tell exactly where he was headed: the so-called Perm triangle, a cluster of three prison colonies in the forested countryside outside Perm, a drab manufacturing center seven hundred miles from Moscow. In those days, Perm was home to an important munitions factory, and therefore a closed city, sealed off to foreigners.

The Perm camps had sprung up not long before, as Soviet authorities looked for an alternative to the prison colonies in Mordovia, a region closer to Moscow. By the mid-seventies, the massive Stalin-era purges were long over, and repressions had become more targeted, on a smaller scale. Those imprisoned for what were known as "political" criminal statutes, several hundred people or so, could be held all together in a tight constellation of camps. But the Mordovia colonies were too close to nearby population centers. Prisoners were able to maintain ties with the world beyond, and information kept leaking out. Plus, with the 1980 Olympic Games in Moscow looming, the Soviet state didn't want to risk uncomfortable questions from foreign officials and media by having political prisoners in any sort of proximity to the capital. Kovalev would serve his sentence in Correctional Labor Colony VS 389/36, or Perm-36 for short.

Perm-36's history in fact began much earlier, in 1943, when it was founded as a camp for those caught up in the later years of Stalin's repressions. In the years after the Second World War, prisoners cut down trees and sent the lumber downriver to rebuild Soviet cities damaged in the fighting. After Stalin's death, the facility took on a second life as a prison for convicts from within Soviet law enforcement bodies. Many of those were midlevel officers who had carried out the purges in the thirties and forties, only to be blamed for them when the Soviet state decided to paper over that history. Then, in 1972, on the orders of Yuri Andropov, the head of the KGB, the site was refashioned as a prison for those convicted of treason, anti-Soviet activity, and other political offenses. By then, Soviet prison colonies were no longer home to the barbarity of the Gulag. The cruelty was more psychological than immediately physical—though when camp bosses wanted, there could be plenty of that, too.

Kovalev had assumed he knew just about everything about life in the "zone," as the camps were commonly known in the informal Soviet lexicon. But as he came to realize, "there were some things I didn't understand." In particular, one detail had always bothered him when he was still on the outside, compiling reports from Soviet prisons for the *Chronicle*. He would regularly learn of a political prisoner who was sent to the camp's punishment cell, the dreaded "isolator," for silly infractions, like wearing house slippers outside the barracks or having the top button of his work shirt undone. Kovalev could understand taking a stand on unjust conditions or going on a hunger strike to promote a broader political cause—but the right to wear slippers where you wanted? "Why pick this battle?" he thought. "What's the point? Is that worth getting sent off to the punishment cell? It just seems silly." Better to save your strength and fight the prison administration on more meaningful points.

But now he understood. Slippers and buttons and all the rest were just pretexts, technical infractions the guards would blithely ignore for months, and then one day, when they decided they needed to act against this or that inmate—or, more precisely, their bosses in the prison administration gave them such an order—they would catch you in slippers on the front steps of the barracks and write up a report. No one cared about the rules until suddenly they did, and it was off to the punishment cell for you. Kovalev had been in Perm-36 for three months when his time came. As a means of retribution for his sticking up for another prisoner, the camp bosses confronted him with some absurd violation; he got seven days in the punishment cell, which the guards lengthened to fifteen for good measure.

Kovalev and other dissidents, or "politicals," as they were called, were actually in the minority at Perm-36, ten or fifteen people out of an overall population of 250 or so inmates. The rest had tangled fates and putative crimes even more opaque, often dating back to the Second World War, especially as it was fought on the Soviet Union's western borderlands. The collision of the Nazi and Soviet armies, and ideologies, in places like Ukraine and the Baltic states, led to heinous bloodletting—and hotly contested historical narratives over who should be considered a hero or a traitor. For a number of local populations on the outer reaches of the Soviet empire, the Red Army was no less an occupying force than the Nazis; when the Germans showed up, some saw their chance for national self-determination, while others collaborated with the most gruesome crimes of Fascism.

For the Soviet state, fighting alongside Nazi troops and distributing anti-Soviet literature were comparable offenses, which is how people convicted of each of these crimes ended up sharing the same prison yard at Perm-36. And, as Kovalev came to learn, even among those who took up arms against the Soviet state during the war, it was hard to generalize too broadly about motives and circumstance. Each case had its own backstory and moral cast; sadists and outright murderers intermingled with sincere nationalists and those who were simply powerless and confused. But these were debates the Soviet Union was thoroughly uninterested in having, which meant the legacy of this historical period was never really settled, and remains so today.

In the mid-seventies, the oldest prisoners were finishing up twenty-five-year terms for having fought against Soviet forces in territories annexed by the Soviet Union after the war. In the Baltic states such local militias called themselves the forest brothers; in Ukraine, the insurgent army. They became a sustained nuisance to Soviet authorities, and oftentimes proved just as brutal in their tactics. But it wasn't long before such nationalist movements were overwhelmed by ruthless Soviet campaigns, and by the fifties, thousands of self-proclaimed freedom fighters had been captured and executed. Others ended up at Perm-36, where, by the time Kovalev arrived, they stayed quiet and kept to themselves. Besides the nationalists, Kovalev came across a scattered collection of prisoners whose ties to Nazi crimes seemed obvious and inarguable; some didn't even try all that hard to deny them. There was Zagrebayev, who had a faded SS tattoo under his armpit; Potemin, who had worked as a translator for the Nazi military command on occupied Soviet territory, and was whispered to have raped a prisoner during the war; and Katok, who had served in the Nazi *polizei,* and, having taken two female partisan fighters as lovers and impregnated both, led them to the forest and shot them. Like many of those at Perm-36 implicated in war crimes, Katok was a ruined and hollow man, easy for the camp administration to manipulate and deploy as a *stukach,* an informant. In a rather transparent ploy to gain the trust of other prisoners—so he could then report on them to the guards—he would offer a cigarette, a luxury as rare in the zone as a ripe peach. But, perhaps belying his true personality, he never provided a match, making his attempt at pseudo-generosity cruelly useless. "But we still managed to light them, though," Kovalev said.

As the years passed, Kovalev also encountered plenty of purported war criminals and Nazi accomplices whose transgressions seemed more tenuous. The Soviet state launched a wave of new prosecutions for wartime offenses and dredged up old ones. Perm-36 filled with a fresh influx of prisoners—old men punished for the alleged crimes of their youth. Kovalev came to know a man in his fifties named Mikhail Tarakhovich, who grew up on a communal farm in Belarus. His village was captured by the Nazis early in the war. In 1944, when he was seventeen, he was forcibly conscripted into German military service. But before Tarakhovich could fire a shot, his village was taken back by the Red Army, who, having freed him, enlisted him to fight on the Soviet side. He ended up taking part in the capture of Berlin the next year—the heroic capstone to Soviet victory. After the war, he returned to farm life in Belarus, where investigators grabbed him three decades later, having remembered his brief forced service in the German ranks.

Perhaps the most telling was the case of Pavel Boguk, who, in the 1970s, was a witness for the prosecution in several trials of defendants sent to Perm-36 for alleged wartime crimes. He testified how, as a teenager, he had seen this person burn down a house, that person shoot into a crowd of people. After three or four such trials, a state investigator approached Boguk and said it seemed strange that Boguk had supposedly stood around and witnessed all these crimes but was still free. To smooth things out, Boguk should confess to some wartime atrocities of his own, and he would get a minimal, purely symbolic sentence. That was a ruse. In the end, he got ten years and was sent to Perm-36, alongside those he had helped condemn to such a fate. "He was always spooked, expecting revenge at every moment," Kovalev said. Boguk would beg to spend the night in the infirmary, even the boiler room—anywhere but the general barracks. Yet his fellow inmates didn't react with violence or hatred. "It's the intelligentsia who don't forget every offense and slight," Kovalev explained. "Simple people, those who aren't so educated, they understand the villainy of other people quite well. They know that in his position, they would have done the same."

JUST ABOUT ALL THE DISSIDENTS and those charged with political crimes in the seventies and eighties ended up in the Perm camps; they were the only prison colonies in the Soviet Union designed to house such inmates. Inmates included Vladimir Bukovsky, a prominent dissident who brought to light the abuses of forced psychiatric treatment in the Soviet Union; and Vasyl Stus, a Ukrainian poet of towering ability, who died in 1985 while on hunger strike in the middle of a long spell of solitary confinement, unaware that a number of supporters and literary critics had nominated him for the Nobel Prize in Literature.

By then, the authorities were concerned that abusing the prisoners would draw further attention to their cause or create pressure from Western governments. That gave the prisoners a wedge they could exploit. They regularly threatened to go on hunger strike, which would embarrass and frighten the camp administration—how would they explain a starved prisoner to their superiors?—and wrote an endless stream of official complaints, which the Soviet bureaucracy was compelled to process and formally address.

Relations took on the form of ritualized battle, in which inmates were trying not so much to win as to frustrate and madden their jailers; and the jailers sought nothing more than a surface image of order, keeping things quiet so they didn't face problems from above. As Bukovsky wrote in his memoirs, by then no one cared about Marxism or talked of a "radiant future." The guards at Perm-36 were interested only in a simple acknowledgment of their power. "And when they tried to starve us into it in the camps, or threw us into the punishment cells to rot, they were demanding not a belief in communism, but simply submission, or at least a willingness to compromise."

Kovalev was among those unwilling to compromise. For that stubbornness, he did stint after stint in the punishment cell, totaling as much as three out of the seven years he spent there. He continued to pass information on prison conditions to the *Chronicle,* which drove the administrators crazy. They could not figure out how Kovalev was able to get messages out, and regularly had to deal with screaming phone calls from higher-ups. His method, as Kovalev would delicately put it, was "unappetizing." Before his wife and son would come to Perm-36 for visits, Kovalev would write out small texts on excruciatingly tiny folds of paper and wrap them in two layers of polyethylene. He would be searched before being given an audience with his guests, which means his only way to pass the papers along was to swallow them—timing the ingestion so that he would defecate during the scheduled family visit, which could last a day or two. His wife and son, who were also searched on their way out, would take off one layer of wrapping, swallow the papers again, and expel them some days later, already on the outside. In the most voluminous such operation, Kovalev swallowed eight wrapped notes, seven of which made it to their ultimate recipient, what he considered a successful percentage. After his release, in 1981, his colleagues at the *Chronicle* who typed up the smuggled messages told him the stench was unbearably foul—a small price for passing news from inside a Soviet prison camp to the outside world.

Among the last wave of convicts to make their way to Perm-36 was Mikhail Meylac, a victim more of happenstance than purposeful resistance. Meylac was thirty-eight at the time of his arrest in 1983, a linguist and literary scholar in Leningrad. He and his friends were thoroughly hostile to the Soviet system, but they were by no measure dissidents—an important distinction in their minds, but one of less consequence to the state itself. "It would be impossible to imagine a single person in my circle holding any, shall we say, Soviet ideas," Meylac recalled years later. "Everyone hated Soviet power, but we didn't allow ourselves to act against it."

Meylac had a repository of samizdat—Solzhenitsyn's *Gulag Archipelago* and the novels of Vladimir Nabokov, along with assorted poetry and essays—which he kept in the apartment of an older woman he trusted. No one would ever suspect her, so Meylac could come by every now and then to trade, say, a volume of Akhmatova's poems for Mandelstam. He would have a read, maybe pass it to a friend, and the cycle would repeat. But the woman fell ill, and as she was nearing death, she asked Meylac to come retrieve the collection. He did, but wasn't sure where to take it next. His family's dacha outside town was an option, but he didn't want to create any problems for his father, an esteemed literary historian. In the end, Meylac left it at the apartment of a distant friend, who, as he later said with some bitterness, turned out to be a "rather irresponsible person." This friend started passing around books to anybody who showed up, and it wasn't long before the KGB learned of the underground literary stash. The friend quickly repented, and got a minimal sentence; Meylac was given seven years.

He arrived at Perm-36 in 1984. It would be hard to say he had fought against the Soviet state: he certainly wasn't among those who had actually picked up arms, nor had he waged a conscious and open struggle of ideas, like Kovalev. Meylac was to lose several years of his life for a trunkful of fiction and poetry he and his friends shared among themselves. The isolation of Perm-36 was hard for him, as were its arbitrary and punitive rules, the caprice of the guards, who could march in the barracks and drag you off to the punishment cell because your bedsheets weren't tucked in according to camp regulations.

Meylac had practiced yoga for many years, and in the evenings, he often stood in a pose with his head on the ground and his feet sticking up in the air. Prison authorities were driven mad by this behavior—surely standing on your head can't be allowed, even if this wasn't specified anywhere. Finally, they decided that Meylac wasn't observing the rule that prisoners must rise when a prison guard or camp employee entered the room. He tried to argue that standing on your head is in fact standing—a point over which he would have plenty of time to ruminate in the isolator. He was freed in 1987, part of a wave of commuted sentences during perestroika. The last prisoner left Perm-36 a year later.

IN 1992, A YEAR after the Soviet collapse, a group of twenty or so historians and activists from Perm drove several hours out to the area of what had been, just recently, the Perm triangle. People across Russia were curious about all the moments of the country's history that had been kept hidden. Over successive generations, nothing had been kept darker than the facts of Soviet repressions and its political prisoners. Most people in Perm didn't know the three camps in the forest outside town even existed. In Perm, as in many cities around the country, a local office of Memorial—the organization founded in the late eighties, with the mission of documenting the state's mistreatment of its citizens—had opened up, and was beginning to research the stories of repressions in the region.

On their trip, members of Memorial and like-minded supporters visited the "zone." At Perm-35, they went into the medical ward and encountered a number of older, infirm prisoners confined to their beds—the last remnant of those convicted of fighting the Soviet state in postwar Eastern Europe. Perm-37 was off-limits; it had refashioned itself as a regular prison for inmates sentenced for standard criminal offenses. Finally, they drove another hour and a half to the site of Perm-36. The wooden barracks that had housed prisoners were in a state of decay; the roof had collapsed, and the foundation was beginning to rot. They walked across a field of thick mud to what had been the "special regime" area, an even more restrictive zone. Here the buildings were half swallowed up by the trees and damp earth—it was like coming across Mayan ruins in a jungle clearing. The members of the expedition walked down to a swamp behind the prison. They found a rusted tangle of barbed wire and iron gates. Before abandoning the place, the last remaining guards had bulldozed what remained of the perimeter fence, dumping its gnarled remnants and leaving them to be swallowed up by the brown mush.

Among those on the trip was Viktor Shmyrov, the head of the history department at a local university in Perm. On successive visits it became clear to him that the site reached back to the 1940s, making it the only extant physical object dating from the time of Stalin's Gulag. That made it an astonishingly rare and important historical artifact, the only place in all of Russia, once dotted with such camps, that allowed for an immediate and tactile communion with the memories of the past. Shmyrov; his wife, Tatiana Kursina; and others from Memorial became committed to the site's preservation. They cobbled together some funds from their own savings and loans from friends, which they spent on repairing the camp's sawmill and used it to cut timber. Half the finished wood they sold, using the profits to pay for materials and equipment; the other half they used to restore the barracks and the camp's administrative buildings. They didn't have enough nails, so Shmyrov pulled old, bent nails out of ruined pieces of wood and straightened them out so they could be reused. "The first task was to preserve this place as a monument," he said. "Then, if we managed to do that, we must use it somehow. That was obvious."

Perm-36 opened as a museum in 1995, eight years after the last prisoner had walked free. Its first exhibit showcased the prominent dissidents who had been held there: Bukovsky, Stus, and Kovalev. In the nineties, Kovalev had become a high-profile human rights activist, for a while even serving as a deputy in the Duma and an advisor to Yeltsin. Next, Shmyrov began work on an exhibition that would tell the story of the Stalin-era purges and the vast network of Gulag camps, which stretched far beyond the snowy forests of Perm.

Leonid Obukhov, a local historian and cofounder of the Perm-36 museum, noticed that among the older generation—those who actually lived through the worst and most ferocious years of Stalin's Terror—a residual fear remained, an inability to talk about what they had experienced. More worrying was what he saw among successive generations, their children and grandchildren. "They didn't have this fear, but they also didn't have any knowledge," he told me. Obukhov observed visitors as they made their way around the museum. "They would walk through the barracks, see the cells—but for them, it was history; they didn't see a connection to themselves or the present day."

The comparison between Perm-36 and a place like Auschwitz is unavoidable: both function as memorial complexes and museums, set on the immediate site of camps run by totalitarian regimes. The ultimate function of Auschwitz, of course, was the murder of its prisoners; Perm-36 was meant to isolate and punish those the state considered its enemies, but unlike the Soviet camps of the thirties, it did not seek their physical destruction. For the purposes of historical memory, the more meaningful distinction is that, whereas today's Auschwitz is representative of a broader societal consensus in Europe, part of a collective effort to remember and draw lessons from the recent past, Perm-36 was more discordant. It was not one among many such sites in Russia; it did not slot into nationwide educational and civic programs on the subject of repressions, because such programs did not exist. Perm-36 was an anomaly, and, set in a forest several hours from the nearest city, a hidden one at that.

The manner in which postwar Germany and post-Soviet Russia confronted and tried to exorcise—or bury—the demons of their respective histories could not be more opposed. The reasons are multitude. Much less time has passed since the fall of the Soviet Union than since the end of the Nazi regime, which lasted decades fewer than Soviet power. Postwar Germany had been defeated militarily and was under foreign occupation—which made possible the prosecutions of many former Nazi officials accountable for mass crimes. No outside force administered Russia in its transition, and no legal processes were ever held to sort through the responsibility of officials from the Communist Party, KGB, and other state organs.

But perhaps the most important factor was the nature of Soviet repressions: they were directed at enemies within, whether supposed traitors and spies inside the Communist Party or would-be saboteurs and "wreckers" on the factory floor. "If the Nazi Holocaust exterminated the Other, the Soviet terror was suicidal," notes Alexander Etkind, a professor at Cambridge University, in *Warped Mourning,* his probing work on how modern Russia remains haunted by its unfinished examination of the past. The Soviet terror's cannibalistic quality was laid bare in all its absurdity in 1992, during a lone attempt to declare the Communist Party unconstitutional. At the trial, the party's lawyers argued that since party members disproportionately suffered from repressions, the party had already been punished. Party members were both executioners and victims in the same historical process, the argument went, so let's just call it a draw. Etkind describes how the "self-inflicted" nature of Soviet terror complicates the impulses that usually appear after violent societal catastrophe: striving to understand the calamity, mourning for its victims, and yearning for justice.

In the Soviet Union, people were killed or imprisoned for reasons that did not comport with observable reality. As Etkind notes, a Jew caught in the Holocaust understood himself as a Jew; he recognized the category and his belonging to it, even if he obviously

NOTES ON CAMP | 223

did not find this a reason to exterminate him. But who was a kulak, an enemy of the people, a counterrevolutionary element? These were paranoid fictions that did not exist in actual life, yet carried deadly meaning. In *Warped Mourning,* Etkind quotes another historian, Mikhail Geller: "The difference is that in Hitler's camps, the victims knew why they were killed," whereas those who perished in the Gulag "died bewildered." That bewilderment, that inability to explain—except by pure chance—who lived and who died, meant that all those who took part in the Soviet project were in some way implicated. In 1956, after Stalin's death and the emptying of the Gulag, the poet Anna Akhmatova observed: "Now two Russias are eyeball to eyeball—those who were in prison and those who put them there."

At one point in the mid-nineties, a group of German university students came to Perm-36 as volunteers to help with repair and construction projects. They were a motivated, enthusiastic bunch, full of well-intentioned notions of memory and historical justice. Kovalev was there, too—he came often to work through ideas with Shmyrov and Kursina and to offer up old memories. The German students began to ask him about his time as a prisoner at Perm-36, and he told them stories of how he was sent to the punishment cell for an unfastened shirt button. Kovalev called over someone else who worked at the museum, Ivan Kukushkin, a bearded and lumbering man in his fifties. The two shook hands warmly. "Tell them, Kukushkin," Kovalev said.

Kukushkin was a former guard at Perm-36, and had watched over Kovalev during his years as a prisoner, had even ordered him to the punishment cell more than a few times. He still lived in the village near Perm-36, and had reinvented himself as the museum's security guard, doing some odd jobs around the property. He helped Shmyrov reconstruct the room where prisoners were inspected for contraband and forbidden materials. Kukushkin was honest, and a hard worker, and had the respect of Shmyrov and Kursina, even Kovalev. He answered Kovalev by saying he only sent him to the punishment cell for good cause, which he went on to define as "discipline." It wasn't that Kovalev had necessarily done anything wrong—or maybe he had, that wasn't important—but the camp bosses said he should be sent off to the isolator, and so that's what Kukushkin did.

The Germans were stupefied. They seemed deeply upset, and wanted to leave Perm-36 immediately. It wasn't the story of Kukushkin following orders that so disturbed them, but the handshake the two men shared, their bonhomie. Kovalev tried to explain that Kukushkin was not a sadist or a torturer, or a guard at Auschwitz; "He didn't chase people to their deaths in gas chambers or shoot them in the middle of the prison yard." Rather, he had been a young man trapped by circumstance and zombified by Soviet propaganda. If anything, Kovalev empathized with Kukushkin. When you think about it, Kovalev went on, "his status wasn't much higher than ours. He was not really a free man, but captive to the same whims of the camp administration." He lived in barracks that weren't much different from those housing the prisoners and, for the most part, ate the same lousy food on which nearly everyone in the Soviet Union subsisted at the time. "In a certain sense we shared a common fate," Kovalev said. The Germans were not convinced. They were bound by strict, categorical norms, an ethical prism born of Germany's admirable—if often inflexible—attitude toward totalitarianism and those who serve it. A political prisoner and his guard should not shake hands, and from that flows a whole way of seeing the world.

Kovalev tried one last argument. He told the German students of the time, before his arrest, when he was a researcher at a biophysics institute in Moscow. He depended on the institute's in-house workshop to make him microelectrodes, detailed parts that he needed for his experiments. There was always a long wait, months that could stretch on to infinity—which could be circumvented if you gave the guys at the workshop a bit of booze. So Kovalev would fill out procurement orders with descriptions of experiments he had no plans to ever carry out, but which required several liters of laboratory-grade spirits. He'd pour it into smaller bottles and bring them to the workshop as a bribe to get the parts he actually did need. "If life is arranged this way, if I can't carry out my scientific work without theft, then how can I judge Kukushkin?" Kovalev asked the Germans. "I can't look at him from on high when I'm part of the same system. I'm just as implicated in lies."

Shmyrov and Kursina understood that Russian society hadn't really grappled with the myriad lessons and complications of this legacy. After the Soviet collapse, freedom had descended on the country too effortlessly, and wasn't appreciated or understood. Most people, Kursina said, remained infected with "all signs of the disease" that was the Soviet condition: fear, ignorance, powerlessness, irresponsibility, aggression. A systematic treatment protocol was required. "One of the most bitter medicines is knowledge of what the Soviet regime really was," Kursina said. She felt that it was impossible to narrate this history with scientific disinterest, weighing the suffering of victims with, say, the needs of a rapidly modernizing country or the urgent war effort. "I'm supposed to be neutral about this? When I talk about these terrible things I'm not being overly dramatic."

Shmyrov and Kursina became convinced that Perm-36 should function as a civic platform, a place to work through Russia's undigested history and its meaning for the present day. You couldn't just show where prisoners lived and ate and made parts used in the manufacture of Soviet irons and not address the deeper questions: Why did the state imprison people for a book, or for passing on the facts of the country's court system? Why was that so threatening, and what does that say about the system itself? "The museum isn't meant to be a haunted house: 'Oh, look at how scary it is. How they were imprisoned. What they were fed,'" Shmyrov said. Its mission was something else: to tell the story of "resistance to unfreedom."

In 2005, Perm-36 hosted the first annual event called Pilorama, named for the Russian word for "sawmill," the machinery that camp prisoners and then the museum's founders had used to cut timber. Over the next seven years, Pilorama grew into a multiday festival and conference, combining performances by acclaimed poets and musicians with roundtable discussions on political repressions. Participants slept in tents set up in an open field on the prison grounds. Pilorama combined the grime, booze, and louche, skeptical attitude toward authority of a rock festival with the fervency and ideological stubbornness of a university debate club.

One year, the British theater director Michael Hunt staged a performance of *Fidelio,* Beethoven's only opera. The libretto tells the story of Leonora, who disguises herself as a guard to rescue her husband, Florestan, from prison, where he is held on false, politically motivated charges. It is a rebuke to cruelty, injustice, and the abuse of power, with an ending that celebrates the triumph of freedom and love. The moral argument is clear and resonant; *Fidelio* was banned in the Soviet Union until after Stalin's death. At Perm-36, Hunt made the work immersive, with no stage or seats. The audience roamed the territory of the camp, surrounded by performers dressed as prisoners and guards singing and enacting the rituals of prison life. At intermission viewers were fed a meal of soggy buckwheat porridge. The second act took place in the cramped, dark corridors of the "special regime" zone, where Leonora cried out in search of Florestan, an intimate and moving spectacle for those standing just inches from Leonora as she moved from cell to cell.

IN ITS EARLY YEARS as a museum, Perm-36 was celebrated by the local authorities, who welcomed it as a tourist draw for the region as much as a civic institution. The governor of the Perm region gave Shmyrov an award for "merit to the Fatherland." He got a medal and a congratulatory decree signed by Yeltsin. Kursina was approached by a retired KGB officer who, repeatedly and persistently, asked for an audience with Kovalev. It turned out the retired officer had overseen Kovalev's case in the seventies. Kursina arranged a meeting; the officer, by then aging and unwell, had Kovalev and Kursina over to his apartment, where they met his wife and adult children, and sat for a meal of endless *zakusky*—dill-flecked salads and cold cuts and sour pickles—washed down with a bottle of fine cognac. "I'm now certain that he needed a kind of papal indulgence," Kursina told me. "Having met and shaken hands, he washed off all that rubbish and dirt." Afterward, the man donated his private memoirs of his years in the KGB to the archive at Perm-36.

The ascendance of Putin to the presidency did not change things right away, but it was clear from the beginning that the state's interest in discussing the ugly and more uncomfortable moments from the country's past had narrowed, and that a new set of values was on the rise. Confidence and patriotic swagger were to replace the insecurity and self-flagellation of the nineties, not least in the study of Russia's own history. New textbook editions brushed past the worst of the Stalin-era repressions, painting them either as outlying exceptions or necessary sacrifices for modernizing the country and defeating Nazi Germany.

According to the hodgepodge ideology that undergirds Putin's rule, today's Russia is the inheritor of the Soviet Union's great-power status. A through line follows from the Soviet victory in the Second World War to the exploration of space and the Cold War rivalry with the United States: in this worldview, what matters is the history of empire and the power of the state. No one longs for Marx or bread-lines, but the nation, no matter the historical epoch, is sacrosanct. Over time, this attitude filtered through the country's political bureaucracy, making its way from Moscow to Perm and parts far beyond. "The administration in the Kremlin changed," Shmyrov said. "And then things began to change here, too, but slowly and more quietly."

At one point, the former KGB officer stormed into the museum's offices in a huff and demanded they return his papers. He didn't want the museum to hold them any longer, and was breaking off all relations with Kursina and Shmyrov. For Kursina, he turned out to be a "barometer"—when it seemed to him that the awakening of the nineties was "serious and permanent, he tugged at me constantly," but with time, things changed. "He felt where the wind blew, that the trend is changing. No one else had noticed this yet, but he did." Under Putin, who himself came from the security services, the *siloviki*—the "men of power," with backgrounds in intelligence, military, and law enforcement—took on positions of influence in running the country. In a telling moment of irony, one of them was Viktor Cherkesov, who came to occupy several high-ranking posts, including the head of Russia's anti-drug agency, with informal powers that were far wider. He began his career as a young KGB officer in Leningrad in the seventies, in charge of hounding dissidents and traders in underground samizdat. One of his early cases was the prosecution of Mikhail Meylac.

Although Putin tries to avoid overly categorical statements on the history of Soviet repression, a certain understanding has emerged. Within measure—that is, without questioning the legitimacy of the state itself—society can remember and mourn victims of political repressions, but discussing the perpetrators is off-limits; that chain of guilt, if fully examined, would lead uncomfortably back to the state and those who serve it. It is memory in the passive voice. Speaking in 2017 at the opening of a memorial to victims of state terror in Moscow, Putin declared, "We and our descendants must remember the tragedy of repression and the reasons that gave rise to it. But that does not mean we should call for the settling of scores. We must not push society back to a dangerous point of confrontation." Remarking on this phenomenon, Arseny Roginsky, one of the founders of Memorial, spoke of "the Stalin paradox": somehow, the Stalinist machine produced millions of victims but no criminals.

When I visited Alexander Kalikh, the founder of Memorial's Perm office and one of those who discovered the abandoned Perm-36 complex and built the museum, he mentioned the Solovetsky Stone in Moscow. The stone, a hulking mass that weighs about ten thousand pounds, comes from the Solovetsky Islands, in the White Sea, the site of the first Gulag camp, dating to 1923. It was brought to Moscow in 1990 and now sits on a corner of Lubyanka Square, across from the former headquarters of the KGB, now home to the FSB. An inscription beneath the stone explains that it was "installed in memory of the millions of victims of the totalitarian regime." That message, and the Solovetsky Stone's location, make it an important symbol, but also one devoid of context or interpretation. It is a memorial to the past, a finished and sealed history that, if one chooses, can be used to make inferences about the present—or not. It is the sort of historical marker with which the Russian state is comfortable, but that's not what Perm-36 aimed to do. "We weren't just laying a stone—though that's also important—but making a direct appeal to the state, and society as a whole," Kalikh told me.

It wasn't enough to talk about political repressions as having been a manifestation of a particular time, Kalikh said, to "talk only about the misfortune and tragedies of the past. We want to understand the system that created this terror, the reasons this happened—and yes, you could say this is politics." Kalikh understood that "politics" was a loaded term, and one that meant different things to different people. But with no settled, mutually accepted version of the country's history, any attempt to come up with one was, by definition, a political gesture. The truth, Kalikh said, is that "there are no clear borders between civic and political activity," but for the museum's enemies, the distinction didn't matter anyway. "The presence of politics in our actions was falsified as a fact of a crime, and used as a pretext to destroy us."

IN 2012, PUTIN RETURNED to the presidency, and the Perm region's longtime governor, a relatively modernizing figure, was replaced with a by-the-book functionary. The new governor's office moved to make Perm-36 a state institution, which would exist alongside an NGO set up by Shmyrov and Kursina to administer the museum. The two bodies would operate in forced coexistence, a wary and increasingly unhappy arranged marriage. Tensions became all the more acute when Shmyrov and Kursina's organization was charged with being a "foreign agent," a Stalin-era locution that had been revived for a new, repressive law governing foreign funding for NGOs working in politics and public opinion.

At the same time, the museum's finances, never extensive to begin with, became more precarious: for the first time in a decade, authorities in Perm raised questions about continued support. A member of the regional parliament asked why the government was backing an institution that taught schoolchildren that Hitler had been on the right side in the Second World War, and that Fascism was a more virtuous ideology than Communism. "Before, everyone understood this was nonsense, that it was shameful to say such things," Shmyrov said. "But suddenly there was nothing to be ashamed of anymore; it turns out it's not nonsense at all." In the end, the museum's funding was cut by 80 percent.

The museum also faced attacks from members of a group called Sut Vremeni, or "Essence of Time," a Russian nationalist movement with philosophical pretenses, which at times outflanked the Kremlin in its neo-Soviet zeal. It was founded by a Soviet-educated scientist who became interested in experimental theater and later turned himself into a political gadfly, and it had chapters all over the country. Activists from Essence of Time went to Pilorama to shout down the panel discussions. They published a newspaper that featured interviews with former guards from Perm-36, who defended the honor of their work at the prison and decried the supposed manipulations of Shmyrov and Kursina.

One afternoon in Perm, I stopped by the group's local headquarters, a single room in a Soviet-era office block outside the center of town. I was met by Pavel Guryanov, a thirty-four-year-old teacher at the city's pharmaceutical academy. He has a smooth, boyish face, and although he talked with great animation, his voice was quiet, even soft. Guryanov told me he had been interested in history and politics for as long as he could remember, and joined Essence of Time in 2011, the year it was formed. "If other parties and movements work to simplify things, here we seek to answer deep questions," he said. The attraction of Essence of Time was that it gave an intellectual veneer to Stalinist revanchism, as if only its members are bold enough to get to the "essence" of things.

Guryanov told me that, under Shmyrov and Kursina, Perm-36 had "turned history all around, acting as if seventy years of Soviet history represented a solid black mark." Echoing the standard line of attack, he said he was most aggrieved by the museum's treatment of those prisoners from Ukraine and the Baltics who were charged with wartime crimes: they weren't activists or freedom fighters, but Nazi collaborators and executioners. In Perm-36's backward telling, Guryanov explained, "it turns out the Fascists are considered heroes, and those who served the state that defeated Fascism are antiheroes, the ones who should apologize for their actions."

Leaving the thorny questions of wartime guilt aside, I asked Guryanov how today's Russia should remember the history of the Gulag and political repressions. He acknowledged that some innocent vic-

tims were swept up in the whirlwind of the Soviet project, and that
was a tragedy. Yet what mattered was that this project, Soviet Communism, was animated by aims that were good and just. "Okay, in
putting this system in place there were some victims," he admitted,
before falling back on whataboutism: "Were there not victims in the
French Revolution? Does that mean we should say the French Revolution was a wholly terrible event?" As for the purely political prisoners held at Perm-36, people like Kovalev, he was nonchalant.
"These were people who were working for the overthrow of the
state. All regimes react to this negatively." These historical deviations
at the museum might not have been so objectionable, Guryanov said,
if it weren't for the ultimate purpose they were meant to serve. "A
union of liberal groups wanted to unseat the president, to organize a
coup through protests. They made calls for this," he told me. "It is
clear the museum was being used as cover for creating a base dedicated to regime change—and all of this was being done right under
the nose of the authorities, and on their dime." For a while, the administration in Perm was oblivious to this danger or tolerated it as
immaterial; and then, as the mood shifted, it changed its mind.
"Events allowed us to have our ideas listened to," Guryanov said.

Those events were the annexation of Crimea and the outbreak of
war in the Donbass, which created an opening for a final, and decisive, round of attacks on the museum. The country's politics curdled
into an acrid mixture of cocksure patriotism and proud xenophobia
directed against the West and its values. Perm-36's enemies could sense
that momentum was on their side: Essence of Time escalated its attacks; NTV aired its documentary aimed at discrediting the museum;
and the Perm government further stalled its funding before declaring
that the museum owed back payments for misallocated subsidies. The
museum saw its water and electricity shut off and soon had no money
to pay its operating costs or salaries. It stopped accepting visitors. Finally, Kursina was called to the office of the regional administration
and fired. She was locked out of the museum's archives—the collection she and Shmyrov had assembled over the years.

That same day, the Perm government announced Kursina's replacement as director of the museum, which now belonged entirely

to the state. Natalia Semakova was a thirty-eight-year-old midlevel bureaucrat from the provincial town of Kirov. She had been an aspiring opera singer in her youth, and since then had worked in state cultural bodies for nine years, running children's theaters and arts festivals and the like. In her most recent position, she had served as deputy to the Perm region's minister of culture, a crude and uncouth reactionary who had helped arrange the state's takeover of the museum. Semakova emerged from a stay in the hospital, where she had been treated for heart problems, to be told she was now in charge of Perm-36. She had no expertise or particular knowledge of the Gulag or Soviet-era political repressions, which was likely a plus for those who had named her to the job. As she understood it, her mission was effectively to "look after the pipes"—that is, keep an eye on the physical infrastructure of the museum—while authorities figured out what they wanted to do with the place.

Shmyrov and Kursina, along with their supporters in Perm and around the country, weren't sure what was worse: that the local authorities might decide to close the museum entirely, or, as some trickles of information suggested, keep it open but flip the logic of the old museum on its head, making it a memorial complex told from the perspective of the camp guards who had worked there and of the state itself. It would be a museum to Stalin and the internal security troops who kept watch over the place. Another related rumor held that Perm-36 would be transferred to the federal prison service, and would tell the story of the country's penitentiary system, starting in the eighteenth century and moving through the Tsarist and Soviet periods with a tone of statist, bureaucratic pride.

As it happened, the early days of the museum's second life were mixed: no one put up Stalin posters or removed language on political repressions, but the museum's staff did wall off a display that featured Kovalev and various prisoners from Ukraine and the Baltic states— their biographies were deemed too controversial for the moment, with talk of Fascists in Kyiv all over state television. Semakova proved an unsure and panicky boss, in one case calling the cops when Kursina showed up with a visiting delegation from the museum at the former Bergen-Belsen concentration camp.

A year after Semakova's appointment, the museum opened a new exhibit on the use of prisoners in the local timber industry. Throughout the 1940s, those held at Perm-36 were deployed as forced laborers in the surrounding forests—a history that was told with blown-up black-and-white photos and a scattering of original artifacts. The exhibit did not offer open or direct praise of the merits of the Gulag, yet neither did it offer a moral condemnation. It simply told of how prisoners used saws and canoes to send timber to where it was needed across the Soviet Union. The air of careful neutrality—on the one hand, conditions were brutal; on the other, the camp was a key node in supplying the country with wood—was itself a dramatic break from the unabashedly ideological view imparted by Shmyrov and Kursina.

On the day the exhibit opened, the Perm minister of culture, Semakova's former boss and one of the instigators of the campaign against the museum, came to give a speech. "During times of great tribulations, during times of profound decisions for the country and the fate of the people, no one remained indifferent," he said, positioning the Gulag, above all, as a means to victory in the Second World War. "Glory to the heroes," he said in conclusion, linking the sacrifice of Soviet soldiers in battle to prisoners engaged in what was essentially slave labor. A local journalist in Perm told me that when he visited the exhibit, a male guide spoke of how female prisoners made for better laborers: they were more disciplined and resilient. (Women are also the "source of life on earth; they are more prudent," the guide added.) A printed display boasted of how, in the years after the war, prisoners at the camp sent thousands of cubic meters of timber to Stalingrad to rebuild the destroyed city.

Did the prisoners at Perm-36 contribute to the war effort, and thus to victory? Quite possibly yes. Did that mean the camp, and hundreds like it, were justified? Depends on whom you ask. In April 2016, on Russia's annual cosmonauts holiday, a post appeared on the museum's website. It was dedicated to the achievements of the Perm region's *sharashki,* the name for closed scientific communities that functioned as prisonlike clusters for researchers and scientists in the thirties and forties. Instead of a stint in the Gulag, a useful technical specialist could do his or her term in one of these facilities. "From the point of view of effectiveness, the 'sharashki' justified themselves," the post read. "The concentration of talented people in one place" produced "brilliant results." With its position on *sharashki*—effectively prison camps in all but name—the museum seemed to make clear its thinking on modern Russia's questions of historical purpose, meaning, and responsibility.

THE TROUBLES SURROUNDING PERM-36 got the attention of Russia's leading historians and cultural figures. The country's flagship institution dedicated to the memory of the Gulag and Soviet-era political prisoners was under threat of turning into a center of historical revanchism. Word got back to Mikhail Piotrovsky, who, as director of the Hermitage Museum in St. Petersburg, is at once respected by the intelligentsia and favored with access to powerful officials. He came to Perm-36 for a visit. Afterward, he asked one of his colleagues, Yulia Kantor, a historian with a specialty in political repressions, to serve as outside curator for the museum. The position did not previously exist, and it took on much more significance than its title would suggest. Kantor was at once a crisis manager as well as a mentor for the museum's new employees and their emissary to the outside world, adding a measure of respectability and professionalism at a time when many feared Perm-36 was in danger of permanently losing both.

Kantor, as she told me, traveled to Perm without particularly warm or optimistic feelings—like many of her friends and colleagues back in St. Petersburg, she was wary of the museum's new orientation, and braced for the worst. But she wanted to give it, and Semakova, a chance; in any case, the situation seemed critical, and there was no choice but to do what she could to save the museum and its reputation. When she met Semakova, the director came across as out of her depth, "completely unprepared for the topic at hand, and for the task that had been entrusted to her." If one of the options the local authorities were considering was closing the museum entirely, Semakova had been "invited to the job quite literally as a liquidator."

Semakova was a bureaucratic placeholder and, by her own admission, hadn't thought much about the Gulag and political repressions until her appointment to head the museum. "This topic was foreign to her, and maybe even unpleasant," Kantor said. Semakova's task was different. "She was feeling her way blind, acting like a caretaker: lay pipes, repair the roof, pay for electricity."

But Kantor also saw that the museum had not turned into a paean to Stalin or contorted itself to show a balanced view of the Gulag. Most of the old exhibits were intact, and with state funding and official status, Perm-36 had the potential to become something new, certainly different from what it had been, but also useful and important: not a civic platform but a history museum, one that could fulfill this function capably and honestly, if without the ambition and audacity of what came before.

With time, Semakova grew into the job. She fired the employee who wrote the post on Perm's *sharashki* and hired a new deputy, a qualified local historian. Kantor talked to Semakova about the importance of the museum, how it was needed as a "vaccine" for Russian society. She invited Semakova to St. Petersburg, where she made introductions and took her to the Museum of Russian Political History; at one point, Kantor found Semakova stopped in front of a display on the many children caught up in the maelstrom of the Gulag in the 1930s and '40s. She was crying. Semakova thought about her own young daughter, who was studying in second grade, and about how, in the thirties, every student in class got a present for the new year—except for the children of enemies of the people. Up until now, Semakova hadn't really paused to consider this history, but now that she had, she found it moving and energizing. A new impulse and understanding of her job was developing inside her. Kantor was struck by what she saw as an amusing paradox: those officials who were betting on the museum's demise—the "masterminds of the whole debacle"—had made the opposite come true. "They ended up in a funny situation: they wanted the worst, and got something better."

At her core, Semakova remained a person of the state, one who thought primarily of how the museum should best fit into the official agenda of the day. The status of Perm-36 as a state body was certainly more familiar to Semakova, but also, as she saw it, safer and more reliable: "What is a nongovernmental organization? Today you exist, tomorrow you don't. You have money, then not." But a state organization is "under protection." As Semakova saw it, the museum was protected by a federal policy, enacted in 2015, that created a formal structure for memorializing the victims of political repressions. The nationalists from Ukraine and the Baltic states would be downplayed, just like any subject that caused undue controversy. Her museum would be competent and professional, if muted and neutral; she favored the "depoliticization" of Perm-36. "All this yelling without structure," she thought, "it doesn't bring anything good."

I FIRST VISITED THE museum on a gray and windy day in March. A film of melting ice covered the center of town, but as I drove out of Perm itself, toward the site of the onetime prison, the slush gave way to forested slopes covered in the clean white snow of midwinter. The monotony of the Russian countryside can be disorienting, but in the hypnotic, even calming sense of deep meditation: the snow, the trees, the wooden houses with wisps of black smoke snaking their way to a heavy sky, could have placed me anywhere in the thousands of miles of the expanse between Smolensk and Khabarovsk. The drive took two hours. When Shmyrov and Kursina first came, Perm-36 was more than four hours away; only in 2016 did local authorities build a more direct road to the site, saving eighty miles of circuitous driving.

I entered the museum—or just as fair to say, the prison—as visitors did in the seventies and eighties, through a heavy door that leads to a corridor walled off with iron bars where guards would inspect those coming and going. Having made my way through the passageway of metal gates, I walked out into the prison yard, an open expanse of low-slung buildings encircled by a series of perimeter fences. A shabby wooden fence, topped with a ring of rusted barbed wire, stood before a taller, much more solid metal one. (As museum guides always mention, there was not a single successful escape at Perm-36.) An empty guard tower watched over the grounds, which that morning were empty and still except for the presence of Semakova; her new deputy, the credentialed historian Maxim; and me.

We set off for the residential barracks, where prisoners lived and slept. Maxim's narration was voluminous and matter-of-fact, and he did not avoid or soften the ugliness of Soviet-era repressions: the caprice and horror of the Stalin purges, the conditions in the Gulag camps that amounted to a death sentence, the banal cruelty of the prison in its final years in the seventies and eighties. He showed me the dark cement cave that was the punishment cell, where Kovalev served nearly half his time. We also talked about Balys Gajauskas, a Lithuanian nationalist and dissident who was given a ten-year sentence for, among other crimes, translating a copy of Solzhenitsyn's *Gulag Archipelago* into Lithuanian. He did seven of those years at Perm-36, and after his release became a prominent politician in independent, post-Communist Lithuania. We made our way toward the dark cell where Stus, the Ukrainian poet, had been found dead. Semakova came along but largely stayed quiet, except for every now and then dealing with some administrative matter on her cellphone; it was clear that she acknowledged Maxim's historical expertise and thought it better to leave the tour to him.

After several hours, with my feet chilled to the point of numbness inside my boots, we walked over to what was known as the "club": a restored building that once housed the prison's small recreation hall and cafeteria. The museum's cook, a friendly and chipper woman in her fifties named Lidia, had been working here since Perm-36 was still a functioning prison. She served us bowls of boiled kasha flecked with pieces of tinned meat; the menu, she said, had remained relatively stable over the decades. (I would stay the night, eating this same meal for dinner that evening and for breakfast the next morning.) Semakova pulled out a bottle of vodka and opened a glass jar of homemade pickles she had made from cucumbers grown in her garden. There was something charming, if unearned, in her hospitality: she was a warm and generous host, but the backstory of how she had ended up in charge of this place, able to show me around and offer a spread of food and booze, was left unspoken, lurking just in the background.

I asked Semakova what she understood her mission to be—certainly the state officials who summoned her to offer her a new position had some idea of what they expected? She spoke of the task of "museumification," of creating a "state institution" that would bring itself in line with the norms and expectations of everything that definition entailed. In the past, she said, Perm-36 was home to "a lot of things which, maybe, were too complicated: the museum had become a place of lectures, debates, panel discussions." As she understood it, "We needed to rethink the nuts and bolts, to get back to the roots a little bit."

Semakova danced around the question of Shmyrov and Kursina, and where exactly she thought they might have erred in their boldness. But it was clear she thought their style of running the museum had been extravagant and at times self-indulgent. She told me that Kursina would spend millions of rubles in state budget money on Pilorama and seemed less interested in securing the funds to maintain and operate the museum complex. "In my understanding, as a bureaucrat, it simply doesn't make sense," she said. "You want to crap all over the government? Find some money and do it. But not on government territory and not with government funds." She told me of the two opposing visions she is stuck between: "There is the liberal position, for the museum to yet again become a political forum, where you say everything you think and do anything you want. The other is to close this place down, bulldoze everything, so as not to defile the honor of Stalin. Neither will lead to anything good."

As Semakova saw it, the fact that she comes from the particular world of Russian bureaucracy, that she speaks its language and knows its mores, is only an advantage. She can extract benefits for the museum from the state apparatus while avoiding unnecessary dangers and traps. "I know where to go, and for what, how to make sure we're not hindered in our work," she said. "If I'm going to explode, jump with every sneeze, then I won't last long, and if I leave, it's unclear what would happen here. Those who came before me aren't coming back—and who knows what sort of aims those who come after me will bring." I felt a pang of sympathy for Semakova, or, more exactly, a feeling that if I wanted the museum to survive and this place to remain as a living totem of historical memory, that meant, in some unavoidable sense, rooting for her. I knew it was a dirty and unfair trick perpetrated by the state, effectively making me cheer on the new managers sent to look after stolen property. I proposed a toast to the museum, and we knocked back another glass of vodka, chasing the numbing bitterness with the snap of one of Semakova's pickles.

A COUPLE OF DAYS LATER, back in town, I paid a visit to Shmyrov and Kursina, who live in an apartment tower on a hill overlooking Perm's concrete-and-brick silhouette. Shmyrov's health is poor; he has heart trouble and has undergone four surgeries over the past several years. Kursina was at the hospital visiting him when she found out she had been fired from the museum. When we met, they had just returned from yet another doctor's appointment. "First, you are very lucky that he's not in the hospital. Second, that's he alive at all," Kursina told me. We shared a pot of black tea and picked at a piece of honey cake. She and Shmyrov told me that just before the museum was taken from them, the regional administration had been interested in pursuing UNESCO status for the site, and they were in talks with a distinguished American architectural firm about a wholesale redesign of the exhibition space. All those plans were quashed now.

I broached the idea that perhaps the museum, in whatever incarnation, would be well served by reaching a form of coexistence with the state. Shmyrov insisted he and Kursina were capable of exactly that, and told me of his hours of talks with local officials. "They would say it should be like this, we'd say it should be like that. A few days would pass, we'd take a break, then come back. Okay, so let's edit this, fix something here, put this in writing." But there was a limit, and Shmyrov would oftentimes say no—which, for a while, seemed to work. "They knew perfectly well there were some things on which we would never back down." He insisted the reason the old museum was shut down and he and Kursina were kicked out was not Pilorama, or any one particular exhibit or program, but a more fundamental issue: that Perm-36, at least under their direction, was increasingly an aberration, an island of inquisitive and critical reflection, surrounded by ever-higher tides. "Everything we thought up, all that we did, stuck in the throat of this regime."

I asked Alexander Kalikh, the head of Perm's Memorial office, if he thought Shmyrov and Kursina, his old friends with whom he had founded the museum all those years back, could have saved their institution, and their place in it, by being a little more accommodating. "Maybe I would have been more shrewd in some cases, struck some compromises, not gone head-to-head with the enemies of the museum," he told me. "I would have acted more flexibly," he said, but then added, "I know that if Viktor Alexandrovich heard me right now, he would laugh loudly." The truth, Kalikh knew, was that nothing could have saved the old Perm-36. No concession or retreat would have kept the state at bay. Kalikh spoke with sadness for what they had all built together, and what had been lost. Even if he questioned their stubbornness, he held Shmyrov and Kursina in deep admiration: "They are more radical than me, but radicalism has its own truth."

IT IS IMPOSSIBLE TO separate the story of Perm-36 from the broader arc of the city's so-called cultural revolution. In the span of a few years, Perm whipsawed from a burst of experimental energy to reactionary backlash. That was in part due to the shifting climate set by the Kremlin—the moderate and piecemeal modernization of the Medvedev era gave way to the conservative revanche of Putin's return to the presidency—though perhaps even more due to the handover from one regional governor to another. The most high-profile manifestation of that earlier, short-lived period is a contemporary art museum called PERMM. When it opened, the museum was housed in the city's disused riverfront terminal, a gem of Stalin-era baroque architecture set along the banks of the Kama River. Its director was a well-known Moscow gallerist named Marat Gelman, who, upon his arrival in Perm, helped turn the city into what *The New York Times* called "Bilbao on Siberia's Edge." His tenure did not last long. An irreverent exhibit on the theme of the 2014 Sochi Olympics played

with Olympic imagery and Soviet aesthetic motifs, mocking everything from Russia's corruption to its alcohol consumption. Gelman
was dismissed and the museum was kicked out of the river station.
That space was taken over by a big-budget, patriotic historical exhibition, funded in part by the Orthodox Church. PERMM now makes
its home in a converted three-story shopping mall. Yet it has not entirely lost its verve or boldness.

On the day I visited, PERMM was in the middle of an exhibit on
the theme of revolutionary utopias, their ultimate impossibility, and
the inevitable disappointment that follows. I was shown around by its
director, Nailya Allakhverdieva, a curator who was invited to work at
the museum by Gelman and who took over after his firing. She told
me that, these days, "everything is oriented around preservation,"
which means avoiding risky topics and events, anything that could
rouse suspicion among civic groups and politicians who are waiting
for the slightest provocation. As she explained, "We all understand
that the appearance of any conflict at all could lead to our destruction. And our task is to survive."

Allakhverdieva described the logic of topics to be avoided: not
just politics, but anything that touches on sex, children, religion. "It's
hard to articulate, but I understand a certain methodology." Yet that
guessing game often proves impossible, and thus rather pointless.
"The situation changes all the time, which means the same tactics that
were effective before become counterproductive. What's clear,
though, is that contemporary art is definitely not the priority of the
state at the moment." She told me of a scandal that erupted after the
museum put on an exhibit of contemporary Azeri art that included
an array of children's dolls in grotesque poses. An investigation
dragged on for two years, with the museum premises inspected numerous times and Allakhverdieva questioned by investigators. Ultimately, she told me, "we have to think of how some village idiot will
use the prevailing agenda." Oftentimes, she explained, "the state sees
not with its own eyes, but through those of the most contentious and
bellicose character possible, and so we have to try and anticipate the
reaction of such a person."

As Allakhverdieva spoke, I thought of what had happened at

Perm-36 and the role of Essence of Time, how extremists had seized on the official mood to further their own obsessions and agenda. When I spoke to Ilya Rogotnev, a literature professor and activist in Essence of Time's Perm branch, he acknowledged that exact dynamic in the group's campaign against the museum. "Of course the state used us as their instrument—but maybe we used them, too," he said. He thought of the campaign against Shmyrov and Kursina and the previous incarnation of Perm-36 as a "situational alliance of mutual benefit," something that accomplished the political goals of the authorities while allowing Essence of Time an ideological victory. Rogotnev was satisfied with how things turned out. "The point of view of the new museum is closer to ours than what came before," he told me.

The dilemma of PERMM is essentially that of Perm-36: how not to betray the institution, as Allakhverdieva put it, without bringing about further problems. Gestures of irreverence and bravery are only so useful, lest they lead to the closing of the museum entirely. Today's Perm-36 has settled on a formula of carrying itself quietly and unobtrusively, while putting on exhibits that are sober and historically sound. In 2017, on the occasion of the hundred-year anniversary of the Bolshevik Revolution, the museum opened an exhibit called "Between Dreams and Reality," organized in cooperation with a pair of German cultural foundations. It showed the slide from revolutionary zeal to the creation of the first labor camps and the launching of the purges. The German consul attended the opening. On one of my trips to Perm-36, I visited a gripping and deeply fascinating exhibit on "material evidence"—that is, the artifacts confiscated by Soviet police during arrests and then used at trial, like a poster of Stalin that a factory worker had torn through with a pencil.

These days, supporters of Perm-36's founders and those who back the new incarnation of the museum seem further apart than ever, with each camp dug into a bunker of stubborn, principled certainty. The current administration has ever less patience for the complaints and sense of moral injury of Shmyrov and Kursina and their allies. Kantor, the outside curator, came to believe that their intransigence presents as much a threat to the museum as the apologias to Stalin circulating in society. If even the museum's founders are critics, Kantor fears, then state officials have a ready-made pretext to argue "What's the point?" and to walk away from the place once and for all. "The most terrible thing in this whole story," Kantor told me, is that "our opponents turned out to be the people who should have been our friends."

A mood of bitter resignation has settled over those who are still close to Shmyrov and Kursina and were once involved in the running of Perm-36. They miss the old museum, and wish there were a way to continue to offer their ideas and expertise. But the removal of Shmyrov and Kursina and the state takeover of the museum remains an open wound, one that is unlikely to heal any time soon, and leaves them feeling morally obligated not to abet the new regime. Obukhov, who was among the cofounders of the museum in the mid-nineties, said, "If I go work with them, I will be acting incorrectly, against my principles." It's a shame for all sides: the museum loses out on knowledge and expertise, while Obukhov and others with a long, shared history with Perm-36 are effectively cut off from the institution that once meant so much to them. But Obukhov is categorical: "As long as the situation with Shmyrov has not been resolved, I cannot cooperate with them."

Obukhov and I were sitting on a bench in front of the history department at Perm State University, where he still teaches. He said the idea that the museum can avoid or otherwise recuse itself from politics is false— you can't engage the history of political repressions without fostering a conversation that leads straight to the present day. "When you talk about what a person went to prison for, willfully or not, some analogies come to mind. If a person is sensible, he will come up with these convictions on his own," he said. The museum can claim publicly and officially—which may be all that matters to those higher up—that it takes no interest in questions of immediate political and civic concern, but that is a delusion.

Perhaps no one I spoke to in Perm was more conflicted on the subject than Sergey Shevyrin, who was a PhD student of Shmyrov's and wrote his dissertation on labor productivity in the work camps around Perm. Shevyrin is in his fifties now, with a thin white beard, and narrow wire-frame glasses that perch over his nose. He told me he was initially wary of Perm-36's new direction, and found the exhibit on timber production distasteful and one-sided. But he agreed to help curate an exhibit on the lives of former Gulag prisoners after their release and their struggle to reintegrate into a Soviet society that did not particularly welcome or understand them. He had a positive experience. "What we wanted to say, we said," he told me. After that, he became convinced, despite his feelings about Shmyrov and Kursina's removal, that it was still possible to do serious and accurate historical work there. When Semakova asked him to lead the museum's historical research department, he agreed. Shevyrin had a fairly functional understanding of his role and the opportunities it would allow. "There can be no compromises in the telling of history. It has to be the full truth, as close-up as possible, with no retreat," he said. But, as for the civic activity of the museum, Pilorama, and the like, "I don't really need this. I'm a historian, I like to sit in the archives and study materials."

Shevyrin retained a sense of moral fealty to Shmyrov and had no illusions about Semakova's abilities. Shmyrov was an "engine, a real locomotive, he delved into this history," he told me, whereas Semakova is "someone else: an administrator," who knew why she had been named to her job and would avoid the pitfalls of those who preceded her. "She understands perfectly well the example of the previous team. They did everything themselves, never asking permission or what anyone thought," Shevyrin said. By contrast, Semakova "will run ten times back and forth to the Perm administration, asking can we do this, can we do that." Yet all the same, she largely left Shevyrin alone to carry out historical research and put on the exhibits that he finds important and compelling. "She doesn't get in the way, she allows me to bring the essence of the Gulag to the people. And since this is possible, why shouldn't I?" But he could not get over knowing that Shmyrov was upset with him and considered Shevyrin working at Perm-36 akin to personal treachery. Shevyrin would never be truly comfortable in his position at the museum. "My logic does not agree with my convictions. Sometimes I think that I should leave, that it will be easier for everyone—including me."

When the museum announced its plans to develop a series of exhibits documenting daily life in the camp, Semakova and Kantor were especially pleased that Mikhail Meylac, who had been reluctant to cooperate with them, agreed to consult on questions of historical accuracy. Given his biography, Meylac is a figure of automatic respect, and his participation lent an air of legitimacy to the era, now several years on, of Perm-36 as a state museum. One rainy summer afternoon, Meylac and I met at his family's dacha in the woods outside St. Petersburg—the same place to which he fatefully decided not to bring his collection of illegal literature back in 1983. Since his release, Meylac, now in his seventies, has lived a phenomenally active life—still making up for the time he lost at Perm-36, he is fond of saying—moving to Strasbourg, France, where he taught Old Church Slavonic and Russian literary history, and published poetry and a half dozen academic volumes. He takes a sublime pleasure in theater and classical music. Every spring, he comes to Perm, where he attends an annual music and arts festival held in the city. The ten days of avant-garde performances are the last vestige of Perm's "cultural revolution." On his last trip, he went to Perm-36 and toured the museum. "I had mixed feelings, let's put it that way," he told me. "But the most important thing is that it exists at all."

Meylac reminded me of Pilorama's slogan and motivating idea: "Freedom in a place of unfreedom." That sense of purpose is gone now, he said. Perm-36 no longer makes such sweeping moral claims, and does not position itself as a repository of experience and lessons of immediate importance for present-day Russia. The greatest change, of course, is the absence of Shmyrov and Kursina, and the sense of vitality they gave to the museum. "They were the soul of the place, and that's more important than any exhibitions," Meylac told me. Nonetheless, when Semakova and her colleagues asked him to offer his memories of the place, he agreed. "I'm no longer a young man; if I can be of use, it's my duty to do so, to offer some advice, explain some things." He made his own small compromise: he would act as a consultant on a set of limited and defined questions, but refused to join the museum's outside advisory council or participate in conversations about its larger, strategic direction. Meylac can't shake a feeling of discomfort with Perm-36 in its current form, and was uneasy with Semakova, "an absolutely official figure from inside the state." He paused and shifted in his chair. "Actually, it's all so unpleasant for me, I don't really want to talk about it."

I asked Meylac to tell me more about the years he spent at Perm-36, a much easier topic for him to discuss than the present. Then, as a prisoner, the moral boundaries were clearer. There was no reason for confusion or doubt, no need to balance the demands of one's conscience with the opportunities of the moment. He found a kind of peace in the prison's boiler room, where he would work a daily shift, breaking apart heavy blocks of coal and shoveling them into the furnace. He liked the physical work, being left relatively alone. Outside, in the few spare moments of the day, he could find, if not beauty, then at least reminders of life's essentials, over which the guards and their bosses could not seize control. He took pleasure in the "air, the landscape beyond the fence, clear sky, the trees, and most of all, the stars." Before his imprisonment, he had been friendly with Joseph Brodsky, and at Perm-36, often thought back to his poetry. He liked one of Brodsky's lines in particular, about the winter in Yalta, on the Black Sea coast of Crimea: "There is life everywhere, and this place had its own."

CHAPTER 6

HELL ON EARTH

—

LIZAVETA GLINKA WAS TIRED, WORN-OUT BY MORE THAN TWO years of regular travel in and out of war zones, by how every journey became an odyssey, by the injured children and bombed-out hospitals and pitiless indifference, or just recklessness, of those who lob artillery shells in the direction of orphanages. She didn't understand war, and felt a kind of confused loathing for those who wage it, but that is where those in need are. She was instinctually on the side of the victim, of the weak and powerless, of anyone whose suffering she might be able to mitigate or lessen, even by just a small degree.

By the winter of 2016, Glinka, a doctor by training, had made innumerable humanitarian trips from Moscow to the Donbass, where the war between Russian-backed separatists and Ukrainian forces had ground to a temporary and flimsy cease-fire. Earlier that year, in September, she had also gone to Syria, where Russia had intervened on the side of Assad, visiting hospitals and noting which medical supplies were most needed. Doctor Liza, as everyone called her, gained a following in Russia for her selfless care for the homeless and critically ill, running what amounted to a one-woman charity organization that provided clothing, medicine, or just a hot meal to those who needed them—a population the rest of Russian society preferred not to see. Glinka was fifty-four, with a cheerful bob of blond hair and wide, deep-set eyes that, when they focused on you, made you feel like you were the subject of a deep and enveloping empathy.

She had spent years at the bedsides of the sick and dying. It was quixotic, draining work, but it gave her a sense of deep meaning and satisfaction. There was something at once viscerally human yet also mystical about accompanying a person to the exit from this life. The writer Ludmila Ulitskaya described first meeting Glinka at the hospital bed of a mutual friend, who lay dying after suffering a stroke. Glinka had come to spend the night sitting by the friend's side, but the room had only one chair, which Ulitskaya was already occupying. So Glinka stayed for a few minutes, offered some words of comfort, and left. Sometime later, Ulitskaya stepped out into the hallway of the ward. She saw Glinka lying down on a hospital cot next to an old man who had just been admitted that evening and was clearly on his last breaths. She was gently caressing this stranger's head, though it struck Ulitskaya that the man, close to death, probably couldn't feel anything at that point. "Liza's behavior at that time seemed a little weird to me," Ulitskaya recalled. But, she added, "ordinary people tend to find the behavior of saints a little weird."

War, however, felt very different from a hospital ward: it left Glinka exhausted and deprived of vitality, not so much by the work itself, but all that came with it—rubbing shoulders with unpleasant men in camouflage, the constant negotiations with bureaucrats, and, most of all, the way everyone now assumed there was something political in her activities, and thus demanded a political stance from her, something she had deliberately avoided all these years. She told her husband, Gleb, a tax lawyer, that she wanted to slow down in the new year, delegate more responsibility, and spend less time on the road. Yeah, right, Gleb said, knowing his wife's boundless energy and almost manic need to be where her help was needed: So we'll get you a rocking chair and you'll knit socks for our grandchildren? "I'm serious, Glebushka," she said.

It was late December, and the Glinkas were preparing for the New Year's holiday, which they planned to spend in Crimea, as they had for years. Three months had passed since Glinka's first trip to Syria, and now a call came asking her to take another. A humanitarian delegation organized by the Russian Ministry of Defense was leaving in three days—would she join? "I don't think she really wanted to go," Gleb told me. He could tell she was less than enthusiastic; he heard a certain hesitation in her voice when she told him she had agreed, but she kept whatever doubts she felt to herself "You live with someone for thirty years, you pick up signals, you learn to tell when something is being held back," he said. But, having been asked, Glinka couldn't say no.

Russian warplanes had been pounding Syrian targets for more than a year. Russia had formally entered the war in the fall of 2015, sending its fighter jets to a base near the port city of Latakia. The ostensible aim was to lend the Assad regime a hand in fighting ISIS— that was how Putin presented the campaign to the world, and how it was sold to the Russian public on state television. But the target list suggested the mission's real purpose. One analysis showed that only 20 percent of the targets hit in the first weeks of the air war were in areas held by ISIS; the rest struck other rebel militias fighting the government of Bashar al-Assad. Putin had a visceral aversion to anything that looked like regime change—his support for Assad since the outbreak of fighting was philosophical, not personal. He dispatched the country's military to prove this point and, at the same time, to restore Russia's position as a central and necessary player in the Middle East—as he saw it, another historical birthright Russia had been unjustly denied by the country's temporary, post-Soviet weakness. Given Western efforts to isolate Russia in the wake of Ukraine, Putin's Syria gambit was a way of forcing himself, and Russia, back into the league of geopolitical superpowers. On that score, and in staving off a battlefield defeat for Assad, the campaign seemed to be working.

Late in the evening of December 24, with wintertime Moscow entombed in a heavy, black stillness, Glinka left her apartment on the city's central Boulevard Ring and drove twenty miles out of town, to the Chkalovsky military air base. Waiting on the tarmac was the usual retinue of generals and flight engineers and state television crews, along with sixty-four members of the Alexandrov Ensemble, more popularly known as the Red Army Choir, a storied musical troupe that regularly traveled the world performing its repertoire of folk tunes, military hymns, and spirited dances. They were headed to the Russian base near Latakia, on Syria's Mediterranean coast, where they would put on a holiday concert for the troops stationed there. At 1:40 in the morning, the Tupolev Tu-154 jet, with eighty-four passengers on board, along with eight crew members, took off and headed south. Two hours later, it landed at another military airstrip in Sochi, on the Black Sea, for a scheduled refueling stop.

At five thirty, with the first rays of dawn rising over the sea, the plane started its engines and sped down the Sochi runway. It lifted into the sky, a shrinking dot streaking across the horizon. Within seconds, as the plane ascended, the chief pilot became disoriented: he thought they were climbing too sharply and pushed the controls forward, sending the aircraft into a dive. The plane lost twenty feet of altitude every second. The pilot, confused about the Tupolev's orientation in the sky, banked sharply to the left. The crew's navigator unleashed a slew of profanities over the onboard communications system; by this point, as the plane dove and swerved haphazardly, the passengers must have been in a state of terror. Seventy seconds had passed since takeoff—and the plane was now just a couple hundred feet above the water, hurtling even farther downward. It hit the surface at 330 miles per hour and broke apart, spraying metal and debris over more than a mile. Back at the base, the crew at air traffic control saw the blip representing the plane flash and then go dark. The flight had disappeared.

In Moscow, as news of the crash began to circulate, Gleb, along with Glinka's many supporters and admirers, hoped for the impossible: maybe she wasn't on board; perhaps, as one short-lived rumor had it, she had been held back during an additional security check in Sochi, and had taken another flight. But the hours stretched on, and Glinka's mobile phone was still switched off. Finally, Gleb heard the doorbell ring: his wife had indeed been on the plane, and she, like the others, was gone. The news was delivered by Mikhail Fedotov, the head of the Kremlin human rights council, a body that Glinka had joined three years earlier. The two had grown close, bound by mutual admiration and a sense that each complemented the other: Fedotov's formal title provided access and influence; Glinka's reputation ensured respect and legitimacy. Fedotov himself was supposed to join Glinka on the flight. But he had been kept from going by the defense ministry, and was now left in the role of announcing Glinka's death. "We were hoping for a miracle until the very end," Fedotov said. "She herself was a miracle, a message of virtue sent from heaven."

GLINKA'S MOTHER, GALINA, was a doctor, and for as long as Glinka could remember, she wanted to become one, too. She enrolled in medical school, and, in the early eighties, not long after she finished, met Gleb. He was fourteen years her senior and had come to Moscow from Vermont, where he had grown up, the child of a Russian father and a Polish mother. He was entranced by the mysteries of the land he had known only from his parents' stories. Adding to this swirl of romanticism was his love for Liza. He wanted to stay; she laughed and told him there was no way he'd survive. In 1990, she moved with him to Vermont, settling in a farmhouse in Cabot, a small town deep in the Northeast Kingdom, home to a number of glassy ponds and even more dairy farms. Glinka busied herself gardening, and raising the couple's two boys, Constantine and Aleksei. Before long, Liza felt the itch to practice medicine, but to qualify in the States would require attending medical school all over again. Gleb recommended she visit a nearby hospice as a start, to see if she could pick up some volunteer shifts.

Glinka went to have a look, and was immediately transfixed. She had never imagined such a place was possible. A few dozen patients lived in private rooms, each with a photograph and short biography of its resident on the door. Staff members did not hide or particularly resist the undeniable fact that those under their care would soon die, but treated them as worthy of honor and respect, an approach that was neither patronizing nor overly doting, but marked by compassion and grace. "I saw blissful, clean, well-fed patients, whose dignity was respected, and who were able to contemplate the eternal," Glinka said later. It was nothing like the Soviet approach to the dying, which modern Russia had inherited, in which those with terminal illnesses were shunted out of view, ignored by a medical system that treated death as taboo, as if the act of dying was not a natural and inevitable phenomenon but something contagious. Glinka understood right away that she had found her calling. She enrolled in a course in palliative medicine at Dartmouth.

In the late nineties, Gleb, who by then had built a successful law practice in Vermont, was offered a job working on legal reforms in Ukraine. The family relocated to Kyiv. Now Glinka could open a hospice of her own, in a place where nothing of the kind existed. In 2000, the hospice admitted its first inpatients. The number soon grew to thirty, with more than a hundred receiving care at home, but Glinka kept up the daily, tactile clinical work she loved. Or rather, her friends would say, the work she couldn't live without, no less than a person could live without breathing: holding the hand of a sick child, changing the dressings on the wound of an elderly man, listening to the grievances and regrets that rise to the surface in a person's last days.

Despite her years at the hospice, Glinka could never accept death or pretend to understand it. She saw her first coffin at the age of seven, when a teenage boy, Seryozha, who lived in the same apartment building, had died of cancer. The unexpectedness of it frightened her, as did the seeming injustice of Seryozha leaving this earth so early. And no matter how many terminal patients she comforted, she could never shake a deep fear of the total, existential void that death represented. She was a religious person, but never announced her Orthodox faith, and wasn't even sure what it meant for her own understanding of what, if anything, follows when we die. "I'm afraid, terribly so, of not knowing what awaits . . . there," she told a filmmaker in 2009. "I have a sense, as a religious person, that it should be better somehow," she said. "But at heart, I'm afraid of death, because I don't know how it will happen: Will it come unexpectedly, or will I suffer? All of this is unknown, and it frightens me." She could never be sure she wasn't lying when she told her charges that there was nothing to be afraid of.

Her great gift was to take some piece of her patients' dread and sadness and make it her own. By making the burden of death just a little bit hers, she made it that much less for others. At the hospice, she learned each patient's name, profession, and talents, who they were before their bodies failed them, and, most important, how they wanted to spend their last days—whether it was the Orthodox priest who asked for a *shashlyk* kebab or the lonely woman who surrounded herself with relatives and hangers-on clearly set on taking advantage of her, but who told Glinka to let them in all the same. She buried the men who died in her care in fine clothes, sometimes by raiding Gleb's closet—her husband might search for his favorite navy wool suit only to learn it was being worn by a man already in the ground.

Glinka started to keep an online diary in which she narrated the stories of those who passed through the hospice. The only difference between them and us, as she put it, is that they know when they are going to die and we don't. Otherwise, we're all the same, with the same desires and weaknesses, the same capacity for wisdom and generosity, and for pettiness. "The sick and dying also fall in love, get married, feel hatred, suffer, get anxious, make telephone calls, eat, listen to music, watch television," she wrote. In one post, she described a woman named Elena, who, in her forties, was dying of cervical cancer. She had two children, a son and daughter. One day, Glinka brought in a wealthy man who had asked how he could be helpful. He wanted to donate to only the most difficult cases, he told her. Glinka led him to Elena's room. Go on, Glinka encouraged her, let this man help you, ask him for something, whatever you want. Without thinking, Elena replied, "My boy is dancing in *Raymonda* on the twenty-eighth. Be sure to go see it. You'll enjoy it."

Everyone dies differently, Glinka learned. Some cry out and want to be held, asking for Doctor Liza to squeeze their hand or wrap her arms around them. Others are quiet and withdrawn. Children tend to pass as if they are falling asleep—"as if their breath just flies away," Glinka once described it. The aphorism of how death is hardest on the living struck her as undeniably true. Some find themselves trapped in a spiral of grief and become self-destructive, intent on destroying their lives even further; others cope by becoming angry at the deceased, wondering how such a person could depart and leave them here alone. The most difficult, of course, were the parents of a dying child. The worst was a man whose young daughter, Natasha, was in the final throes of a long and torturous illness. He tore through the hallways, yelling to himself; his wife said he had smashed all the Orthodox icons at home. It fell to Glinka to try to keep him from seriously damaging the hospice or himself. "You know," she told him, "if you sit down, you can hold Natasha in your arms." "Really?" he said, his attention focusing. "May I?" "Of course," Glinka replied, unplugging the various tubes and cords from his daughter's small body and handing her to him. She didn't even see when the child died, Glinka recalled later. "He himself said, 'She's gone.' "

IN 2006, GLINKA WAS in Moscow visiting her mother. After a week, as she was headed to the airport to leave, she got a call: her mother, who was seventy-one, had suffered a massive brain hemorrhage. Glinka told the taxi to turn around, and ended up staying in Moscow another year and a half. She visited the hospital twice a day, sitting with her mother, talking with her, holding her hand—even though she was in a deep coma and couldn't respond or even acknowledge that she understood her daughter was by her side. The doctors and nurses had seen this before: everyone comes in the beginning, but then they slowly stop, drawn back to their own lives, ever more aware of the futility of their visits, depressed by their own impotence. But Glinka came day after day, all the way until the morning in April 2008 when her mother finally died. As the orderlies wheeled the body out into the corridor, with Glinka walking alongside, the hospital's doctors and nurses stood in a long line, honoring Glinka as she walked past. The next day, she published a post on her diary: "I remain here, where my life is formed by the pain and suffering of others."

While in Moscow, Glinka formed an organization she called Fair Aid, which would provide medicine and palliative care to the terminally ill, especially those who couldn't afford the city's private clinics and would otherwise be left to die on their own, in pain and a burden to their often overwhelmed families. It would be like the Kyiv hospice, but instead of having one fixed address, Doctor Liza would make house calls. A remarkable documentary shot in this period captures her as she travels around Moscow to care for those with late-stage illnesses. She visits Oksana, a translator in her thirties dying of tongue cancer, who can no longer speak and instead writes out notes on a pad she keeps near her bed. Glinka replaces her neck bandage and pats her on the temple. Spending time with the dying is a privilege, she says. "We will be the last people to come into her life, the last people she trusts, the last people she loves."

One day, Glinka received a report of a homeless man who was near death at Paveletsky railway station, on Moscow's central Garden Ring. When she got there, a number of other homeless people came up and said to her, Hey, what about us, we also need help. Glinka began coming by Paveletsky station every Wednesday, serving a hot meal and offering on-the-spot medical checkups. Readers of her blog brought warm clothes, or sometimes just cash for Glinka to buy medicine and food. The Paveletsky gang were among the most marginalized people in all of Moscow—those left behind by the city's fantastical transformation into the world capital of billionaires—but Glinka treated them no differently than her hospice patients. She learned their names, and made sure no one among the small cohort of staff and volunteers at Fair Aid called them bums. "Any homeless person was once someone's child," she once said. "In this, he is identical to me and you."

Local residents near the station filed reams of complaints, certain that Glinka was ruining the neighborhood. They asked the municipality to kick her out. City officials were no more understanding, and periodically appeared on television to shriek about how Glinka was only increasing the numbers of derelicts for the city to deal with. Her blog readers left nasty comments, accusing her of undermining the strength of the nation, writing that helping the homeless and the terminally ill ran against natural selection: a new Russia was on the rise, wealthy and strong, and Doctor Liza's band of miserables didn't fit in with the mood.

But the blog also attracted ever more supporters, people who sent small donations amounting to a few dollars. Every now and then, someone would give a thousand rubles, around thirty-five dollars, a noticeable sum. With time, as Glinka's fame spread and Moscow became an ever wealthier and more glamorous city, the donations got bigger, with people hopping out of idling Mercedes to drop off envelopes containing a thousand or even five thousand dollars. Glinka bought medicine for the sick, diapers for their babies, heavy parkas for the homeless at the station. When a forty-two-year-old computer programmer named Sasha, who had late-stage liver cancer, needed an oxygen machine that cost seventeen hundred dollars, Glinka appealed to her readers: If everyone pitches in one dollar, we could have enough by the evening. She didn't even need to wait that long. A wealthy businessman and his wife offered to pay for it themselves.

One day, Lana Zhurkina, who first met Glinka at a fund-raising event for Fair Aid, showed up at the basement office near Paveletsky station and asked how she could help. Glinka asked whether she could make buckwheat kasha. Yes, Zhurkina answered, and she spent the rest of the winter cooking in the back kitchen. "I liked this, let's say, systematic aspect of Liza's organization—that it functioned as a kind of membrane between those who give and those in need," Zhurkina told me. "A person brings a donation of kasha, and you feed it to someone who is hungry; a person drops off a winter coat, and the next day a homeless person is wearing it." Zhurkina was also struck by Glinka's even temper, the way she treated everyone the same, whether the person walked into the basement headquarters wearing a fur coat or a smelly parka. "Everyone heard the same jokes, fell into the same soulful embrace, had the same chance of getting cursed out."

Another time, Mikhail Gokhman, a middle-aged journalist and editor, stopped by. He had been following Glinka's blog, and like countless others wanted to see what he could do to help. He asked Glinka a question that she got a lot in those days: Isn't it the worst thing for a doctor when a patient dies? That must be awful—how do you reconcile yourself to it? "It makes no difference whether a person dies now, or in two years, or fifty—in the scheme of human civilization, it's irrelevant," she answered. "What's more important is that a person's death, whenever it happens, should not be undignified. If a person is destined to die, the person shouldn't suffer, but should die in humane conditions, in a clean bed, surrounded by people one wants to see,

and with one's wishes carried out." Gokhman became a regular supporter of Fair Aid, sending Glinka money here and there to buy medical supplies and food; he organized his fiftieth birthday party at the
Paveletsky basement, and instead of presents asked his guests to all
chip in small donations. When we spoke, he took care to emphasize
that Glinka was not an otherworldly being. "She allowed herself the
occasional profanity," he said. "She liked to smoke, and drink, especially Armenian *tutovka*," a heady liquor distilled from mulberries.

Glinka became one of a number of philanthropists and humani-
tarians who, by their example, changed the perception of charity in
modern Russian society. For a long while, the paternalistic inheritance of the Soviet period continued to prevail; people subconsciously expected the state to take care of them, and didn't imagine
that they should—or even could—organize themselves to take care
of each other, filling in the gaps where the state proved incompetent
or unwilling. What's more, many of those who did emerge in the
early post-Soviet years to profess their benevolent, civic-minded intentions turned out to be hucksters and frauds. An organization raising money to carry out charity work was seen as just another scheme.
"If you work with money, you are a swindler by definition," one
nonprofit executive told me, paraphrasing the view widely shared by
many Russians in the 1990s and early 2000s.

The cynicism was understandable. A friend of mine was once sitting in a taxi in Moscow's famously snarled traffic; behind him, an
ambulance was trapped in a sea of cars, its siren blaring impotently.
My friend asked the taxi driver, Why is it that Moscow drivers never
give the right of way to ambulances? That's easy, the driver replied.
Everybody knows that ambulance crews started selling themselves as
VIP taxi services, accepting a wad of cash to ferry some aspiring oligarch around town while avoiding the traffic jams all the plebes sit in
for hours.

Glinka overcame this ingrained skepticism with her own credibility, a force of personality that could not easily be dismissed. If, at the
outset, donors were willing to support a particular individual or
case—like Sasha and his oxygen machine, say—with time, people
started to give to Fair Aid as an organization, trusting Glinka to dis-

burse funds as she saw fit. Communities of self-organized donors and volunteers formed around particular emergencies, like the choking wildfires outside Moscow in the summer of 2010 that turned the skies an acrid black, or a flood in the southern city of Krymsk in 2012. Glinka collected food and clothes and medical supplies at the offices of Fair Aid and packed them into a fleet of vans headed for Krymsk, accompanied by dozens of volunteers.

Slowly, the state came around, if not quite becoming an outright friend to Glinka and her activities, then at least not acting as an antagonist. She was constitutionally uninterested in politics, had no conception of how individuals assemble and wield power, of the intrigues and alliances and coalitions that people dip in and out of in search of influence. "She wasn't able to think in those categories even if she wanted to," Gleb said. "They were bewildering to her." Yet as her fame grew, Glinka fielded periodic inquiries from representatives of various political parties and movements: Might she join them, sign on to this or that initiative, maybe even add her name to the party list in upcoming elections, lending her credibility in exchange for, say, a seat on the city council, or even parliament? "She said no constantly," Gleb recalled.

Glinka found her dealings with various municipal bureaucrats uncomfortable and best dispatched with quickly, though she acknowledged that they were necessary, especially for an organization that wanted to expand its activities. She couldn't personally visit every sick and dying person in Moscow, and if a patient needed treatment at a state-run oncology clinic, or a homeless person was waiting for a place at a government shelter, she would have to involve the state. She documented on her blog an exchange with a midlevel official, who had signed some sort of formal document that Fair Aid needed to carry out its charity activities. "You should be grateful to me," the official told her. Glinka was bewildered. "For his work!" she wrote in the post. "For work, do you understand? Society has reached the point where people require gratitude for doing simple, normal work."

For all her ignorance of politicians and their motives, Glinka had an innate skill for dealing with them. It was the same way she dealt with everybody. What help can this person offer, and what do I need to do so that he provides it? "She had a clear understanding for how people can be useful: what to expect from them, who is capable of what, who can provide the motor for her locomotive," Zhurkina said. The state and its functionaries were neither inherently good nor bad—they just had certain resources that she needed in order to help more people, and getting access to them was more important than taking a moral or political position, which struck her as abstract and pointless.

"Her battle was not for the state or against it, for Putin or against him. Her battle was against injustice, suffering, pain," said Dmitry Aleshkovsky, a photographer and charity organizer who became close with Glinka. During the protests in the winter of 2011–12, she prepared hot soup and tea to take to demonstrators as they stood outside in the frigid, subzero temperatures. Her sympathies lay with those out in the streets, not out of some deeply held conviction about the evils of Putin's rule, but from an instinct to always take the side of the weak. When protestors were being beaten and rounded up by riot police, of course Glinka would do what she could to help them; that struck her as self-evident. She didn't think in big, abstract categories, but in very concrete terms: the Putin system as such didn't exist for her. At a moment when the Moscow city administration was making noises about kicking Fair Aid out of its basement offices, Aleshkovsky introduced Glinka to a high-ranking official, who took a liking to her and her cause. The city ultimately agreed to lease the basement space to Glinka for ten years, rent-free. As Aleshkovsky put it, "These connections would come to give her all sorts of possibilities she didn't have herself—and, in the most unavoidably direct sense, were the thing that ultimately killed her."

MIKHAIL FEDOTOV IS PERHAPS the only high-ranking functionary in the Russian presidential administration who keeps portraits of both Sakharov and Putin in his office. Descended from a long line of Russian legal scholars, he is sixty-nine, a warm and intelligent bear of a man with a white beard and a genteel manner that affirms his pedigree. In his youth, Fedotov worked as a journalist, then switched to law: in the early nineties, he represented Yeltsin in his ultimately failed bid to declare the Communist Party unconstitutional. Since 2010, Fedotov has been the chair of the Kremlin's human rights council, a position that gives him a degree of access and influence on certain questions and no small amount of distress over the many others he feels powerless to resolve. Fedotov has the opportunity to make his case to Putin personally, and every now and then this "proximity to the body," as Russians like to put it, yields results. But just as often, Fedotov's council serves as a decorative token, held up as proof of the Putin system's humanistic side.

In his office, Fedotov told me that in approaching his job, his motto is "Less politics, more concreteness." Take the problem of landfills outside Moscow, he said. These garbage dumps had become the source of angry protests from local residents in a number of towns outside the capital, especially after scores of children fell ill from chemical toxins in the air. Now, Fedotov asked me, what could he and his council push for? They could demand that the governor of the Moscow region be fired, that a new candidate be put forward at upcoming elections. Or they could make sure that landfills operating illegally or without proper regulatory oversight were closed, and that residents were no longer in danger or made unwell. That was his approach. "I don't care who the governor is—what's important to me is that the garbage dumps are destroyed," he said. That sounded sensible, but it overlooked the fact that in today's Russia, a massive garbage dump doesn't operate in violation of the law without ties to local power brokers, politicians, and bureaucrats. You could play Whac-A-Mole with garbage dumps to eternity, but at a certain point, the problem becomes unavoidably, well, political.

One long-running battle Fedotov has waged with the Kremlin is over the law, first passed in 2012, that forces the label of "foreign agent" on any NGO that receives funding from abroad. The law is deliberately designed to cast suspicion on any group with ties to the West, just as it was used in relation to the founders of the Perm-36 museum. Fedotov said he regularly tells Putin about the flaws in the law and explains its fundamental injustice—an NGO with foreign

grants is not doing anything traitorous or subversive. But Putin believes that an organization receiving money from a foreign donor is
automatically acting in the interest of that foreign government. "I
tell him, 'Vladimir Vladimirovich, that's not the way it is, that is a
misunderstanding,' " Fedotov said. "But he says: 'No, whoever pays
orders the music.' He is absolutely certain of this. Argue with him all
you want, but to convince him otherwise is impossible." Since he
realized there was no chance of rescinding the law, Fedotov concen-
trated on minimizing the number of organizations affected by it. He
pled his case with Putin's advisors in the Kremlin and the Ministry of
Justice, and managed to slow down the pace with which new organizations were stamped with the "foreign agent" label. (The overall list
shrank from some 160 names in 2015 to around 80 today.) Fedotov
told the story as an illustration of his guiding thesis: yelling about the
law itself would be politics, and thus counterproductive, but working to get this or that group off the list is concrete action, and thus
more effective. "I prefer small steps in the right direction rather than
big steps in the opposite direction," he said.

No episode better exemplifies the dance of compromise that
Fedotov must constantly perform than the story of how, shortly
after he was named the council's head, he managed to add new members. Fedotov wanted to bring in a fresh crop of public figures and
civil-society activists, but he had to get his candidates approved by
the Kremlin. He sat down in a Kremlin office across a table from
Vladislav Surkov, a shadowy and influential advisor to Putin, with
the following ground rules: each one had the right to propose whatever candidate he wanted, but each also had the right of veto. Fedotov started. He proposed Emil Pain, an ethnographer and expert on
Russia's many smaller nationalities. Surkov said maybe, he'd have to
think. Fedotov then put forward Evgenia Chirikova, an environmen-
tal activist who led opposition to the building of a toll road through
a forest outside Moscow. Surkov said no. How about Sergey Vo-
robyev, who co-chairs an association of Russian business leaders?
Okay. Vladimir Pozner, the television host on Channel One who
spent much of his earlier years in America? Surkov again said no.
Then they traded places, and Surkov read off his list. He started with

a powerful Kremlin-friendly labor activist. Fedotov agreed. Surkov named a few more people whom Fedotov accepted. Then he proposed Vladimir Solovyov, a deeply cynical pro-Kremlin television host. Fedotov said no. How about Sergey Dorenko, another media personality? Fedotov again declined. "Some candidates he axed, some I axed—a perfect compromise," he told me.

In the summer of 2012, when it came time to expand the council again, Fedotov asked Glinka if she would join. By then, she had a rather high profile in Moscow, especially among the capital's liberal intelligentsia, who accepted Glinka as one of their own; without confronting the Kremlin, she had created a functioning organization wholly independent of it. Glinka accepted Fedotov's offer. The two grew close, especially after his mother died. He hadn't told anyone on the human rights council of her passing, but Glinka found out, and came to the funeral. Fedotov was touched by the gesture. "This is the uniqueness of her soul: she needs to be near a person when he is feeling bad, who's having a difficult time, so she can take on part of his pain, absorb some of the burden."

Glinka spent her first couple of years on the council traveling around the country, looking at conditions in provincial hospitals and children's homes. Oftentimes what she found dismayed her—decrepit facilities, lack of necessary medicines, disabled children left to lie on soiled sheets. She scolded regional governors and ministers, who, after some resistance and prevarication, usually provided what she asked for. "Titles didn't matter for her," Fedotov told me. "Governor, minister, president—that wasn't important. She demanded good deeds from them all."

EVERYTHING IN GLINKA'S LIFE changed with the outbreak of war in Ukraine. In the spring of 2014, after Russian-backed separatists seized administrative buildings across the Donbass, Glinka traveled to Donetsk, the regional capital. She was joined by Ella Polyakova, an activist and military watchdog from St. Petersburg who also had a seat on the Kremlin human rights council. At the time, Donetsk, a well-manicured city of nearly a million people, was eerily calm. It had been taken over by rebels, and a feeling of dark premonition hung in the air, but for the moment, actual fighting between Ukrainian forces and pro-Russian militias was confined to the towns in the surrounding countryside. "It was a strange situation, no one understood anything," Polyakova told me. A freezing rain fell in Donetsk all four days the two of them were there. Glinka went from one hospital to the next, asking the same questions of every doctor she encountered: Was the facility ready to accept a large number of trauma patients? Did it have enough supplies and medicines? The short answer was invariably no. Donetsk was short on blood plasma and serums for preventing gangrene; there weren't even enough gauze bandages and syringes to go around. Glinka wrote down everything she heard and came back to Moscow with a long list. A few weeks later, having secured a few hundred pounds of medicine and first-aid supplies, she returned to Donetsk.

As the fighting intensified and rebel fighters mounted an assault on the airport, the direct flights stopped, and Glinka had to travel nearly twenty hours by train to get to the city. She and Polyakova made another trip. But this time Polyakova found herself uneasy with Glinka's connections, with both the rebel leadership in Donetsk and influential figures back in Moscow. At one point, a cameraman working for Russia Today, a state-funded television network, was wounded in street fighting. Glinka got on the phone with Margarita Simonyan, the network's editor in chief, and tried to arrange a medical evacuation on a Russian military aircraft that would exfiltrate her and Polyakova, as well. "This bothered me," Polyakova said. "Why Simonyan? Why a military plane?" For her, Russia's state media, and certainly its armed forces, played central roles in the undeclared campaign in Ukraine. She wanted nothing to do with them.

For Glinka, interested in people and institutions only insofar as they could save lives, the choice was simple. Over the months to come, she returned to the Donbass many times. On one trip, she visited an orphanage in Slavyansk, a city that had been taken over by forces under the command of a man known as Igor Strelkov, a self-styled rebel generalissimo. Strelkov was actually Igor Girkin, a former FSB officer who had served in Chechnya and had developed a taste for costumed military reenactments—he often played the part of a White Army general from the Russian Civil War. In the Donbass, where he assembled a ragtag army of volunteers and war enthusiasts, he brought his battlefield fantasies to life. His nom de guerre translated as "Shooter." Clashes between Ukrainian forces and Strelkov's would-be warriors spilled out across the city. The orphanage was often trapped in the crossfire. Glinka saw dozens of soldiers from both sides who were injured or killed in the fighting—these were wounds far more violent and grotesque than anything she encountered at the train station in Moscow.

"I've been thinking about the pointlessness of war, its cruelty," she told a journalist that spring. "These young men seem so young and strong, but then you see what a single bullet or shell can do to a person." At the next meeting of the human rights council in Moscow, Glinka spoke of what she had witnessed in Donetsk. "Before you begin to discuss what I don't entirely understand," Glinka said, "I would like to inform you that Donetsk doesn't have enough medicines. What's more, there are children injured by bombs and mines." She proposed organizing the evacuation of the most seriously ill and wounded children to Russia, where they could be afforded more professional care.

Two hours later, when she was back at the Paveletsky basement, she got a call from the office of Vyacheslav Volodin, Putin's main advisor on domestic politics, one of the most powerful men in the country. He had attended the meeting of the presidential human rights council and, as one of his assistants relayed, had been moved by Glinka's speech. Could she come to his office tomorrow? When she arrived, Volodin told her that she had the Kremlin's backing to bring wounded and sick children out of the war zone in the Donbass and to Moscow for treatment. He would help with evacuation and transport, and once the children got to Russia, they would have places in state hospitals for treatment.

Glinka arrived back in Donetsk in June. If the war felt distant in the spring, it had now come to the center of the city: the battle for the airport went on seemingly twenty-four hours a day. Booms of exploding ordnance echoed among the high-rise apartment blocks.

Shells whizzed past periodically, landing in a storefront or balcony or bus stop. Shrapnel screamed through the air. At one moment, the streets could be full of life, and you could forget you were in the middle of a war zone; but then everyone would jump and run to cellars and bomb shelters to wait out the latest exchange of artillery fire, and the city became an empty, ghostly shell of itself. Doctors at local hospitals had given Glinka a list of nine children, the ones whose injuries or diseases they couldn't possibly treat given their conditions. She reserved a train car and brought them, along with their parents, back to Moscow. Once she had gotten them admitted to state hospitals around town, her phone rang again. It was the doctors in Donetsk. They had more children. Could she come back?

Another call came from the director of an orphanage in Kramatorsk, a regional hub fifty miles north of Donetsk that had been taken over by the separatists. Thirty-three children, from infants to four-year-olds, were all suffering from serious neurological disorders. Ukrainian forces were slowly beginning to recapture territory seized by the rebels in the early part of the summer, and Kramatorsk, by dint of its geography, was among the first places the Ukrainian army would reach. Its airport was considered a strategic target by both sides—and it happened to be situated right next to the children's home. The crackle of machine-gun fire and periodic blasts from mortar shells landing nearby shook the windows and sent the children into crying fits. The only way out of Kramatorsk was on a road that went through Slavyansk, still held by Strelkov's militia, which was in the habit of issuing capricious and impossible-to-follow edicts.

Glinka somehow managed to get Ukrainian officers and rebel commanders alike to allow her and the children at the Kramatorsk hospital safe passage. She agreed to hand the children over to an orphanage in the Ukrainian city of Kharkov, 120 miles away, but would have to pass through rebel-held territory to get there. Malaysia Airlines Flight 17 had been shot down just a few days before: it was clear the war had entered a new cycle of escalation, but what that would mean on the ground was still unclear. Glinka had to get a sign-off from both sides for every kilometer of the route: here was a separatist checkpoint, there was a stretch of road blocked by mines, here was the point where Ukrainian forces would take the children and drive them onward to Kharkov. Even the time she would set off from Kramatorsk had to be debated and approved; the mutually agreed upon cease-fire would only last for so long.

Glinka was met early in the morning in Donetsk by a driver named Tolik, who showed up in an old, beat-up ambulance. They drove to Kramatorsk and picked up the first five children. Glinka used gauze bandages to strap the older ones into the pair of stretchers that stood in the back of the vehicle; the smaller children she took in her lap, one on each knee. The drive took an hour and a half. She and Tolik were quiet the whole way—they didn't speak until just the two of them were headed back to Kramatorsk to pick up the next carload of children. For two days, they drove back and forth between Kramatorsk and the highway that leads to Kharkov, taking six or eight or even more children at a time.

Glinka later said she was naive to ever think the cease-fire would hold for more than a few minutes. No one shot directly at the ambulance, but bullets and artillery shells flew overheard, exploding in ever-increasing proximity. Out the window, Glinka saw a pair of dead civilians in the grass. She frantically called her military contacts on both sides: "You said you weren't going to shoot, but I'm looking right now at two dead bodies that are still warm!" Her interlocutors asked where she was, what checkpoint had she just passed. Tolik told her that stopping to ask the armed men on the side of the road the location of the particular checkpoint they were guarding was a good way to get a bullet in the head yourself, so she dropped it, and the two drove in silence some more.

At the end of the first day, as Glinka and Tolik were coming back, they became concerned on the approach to Slavyansk. Glinka later recalled the scene: "It was dark, and we got lost. We didn't know where we were driving." They had no GPS. "We had no idea where to go." The flash of a tracer round whizzed past the ambulance. Glinka yelled at Tolik to step on it, and they lurched forward, but that only attracted more gunfire. By then, Glinka had become fluent in the sounds various weapons make when fired, and she heard what she knew to be a shoulder-launched missile. She and Tolik lay on their front seats in terror, before Glinka yelled at Tolik to open the driver's side door and slide out onto the road. The night was cold, and suddenly eerily still. A number of men in military fatigues emerged from the darkness and questioned them: Where were they headed, with what purpose, didn't they know it was dangerous to drive on these roads at night?—the standard assortment of hectoring from men in mismatched camouflage guarding a back road in wartime. Finally the men let them go and pointed the way back to Kramatorsk. There was no running water there, however, and Glinka badly needed a shower: a number of the smaller children, frightened and carsick during the journey, had peed or thrown up on her in the ambulance. She went back to Donetsk, where, at five in the morning, she finally bathed, put on a new pair of scrubs, and, as the morning light washed over the battlefields of the Donbass, headed back to the orphanage. By the end of the next day, she and Tolik had driven all thirty-three children out from Kramatorsk.

In telling the story of Tolik and the children from Kramatorsk, Glinka never distinguished who exactly had been shooting at her: Was it Ukrainian troops, or the Russian-backed rebels? She claimed not to know, or really care. "I can't figure out these people in camouflage," she once said, and you believed her—she wasn't there to determine who was on what side, who controlled this checkpoint or that stretch of road. Were the Sparta or Aidar battalions on the side of Kyiv or the separatists? Such questions were immaterial. "It's probably fair to say she didn't look at the bigger picture," Gleb said. "But that was because she truly didn't understand war. For her, it was senseless in the truest sense of the word. It defied any meaning whatsoever."

But Glinka was no fool; she was not naive about how the world worked. She had to know that the war in the Donbass, the shelling and gunfire and explosions threatening those children, had been instigated by the very people who now promised to help her: Putin's officials in the Kremlin. There was plenty of genuine discontent and anti-Kyiv suspicion in the Donbass, but it took Russian money, weapons, and volunteer fighters—all directed from the shadows by the security services—for tensions to escalate into a full-blown armed conflict. But all that felt murky to Glinka. Not poking around in the details of the war was essential to her mission. "Yes, I purposely keep neutral. I don't want to make clear my position," she said. "I try to separate myself from everything that prevents me from saving a person's life." Not entirely unlike Heda Saratova, Glinka was in the ironic position of relying on the state to help those who, in some sense, were victimized by that very same state. Glinka was driven by a genuine and rare altruism that Saratova lacked—her motives were often more immediate and based in the crude logic of survival—but the two women did share a certain pragmatism, in which the moral value of helping a person in need trumped how that help might be obtained. I got the sense that whereas Saratova often ended up helping, or at least protecting, herself most of all, Glinka—whatever one thought of her compromises—delivered humanitarian aid on a scale that couldn't be denied.

Throughout that summer, Glinka made a dozen more trips to the Donbass, each time bringing out scores of children and their families. When the main water station near Donetsk was bombed, she arranged medical evacuations for three boys who suffered from kidney conditions and depended on regular dialysis treatment, which required two hundred liters of water. Russian officials provided specially equipped medical train cars and even planes, which transported the sick and injured to Moscow and other Russian towns. The government took on the cost of their complicated and lengthy treatment. This amounted to an "algorithm," as Glinka called it, that required the Russian state's willingness to provide its logistical muscle and resources.

No small part of the Kremlin's enthusiasm for her work in the Donbass was transparently cynical: it was easy PR, a way to show that Russia was a benevolent actor, interested in lessening the pain and suffering of the most innocent. The implicit message, as Gleb put it, was "How bad can we really be when we have Doctor Liza?" She became a regular subject on Russian state television, crucial to the Kremlin's information war. "Liza wasn't bothered by the state extracting some propaganda value from her activities," Fedotov told me. "She saw it the other way around—she was using the state to do good."

Glinka proved to have a genuine and powerful effect on high-ranking bureaucrats, even ministers. Part of that was structural, and particular to the logic of power in the Putin system. Once she joined the Kremlin human rights council, "people were afraid that she was one handshake away from the president, and so therefore it's wiser to do what she asks than not," Gleb said. "But she also managed to awaken some deeply repressed vestiges of conscience." Russian officials weren't uniformly cold, unfeeling sadists. She knew that many were capable of empathy and charity, and, if given the opportunity, could act with generosity and care. Ksenia Sokolova, a journalist and editor who became close to Glinka, said Glinka performed a kind of psychological—even spiritual—service for her interlocutors in positions of power. "These people know that they are doing a lot of vile things. Deep down, they feel like sinners," Sokolova told me. "They want an absolution—and Liza could offer it to them. They saw her as a holy figure, and by helping her they could share in this holiness. Atone for their sins."

Fedotov, as the head of the Kremlin's human rights council, used his status and access to pass along Glinka's requests to higher-ups in the state hierarchy. He often found that her name carried more weight than his own. "When I would go to Volodin and say 'Slava, Liza needs us to do this or that,' he answered right away: 'Of course, consider it done.' He understood immediately." The same was true with the defense ministry or the emergency services. If Doctor Liza needed a special plane for medical evacuations or a dozen beds in Moscow clinics, officials responded with uncharacteristic speed and efficiency. "I used her name like a magic key," Fedotov told me. "I would always say, 'This is Liza's proposal, Liza's initiative, Liza is working on this,' and it became a priority." Aleshkovsky, the photographer and charity organizer, told me, "She could open any door, she could solve any problem—there are very few people in Russia who can do this. It's a kind of bureaucratic nuclear weapon, and she used it for good."

As Glinka understood it, she was working the way she always had, just with more resources and opportunities to help a wider number of people. Her cooperation with the Russian state in bringing children out of the Donbass merely represented an expansion of what she had been doing all these years, not any fundamental shift. But as Glinka's reliance on the Kremlin increased, many of her earlier champions began to have misgivings. She started showing up less at Fair Aid's basement office and rarely made it to the regular Wednesday missions at the train station.

The Donbass was, at best, a distraction from what she and Fair Aid were known for. Some feared it was worse than that, a moment of bartering one's reputation and conscience for unclear benefit. Others found Glinka's willful blindness to the Kremlin's culpability in Ukraine not just upsetting, but perhaps even disqualifying. If some years before, Glinka had gotten donations from people who said she could spend the funds on anything but the homeless, now she heard the opposite: donors began sending money on the condition that she would spend it only on the Russian homeless and on nothing to do with the war. The nasty messages changed, too—they weren't about Glinka undermining natural selection, but about what might, or should, happen to her on her missions to the Donbass: "Die, bitch!" "I hope your children drop dead!"

Glinka was confused, and upset. "It didn't make sense to her," Sokolova said. She was worn down, physically and emotionally exhausted. As the fighting on the ground escalated, her trips became more fraught and logistically complicated. They stretched from a few days to a week or more. Emotions were raw; her attempts at neutrality were taken as the exact opposite, with each side certain the other was to blame. Either Russia was a nefarious and meddlesome power, a warmonger, and so was anyone who had anything to do with the state, or, alternatively, Ukraine was a Fascist oppressor, and anyone who didn't acknowledge that was complicit in the suffering of the people of the Donbass. Lana Zhurkina, the Fair Aid volunteer who became its spokesperson, accompanied Glinka on a number of trips. They were once riding in a bus that became trapped between two opposing troop positions, bullets and shells flying past them in a terrifying rumble. Zhurkina told Glinka that she looked terrible, like a squeezed lemon. She needed a rest. Glinka agreed, but never managed to take one. "Liza loved flowers, perfume, beautiful dresses, talks with her girlfriends," Zhurkina told me. "But with the war all of that went away. Her levity was gone."

One day, I met up with Svetlana Sergienko, who introduced herself to me as "a member of the liberal intelligentsia—I'm not afraid of this word." She first encountered Glinka on a television program speaking about hospice care, and began to read her blog. Sometime later, Sergienko ran into Glinka at a party for an independent, opposition-minded magazine in Moscow and, after that, became a regular volunteer at Fair Aid. Sergienko said that she understood, of course, that a doctor doesn't always have the pleasure of moral choice: if you come across the scene of a car accident, you treat the wounded, starting with whoever is most in immediate need, even if that is the driver who was drunk behind the wheel. That was obvious, and, in Glinka's work with the most marginal and forgotten members of society, deeply admirable. Still, Sergienko found her involvement in the war in Ukraine worrying and unpleasant. She once tried to raise her concerns in a quiet moment with Glinka—"an emotional protest," as she described it to me. "I wasn't upset that she was going to the Donbass to try and save these kids," she said. "Rather, I was upset that by doing so, she was creating a romantic image for people I consider, well, bandits. This confused and frightened me." Glinka quickly ended the conversation, and Sergienko never raised the subject again. "I got the sense that the more she understood, the less she wanted to talk about it," Sergienko said. "She knew everything perfectly well on her own."

AT THE END OF the summer of 2014, with Ukrainian forces poised to overrun a number of strategic positions held by the rebels—including the city of Donetsk—Russia launched an unambiguous, if still officially denied, land invasion. A number of regular Russian army units, including tanks and heavy artillery, poured across the border, decimating Ukrainian forces and forcing then president Petro Poroshenko to agree to immediate peace talks. In October, with the shaky cease-fire in place, the members of the Kremlin human rights council gathered for a regular working meeting. This time, Putin himself showed up.

Fedotov opened the proceedings with a verbose preamble, a defense of humanistic values. He is a sound and forceful speaker, and listening to him, one can think that if a person with direct access to Putin is saying such things, things in Russia can't be all that bad. "You don't have to love civil society," he said. "But you can't ignore it, or try and subdue or replace it." The modern world is determined by the value of the individual. "It is the main resource of the future, and, therefore, the main object of our common concern," he went on. "These are my opening remarks, Vladimir Vladimirovich," he said, turning to Putin. "And now, if you will allow me, I will give the floor to Elizaveta Petrovna Glinka, our beloved Doctor Liza."

Glinka's tone was serious and clinical, befitting a doctor. "I will speak about children and the wounded," she said. She went on to tell Putin and the council members about the patients from the Kramatorsk children's home and plenty more cases: the young epileptics who lost access to antiseizure medicine and are regularly driven into uncontrollable fits by the constant explosions and blast waves; the five children who, two days earlier, had been hit with a cluster bomb, two of them killed on the spot and another sliced from head to toe by shrapnel; fifteen-year-old Yulia from Gorlovka, a town under rebel control, who survived an artillery fusillade that killed sixty-one people and left her with blown-out eardrums and wounds all over her body. Glinka's organization had arranged transport out of the Donbass for these children and their families and supplied them with basic medicines and treatment. But there were things Glinka couldn't do for them, like find them long-term places in hospitals and rehabilitation facilities, let alone pay for the months, if not years, of surgeries and treatment they would require. Such children are "the most innocent victims in the truest sense," she said, "and until we find ways to solve the conflict, their number will only increase." She had just received word of sixty-two more children who doctors in the Donbass said needed urgent evacuation. She would be leaving shortly to retrieve them.

Most urgently, Glinka told Putin, children were suffering for purely bureaucratic reasons, and here, Putin, as Russia's president, could help them with the stroke of a pen. Russian law did not allow for citizens of foreign states to receive advanced medical care in Russia unless they asked for refugee status. Not all families evacuated from the Donbass wanted to become refugees; many hoped that once the war was over, they could return home, and didn't want to become stuck in Russia forever. "Perhaps you can pass a temporary law or issue some kind of decree?" she asked. One word from Putin, and everyone Glinka brought out of the war zone would have access to the best trauma clinics and specialists in Russia. She finished her address with one last request to Putin. "I want to ask you to express your gratitude to certain people," she told Putin, going on to list a number of state officials who she said had helped her in her missions to the Donbass—Volodin, Putin's top aide, most of all.

Putin thanked Glinka for her presentation, and listened to the other members of the council. He played the role of a paternal tsar, deeply moved by the tales of human suffering, as if he was as confused as anyone gathered there as to how such a vicious war could erupt just like that, how such terrible forces had taken hold, how neighbors could begin shooting at each other with such lack of pity. "We can't just stand back and watch people die," Putin said. He promised the full support of the Russian state for Glinka's initiatives and said he would make sure to find a legal mechanism to pay for the medical care of the sick and injured. It was a transparently cynical ploy—Putin seemed to relish his chance to act the concerned humanitarian, tending to the injured in a fire he himself helped to start—but Glinka had gotten what she wanted. Putin issued Government Order 1134, giving state money and backing to the evacuation and treatment of children from the Donbass.

The apparent cynicism of the exchange confirmed the suspicions of those who had grown wary of Glinka's new profile. She had tried to steer clear of politics, but the thing about war is that it is an inherently political event. Neutrality itself is a position: refusing to apportion blame for violence means letting one side or the other off the hook. Yuly Rybakov, a human rights activist who had been imprisoned as a dissident in the seventies—among other anti-Soviet acts, he had scrawled "You may crucify freedom, but the human soul knows no shackles" on the wall of the Peter and Paul Fortress in Leningrad—watched a recording of the Kremlin meeting and was repulsed. He listened to Putin commiserate with the Ukrainian people, and wondered, "Does no one have the courage to say, Mister President, it's terrible, but after all it's you who provoked this carnage, you who splashed kerosene—weapons, money, soldiers—onto the spark of discontent in Donetsk." Rybakov understood the logic of staying silent, that the positions of those on the human rights council were fragile and uncertain, and that such a statement would force their immediate resignation without changing Putin's policy in Ukraine one iota. But still, Rybakov, who spoke for many in Russia's liberal and civil-society quarters, was uneasy. "When not a single holy fool dares to say that you shouldn't worship a murderous tsar," he said, "then the tsar remains assured that he is righteous and universally loved, and the country sinks back into the middle ages."

It boiled down to how one should use one's audience with the sovereign. Glinka chose to extract as much utilitarian benefit as possible. Yes, she said later, I singled out Volodin for praise. "I believe that even if Volodin and other powerful people who help me have done atrocious things in their lives, then, by saving from death Bogdan, Ksenia, Masha, Kolya, Vasya, Danila, and all the other children who would have surely perished there under bombardment, they have bought themselves a place in heaven."

Some weeks later, when Glinka was briefly in Moscow in between trips to Donetsk, she got a call from Volodin's office. The Kremlin was planning to organize a peace march in the center of Moscow. Would Glinka sign an open letter in support of the demonstration? "If it's against war, I'll be the first to sign," she said. But the march was, of course, a more complicated affair, not so much a call for peace as a choreographed gesture of solidarity and loyalty, a way for the Kremlin to convince society—and itself—that the Russian people were united in their support for its policies in Ukraine. Glinka was in Ukraine the day of the demonstration, but she saw coverage afterward, and recognized its political cast. Although she never made her frustration public, her friends and colleagues could see that she was upset. Zhurkina, her longtime colleague, told me that Glinka knew she had been used but blamed herself: she was terribly exhausted, too overextended to properly focus, and had naively trusted those who asked for her signature on the letter. "She signed up for this from the very best motives," Zhurkina said. "And once you do that, you have no choice—you follow through to the very end."

That meant speaking in ways that loosely paralleled the Kremlin's own narrative for the war, or at least didn't contradict it. "As a person who regularly visits Donetsk," she told an interviewer, "I have not seen Russian troops there, whether people like to hear that or not." The Kremlin persistently denied the presence of Russian soldiers on the battlefield, even as it was clear that intelligence officers and special forces were guiding operations behind the scenes; and at a number of key moments in the war, regular Russian army units propped up separatist forces and pushed back the Ukrainian military. She later explained that she was speaking only from her own impressions or experience, not making a larger statement about Russia's role. All she saw was a bunch of men in fatigues running around with weapons. "Who am I, an OSCE monitor or war correspondent?" she asked. "Why should I distinguish what troops are whose when I'm busy transporting wounded children through several checkpoints in an old jeep?" It's not like the Russian soldiers in the Donbass announced themselves, and even journalists who were set on finding them found only glancing traces, rather than conclusive proof. If Glinka indeed never saw anyone who was clearly and unambiguously a Russian soldier, it's also true that she had every reason not to look too closely.

Glinka never fully came out and said it, but her understanding of the war and how she spoke about it came to match, quietly and subtly, Moscow's preferred version of events. "There are militia fighters, and there are Ukrainian troops, who are sorting things out between themselves," she told a reporter from a Russian Orthodox news portal. It's a civil war, she explained: two opposing sides from within Ukrainian society are fighting each other, she implied, with the war's causes rooted in long-simmering discontent in the Donbass and social and political cleavages within modern Ukraine. This version of events, favored by the Kremlin, made Russia a concerned observer but ultimately an external actor. As with so much about the war and its causes, that narrative was partly true but woefully incomplete—Kyiv's neglect and mismanagement of relations with the population of the Donbass was the kindling, but Russia added the kerosene.

Inevitably, Glinka was drawn into discussions of geopolitics. "Russia now faces a very difficult environment," she told an interviewer, referring to escalating sanctions and diplomatic opprobrium from Western capitals. "These accusations are not substantiated by anything." She was not on anyone's side, she constantly repeated—but, as she put it once, if Western governments say Russia is so terrible, why don't they help Ukraine's most innocent and vulnerable themselves? "Why is there no German or British humanitarian aid? Why doesn't everyone who has imposed sanctions against us go help those whom, they believe, we have harmed?" The question was fair but ignored the reasons the sanctions were enacted in the first place. Western countries and institutions were by no means above criticism, but to be credible, some portion of scrutiny had to be directed at Russia, too. In that same interview, Glinka said that the Moscow office of the Red Cross declined to provide a letter of support for her missions to deliver medical supplies to the Donbass; when she asked why, she said, the head of the office told her, "We don't like the policies of your president." The Red Cross denied that such an exchange ever took place, and explained that it carries out only its own aid missions and is not in the business of approving or disapproving of those led by others.

Glinka grew withdrawn and suspicious, coiled in a defensive crouch. One night, she showed up at Ksenia Sokolova's apartment in Moscow and started bawling. Sokolova had known her for almost a decade, but had never seen her like this. She had a tired, gray face, but Sokolova noticed her eyes most of all: they were Glinka's most pronounced feature, those wide and bright spheres of energy, but now the fire had gone out and they moved with a dull, mechanical rhythm. She was worn down by having every utterance of hers dissected, every action parsed for signs of malevolent intent. Even as she opened up to Sokolova about the pressures she was under, she remained on guard, careful in choosing her words. "I got the sense that, having chosen to walk on this thin ice, she understood she had to take certain precautionary measures," Sokolova told me.

When I spoke with Sokolova, she suggested that it was inevitable that Glinka would drift away from the world of Moscow liberals and draw closer to her new benefactors. As many liberals disowned her, officials in the ruling apparatus welcomed her to their side—and opened their wallets to prove it. "What did the state represent for her?" Sokolova asked. "It expanded the scope of possibility. No one besides the state could provide her with planes, train cars, hundreds of millions of rubles every year to pay for the medical care of these children—and the influence to make all of this happen. This raises the stakes, and it gets harder to get out of the game."

Glinka told Sokolova that she missed the way things used to be, before the war, when she could spend a whole day in the freezing cold at Paveletsky station ladling hot soup into Styrofoam cups and stitching up head wounds of the homeless men she had come to know by name. But of course there was no going back. "She understood that in the end this resource will cost her something," Sokolova said.

Sokolova, an accomplished and high-profile interviewer who has worked for Russian television and glossy magazines, proposed that Glinka sit for one big, formal interview—let Sokolova ask her all the tough questions in a candid and all-encompassing conversation. Then Glinka could go quiet, freed from the pressure of having to respond to every snipe and attack on her and her fund. Glinka agreed. In the interview, Sokolova articulated what many Russian liberals found distasteful about Glinka's newfound proximity to Kremlin officials. "With your reputation, you give these people a kind of indulgence—that is, the opportunity to continue to sin," she told Glinka. "They continue this war, which leads to the death of hundreds, perhaps thousands of children—a few of which you will then be able to save thanks to their help. You become a tool they employ to buy their place in paradise, as you have said. And to buy it so cheaply! The price is to simply allow Glinka to go to the war zone, dodge some bombs, and save a few children. And you convince the villains that this cancels out all their sins."

Glinka weighed the thesis. "This is certainly a tough ethical inter-play," she told Sokolova. "But I'm sorry, I don't have the energy, time, or desire to analyze it all that closely. I have a specific goal. My task is to take out the wounded and sick children so that they receive professional medical care, free of charge, along with warm clothes, food, and medicine. And I do not care how it will be done." Doing battle with the "bloody regime," as she ironically put it, was not her job: it's not like the sign on her basement office reads "Doctor Liza's Fund for Fighting Putin." As for those who do see that as their mis-sion, well, God bless them. "Do they want to overthrow their rulers? Great, let them get to work! Let them risk their lives, follow their convictions to prison, come out as heroes, bring millions of support-ers to the streets inspired by their courage and heroism."

Glinka could never understand the focus on the political over the concrete. As a doctor this struck her as absurd, even immoral: Are we really going to have an unresolvable argument over political values instead of concentrating on the value of a human life? She couldn't make sense of what her opponents wanted. "Do you think it would be better if the children I brought out had died?" she asked Sokolova angrily. "Let's take Nikita Teplyakov, who needed a kidney trans-plant, and whom I was able to evacuate by train—thanks to Volodin, no less, I am not ashamed to say. Would you live better? You would get the opportunity to write a post: 'Putin's bloody regime crushed Nikita Teplyakov.'"

Their interview lasted a couple of hours. It was perhaps a cathar-tic experience for Glinka, but not one she particularly enjoyed. "She said that she didn't want to speak on this abstract level, that she didn't understand these conflicts," Sokolova told me. "But I think that of course she understood them. It's just that she had made her choice."

GLINKA'S REGULAR VISITS TO the long, hushed corridors of power, lined by cavernous offices with their heavy wooden furniture, didn't leave much of an impression on her. Friends and colleagues got the sense that she viewed these meetings as mere distractions and annoyances. Yet Glinka, like her interlocutors, was human, and it was impossible not to form relationships, even if ultimately of a delicate and circumscribed kind. She and Volodin developed a rapport. His family is from a village near Saratov, a city on the Volga, and he opened up to Glinka about the experience of his grandparents, who suffered during the Stalinist anti-kulak campaigns in the twenties and thirties, when peasants judged to be too prosperous had their land seized and faced repressions. This history weighed on Volodin, and led him to want to help people in need as a way to remember and honor the misfortune of his family, or so he said. (Volodin is not the cold, Machiavellian figure he seems, Mikhail Fedotov insisted: "This person has some very kind and good qualities, and Liza used these qualities to advance her own cause.")

Glinka was most comfortable, and most pleased, when she could leave behind her organizational duties and again serve as a simple doctor. "The scale exhausted her after a while," Gleb told me. "She was all about the intimacy of medicine." She felt most herself when she was holding the hand of a scared child, not letting go for hours and hours as they rode a bus out of the Donbass; or, back in Moscow, making the rounds at a hospital, learning everyone's names and asking how they felt today, who had what pain where, when they were scheduled for this or that operation.

In December 2014, Nadezhda Savchenko, a Ukrainian helicopter pilot awaiting trial in Russia, announced she was going on a hunger strike. At that point, Savchenko had been detained for five months. Russian prosecutors claimed she had acted as a spotter for a mortar attack in the Donbass that had killed two correspondents from Russian state television; Savchenko, however, said she had been kidnapped by separatists and brought across the border to Russia, where she was handed over to the security services and presented with made-up accusations. After two months of refusing food, Savchenko was weak and in ill health, and had lost more than forty pounds. Fedotov arranged with investigators overseeing Savchenko's case for him and Glinka to be admitted to see her in the hospital wing of Sailor's Rest, a notorious prison in northeast Moscow. The head of

Sailor's Rest agreed, but warned them not to expect much: Savchenko had brushed off earlier entreaties from other human rights advocates, and insisted on speaking Ukrainian, not Russian.

When Fedotov and Glinka showed up, Savchenko was withdrawn and hostile, refusing their attempts at making contact. But then Glinka, in Russian, started to ask her purely medical questions: What was her overall condition, where did she feel pain, could she sit in this position, or how about that one? Savchenko answered matter-of-factly. Glinka switched to the informal *ty* form of address, and spoke to Savchenko with a kind of motherly care, but without patronizing or belittling her and her ideals. It will be unpleasant, Glinka warned. They'll stick a tube down your throat and feed you all the same. Why not at least eat a little something yourself? Savchenko agreed. And so, every week or so, Glinka came to Sailor's Rest with packs of nutritional mixtures she picked up at a pharmacy in town. Savchenko accepted them, and gradually her health improved. The two women would often speak about the war, not so much its political causes as its human toll. At one point, Savchenko volunteered to write a letter from jail to President Poroshenko in Ukraine asking him to lift the blockade on medicines and supplies that Ukrainian border guards had prevented Glinka from bringing into rebel-occupied territory.

It's hard to know what to make of the relationship. Nikolay Polozov, Savchenko's lawyer, warned of a certain "mythologizing" of Glinka's role: even if she acted out of genuine compassion, it's clear the Russian authorities had their own interests in allowing her visits. "I'm quite sure that the calculation was to stop Savchenko's hunger strike, which at the time was causing no small amount of political pressure on the Kremlin," Polozov told me. Savchenko was circumspect and distant with Glinka, he said, just as she was with anyone she understood as representing the Russian side in Ukraine. What's more, Polozov said that Savchenko had described Glinka nudging her to admit her guilt and accept a pardon—an offer Savchenko rejected, but that certainly would have been preferable for the Kremlin to the uncomfortable spectacle of the drawn-out, open trial that resulted. (She was eventually found guilty by a Russian court, but two months after the verdict she was freed in a prisoner swap with Ukraine.)

The longer the war dragged on, the more Doctor Liza's legend grew among the vast majority of Russians who were untroubled by her new connections. She became a phenomenon, the most well-known and beloved charity worker in the country. "She disliked being at the center of attention, but she knew this was the only, or at least best, way to pull in more resources for the fund," Gleb told me. (Glinka's new position did not shift her policy of never accepting a single ruble of state money; all the funds for Fair Aid came from volunteer donations.) Among the public at large, the name "Doctor Liza" carried an inarguable moral weight, a testament to the startling and magnetic power of altruism in a country where venal self-interest had long become the norm, especially for those with a modicum of fame or influence. Being kind didn't make Glinka a sucker or a dupe, as had been the general presumption in Russia. Quite the opposite: she was ennobled by her generosity and care for others, the rare public figure in Putin-era Russia who seemed genuinely motivated by compassion and service. A polling firm put out its rating of the most promising political candidates, should they choose to run. Glinka was at the top of the list. She thought the idea ridiculous.

Given the power of the Doctor Liza brand, it was perhaps unavoidable that with Russia's entry into the war in Syria, Glinka would be pulled into that conflict as well. The idea came from the defense ministry: Perhaps Doctor Liza would join a humanitarian mission organized by the Russian military? She could visit hospitals, deliver medicines—and lend her gentle and caring image to the news programs on Russian state television. She was reluctant. "It was the first time she was being asked to do something that wasn't her initiative, but theirs," Gleb said. She worried that the scope of her work was getting out of control. "But she was tired, really drained, her guard was down." She and Fedotov traveled to the Russian air base near Latakia that fall.

In early December 2016, the Kremlin announced it would be issuing a new presidential award, to honor achievements in human rights and charity work. Glinka would be the first recipient. The ceremony was held in the Kremlin's Saint Catherine Hall, a soaring space with vaulted ceilings supported by gleaming white columns. Putin stood at the lectern and delivered a speech. "We can see what people can achieve when they answer their heart's call," he said. "Today, the values of humanism, compassion, and mercy find ever-greater resonance among our people and serve to unite them." It was hard to listen to Putin talk of compassion and mercy, but in that moment his admiration for Glinka seemed genuine. In any case, the award was hers, not his. "Elizaveta Glinka is a familiar figure to hospital patients, people facing hardship, children in the Donbass and Syria," Putin said. He pinned a medal on her lapel and handed her a bouquet of pastel-colored flowers. She didn't find a place to set them on the lectern, so turned to Putin and said, "Hold these, please." "With pleasure," he said, smiling as he took them and stood off to the side. The crowd murmured with delight: it's not every day a Kremlin visitor asks Putin to hold her stuff. ("That's what gave her such moral authority," Gleb told me. "She was exactly the same with everyone.")

Glinka unfolded a piece of paper and began to read, glancing over to look at Putin and out into the hall. "The greatest right of all is the right to live," she said. "This right is constantly being trampled underfoot in these difficult times." She acknowledged that the past years spent in war zones had taken a toll on her, but such was the mission. "Our job is to protect human rights and we are outside of politics, just like the people we protect. We are on the side of peace, dialogue, and cooperation with all." She spoke of her next trip to the Donbass, scheduled for the following day, and, after that, another visit to hospitals in Syria. Her voice was soft but forceful. "We never know if we will return alive, because war is hell on earth, and I know what I'm talking about." Two weeks later, she boarded the flight to Syria.

CHAPTER 7

SUBTLE CREATURES

—

ONE SATURDAY EVENING IN DECEMBER 2017, AS IT HAS REGU-larly for nearly two hundred years, the stage of the Bolshoi The-atre, draped by its famous scarlet and gold curtain, featured the long-anticipated premiere of a new ballet. Tickets sold out within hours of going on sale, with many left waiting in the cold in a long line outside the box office. The Bolshoi's capacious hall, ringed by teetering loggia boxes, was filled with so many members of the ruling elite—from Dmitry Peskov, Putin's press secretary, to Konstantin Ernst, the head of Channel One—that the event seemed an updated version of an old Communist Party Central Committee congress.

The highly awaited ballet was a staging of the life and work of Rudolf Nureyev, the famed dancer and choreographer whose defec-tion from the Soviet Union, in Paris, in 1961, made international head-lines. The director was Kirill Serebrennikov, who, at forty-eight, was Russia's most celebrated theater personage, an artist whose tastes run to the experimental and provocative. *Nureyev* portrays its hero as a genius whose talent, like his idiosyncrasies, made him difficult for the bosses of the time to understand—an inevitable object of suspicion. The dancing is broken up by the intermittent reading of text aloud, which muses on the ideas of art and exile. One passage, which quotes a letter received by Nureyev after he had emigrated to Europe, la-ments how Russia is a country that "does not value its heroes." The close of the first act features a sensuous and lyrical pas de deux between Nureyev and the acclaimed Danish dancer Erik Bruhn, Nureyev's partner of many decades.

Serebrennikov missed the performance. He was at home, in his two-bedroom apartment on Prechistenka Street. The previous spring, prosecutors accused Serebrennikov of fraud, alleging he had embezzled 68 million rubles, or more than a million dollars, in state money during the production of theatrical festivals and performances over several years. He was now in his fourth month of house arrest. If found guilty, he could face up to ten years in prison. He was one of four defendants charged in a wide-ranging case that was at once numbingly typical (the Putin state regularly makes a show of putting on trial those it says misallocate budget funds) and deeply abnormal (before Serebrennikov, the last Russian theater director to be arrested was Vsevolod Meyerhold, who was repressed on Stalin's orders in 1939 and shot the next year). Few in Moscow believed that Serebrennikov's real problems had anything to do with money.

After the dancers took their bows, receiving a standing ovation, the production team came onstage wearing shirts reading "Freedom to the director!" with Serebrennikov's face on them. Some in the crowd shouted, "Bravo, Kirill!"—cries of praise for the one person not present onstage, as if shouting his name could, in an act of fitting surrealism, return him to the theater.

The facts of Serebrennikov's criminal case were overshadowed by public speculation about its import. What message was the Kremlin trying to send to the country's artistic and cultural figures? If Serebrennikov did commit a transgression, what was the true nature of it? Or was the randomness of the charge the point, the idea that any director or artist or performer could end up in Serebrennikov's position? No matter the answer, his case appeared to be a sign of a deeper and troubling shift in Russian political life, a symbol—and a warning—of a state that had grown more inflexible, rapacious, and unpredictable, liable to turn even on those it once feted. It was not accidental that Serebrennikov came to face criminal charges at a time when Russia's ruling ideology had turned inward and conservative, at times veering toward the outright retrograde and obscurantist.

Nureyev should have premiered the previous July. But two days before the first show, the director of the Bolshoi suddenly announced its cancellation. The supposed reason was that the production was "not ready." That seemed unlikely. A dance critic at *Kommersant,* a Russian daily, who had seen snippets of rehearsals declared that the world of ballet had not produced anything "bigger and more significant" in years, and that its choreography was like "breathing." She predicted that *Nureyev* would be the Bolshoi's most "successful and profitable ballet since the fall of the U.S.S.R." A more probable culprit, then, was the ballet's nudity and overt theme of homosexual love. (Nikita Mikhalkov, a powerful film director close to the Kremlin, told *Vice* that the Bolshoi was not the place to "hang Nureyev's cock.") Rumors swirled of a call to the Bolshoi from a high-ranking Kremlin official, or a politically influential Orthodox cleric, which could have led to the theater's abrupt decision not to stage the work. That Serebrennikov had by then clearly fallen out of official favor made his ballet an obvious target.

Yet Putin's Russia is marked by a discursive, nonlinear quality, full of contradictions for anyone trying to decode the meaning of events. And so, after a five-month delay, the Bolshoi presented *Nureyev* after all; but Serebrennikov remained out of sight, awaiting trial, the outcome of which would define the relationship between art and the state in the Putin era going forward. The question is, What is the aberration and what is the norm—that a ballet like *Nureyev* was celebrated on the main stage of the Bolshoi, or that its director was under house arrest?

SEREBRENNIKOV WAS A PARTICULARLY Russian type of rebel: one who sought, and attained, mainstream success, often with the blessing and support of the state. He was, for a while, the house avant-gardiste of Putin-era Russia. Serebrennikov grew up in Rostov-on-Don, a city in southern Russia known for its scrappy, mafiosi-tinged local folklore. His mother was a schoolteacher of Russian, his father a urologist—in other words, archetypical members of the late-Soviet provincial intelligentsia. Serebrennikov was educated as a physicist, but showed a talent for theater from an early age, and was a popular director of local plays and televised films.

In the early 2000s, when Serebrennikov was in his thirties, he came to Moscow, where he staged a number of successful performances at the Sovremennik, a theater founded during the Khrushchev thaw, in the 1950s, and the Moscow Art Theatre, the historic stage made famous by Konstantin Stanislavsky and his eponymous acting method. I spoke with Mikhail Shvydkoy, Russia's minister of culture at that time, who remains a high-profile and influential figure in the arts. Shvydkoy presided over a relatively laissez-faire period in the state's role in culture, including support for innovative, and at times unconventional, art forms—sometimes making the ministry more progressive than other arms of the state, or even the viewing public. As he put it to me, "I always repeat the words of Alexander Pushkin: 'The government is the sole European in all of Russia.'"

Shvydkoy watched Serebrennikov's career develop and appreciated not only his thoroughly modern sensibilities, his desire to push against the conservative strain in Russian theater, but also his professionalism and creative ability to execute that vision. "Kirill is very talented and very genuine," Shvydkoy told me. "Yes, he is extravagant, and he creates a certain element of provocation in his art, but this is natural and correct." All the same, Shvydkoy went on, "he always existed inside the system: he worked with Moscow's largest theaters, or at the Bolshoi, he filmed movies."

Serebrennikov's star rose in tandem with the Putin system's purposeful dalliance with contemporary art. For a time, in the mid- to late 2000s—during Putin's second presidential term and Medvedev's short-lived reign—the Kremlin launched a kind of stage-managed social modernization, which came to include state support for innovation and experimentation in the arts. Anna Narinskaya, a longtime journalist and arts critic, told me that by fostering the avant-garde, the Kremlin hoped to send different messages to different audiences. For the West, it was an "invitation to get involved," as Narinskaya put it: foreign curators and architects and contemporary artists regularly passed through Moscow to present or oversee large-scale projects. Russia's own intelligentsia and creative professionals were meant to see the state's interest as a "call for collaboration—come work for us." And the country's young people got a relatable style, an aesthetic that was attractive and modern.

Not that Serebrennikov and others had any real choice. Much of Russian cultural life is dependent on state funding; nearly all of the country's more than six hundred major theaters are state institutions, and rely on government support for 70 percent of their budgets. Fund-raising and endowments are almost nonexistent. "You don't have a choice between making a film with state participation or without," Narinskaya said. "The question is: Do you want to make a film at all?"

In the mid- to late 2000s, the person behind the Kremlin's efforts to attract—some might say co-opt—artists and cultural figures was Vladislav Surkov, the influential advisor to Putin who did the most to construct the country's postmodern, make-believe politics. Surkov is a self-styled cultural sophisticate, whose tastes range from William S. Burroughs to Tupac Shakur. He and his deputies would regularly fly to Salzburg for the opera. It was Surkov who came up with the term "sovereign democracy" to describe the Putin system, essentially a clever way of masking soft authoritarianism. He deftly created stylish youth groups and political parties. He arranged for a beloved Russian alternative rock singer, Zemfira, to perform at a pro-Putin youth camp in the countryside. In Moscow, he organized a regular evening of poetry and experimental theater with actors who trained with Dmitry Brusnikin, a director and pedagogue with a cultish following.

It wasn't long before Surkov took an interest in Serebrennikov, and Serebrennikov in Surkov. Alexey Chesnakov, a former Kremlin political advisor who worked for Surkov, told me that Surkov knew that Serebrennikov and other artists of his type "felt things very subtly, in a way that Surkov understood, but other officials did not, and could, in a way, elevate the state." The two men were not especially close, but their interests overlapped to some degree. Serebrennikov could use the resources of the state to realize his creative ambitions; and Surkov could harness the talents of such people like Serebrennikov to further his own vision of Putin-era cultural life, at once vibrant and edgy, yet within prescribed boundaries. "It was a time when a lot of people were attracted to the state, to the process that was taking place," Chesnakov said. "It wasn't merely profitable to be close to the state, but interesting."

Narinskaya, the journalist and critic, recalled Surkov as "this kind of gray cardinal." He seemed to run the whole of Russia from behind the scenes. "He was demonic, mysterious. How could you not be interested in him? Plus, he had the power to give you a lot of money." As for Serebrennikov's part, Narinskaya went on, "He knew how to make nice with the bosses. He was friends with ministers and oligarchs and beautiful socialites."

In some ways, the relationship between Surkov and Serebrennikov resembled that between Trotsky and Meyerhold, the avant-garde director; or between the writer Isaac Babel and Nikolay Yezhov, the sociopathic head of Stalin's secret police. Both Meyerhold and Babel were, for a time, bathed in the attention of the Soviet state, only to perish during the purges. Serebrennikov's rise and fall was far more subdued. And he never had any ideological affinity with the regime. Quite the opposite. His politics were openly liberal, and in 2011 and 2012 he even frequented the anti-Putin protests. Surkov's innovation was to downplay ideology and bet on style, not substance. This, after all, is how someone like Ernst was able to rise inside the state system; despite his refined, art-house tastes, he was an aesthete, not a liberal, as one of his friends pointed out to me. The key difference between Ernst and Serebrennikov is that Ernst was ultimately a statist, who recognized and accepted the state's primacy, whereas Serebrennikov was just happy to use the state's resources to carry out big and ambitious projects. He didn't ascribe to the state any greater metaphysical importance beyond that. Ernst entered into an alliance of belief; for Serebrennikov, this alliance was merely tactical, and thus perhaps destined to be impermanent.

The height of Serebrennikov's dalliance with Surkov came in 2011, when Serebrennikov staged a theatrical production of *Almost Zero,* a novel likely written by Surkov under a thinly disguised pen name. I heard various explanations for how Serebrennikov came to direct the play: one person suggested it was an implicit condition of being given the budget to stage a large-scale contemporary arts festival; others said that Serebrennikov saw something curious, even subversive, in the text, and set out to make a play that was less than flattering to its author. In his book on Putin-era Russia, *Nothing Is True and Everything Is Possible,* Peter Pomerantsev describes the sold-out premiere, in Moscow. The crowd was full of "hard, clever men who rule the country and their stunning female satellites," Pomerantsev writes. For the play, Serebrennikov cleverly switched out the main character's cold cynicism, the theme of Surkov's novel, and made him racked with doubt and self-loathing. Serebrennikov's actors talked directly to the audience, accusing them of being "at ease in a world of nepotism, corruption and violence." Pomerantsev described their reaction: "The bohemians in the audience laughed uncomfortably. The hard men and their satellites stared ahead unblinking, as if these provocations had nothing to do with them." As he writes, "Thus the great director pulled off a feat entirely worthy of the Age of Surkov: he pleased his political masters—Surkov sponsors an arts festival that Serebrennikov runs—while preserving his liberal integrity."

Not long after, Oleg Kashin, a Russian journalist fond of provoking his subjects, asked Serebrennikov why he had chosen to collaborate with Surkov. Serebrennikov's answer was, effectively, why not? He said that *Almost Zero* was a "talented, representative, and interesting work that, in a very serious way, speaks to our time." He went on to tell Kashin, "I don't think that theater should only engage in pure art, stuck in its ivory tower. I'm interested in theater, and cinema, that deals with life, is right in the thick of it, asking disturbing questions, ready to pronounce some unpleasant words."

IN MARCH 2011, not long before the *Almost Zero* premiere, aides at the Ministry of Culture passed a message to Serebrennikov: he should ask for the state's blessing. Medvedev was then president, and he was as responsible as Surkov for the state's interest in and support for cultural projects and contemporary art. Medvedev had championed the idea of building a top-down, state-led business incubator called the Skolkovo Innovation Center, and now he wanted to do something similar in the arts—a state-supported initiative called Platforma. Sere-brennikov would be one of its directors. "Serebrennikov was told that if he were to come forward with this request, it would be ap-proved," a former employee of the Ministry of Culture told me.

For a time, the experimental stagings at Platforma—which also featured dance, music, and media art—were among the most relevant and energetic in the country. Serebrennikov's production of *Scum-bags,* a raw, cruel play about Russia's lost generation of the 1990s, was particularly successful. Surkov imagined that the project would in-spire a network of cultural centers around the country, provincial hubs for contemporary art and innovation. Around the same time, in 2012, I went to the Bolshoi to see *The Golden Cockerel,* Nikolay Rimsky-Korsakov's opera from 1907, which Serebrennikov turned into a satire of contemporary Kremlin politics. A military parade fea-turing huge missiles being towed across the stage was an allusion to Russia's annual Victory Day celebration; a horde of children glorify-ing the tsar was a nod to the pro-Putin youth groups fomented by Surkov.

Perhaps no bureaucratic appointment did more to remake the sur-face experience of life in Moscow over the last decade than the nam-ing, in 2011, of Sergei Kapkov as the city's minister of culture. Kapkov, then in his late thirties, was close to the oligarch Roman Abramovich, who had kept his fortune intact throughout changing political winds and had developed a taste for contemporary art. The first large-scale project Kapkov oversaw in Moscow was the widely loved renovation of Gorky Park, in which rows of decrepit Soviet-era arcade games were cleared out; in their place came businesses like the café opened by my friend and neighbor Dasha, who set up an outdoor bar alongside gravel lanes for playing *pétanque,* which proved immediately popular with twentysomethings and young families. A program to refresh the city's network of public libraries followed. Kapkov's name became shorthand for a benevolent and tasteful form of authoritarian modernization, a top-down makeover of the capital that wasn't necessarily democratic—Kapkov relied more on his own judgments than on any sort of open civic process—but was worldly, clever, and attractive.

In 2012, Kapkov asked Serebrennikov to take over the Gogol Center, a struggling venue on a side street behind the Kursky train station. The theater had trouble drawing sizable crowds and had taken to blocking off half the seats in the main hall. The appointment was controversial, especially among the theater's actors, a conservative bunch, who staged protests in front of the mayor's office and sent protest letters to the Duma and the prosecutor's office. Serebrennikov fought back and eventually turned a core group of his former pupils into Gogol's primary troupe.

"In those years, the main enemy was not the state, but the rather terrible old guard in the country's theater scene, people with Soviet brains, who were the enemies of all modernizing trends," said Marina Davydova, a prominent theater critic and the editor of *Theater* magazine. She is close to Serebrennikov, and was buoyed by his rise in the country's drama scene. She perfectly understood the logic in his dealings with the authorities. "The state shows up and says, 'We will give you money to do all the projects you've been waiting to do,'" she said. "Why should you say no?" Davydova suggested that, in a way, the state needed Serebrennikov more than the reverse. "There are few such people in the world of Russian theater, who are thoroughly modern and innovative, who can pull off art-house productions, but can do it on big stages, where thousands of people will come and see it."

Under Serebrennikov, the Gogol Center staged a number of successful performances, including *The Idiots,* which was inspired by the 1998 Lars von Trier film and subsequently played at the Avignon Festival. Serebrennikov's version of Gogol's *Dead Souls* is three hours of rich and cutting satire, not so much contemporary as timeless. One night, I went to see the Gogol Center's staging of Ivan Goncharov's *A Common Story,* a tale originally written in the 1840s, which Serebrennikov turned into a punkish rebuke of conformism. A spirited young man comes to the capital full of vigor and ideals, but he slowly becomes seduced by the power and comforts of the ruling system, his character growing ever darker and more cruel. Aside from individual productions, which varied in quality and were far from universally loved, the Gogol Center was most significant for the kind of venue it came to represent: a cultural space in the most sweeping sense, where people could gather not just to watch a play but to listen to lectures, participate in seminars and master classes, or simply sit around and talk in the café.

Davydova told me that she warned Serebrennikov that this period could not last long, just as the freewheeling cultural age after the Bolshevik Revolution gave way to the stifling artistic controls of Stalinism. "Don't get too close to power," she told him. "There are people inside the system who are supporting you now—but others will come to fight them, and, when they do, they will destroy you in the process." As she put it to me, "This was not a moral demand, but an understanding of the algorithms of history." At the time, Serebrennikov waved off her concern. "Don't worry," he told her. "We're not that close."

THE ALGORITHMS BEGAN TO shift in late 2011 and early 2012, with the appearance of the protests on the streets of Moscow. The demonstrators were largely middle-class professionals: Serebrennikov's audience, and the sort of people whom Surkov thought he could cleverly manage. Putin's response—turning to a new ruling ideology that blended conservative values, anti-Western resentment, disdain for urban elites, and an elevation of the Orthodox Church—heralded the end of the state's enthusiasm for experimental and avant-garde art forms. Putin demoted Surkov and named Vladimir Medinsky as Russia's minister of culture. A nationalist ideologue with spurious academic credentials—amateur researchers provided evidence that one of his dissertations was poorly sourced and full of errors—Medinsky shifted the ministry in a strongly conservative direction. His arrival was "abrupt and palpable," said the former ministry employee. "We started to get all these questions about why we are supporting this strange and unnecessary art."

A period of political revanche followed, both inside the Kremlin and outside. In 2013, Serebrennikov wanted to host a screening at the Gogol Center of a documentary sympathetic to Pussy Riot, the punk group who had staged a protest in Moscow's Cathedral of Christ the

Savior. The movie would be followed by a public discussion with two of the women from Pussy Riot, who had just been released from prison after serving terms of nearly two years. Kapkov intervened and forbade the event. He wrote Serebrennikov a formal letter: "I deeply believe that a government cultural institution should not associate with those people who provoke such an ambiguous reaction and whose activity is based on the provocation of society." Serebrennikov decried the move as censorship—"cynical, pointless, and stupid," he said—but given that the Gogol Center was formally a state theater under Kapkov's remit, he had no choice. In a public statement, Serebrennikov described how, even in the country's gathering conservative revanche, it had seemed that some "free air" remained, if only "in fashionable cafés, at home, with friends." But now he changed his mind: "That's it! Fuck! There's no air!"

When I spoke with Kapkov, he responded to my questions more frankly— and more cleverly—than most Putin-era officeholders. He acknowledged that his move was an act of censorship, but presented it as a paternal gesture, an unpleasant but necessary decision to protect Serebrennikov and the Gogol Center. "They were silly," Kapkov said. "They didn't realize how seriously they could get hit over the head." Kapkov's aversion to Pussy Riot was not ideological but rather bureaucratic—their appearance at the Gogol Center would be fuel for the theater's many enemies in the state apparatus, those already predisposed to dislike Serebrennikov and everything he was involved with. Why hand them the revolver they'll use to shoot you? At least pick a grander and more meaningful kamikaze mission than a film screening, Kapkov thought. "Don't choose to die under other people's flags."

Kapkov is the archetype of the enlightened Putin-era bureaucrat, at home among Moscow's beau monde, regularly dropping stories of how he'd just gotten back from New York or Tel Aviv, but with a dispassionate recognition of how the country's byzantine politics work, the intrigues and power struggles that decide people's fates. He told me the scenario he feared if Pussy Riot were to appear at the Gogol Center: "They will upset the patriarch, let's say. The patriarch calls Putin. Then Putin's chief of staff calls the mayor and gives him an earful. The mayor calls me and says, angrily, 'What have you done?'" After that, Kapkov explained, it would be that much harder for him to defend Serebrennikov's next production, to explain why this or that staging isn't too inflammatory or transgressive for a state theater—or to keep Serebrennikov in his job at all.

Did I know, Kapkov asked, about the special-issue telephones in Russian government offices? They don't have any keys or a way to dial, just a name on each: "Vladimir Vladimirovich" for Putin's office, "Sergey Semenovich" for Sobyanin, Moscow's mayor, and so on. "So the phone rings in Sobyanin's office," Kapkov said, unspooling his imaginary story. "The one labeled 'Vladimir Vladimirovich.' He picks up. 'Greetings, Sergey Semenovich. Fire Serebrennikov.' And then Putin hangs up the phone. What then?" Serebrennikov didn't understand or even imagine these dangers. That was Kapkov's job: to know where such threats lurked and to help Serebrennikov steer clear of them, even if that meant sometimes acting the overbearing censor. "I'm not making excuses," Kapkov told me, recounting the Pussy Riot episode. "But I know that I acted in his defense."

In 2014, with Russia caught in its geopolitical standoff with the West over Ukraine, the reactionary wave intensified. Politics and cultural life became marked by reflexive aggression and paranoia: this was the period when Channel One aired its false report on the crucified boy, the campaign against the founders of the Perm-36 museum reached its frenzied denouement, and whatever enthusiasm had once existed for the avant-garde and risqué in the arts shrank into oblivion. As Kapkov understood it, the Kremlin had been interested in building up a new generation of artists as a way of engendering civic pride, but annexing Crimea had solved that problem. Russians were now a proud nation. "That's it, we don't need anything more from you," Kapkov said, paraphrasing the Kremlin's shift in tone toward the cultural community. "We're at war now." A policy document proposed by Medinsky's Ministry of Culture called for "a rejection of the principles of tolerance and multiculturalism." Contemporary art was unwelcome: "No experiments with form can justify substance that contradicts the traditional values of our society." Meanwhile, the regional cultural centers that Surkov had conceived would promote traditional values and social cohesion. Many never opened at all. Medinsky ordered the ministry to end its support for Serebrennikov's Platforma festival.

It was only a matter of time before Kapkov left office as well. He stepped down as Moscow's minister of culture in March 2015, his departure as much a reflection of the end of a particular era as his arrival had been of its beginning. He presented his decision to leave office as a protective measure, similar to canceling the screening of the Pussy Riot movie. His presence inside the state structure was becoming increasingly tenuous, with many officials primed to see him as a kind of double agent, a person of questionable loyalties who was providing cover for all manner of louche and unreliable cultural figures, Serebrennikov among them. Those who wanted to see Kapkov's downfall would go after the artists seen to be under his protection. "I understood that at a certain moment I would be told to fire Serebrennikov," he told me. "Honestly, I got scared of this choice." After he quit, Kapkov heard from lots of people who thought he had acted cowardly; he had abandoned ship with his men still on board, and it was his responsibility to go down with them. I wasn't necessarily one of those people, but I did wonder how things might have turned out had Kapkov hung on to the bitter end. "By leaving, I saved Serebrennikov's job for another two years and another two seasons at the Bolshoi," he said.

Serebrennikov kept working as if nothing had changed. If anything, he responded to the aggressive and intolerant political environment with confrontational works that did not hide their concern—derision, even—for the direction in which Russia appeared to be heading. It wasn't that he had become overtly political. The change in the national mood just made his extravagance and irreverence seem more egregious. In 2016, I went to the Gogol Center to see a one-off performance that Serebrennikov had put together on the theme of Stalin's funeral, a piece that blended historical reenactment with apolitical testimonials on the legacy of Stalinism in present-day Russia. I found it uneven, and preachy in parts, but probing and sincere. That same year, he directed *The Student,* a film that mocked the country's increasing clericalism and intolerance. It was visceral and unpleasant viewing, and won the François Chalais Prize at the Cannes Film Festival. Serebrennikov and the state that effectively employed him were moving in opposite directions.

INVESTIGATORS BEGAN POKING AROUND in the accounting ledgers at the Gogol Center in the spring of 2017. The first arrests came in May, when three of the theater's employees, including its financial director, were taken into custody. At that point, Serebrennikov was only a witness, but it was clear that he would end up a target. The crux of the accusation was that his production studio embezzled state funds meant for Platforma. It appeared to be an absurd charge. At one hearing, prosecutors claimed that a performance of *A Midsummer Night's Dream* had never happened at all. But the play had won several awards, been performed abroad, and been reviewed widely. Prosecutors dismissed news clippings presented by the defense, saying, "A newspaper article cannot confirm that the performance took place."

Hopes of the theater's supporters were buoyed in May, when Evgeny Mironov, the influential director of Moscow's Theatre of Nations, handed Putin a letter in support of Serebrennikov and his colleagues. Putin, accepting the letter, was heard to utter the word "fools," presumably about the overzealous investigators leading the case. But maybe Putin's insult was directed toward the defendants and their sympathizers. Or, perhaps, Putin himself no longer had the same omnipotent hold over the country's investigators and secret policemen.

As the investigation continued, Serebrennikov kept up a ferociously busy schedule. He spent much of the summer of 2017 in St. Petersburg, where he was directing *Summer,* a movie on the life of Viktor Tsoi, a Soviet rock legend and counterculture hero from the 1980s. On the evening of August 22, Russian investigators showed up at Serebrennikov's hotel room in St. Petersburg. They took him into custody, placing him in a police van and driving through the night back to Moscow. In the morning, a judge sentenced him to house arrest while awaiting trial. At the hearing, Serebrennikov said, "The charges brought against me are impossible and absurd. I thought that we were engaged in a bright and powerful project for our country, our homeland." He finished by asking for his release on bail—an appeal that was denied. "I am an honest person, and I ask the court to allow me to work," he pleaded.

The indictment centered on the studio's use of *obnal,* or off-the-books cash. It's a tricky question, because *obnal* is, in essence, a way of turning entirely legal funds into illicit funds, which can be spent on whatever you choose: to line one's own pockets, or simply to procure necessary goods and services. State funds can be released only a certain period of time after a particular good or service has been delivered. But for a large theater, all sorts of venders demand payment right away: repairmen, prop studios, lighting technicians. Thus, in principle, Serebrennikov and his colleagues at the theater studio could be left with the need for technically illegal cash for entirely legal needs. The law itself became a kind of trap.

"It's quite obvious to me that they did not create a criminal group in order to steal money," said Mikhail Shvydkoy, the former minister of culture. "They created their company in order to make plays and works of art—and, in the process, it's possible they could break the law somewhere." If anything, he suggested, Serebrennikov was led astray by his own success, imagining that he was more protected and secure than he really was. Shvydkoy offered a riddle in the form of a Latin saying: "What is allowed to Jupiter is not allowed to the bull," he said. "And the moment when a bull begins to feel like Jupiter, all manner of funny things start happening."

IN SEPTEMBER, A MONTH after Serebrennikov was sentenced to house arrest, his latest work premiered at the Gogol Center: *Little Tragedies,* a series of small dramas of Russian life, based on Pushkin's verse. It begins with an act of violence at a train station, shocking not so much in its gore as in the lack of reaction it elicits onstage, or in the audience. "Staging a play without its director is, of course, frightening, and a great responsibility," said Alexei Agranovich, the actor playing the Miserly Knight, who, in the play, hoards not gold, as Pushkin wrote it, but books. We met in the Gogol Center's café, an open space of wood and brick, which hums with the ambient busy-ness of actors waiting for rehearsal and people stopping in for a coffee or slice of cake. Agranovich told me that, as he sees it, those wielding influence in the Kremlin today "don't understand why they need a place like this, what the benefit is for them."

He said that the officials in charge simply don't have a clue what Serebrennikov and his art are all about—and that scares them. "It's like an old person flipping through some Salinger," Agranovich said. "For them, this is just some incomprehensible shit. And if this shit begins to stink, and spreads around, they decide to have a look. Where do they look? At the money side of things. Because that is a language the state understands." I asked Agranovich if he thought Serebren-nikov's success had led him to danger, and if he and his team were inattentive to the shifting reality around them. "Who knows?" he said. "Maybe some mistakes were made—but they were sincere ones, childish, naive. Anyway, it's impossible to play a game successfully when the rules change four times in the course of a match."

A few days later, I went to see Sophia Apfelbaum, the director of Russian Academic Youth Theatre, a storied state theater across from the Bolshoi. She had previously worked at the Ministry of Culture, where she led the department that provides support to contemporary art, including the Platforma festival. That made her a witness in the case, and some weeks prior she had gone to the Investigative Com-mittee for questioning. We spoke in her office, an airy space filled with a century's worth of framed playbills of the theater's produc-tions. "For a certain while, Serebrennikov was in favor, but that turned out to be a disappointment," she told me. Ultimately, she blamed the state's own capriciousness: what it had championed in one moment, it recoiled from in the next. In her office, she handed me a copy of a 2011 decree, with Putin's signature, calling on the state to fund Platforma. She emphasized that she had acted in accor-dance with the instructions she was given by the government. Plat-forma, she said, was an "outstanding, absolutely preeminent art project. It's sad this story ended in such a way."

I asked her what sort of effect the charges against Serebrennikov had on those inside the Russian arts and theater scene. "The idea of having a rational conversation with the state is gone," she said. "Now everyone feels tight, like they're in a fishbowl. At any moment the authorities could show up with some sort of economic charges for them, too." A few weeks after we spoke, Apfelbaum was again summoned to the Investigative Committee. She was told that she was no longer a witness but a suspect herself. Like Serebrennikov, she was placed under house arrest, and would await trial for allegedly serving as an accomplice in the theft of millions.

AS THE CASE INCHED slowly along, I met up with Michael Idov, a Soviet-born American author and screenwriter who, along with his wife, Lily, wrote the script for *Summer,* the film about Tsoi and the Leningrad rock scene. "I was hopelessly naive about Kirill's prospects," Idov told me. They were all on set together in St. Petersburg the day before Serebrennikov's arrest. "Like an idiot, I kept saying, 'We'll be seeing much more of you.' The conversation covered every topic in the world except for his predicament." Serebrennikov's arrest set off a flurry of speculation and guesswork inside the close-knit world of Russian film and theater, Idov said, with everyone trying to answer the most basic questions: "Why Kirill? Why now?" There was a natural impulse to try to pinpoint Serebrennikov's transgression, whatever it may have been, as if by identifying the source of this strange new illness, you could convince yourself you were not in danger of catching it. But those details remained unknowable, which left everyone all the more on edge. Idov told me that nonetheless, some broader lessons were already clear. "Before," he said, "the risk was being unable to get funds or coverage for your next project—but not jail time." What's more, he went on, "if the system has its sights on you, no amount of previous compromise will help you. And so maybe all the previous compromises aren't worth it."

After wrapping up *Summer,* which finished shooting in Serebrennikov's absence, Idov wrote and directed a film that confronts the impossible trap that compromise poses for an artist. *The Humorist* stars Agranovich, the Gogol Center actor, as a successful comedian at the height of his fame in the mid-1980s. Agranovich's character performs utterly benign and schmaltzy routines for sold-out audiences on subjects like the amusing mishaps that can happen while on vacation in Sochi. He is awarded all the accordant benefits of late-Soviet privilege: a spacious apartment, wads of rubles in an envelope, a table covered with the kinds of delicacies you couldn't find on a grocery shelf anywhere. Yet lurking just beneath the surface of his studiously apolitical routine is his, and all of society's, reliance on humor as a defense mechanism, a balm for the mounting absurdity of the stagnation years. Success for the film's humorist comes at a price: he's pulled out of bed in the middle of the night to put on private shows for Soviet cosmonauts and Communist Party bigwigs. Far more ruinous for his psyche is the dissonance between what he wants to joke about and what he's allowed to joke about. He finally explodes in a fusillade of off-color political jokes in the presence of a Red Army general. You'd think that would be the end of him, but the film's coda reveals otherwise. The action takes place in the present: Agranovich's comedian has aged thirty years, his face saggy and tired, but there he is, delivering the same tired Sochi routine to a packed hall. *The Humorist* portrays the ugly toll of conformism but is equally honest about its frequent inescapability. If anything, the film seems to argue that this is a false binary: one can play by the rules of the game yet also subvert them, and it's silly and unhelpful to label anyone who isn't an outright insurrectionary an irredeemable collaborator. Humor can be a means of having it both ways: a winking and knowing irony that allows you to eke out a space of personal freedom even when that freedom is restricted.

Ultimately, Idov suggested, an individual artist has control only over his or her own creative output, not the actions of an amorphous and impossibly large state machine. "All I can do is protect the integrity of my own work," he told me. He gave an example: Some years back, he was an advisor at a production studio run by Fydor Bondarchuk, an actor close to the Kremlin. Idov had free creative control on his own projects, including *Rushkin,* a surrealist autobiographical sitcom about an American writer seduced by Moscow's money. But while he was there, the studio was also developing *Sleepers,* a conspiratorial show for Channel One about how the United States is plotting a revolution to upend Russia. Idov came up with a personal rule reminiscent, as he put it, of a "mafia lawyer's": any time *Sleepers* came up at a meeting, he would get up and leave the room. "Is that hypocrisy?" he said. "Sort of, yes—but at the same time, it allowed me to do my own work and not have anything to do with this utterly awful show."

Sleepers presented a particularly interesting case, because Yuri Bykov, its director, was a respected auteur, known for his unflinching and critical approach in depicting modern-day Russia. In particular, his film *The Fool* was praised as a darkly prescient fable of Russian society's deep rot: A plumber in a provincial town realizes a local apartment block is on the verge of collapse, and spends the duration of the film on a mad and quixotic effort to force the mayor to order an evacuation. The mayor and other officials are concerned only with covering up their own corruption and mismanagement; what's more, even those who live in the doomed building aren't especially grateful—the film ends with them beating up the plumber on the street and heading back upstairs to their apartments. The plumber is the movie's "fool." In today's Russia, only an idiot would think he could defeat the bureaucratic class and be rewarded for altruism.

Given Bykov's reputation, many of his fans were left confused, if not outright angry, when *Sleepers* premiered on Channel One. The show's message was not hard to miss: a heroic FSB agent saves the country from succumbing to a Maidan-style revolution organized by the CIA and carried out by sleeper agents made up of Russian journalists, human rights activists, and traitorous politicians. The plot was a distillation of the Kremlin's paranoid fantasies about the West's determination to undermine the Russian state, buttressed by the notion that anyone who opposes the ruling authorities must be a Western patsy.

How did Bykov end up directing such schlock? It seems that even he did not fully possess the answer. After *Sleepers* had run for only a week, subject to derision and mockery among intelligentsia circles, Bykov publicly disowned the show and his own role in creating it. "I am a weak person, full of doubts, and a moment of meekness and disorientation led the best minds of the country to turn away from me once and for all," he wrote in a statement he posted online. His open letter was a remarkable expression of self-flagellation, full of shame and self-doubt—emotions rarely put on such public display in Russia. "I betrayed the entire progressive generation that wanted to change something in this country," he said. "I will have to retreat into the shadows for a long while, and not so that my crimes will be forgotten, but in order not to upset the world with my presence, let alone confuse people who really want to believe that something can change. I fucked everything up because of my own stupidity and cowardice."

Some months later, long after *Sleepers* finished its run on Channel One and the scandal had largely faded from memory, I caught up with Bykov at an outdoor café in a leafy neighborhood in the center of Moscow. He is in his late thirties, with a sincere, boyish smile and an unkempt salt-and-pepper beard; there is something both naive and mischievous about him. Bykov told me that at a certain point in his career, he realized his popularity among Russia's cultural sophisticates was destined to remain limited. His views were far from straightforwardly oppositionist: he had plenty of criticism for the decay of Russian society and the many failings of its rulers, but he was also skeptical of Western intentions toward Russia, supportive of Crimea's annexation, and sympathetic to the position of the pro-Russian fighters in the Donbass. The country's liberals would never fully accept him, and so he would remain a niche director, not celebrated like Andrey Zvyagintsev, whose 2015 film *Leviathan* was nominated for an Academy Award. "And so I simply got jealous," he told me. "I thought that if this crowd doesn't accept me, okay then, I'll be accepted by another." Bykov imagined he could become a "patriotic critic," a director able to call out the country's problems while remaining fundamentally loyal and thus able to enjoy the favor of the state and the resources it can bestow.

The offer to shoot *Sleepers* was rather straightforward. "The producers said the series must have an unambiguous message: the Russian secret services are trying to save the country from the danger of an 'Orange Revolution.' And they are doing this honorably. End of story." Bykov said yes. Part of him agreed with the show's underlying premise—he was convinced that the West is Russia's geopolitical foe and its intelligence officers really would like to undermine Russia—and the other part simply feared the consequences if he were to decline the project. He had already turned away from the country's liberal intelligentsia; if he similarly disappointed those in the ruling apparatus, then to whom would he appeal? Bykov would be a failed *prisposoblenets*—a person who tried to contort himself in order to fit the demands of the time, but couldn't even manage to do that. "I got scared of ending up all on my own, unrecognized and isolated," he told me. Bykov recalled his state of mind: "If I don't go for this compromise right now, I will end up with the fate of some kind of obscure genius who lives on a miserly salary in a one-room apartment on the outskirts of Moscow."

It didn't take long during filming for Bykov to begin to feel uneasy. He was particularly bothered by a plotline in which a popular anti-corruption activist is revealed to be a CIA-controlled stooge. It was a clear reference to Alexei Navalny, the opposition leader whom pro-Kremlin politicians and media figures regularly try to paint as a foreign patsy. It seemed a low blow to Bykov. Why discredit those who genuinely want change, who are working to improve things in their country? But he had gone too far to turn back. Moreover, he believed in the show's underlying mission: he didn't want to see an "Orange Revolution" in Russia any more than those who thought up the series did, and if this was him doing his part, so be it. Seeing the finished product onscreen, though, combined with the outpouring of hateful and disappointed comments, made him realize he had erred in his calculation.

"I played a very dangerous game," he told me. "I thought I was coming to the defense of Russia and its citizens, roughly speaking, but I ended up defending the system of power that is oppressing the Russian people." If the epiphany seems rather obvious, it was striking to Bykov, who, when we spoke, repeatedly described himself as "completely lost." His short-lived allies from pro-Kremlin circles abandoned him as soon as he published his mea culpa. (In the days afterward, he told me, "some rather significant people" called and asked him what the hell he was doing, why he had made such a mess of things.) And given all the hard-to-follow turns in his career, his onetime colleagues and supporters from the liberal cultural elite were deeply wary of him. Bykov spoke in discursive loops, and didn't have any precise answers to my questions of why he did this or that; he told me he was still trying to make sense of what had happened to him. "Let me try and put it like this," he said. "I don't have the ability to constantly live a lie. This starts to eat at me. But neither do I have the courage or guts to be a hero all the time. So that's how I ended up in this hole."

Bykov and I talked about Serebrennikov. He said the criminal charges against him were evidence of how arbitrary and capricious the state can be in its relations to artists. It can withdraw its imprimatur as quickly and with as little explanation as it proffered it in the first place. If that were to happen, he'd be no less safe than Serebrennikov. "What's stopping them from coming now and saying: 'Yuri, you behaved poorly, so let's have a look, shall we—is everything truly clean in your past?'" For the moment, Bykov said, it was actually a stroke of luck that those in power didn't consider him a traitor but rather some kind of strange and confused fool. He started to talk of what Serebrennikov must be going through under house arrest, but it was clear he was lost in self-reflection, churning over how he himself had ended up a cultural outcast several times over. "After all, artists are not samurai," he said. "They are subtle creatures, very finely put together. They can get scared. I know this from my own experience."

A FEW DAYS AFTER Serebrennikov's arrest, a director named Ivan Vyrypaev released an open letter, addressed not so much to the authorities as to his peers in the world of the arts. Vyrypaev is the former head of the Praktika Theatre, a popular space in Moscow for modern and experimental productions. In 2016, he left for Warsaw, where he is one of the founders of a theatrical studio. His letter is an emotional appeal to refuse further cooperation with the Russian state. Vyrypaev begins by commenting on the actors, directors, and artists who showed up in support of Serebrennikov at his court hearing in Moscow. Many high-profile cultural figures spoke in court, or outside, in his defense.

"In the meantime, most of you continue to shoot your films, put on plays and receive grants from the Ministry of Culture," he writes. "One way or another, by collaborating with this regime while thinking that we can change something in this country, or make a meaningful contribution to change, through our art and our role in society, we are only fooling ourselves and our country once again. And this, I'm sorry to say, looks quite childish."

Toward the close of the letter, Vyrypaev says that those who think they can outwit the state while maintaining a clean conscience are deluding themselves. "Living a double life is actually what put Kirill Serebrennikov behind bars," he writes. The letter wasn't universally applauded by cultural figures in Moscow. Many found it self-serving and simplistic. It was first published on the online portal Snob, whose editors explained that some on staff found it "demagogic, provocative, and insulting."

I reached Vyrypaev at the Polish Theatre, in Warsaw, where he was in rehearsals for a new production of *Uncle Vanya,* whose premiere was scheduled for the same night as *Nureyev.* Vyrypaev feared that he had been misunderstood. "I understand theatrical life in Russia is impossible without the state. I didn't mean that you should stop working, no longer show up at the theater or take money from the Ministry of Culture," he said. Still, he feared that the constant searching for funding had become a kind of flirtatious game with the ruling regime. "I left because I no longer wanted to cooperate, but I can't propose this to all my colleagues. It wouldn't be humane. I had the chance to leave, but not everyone has this opportunity."

Vyrypaev emphasized that the real point of his letter was to make his friends and peers think in advance of Russia's upcoming presidential election, in March 2018, when Putin would run for a fourth term. During Putin's previous campaign, in 2012, the Kremlin had enlisted a number of cultural luminaries to lend their image and reputation to Putin's reelection bid. Vyrypaev told me that he wrote his letter with "five or six" specific people in mind. "These people understood perfectly that I was talking to them," he said. "I know that during the campaign, some officials will ask for help, and I want to see how they react. No heroism is required. You don't have to declare anything, or go for some public feat like I did. When they call, just say you have the flu, or are filming somewhere on location."

Vyrypaev told me that several years ago he was invited to a meeting of cultural figures organized by United Russia, the country's loyal pro-Kremlin party. He replied that he couldn't make it—he was awaiting the delivery of a new washing machine. "Back then, you could joke like that," he said. "Now they might not find it so funny. Maybe there would be consequences."

One of the Putin system's most devious tricks is that the consequences, just like the transgressions they are meant to enforce, are left purposefully vague. Even the unofficial, unwritten rules aren't rules but a whispered language of hints and suggestions. One criminal case with a figure like Serebrennikov is more than enough for people in the world of arts and culture to understand that the state expects something new and different from them. But what? Marina Davydova, the theater critic, suggested one answer. "If you do something a little too radical—and only you can guess where this line is located—then they will show up and look for something," she told me. "And, of course, they'll find something. You think even a place like the Bolshoi is clean? If they wanted to come up with financial violations, I'm sure they could find plenty."

It's hard to say what Serebrennikov's mistake was, if there was one. Perhaps the error was merely that he believed, up until the end, that it was possible to have a conversation with those who had, in fact, long ago stopped speaking with him. Serebrennikov once told an interviewer that, no matter the government or system, "you need to go and talk." As he put it, "You tell them, 'I know that you, the state, are lying, mercenary, but by law you must help theater and the arts, so be good—fulfill your obligations.' For the sake of theater, I'm not ashamed to do this."

FATHERS AND SONS

—

ONE DAY IN APRIL 2019, AT A COURT HEARING IN SEREBRENNIKOV'S case, which by then had stretched on for more than a year, the judge made an unexpected ruling. He ordered Serebrennikov freed from house arrest. The trial would continue to plod toward its eventual resolution, but in the meantime, the defendant could live and work as he pleased, with no limitations other than showing up for court and not leaving the country. It wasn't an acquittal, but given the realities of the Putin-era criminal justice system—a steamroller that, once set in motion, moves only in one direction—it was the closest thing to it.

As he walked out of the courtroom, Serebrennikov looked happy but stunned, as if he couldn't quite believe the idea that he was again a free man, at least for the time being. "It isn't easy psychologically," he told a waiting crowd of supporters and journalists. "But there's much to do." There was no shortage of plays to rehearse, premieres to get ready for, new projects and scripts to think over. "But nothing has ended," he said. Technically, the charges against him remained, as did the possibility of a sustained prison term, even if the specter of immediate danger had lifted. The reason for the court's sudden leniency was as mystifying as the reason for the charges in the first place, but it seemed clear that the Kremlin no longer had much interest in the case—in the intervening period, Putin had won reelection, and whatever short-term utility there had been in sending a warning to the cultural intelligentsia had faded.

A week later, the Bolshoi Theatre hosted a ceremony to mark the close of the annual Golden Mask Festival, a celebration of the best performances in Russian theater. It is a resplendent and glamorous evening, Russia's equivalent of the Tony Awards, an occasion for the country's cultural elite to dress up in glittering formalwear and toast one another's successes. The year before, with Serebrennikov at home under house arrest, he won the award for best opera for his staging of *Chaadsky,* a madcap, satirical work based on the verse of the nineteenth-century writer Alexander Griboyedov.

This year, his attendance came across as the ceremony's marquee event. In keeping with his regular uniform, he wore a black jacket over a black shirt, with a pair of chunky black eyeglasses and a black knit cap pulled over his close-cropped hair. The hosts announced *Nureyev* the winner of best ballet, and Serebrennikov, along with Yuri Possokhov, the production's choreographer, ascended the steps to the Bolshoi stage and looked out at the audience, rapturous with applause. "We had a happy life making this performance, and it goes on," he said with a wide, cheerful grin. Later, he was called back up to accept the best director award for *Little Tragedies,* his Pushkin adaptation at the Gogol Center. He noted that Pushkin is suitable for all occasions in Russia: "When you're going for a walk and when you are under house arrest." He closed with a call to "protect the freedom of the artist in the theater with all our might, against all odds."

Serebrennikov had pulled off a successful and unexpected second—or maybe third—act. Having enjoyed the state's favor and been a subject of its ire, he had wriggled out of its clutches and back onto the Bolshoi stage. The state ultimately retained all the power, yet nonetheless it felt as if the momentum of events had unmistakably shifted in Serebrennikov's favor. That is the potential upside of living in the shadow of the state's capricious and ever-changing demands: just as your downfall may come with no warning or explanation, so, too, can your redemption. Eventually, after many false starts, in June 2020, a Moscow court found Serebrennikov nominally guilty of embezzlement but handed him a conditional sentence, effectively a soft form of probation, and which functions as just about the most benevolent compromise the Russian justice system can offer. He was again a free man.

Not everyone is so skilled, or so lucky. One must know when to cower from the state's blows and when to slyly ask for a favor. The case of Fair Aid, Glinka's charity organization, is instructive. In the months after her death, things were difficult. Fair Aid had been so dependent on Glinka's spirit and personality that her sudden absence left its staff frozen in place, unsure of which projects to continue, or how. The books were a mess, and so were fund-raising operations. Glinka had somehow kept it all in her head: the cash donations dropped off by strangers at the Paveletsky basement, which Kremlin official had promised what, how to fill out the necessary documents to get a wounded child admitted to a state hospital. Her saintly—people now used the word freely—demeanor allowed her what the rest of us mortals couldn't pull off, at least not so convincingly and with such grace.

Ksenia Sokolova, Glinka's friend and confidante who had interviewed her at the height of the war in the Donbass, took over as head of Fair Aid. At first she saw her job as that of a temporary crisis manager. She would keep things afloat until the organization had found its way again and then move on after a few months. But her sense of mission quickly expanded. She wanted to arrange for a new children's hospital in the center of Moscow, a modern and well-equipped clinic to be named after Glinka, who had desperately wanted to open such a center. Building it now would be the best and truest way to honor her memory, Sokolova thought. She felt the state owed Glinka a posthumous debt: if she hadn't become a part of the system, she wouldn't have been on that ill-fated flight. To push through the hospital project, Sokolova would have to appeal to powerful figures from within the state apparatus, the kinds of people who could grant the necessary parcel of land and the funds for construction. Presumably that shouldn't be difficult. "I knew they loved and respected Liza," she said. Volodin, who had since left the Kremlin to take up a position as Speaker of the Duma, liked the idea, as did other well-placed officials. But Sokolova ran afoul of a man named Igor Komissarov, a major general in the country's Investigative Committee, a powerful law enforcement body.

Komissarov was distrustful of Sokolova. He couldn't make sense of her motives. It wasn't possible that she didn't have an underhanded personal interest in the hospital project—presumably financial, though he never quite managed to articulate his suspicions. Sokolova didn't help her cause by telling a reporter that she wouldn't be flying to Syria, as Glinka had: Russian military airplanes lack onboard toilets, and she wasn't going to fly three hours to the Latakia air base without being able to go to the bathroom. She was unapologetically glamorous—she didn't think it necessary to get rid of her fur coat just because she took over a charity organization, she said—and her efforts to routinize the work of the fund, by raising salaries and hiring outside lawyers, looked somehow untoward to many inside the state apparatus who had been so smitten with the selfless aura around Doctor Liza.

Sokolova's position became tenuous; she was a target in the exact and opposite proportion with which Glinka had once been protected. It was not that Sokolova was without talents in communication and negotiation, but that they were ultimately earthly traits, professional and dispassionate, whereas Glinka had offered her interlocutors temporary passage into another, holier realm. And it wasn't just Komissarov—soon all Sokolova's dealings with state officials became strained. "They wanted a kind of Holy Liza Number Two: a person who gave them what she had; who could forgive them, let them feel that they are benevolent and mighty," Sokolova said.

Komissarov went on the attack, sending officers for various inspections of the fund and its financial operations. He launched an investigation on charges of fraud and abuse supposedly committed by Sokolova. No one else in the system was able to help her or felt all that compelled to try. Sokolova appealed to Mikhail Fedotov. As she remembers, he told her to continue her work at Fair Aid as if nothing were amiss, to keep up her efforts to open the hospital, that everything would sort itself out. She tried that for a while, but after several months, decided she wanted out. "Mikhail Aleksandrovich, my fit of masochism has dragged on long enough—and is now over," she told Fedotov. She left her post at Fair Aid, and soon, the country. As long as Komissarov's criminal investigation of her remained open, she wasn't going to risk stepping foot on Russian territory. The last time we spoke, I reached her in Rome.

The whole affair reminded me of something I had heard from Mikhail Meylac, the former prisoner at Perm-36 who had agreed to provide some historical advice on the museum's reconstruction projects: how the barracks were laid out, how the boiler room looked, that sort of thing. A year after we first spoke, I returned to his dacha in the woods outside St. Petersburg. Over lunch on the back patio, Meylac told me that he decided to end his cooperation with the Perm-36 museum. He had soured on Natalia Semakova, its new director. The previous winter, he explained, he had received a New Year's card from Semakova on behalf of the museum. She thanked him for his contribution to the "state program to perpetuate the memory of victims of political repression," a reference to a Kremlin initiative launched in 2015. Meylac didn't think of himself as participating in any sort of state program, and had no intention to continue. It was a matter of principle—state programs can be benevolent or murderous, but he wanted nothing to do with either kind. "First comes the order to, say, round up a hundred kulaks or supposed counter-revolutionaries or whomever else in a particular district; and then, some years later, the directive to perpetuate their memory," he said.

To Meylac, Semakova's card suggested she was most comfortable in the realm of official plans, of succeeding in whatever edict is issued from on high that day. Without a clear moral vision, Meylac thought, all that's left are careerism and bureaucratic efficiency. He had made a compromise in agreeing to lend his expertise to the museum—the forced removal of its founders, Viktor Shmyrov and Tatiana Kursina, gnawed at him—but this mention of "state programs" made that compromise impossible. He would have nothing more to do with the museum in its current form.

PEOPLE IN ALL COUNTRIES face difficult moral choices. To be a functioning adult in the world, we all must balance competing sets of expectations and pressures with our own understanding of self. We negotiate the constraints and demands placed on us by our bosses, our parents and friends, internet commenters, the unfamiliar and intimidating people seated next to us at dinner parties. But in the United States and most other countries in the West, such forces emanate from all manner of places: the mores of your social group, your corporation's human resources department, the unrelenting pressures of the marketplace. And none of them can put you in jail.

It is the singular role of the state that gives this dynamic, otherwise perfectly relatable and universal, its particular Russian tinge. In the eighties and nineties, when the state grew weak, Russian society itself did not become stronger (although a number of oligarchs did, if temporarily). When Putin rose to power and reconsolidated the state's authority, the public largely adjusted to a more habitual environment. But that adjustment, as I came to understand, can take many forms, and making sense of the nuanced distinctions is important. Some of the people I encountered, and would come to write about, remained on the outside of the system, making everyday accommodations to the vagaries of their environment, learning when to dodge or outsmart the state and when to acquiesce to its demands. Others went further, effectively joining the system and reaping benefits from their positions on the inside. And for both types, there remains an important difference in the object of your wiliness: Whom are you tricking, and what are the strictures you're trying to avoid or outwit?

As one acquaintance of Serebrennikov's put it to me, trying to explain how Serebrennikov, in his eagerness to mount ambitious and technically complicated plays, could have allowed his theater's bookkeeping to be arranged in such a way that risked putting himself in technical violation of various financial rules: "The fact that Kirill may have been ready to deceive the state doesn't mean he would have ever considered deceiving me." The inclination to outmaneuver the state's obtuse and cumbersome demands does not automatically translate into a universal cynicism, a fallback modus operandi of cheating and deceit. If anything, the opposite: I have long seen how bonds of loyalty and trust between Russians can be deeper and more resolute than those I was accustomed to in America. Wiliness often works vertically, aimed upward; less so horizontally, where relations are often guided by an us-against-them resourcefulness and solidarity.

The sorts of compromises made by the people in this book are not all alike: a retreat made in the face of grave danger is one thing; an abandonment of principles in search of power and wealth is another;

and a lack of any constant guiding set of values, which makes any and all forms of adaptation equally palatable, is perhaps the scariest form of all. As outsiders, we must acknowledge the difficulty, or impossibility, of acting otherwise, while reserving a space for the sober judgment of what such individual choices and behaviors lead to in the aggregate: a society and political system in which nearly every form of initiative risks being co-opted and manipulated, preemptively depriving energy and motivation from those who might seek change.

One afternoon, I discussed all this with Lev Gudkov, the director of the Levada Center, who began his sociology career as a student of Yuri Levada's in the sixties. Do the compromises of the wily man require judgment or compassion? He seized on the example of Glinka and her evacuations of sick and wounded children from the Donbass. "I don't think it's acceptable to throw stones at her, to somehow blame her for what she did," he told me. Her position of insisting that she remained apart from politics was an impossible one—not so much naive as a piece of knowing and self-justifying rhetoric—but the good she did was tangible, real, and unimpeachable.

In this sense, Gudkov's stance mirrored Glinka's own: Would we be better off if Nikita Teplyakov, the sick child whom Glinka saved with the Kremlin's help, had died? Of course not. But compromises such as Glinka's, and those of innumerable others—most of which, unlike hers, are banal and relatively low-stakes—have the effect of trapping society in a kind of utilitarian loop: If results are what matter, then why not achieve them in the benevolent shadow of the state? And isn't that more effective anyway? Gudkov answered, "The consequences are a feeling of no alternative, that nothing can be done, that one way or another you must bow to power or learn to get along with it. Which leads precisely to the corruption of society."

The question of wiliness continues to be "the central problem of Russian modernity," as the well-known political analyst Kirill Rogov declared. (Rogov's term for it was "the dilemma of collaborationism.") The debate crops up with predictable regularity, as one respected public figure or another comes out to announce that she is lending her talents or image to some state initiative. For a week, Moscow's cafés are full of talk over the acceptability, or lack thereof, of the person's compromise. Half the capital's intelligentsia responds with understanding and begrudging, clear-eyed approval; the other half voices its disgust.

A year after charges were filed against Serebrennikov, while he was still under house arrest, another celebrated theater director, Konstantin Bogomolov, declared his support for the reelection campaign of Moscow's mayor, a pillar of the Kremlin's governing apparatus. The decision surprised many. Bogomolov praised the mayor for his approach to the city's cultural life, which he summed up as: "Help and do no harm, help and do not interfere." It seemed an odd formulation, given the ongoing case against Serebrennikov and his colleagues. Perhaps there was nothing mysterious at work: Bogomolov had internalized the lesson of Serebrennikov's prosecution and was acting accordingly. (Not entirely dissimilar to how, say, Semakova, the director of the Perm-36 museum, understood perfectly well why its founders had been removed, and needed no further instruction on how she was to treat her job.)

But what if this was a simplification, a convenient and self-righteous pose of the intellectual who stands off to the sidelines and fetishizes his nonparticipation? "The idea that associating with any state official—or, most of all, offering support—is akin to a betrayal of the highest ideals, equal to denouncing someone to the organs of the Stalinist Terror, is not based on anything," wrote Alexander Baunov, a prominent journalist and editor. "Cooperating with the authorities in the service of enlightenment is as much a long-standing intellectual tradition as obstructing them. If, for the intellectual, an official is an irredeemable enemy of the public interest, then what should keep an official from holding the same idea about the intellectual?" That seems as much a self-defeating trap as the wiliness loop Levada described. Surely there has to be a moral framework that doesn't force those with good intentions to stay cloistered on their side of the barricades, with all manner of good and worthy projects unrealized, lest they be stained by the slightest brush with the state.

But for the logic of compromise to work, both parties have to hold up their end of the bargain. As the Putin system enters its late-stage geriatric phase, becoming ever more clumsy and paranoid in response to its declining faculties, it appears destined to turn increasingly rigid and coercive. The cost of wiliness goes up ever more, and its benefits become less and less. What gave the Putin system its longevity to date was the way it managed to achieve a kind of buy-in, conscious or not, from so many of its citizens. Without that, things begin to look a lot more fragile.

The political uproar that grew out of Moscow city council elections in the fall of 2019 is an example of this process. The authorities simply refused to register independent, opposition-minded politicians who collected the signatures necessary to be added to the ballot. Their candidacies were rejected on flagrantly suspect grounds. These would-be candidates played by the rules—they followed the requirements laid out in the law for gaining access to the ballot—and were rejected all the same. This felt a specific and brazen insult to many people in the capital, where a number of rejected candidates were polling as high as 80 percent in the districts they wanted to represent: We did exactly as your own laws require, and you still shove us aside?

Alexei Navalny, the country's most visible opposition politician, and his associates, a number of whom had tried to run for seats on the city council, called for protests, which led to the largest demonstrations in Moscow in years. The police responded with violence, mass arrests, and intimidation tactics: there wasn't much of an opportunity for wiliness even if you were so inclined. The state had largely removed that option, leaving a much starker choice between total obedience and outright defiance. Such a dichotomy may work to pacify things for a while, but it's not all that promising a recipe for long-term stability. It began to feel as if the state had no positive agenda to offer its citizens, only contempt and force. The Kremlin managed to keep most independent candidates from the city council race, but the resulting months of protest turned what would have been a quiet and largely forgettable election into a rallying cry for civic resistance. Navalny and his compatriots went for their own compromise: barred from the ballot themselves, they settled for a strategy of calling on supporters to vote for anyone but those from the ruling United Russia party, which meant holding their noses and supporting unabashed Communists, complete unknowns, and candidates from the Kremlin-approved soft opposition. United Russia politicians managed to keep their majority on the council, but their share of seats was slashed from forty to twenty-five, with twenty seats won by other parties—

perhaps a draw, but given the Kremlin's earlier ability to manipulate politics and voters with seeming ease, a clear sign that its authority was shrinking, and that the old methods were losing their efficacy.

In the run-up to the Moscow election, before the streets were regularly filled with thousands of disgruntled protestors, Navalny wrote an open letter, touching on the utility and moral acceptability of cooperation with the state. "I understand that these are very difficult times, when people have to decide for themselves the limits of the permissible," he wrote. "And I don't mean only careerists, but decent people who are doing good, and see that in the present conditions they can't make do without cooperating with the regime. The whole problem is locating the border between compromise and conformism."

I would go further, and say the real problem is that this border is not a fixed, observable line, but a limit that each person sets for herself. And the state can move that line, too, making an otherwise acceptable concession feel impossible through its turn toward repression and smothering control. I saw that dynamic among the friends who had gotten involved in urban beautification projects for the city of Moscow. Working to improve public transport routes or to give cultural venues a needed refresh could no longer feel just problematic but impossible when police were smashing heads over a city council election. Even the Orthodox Church, among the most inert and conservative of the country's institutions, was not immune to the shifting mood. In an unprecedented open letter, more than a hundred priests called for leniency in criminal cases brought against several protestors. They cited Paul the Apostle—"The Spirit you received does not make you slaves, so that you live in fear again"—and warned that one "cannot build a society of free, loving people on intimidation." The harsh, indiscriminate justice of the state had awoken a group that had long remained outwardly loyal.

The more I followed the arguments over the permissibility of compromise, the more I became convinced they do indeed hold an urgent and central importance in determining the future contours of Russian society. But they also represent an equation that can't be solved. The measure of wiliness is destined to remain an imperfect and controversial estimation, perpetually fought over by those with even the best of intentions.

AFTER TWENTY YEARS, it is nearly impossible to predict the future contours of Putin's Russia: political systems like his can seem quite externally secure even as they slowly decay and grow impotent from within, one day collapsing without warning. (Consider, for example, the prolonged political and economic stagnation of the Brezhnev era, which seemed stifling and gray, yet ultimately stable—until the Soviet Union fell apart with little premonition under Gorbachev.) Putin is more likely to be replaced in a coup from above than a revolution from below. The danger for his system is that as it struggles to hold on, it quashes the spaces for maneuver, making the kinds of contortions this book describes all the harder.

As Putin's fourth term commenced in the spring of 2018, the old governing model began to show its age, and no one in power seemed to have any ideas for a new one. The combined effect of low oil prices, Western sanctions, and an unreformed, state-dominated economy—in 2019, the state's share in the economy reached as much as 60 or 70 percent, up from around 25 percent at the start of Putin's rule—led to successive years of near zero economic growth, and real wages that had fallen nearly 15 percent since the annexation of Crimea. The euphoria born from that event had long faded, and no new sense of unifying mission or purpose replaced it. State television no longer held the same kind of hypnotizing power: polls showed that trust in television has fallen by 30 percent over the last decade and is now below 50 percent. Popular internet broadcasts received as many viewers as Channel One. In the first year of his new presidential term, Putin's approval rating sank to the lowest figures of his presidency.

Protests cropped up in small cities around the country, focused on local issues like the toxic effects of mismanaged waste disposal and the closing or "optimization" of provincial hospitals, which left scores of smaller and midsize towns without adequate healthcare. As Andrei Kolesnikov, a political analyst in Moscow, noted, "A growing part of society is developing civic consciousness as a result of nonpolitical conflicts in which entities supported by the authorities intrude into ordinary people's private space." Before the fight over Moscow elections in 2019, among the biggest ruptures came in October 2018, when Putin signed a bill raising the pension age from sixty to sixty-five for men, and fifty-five to sixty for women. It may have been an economically prudent measure, but the public viewed it as a violation akin to robbery. The Levada Center recorded up to 89 percent dissatisfaction with the proposal. "It was perceived not only as an extreme injustice, but a violation of the unspoken convention of noninterference in each other's affairs," Gudkov explained. It was easier to remain wily when the state wasn't sticking its hand in your pocket.

A growing civic consciousness represents the antithesis of the sort of wiliness that Levada identified in his 2000 essay. A sober accounting of one's social and political conditions and a willingness to try to confront them are incompatible with doublethink, the wily man's oxygen. "You are no longer only pretending that you're participating while actually sitting off to the side—you're really joining in, getting involved," Gudkov said. "There's no space left for hypocrisy, and the structure of wiliness begins to be demolished." What begins as a local concern can lead to change in political imagination.

These outcroppings of discontent remain atomized and local; the Putin state has managed to wall off particular episodes of frustration or anger from the political system at large. Protests over new landfills didn't really line up with those about, say, fair access to the ballots. There are few vectors through which a burst of civic activity on a concrete issue can gain momentum to become anything more than a stand-alone event. That would require independent media outlets with the resources to bring local stories to national attention; an entrenched opposition party inside parliament that could expose injustices as part of its political maneuvering; and a judiciary that could constrain the actions of top Kremlin officials. None of those appear on the horizon.

IN THE SPRING OF 2020, with the Covid-19 pandemic bearing down on Russia, Moscow's political class was busy with entirely different business. Earlier that year, Putin had dismissed his cabinet and declared the need to revise the constitution, a process that most observers assumed would lay the groundwork for the next epoch in Russian politics. The question of what Putin would cook up for the end of his term, in 2024, had lingered since the moment he was reelected in 2018, seeing as the constitution would keep him from running again. He'd have to change the rules to stay on or find himself a fitting post-presidential sinecure. Putin offered cryptic, contradictory hints about his intentions—too much detail would allow his rivals and foes, whether inside the palace walls or out on the streets, to prepare for whatever he had in store.

And then, in early March, in a tragicomic bit of political theater, Valentina Tereshkova, a former Soviet cosmonaut and a member of Russia's parliament, stood up in the Duma to offer her own amendment to the constitution. The proposal put forward by Tereshkova, who was clearly put up to the job, was simple and brazen: to reset Putin's time as the President to zero, granting him the chance to run again in 2024, and even once more after that, keeping him in office until 2036, were he to so choose. "Given his enormous authority, this would be a stabilizing factor for our society," Tereshkova declared. After her "surprise" proposal, Putin announced that he would make his way to the Duma to respond. "In principle, this option would be possible," he said, with faux modesty: If the people demand it, let it be so. In the span of a few hours, the next sixteen years of Russian political life appeared to lock into place. A referendum was planned for April, when the Kremlin expected the population to duly ratify another sixteen years of Putin's rule.

Those plans were quickly scrambled by the coronavirus. While the pandemic arrived in Russia with some delay—the Bolshoi Theater was still staging operas while Italians were at home singing from their balconies—once it did, cases spiked, especially in Moscow and other large cities. Before long, Russia was trailing only the United States and Brazil in numbers of registered infections. When it became obvious that the referendum would have to be delayed, and that Covid-19 would instead become the central challenge to the state, Putin did not seem all that interested in taking charge, or capable of doing so. "He was preparing for the final act of perestroika of the entire political system, and the virus only got in the way," said Gleb Pavlovsky, a former adviser to Putin who fell out with him and left the Kremlin in 2011.

In the early months of the pandemic, Russia managed to avoid an acute, localized catastrophe of the kind seen in Lombardy or New York City, even as Moscow hospitals were pushed to their capacity for several weeks in the spring. But the response of the Russian federal government was spotty and piecemeal, with individual regions, hospitals, and doctors left to figure out how to deal with the pandemic on their own. In a moment of genuine crisis, Putin's top-down, highly centralized system of rule proved flat-footed, even absent. Putin himself periodically appeared on television to announce a series of rolling "non-working holidays," leaving it up to individual regions to opt for lockdowns—or not—and declining to offer much in terms of economic relief. His video-conference meetings with governors were broadcast on federal airwaves but ended up portraying him as bored and disengaged. One of Putin's signal pronouncements—that doctors and other medical personnel treating Covid-19 patients would receive bonuses from the state—was marred by sporadic and delayed implementation, with scores of doctors all over the country complaining that they have nothing at all.

Rather than coming off as the all-powerful strongman, Putin "looks like an old, sick wolf," the political scientist Alexander Kynev told *The Moscow Times*. That May, the Levada Center found that Putin had an approval rating of 59 percent, a historic low. The wily man had always been rather clear-eyed about the state's numerous inefficiencies and failings, but it turned out that many of those pathologies could feel distant and amorphous as long as a global pandemic didn't strike the country. For so many years, Putin had managed to always look like a man of decisive action, the "commander in chief who is always ahead and manages to outplay everyone," as Pavlovsky put it. "But the virus played a different game."

As the summer wore on, the Kremlin decided to hold its referendum after all. The country's political masterminds had no better solution for what had come to be called the "2024 problem" other than to give Putin the flimsiest legal authority to extend his rule another sixteen years. It was a trend that began earlier but was made all the more acute by the pandemic: The Putin state was looking less nimble at managing the country's politics, repeating its old tricks for diminishing returns rather than think up new ones. There was little genuine enthusiasm for the constitutional changes, but just as little doubt about the results. In the middle of a global pandemic, there was scant opportunity for protest; in any case, the measure to "zero out" Putin's terms so as to allow him to run again felt a distant, far-off possibility—sure, maybe it will happen, but it's a long way off; it's not an affront in the here and now. Passive dissatisfaction with the regime does not lead to active protest, at least not right away. In the end, the constitutional measures passed with nearly 79 percent approval, but it was impossible to measure with convincing accuracy, because voting was held over the course of a week, in impromptu polling places set up in apartment courtyards and even in the back of car trunks. Golos, the main independent election watchdog in the country, called the vote "rigged from the start."

The campaign in favor of the constitutional changes was notable for what was absent: the usual retinue of famous and beloved figures from the world of sports, business, culture, and entertainment lending their notoriety to the state in exchange for favors, access, and riches. Now that YouTube had eclipsed television as the most relevant and impactful media venue, the cost of being overly chummy to the system had gone up. During the Moscow city council elections the year before, the flashy and generally popular Russian rapper Timati was forced to delete a music video that was a thinly veiled paean to the mayor—too many users were "disliking" the video and posting acerbic criticism in the comments. You can't tell Channel One how much its content sucks, at least not in a way that is made plain for all other viewers to see.

Two months after the referendum, with Putin potentially ensconced in power for another decade or more, Navalny was poisoned as he was flying back to Moscow from a trip to Siberia, where he was researching an investigative film on local corruption. He lost consciousness on the plane, which made an emergency landing in the city of Omsk. After a transparently cynical delay, the Kremlin allowed Navalny to be evacuated to Germany, where doctors identified the substance that nearly killed him: Novichok, the deadly nerve agent developed by state laboratories in the late Soviet years, which had been used in an assassination attempt against the former Russian intelligence officer turned mole Sergey Skripal some years before. The use of Novichok was as good as a fingerprint—only the Kremlin and the security services under its direct control could possess such a weapon. The attack was a macabre and terrifying reminder of the changing calculus for both state and citizen in the late Putin era: The former was becoming ever less subtle and ever more cruel while the latter faced a less forgiving and far more harrowing set of calculations in deciding whether to choose confrontation over wiliness.

I have written a book full of characters who spent much of their lives and careers in a gray zone, a murky and complicated in-between world that was never easy to navigate but, if nothing, else provided the opportunity for some maneuvering—"freedom in a place of unfreedom," as the slogan for the festival created by the founders of Perm-36 went. But that zone is shrinking, with the options for wiliness narrowing. The Putin system won't produce another Ernst: A young television producer with talent and vision could only make it on state television today if he or she showed unthinking and subtle loyalty; if not, as is ever more the case, they'd go to YouTube, where the audience is now bigger anyway. In raising the stakes of wiliness, the Putin system may end up scaring many of its subjects into obedience, but it could end up pushing no small number into a position of rejection and confrontation they might not have otherwise chosen.

THROUGHOUT RUSSIA'S HISTORY, the most powerful shifts in the country's political and social life have grown out of generational transition, from the social foment of the mid-nineteenth century— the time of the ill-fated Decembrist uprising and Turgenev's *Fathers and Sons*—to the maturation of the country's postwar generation in the eighties and nineties. Russia's first truly post-Soviet generation, born in the early nineties, will take on positions of power just as Putin's presidential reign approaches its close. These Russians tend to exhibit higher levels of trust, sincerity, and responsibility than previous generations. Thanks to access to worldly educations, travel, and technology, their vision of themselves and the society in which they live is more confident and expansive. They may be less prone to compromise and bending their sense of the permissible, though it may also mean they simply do so in different ways.

In the run-up to Putin's reelection for a fourth term, much was made of Russia's young people, the generation that effectively knows no other ruler or system than his. Those who just turned eighteen that spring and were eligible to vote in their first election were born in Putin's first months in office. A notable core of Navalny's supporters came from students in university and high school; I was regularly struck by the youthful faces at Navalny's protest rallies and marches. "Never before have schoolchildren and students participated on such a massive scale in opposition protests," Meduza, an independent news site that is home to some of Russia's best journalism, declared after a large-scale demonstration in Moscow. A seventeen-year-old named Konstantin explained why he had joined the demonstration: "Teenagers easily experience feelings of envy, unease, of being trivialized—and they go out and they try to do something." In the months before the election, a new genre of videos went viral: recordings of students arguing with their teachers and principals about politics, corruption, and life under Putin. It seemed as if the authorities had lost a certain sway over the country's youth, and no longer spoke their language.

But the surface impression of a roiling generational conflict masked a more placid truth. In a report on Russia's post-2018 politics, the political scientists Ivan Krastev and Gleb Pavlovsky wrote that "contrary to Western fantasies, Russians under the age of 25 are among the most conservative and pro-Putin groups in society." A survey by the Levada Center showed that Putin enjoyed 86 percent approval among those surveyed between eighteen and twenty-four years old, compared to 81 percent for the sample group as a whole. Of those young people surveyed, 67 percent said they thought Russia was going in the right direction, compared to 56 percent among the wider group. Gudkov called them a very "practical" generation. "They are interested in simple things, what you can touch in real life," he told me. "Material well-being, nice food, travel, a car, all these consumer pleasures."

IN JUNE 2017, the summer before Putin's reelection, Russian state television again aired the *Direct Line with Vladimir Putin,* the annual call-in show orchestrated by Ernst and Channel One. Toward the end of the four-hour session, the hosts handed the microphone to a high school student in the audience named Danila Prilepa, who was from Nefteyugansk, a midsize city some seventeen hundred miles east of Moscow.

"Hello, Mister President," Prilepa began. "The fact that corrupt officials and ministers are in the government is not news, and has not been for a long time. Putting them under house arrest for show does not produce results, and you undermine people's trust by doing so." Prilepa, then sixteen, wearing a white shirt and a skinny polka-dot tie, went on to say that such "negligence" affects the majority of the population, including his own father, who had served for many years in the interior ministry, Russia's national police force. Prilepa said that his family—because of his father's job—should be entitled to a subsidy for the purchase of an apartment. But, in his region, from a waiting list of thousands, only ninety families have received the requisite funds over the last five years.

Putin saw that Prilepa had read his question from a piece of paper. He asked if he had thought it up himself: "Did someone prepare it for you?" Prilepa replied, "Life has prepared me for this question." Putin went on to give an answer that was meant to sound convincing, but was lacking in specifics; he vaguely promised to increase housing funds in Prilepa's region, and claimed that the country's judges, not its president, control the sentencing of corrupt officials. For once, it was Putin who looked flat-footed and unconfident. In an otherwise listless ritual, the dialogue made for a rare moment of unscripted— uncomfortable, even—humanity. It also captured the sense of generational shift. Prilepa's confident and unblinking demeanor in the face of the very quintessence of authority seemed to crystallize deeper social changes among the Putin generation.

I was curious to hear more from Prilepa, and some months later, on the eve of the presidential election, I traveled to Nefteyugansk, a compact and prim city of 120,000 people carved out of the snow-covered oil fields of western Siberia. I met Prilepa in a café in a single-story shopping center not far from his family's new apartment—they never got their promised state-subsidized housing, and bought the new place by taking out a mortgage. Danila has a curled wave of brown hair, and a smile that is both earnest and polite. His retort to Putin was simply an "impulse of the soul," he told me. "I didn't think for a second. I didn't expect this from myself. But later I realized it was the most correct thing I could have said."

The exchange left Prilepa feeling dissatisfied, though. He had asked a serious question, and even though he might be a kid, he wanted a forthright answer. Instead, he said, "Putin took it as a joke. He jumped off in a different direction. I expected more." As he put it to me, "I may be young, but I have eyes, and ears, and can make some conclusions. Not just out of nowhere, either, but based on a real situation my family is facing."

Still, Prilepa doesn't consider himself politically engaged—merely curious and not all that passionate. He rarely watches television and gets most of his news, especially on political topics, from various feeds on Telegram, a popular messaging app, and the interview series of Yury Dud, a popular video blogger who puts frank and probing questions to Russian entertainers and public figures. The evening news on Channel One might as well not exist.

"I'm not saying that everything is so terrible in our country, but still, somehow, you want more," he said. He mentioned that researchers at Harvard had recently tested a prototype of a cancer vaccine on mice. "I want this in my country also. We have the resources to allow for it, they just aren't put in the right direction," he said. Sometimes, he told me, it can feel like Russia has become "stuck in place." He was frustrated and wanted better from his country, but in all my conversations with him, he never sounded emotional or aggrieved, and certainly not revolutionary. "As long as I can remember, I've basically been happy," he said.

When I asked Danila about his parents, he mentioned that when he had read Turgenev's *Fathers and Sons* in school, he recognized the portrayal of the generational gap in language and values from his own conversations at home. He never saw or lived through the age that proved most formative for his parents, the Soviet collapse and the hardship of the nineties. Meanwhile, the things that are most relevant for him are things his parents don't understand, and therefore often fear. He told me what he had heard about his father's childhood, in a farming village in the Caucasus. By the time the Soviet Union disintegrated, so had the local economy, and people were reduced to bartering fresh milk for eggs. As a boy, his father couldn't keep up in school because he was too busy tending to his family's small plot of land.

"They had their own worries," he said. "At this moment, we, the new generation—if I may say so—have new needs." But it has proved hard for Prilepa and his peers to marshal that sentiment into something tangible. Prilepa mentioned his experience on Putin's call-in show: "I tried, but it did not bear fruit," he said. "It proved once again that a pug and an elephant are not equal."

One afternoon in Nefteyugansk, I stopped by the city's Center for Youth Initiatives, a space for various artistic and civic projects for young people. I met a cheerful and impressive high school senior named Evgenia Merkulenko, who had raised 2 million rubles, around $35,000, for the building of a new, specially designed playground for disabled children. She gathered the necessary funds from various government offices and local businesspeople. She was buoyant about life in Nefteyugansk, and Russia in general. There are "lots of ideas," she told me. "You just have to develop them, and for that there are resources, there are opportunities."

Her positivity seemed genuine, an optimism forged through what is known in Russian as "social lift," Putin-style—the benefits and resources the state can bestow on those whose talent and ambition line up with the goals of the system as a whole. I thought of someone like Ernst, whose brilliance matched the needs and aims of the state, and was thus awarded nearly unlimited opportunity for it to flourish; or Serebrennikov, a more cautionary and uncertain figure, who nonetheless started as a promising young man in a midsize city and ended up basking in the Putin system's largesse, at least for a while. "I know there was a time when not everything worked so smoothly," Merkulenko told me. "But now I'm confident in my country. We live calmly, and peacefully; life has a certain consistency." As we sat and talked, it was clear that although her values were generally liberal— she spoke of the need for tolerance and the protections of the law— her immediate political outlook was, by definition, conservative: the Putin system suited her just fine, and she was loath to do anything to rock it. "I can't see anything that is necessary to change, because right now, as I can see, there already is everything."

Later, I made my way to a garage for a youth motocross club, and ended up talking with a few of its members about the upcoming elections. Maxim, who was nineteen, said that he would have voted for Navalny were he on the ballot, but seeing as he had been barred, Maxim was thinking of supporting Putin. I asked how he could so easily shift his support from the figure who took on the system to the one who personified it. "It's like this," he said. His first choice would be to see political change. "But those who have prospects are taken out, because they represent competition. The ones who are left are accustomed to the way things are, they've settled in—and they create stability. I am not against this stability." What was important, he said, was that things not get worse.

It struck me as a telling bit of wiliness, and as good a description of the Putin generation as any: they are open, curious, and ambitious, but not—at least not yet—desperate and insurrectionary. On my last morning in Nefteyugansk, I took a stroll around town with Prilepa, passing his school and a row of wooden apartment blocks built fifty years ago for the city's first residents. The sun was out, ricocheting brightly off the snow, and the temperature had climbed to five degrees—delightful spring weather, Prilepa declared. We stopped to warm up with some tea.

Prilepa told me that, as he understood from his father, in the Soviet Union young people had a mania for everything foreign. Today, what's fashionable is "success, having a better life." Achievement is cool. That may explain the duality of being drawn to both Navalny's call for change and Putin's promise of stability. We talked about plans for the future. Prilepa had another couple of years left in school, and then wanted to enroll in a military aviation institute in southern Russia. He'd like to train as a pilot. I asked if he saw a difficulty in serving a state he had begun to sour on. No, he said. "I'm planning to serve my homeland, not a certain circle of people." For as long as Prilepa has been alive, those two things have been inexorably fused. Yet Putin, by dint of biology even if not of politics, will at some point face his last day in power. Whatever Russia's post-Putin future holds, the Putin generation will be its inheritors. Will the wily man be part of that inheritance? So far, he has proved a remarkably enduring creature.

ACKNOWLEDGMENTS

—

I HAD NO IDEA THAT WHAT BEGAN AS YOUTHFUL CURIOSITY with Russia would turn into a pursuit that would shape the course of my life. I'm grateful that I had the chance to discover some of this country's richness, complexity, and depth—an inexhaustible pursuit. My first thank-you goes to those who, at the early stages of my study of Russia, proved skillful and patient teachers: the professors at the School of Foreign Service at Georgetown University, my instructors and hosts at the Smolny campus in St. Petersburg, and the academics and practitioners at the School of International and Public Affairs at Columbia University. It's a pleasure to continue to learn from Timothy Frye, Andrew Kuchins, Stephen Sestanovich, and Angela Stent long after I've left their classrooms.

Friends in Moscow and around the country have taught me far more about Russia than I ever could have discovered on my own, and, in the process, have helped me understand myself and my own thoughts in ways that reverberate far beyond the page. I'm glad to have shared these years with Max Avdeev, Maria and Anatoly Golubovsky, Michael and Lily Idov, Igor Ivanov, Anna Shirokova-Koens, Andrew Ryvkin, Yulia Taranova, Natasha Yefimova, Nina Zavrieva, and Dasha and Katia Zoritch.

I wasn't sure what it meant to be a journalist when I decided I wanted to be one. Among the first to indulge this amorphous goal, foisted on her by a total stranger, was Masha Lipman, who proved remarkably generous in hearing me out and providing early advice and counsel. She was, and remains, the sharpest and most exacting reader I have, and, beyond that, has opened up a wonderful and fascinating world of people in Moscow, including her husband, Sergey Ivanov. At the Columbia School of Journalism, Barry Bearak gave me my first real introduction to the practice of reporting, and instilled in me an appreciation for discipline, shoe-leather rigor, and fundamental decency that I try to carry with me to this day. John Bennet is too wry and self-effacing for such emotive compliments, but it wouldn't be an exaggeration to say he changed my life: he taught me the craft of magazine writing, imparted several tomes' worth of axioms ("a banana is always a banana, never a yellow elongated fruit"), shepherded me through my nervous early days at *The New Yorker,* provided a fulsome and invaluable edit of this book, and serves as the voice of an ever-present editor in my head.

My first attempts at journalism in Russia were made possible by C. J. Chivers, Andrew Kramer, Steven Lee Myers, and Michael Schwirtz, who imparted years' worth of knowledge over the course of one summer at *The New York Times* bureau in Moscow. Vera Titunik at *The New York Times Magazine* published my first long-form piece, taking a chance on a story that began as a student project. At *Foreign Affairs,* I found a group of colleagues who were as kind as they were brilliant. Thanks to Gideon Rose for bringing me on board and building my analytical muscle and self-confidence. Sasha Polakow-Suransky is a dear friend whose mind inspires me regularly; same for Stuart Reid, who is such a good editor that to this day I can't resist sending him drafts of my articles before I file them.

I had no real long-term plan when I left New York and showed up in Moscow in the winter of 2012. Thanks to the trust of Arkady Ostrovsky, I ended up with a job filling in for him at *The Economist.* His were big shoes to fill, but he made it a shade less intimidating by sharing his vast knowledge and feel for Russia's history, culture, and politics. John Peet was a warm, responsive, and accommodating editor.

My writing on the infinitely fascinating well of stories in Russia in long form was made possible by editors at *Bloomberg Businessweek, National Geographic, The New Republic,* and *The New York Times Magazine.* I also owe a debt to the patience and support of Kate Greenberg.

Writing for *The New Yorker* has provided me with the greatest professional satisfaction I have known. It is equal parts inspiring and intimidating to see my work alongside the greats of contemporary journalism. John Bennet, mentioned above, went from being my teacher to being my editor, but remained a guide and mentor throughout. Deirdre Foley-Mendelssohn, David Rohde, and Emily Stokes have made me sound smarter and more graceful than I could hope to be in real life, while indulging many a far-afield idea. The magazine's fact-checkers and copy editors are what make the whole operation click; it's been a particular joy to work with David Kortava and Anna Kordunsky, who appreciably improve my articles every time. And how lucky I am to write for a magazine whose editor, David Remnick, is himself a Russia expert and obsessive. His curiosity and enthusiasm for Russia have allowed me to indulge my own, while making sure I never get away with phoning it in.

Elyse Cheney was willing to hear me out long before I had anything close to a clearly defined idea. Alex Jacobs was responsible for getting me there, pushing me in the best ways possible to think through what exactly it was that I wanted to write. His advocacy made this project a reality. Adam Eaglin is a patient and wise sounding board, who knows just when and how to save me from myself. Tim Duggan had a vision and a confidence in this book that was infectious. His eye—or rather, pen—made its characters, ideas, and stories come into sharper focus. Thanks to him, and Aubrey Martinson and William Wolfslau, for bringing to life the book you're holding in your hands.

Throughout, Ksenia Barakovskaya tracked down crucial sources and pieces of research. Anna Kordunsky made the whole ship airtight; her professionalism is proof that nonfiction writing is only as good as the facts it rests on. Several of the chapters greatly benefited from close reads by people who know the material far better than I do—special thanks to Masha Lipman, Tanya Lokshina, Anna Narinskaya, and Svetlana Solodovnik. An early burst of writing came at the home of Boris and Masha Nikolsky in Tarusa, a fairy-tale town in the Russian countryside.

My initial reporting in Russia was made possible by a grant from the Pulitzer Center on Crisis Reporting, a tremendously important organization that makes possible stories that otherwise would quite likely go untold. New America provided invaluable support as I was embarking on this book project, and I am grateful for the many opportunities provided by the fellowship program. My two years as a fellow were among my most productive and inspired. The MacDowell Colony proved blissfully idyllic; I don't think I ever wrote so much while feeling so happy. From the moment I stepped foot in the American Academy in Berlin, it all seemed too good to be true, and that feeling didn't lessen over the three months I spent in residence. It's no exaggeration to say that this book was made possible by the professionalism and generosity of its staff, and the camaraderie of my fellow fellows.

In Moscow, I have greatly benefited from the friendship, wisdom, and encouragement of my colleagues in the foreign press corps: Miriam Elder, Julia Ioffe, Olaf Koens, Andrew Roth, Simon Shuster, Paul Sonne, Noah Sneider, Anton Troianovski, Courtney Weaver, and Emma Wells. I've passed many a hilarious and terrifying moment— and delicious meal—with Shaun Walker. Russia is home to a coterie of talented and self-motivated journalists, who produce work that is courageous and illuminating. They have my bottomless admiration. A special nod to Mikhail Fishman, Nikolay Kononov, Milana Mazaeva, Daniil Turovsky, and Sveta Reiter. I could talk to Nathan Thrall endlessly, and often do. His example—as a thinker, writer, and father— is never far from my mind. Thomas Williams is more a brother than a friend; we have grown up as writers and journalists together, and have shared our most profound and silliest moments.

My parents, Michael and Ellen Yaffa, instilled in me from an early age a hunger and curiosity for the world, and a sense that one mustn't waste or treat lightly the short time we have to spend in it. They showed me with their example what it means to live with dignity, purpose, and impact. My older sister Jessica is my greatest hero and role model. Taking my seat in 11E next to Yulia was the most profound stroke of luck I've ever had. Thankfully we had more than enough to talk about for the two-hour flight to Berlin, and, all these years later, still haven't run out. This book, and my life, are immeasurably richer for that chance encounter.

SOURCES

—

PROLOGUE | THE WILY MAN

Author interviews with Lev Gudkov, Alexey Levinson, and Igor Yefimov.

Dovlatov, Sergei. *The Compromise.* Translated by Anne Frydman. New York: Knopf, 1983.

Dovlatov, Sergei. *The Suitcase.* Translated by Antonina W. Bouis. Berkeley, CA: Counterpoint, 2011.

Dovlatov, Sergei. *The Zone: A Prison Camp Guard's Story.* Translated by Anne Frydman. Berkeley, CA: Counterpoint, 2012.

Greene, Samuel A. "From Boom to Bust: Hardship, Mobilization & Russia's Social Contract." *Daedalus* 146, no. 2 (Spring 2017).

Levada, Yuri. *Changing times: The subject and the researcher's viewpoint* [*Время перемен. Предмет и позиция исследователя*]. Edited by Abram Reitblat and Lev Gudkov. Moscow: Novoye Literaturnoye Obozreniye, 2016. A collection of works including "The Wily Man: Russian Doublethink" ["Человек лукавый: Двоемыслие по-российски"]; " 'Science life was seminary life' " [" 'Научная жизнь—была семинарская жизнь' "]; "Homo Post-Sovieticus"; "The disappearing essence?" ["Уходящая натура?"]; and "1968: The tipping point" ["Шестьдесят восьмой, переломный"].

Levada, Yuri, and A. Golov. *Got an opinion! Results of a social survey* [*Есть мнение! Итоги социологического опроса*]. Moscow: Progress, 1990.

Solzhenitsyn, Alexander. "Live Not by Lies." Translation of the 1974 essay "Жить не по лжи!" OrthodoxyToday.org, 2004.

Solzhenitsyn, Alexander. *One Day in the Life of Ivan Denisovich.* Translated by H. T. Willetts. New York: Farrar, Straus and Giroux, 2005.

Yaffa, Joshua. "A Russian Writer's Lessons for Being a Nobody While Being Yourself." *The New Yorker,* November 15, 2018.

CHAPTER 1 | MASTER OF CEREMONIES

Author interviews with Konstantin Ernst, Leonid Parfyonov, Artem Sheinin, Anna Kachkaeva, Andrei Boltenko, Yulia Pankratova, Vera Krichevskaya, Arina Borodina, Nikolay Kartozia, Katerina Gordeeva.

Arkus, Lyobov, Konstantin Shavlovsky, and Vasily Stepanov. "Konstantin Ernst: 'I hope the Maya were right'" ["Константин Эрнст: 'Я надеюсь, майя не ошиблись'"]. *Seans* (seance.ru), August 13, 2012.

Baker, Peter, and Susan Glasser. *Kremlin Rising: Vladimir Putin's Russia and the End of Revolution.* New York: Lisa Drew/Scribner, 2005.

Balmforth, Tom. "Russian State TV Edits Out Commentary on Putin and 'Untruth' in Hit U.S. TV Series." *Radio Free Europe/Radio Liberty,* May 15, 2017.

Belov, Kim, and Roman Super. "Person of the year 2014: Konstantin Ernst" ["Человек года 2014: Константин Эрнст"]. *GQ Russia,* September 16, 2014.

Borodina, Arina. "The first buttons of Russia" ["Первые кнопки России"]. *Kommersant,* April 4, 2005.

Channel One. "America for the Russians" ["Америка для русских"]. *Vremya Pokazhet,* September 27, 2016.

Channel One. "Russia vs. the USA" ["Россия vs США"]. *Vremya Pokazhet,* August 29, 2016.

Channel One. "Russia, with Syria as the backdrop" ["Россия на фоне Сирии"]. *Vremya Pokazhet,* October 11, 2016.

Channel One. "Russian elections: The USA's move" ["Выборы в России: Ход США"]. *Vremya Pokazhet,* March 6, 2018.

Channel One. "Slavyansk refugee recalls how a fighter's wife and son were executed in front of her very eyes" ["Беженка из Славянска вспоминает, как при ней казнили маленького сына и жену ополченца"]. *Vremya Pokazhet,* July 12, 2014.

"Conversation partner: Konstantin Ernst" ["Собеседник: Константин Эрнст"]. *Seans* (seance.ru), December 15, 2006.

Ernst, Konstantin. Speech at the GQ awards ceremony. September 20, 2014.

Fossato, Floriana. "Vladimir Putin and the Russian Television 'Family.'" *The Russia Papers*. CERI Sciences Po, 2006.

Gevorkyan, Natalia. Interview with Ksenia Ponomareva. "Whom have you gotten elected for us a year ago?" ["Кого же вы нам год назад выбрали?"]. *Kommersant,* March 23, 2001.

Gorbachev, Alexander, and Ilya Krasilschik, eds. *The history of Russian media 1989–2011. Afisha's version* [История русских медиа 1989–2011. Версия "Афиши"]. Moscow: Afisha Industries, 2011.

Kashin, Oleg. "'I felt it was very important to make Putin not the source of fear but the object of ridicule'" ["'Мне казалось очень важным сделать так, чтобы Путин был не источником страха, а объектом насмешек'"]. *Kommersant,* June 13, 2011.

Kashin, Oleg. "Vladimir Pozner: 'Ernst said that he agrees with my every word'" ["Владимир Познер: 'Эрнст сказал, что согласен с каждым моим словом'"]. *Colta,* February 23, 2013.

Kondukov, Alexander. Interview with Konstantin Ernst conducted in 2008. "RS's archive: Before I kick the bucket" ["Архив RS: Пока не сыграл в ящик"]. *Rolling Stone Russia,* April 9, 2013.

Leontiev, Mikhail. "Moments before the Boeing crash near Donetsk: A unique photograph in the 'Odnako' show" ["За мгновения до крушения 'Боинга' под Донецком—уникальный кадр в аналитической программе 'Однако'"]. Channel One, November 14, 2014.

Myers, Steven Lee. *The New Tsar: The Rise and Reign of Vladimir Putin.* New York: Vintage, 2015.

Ostrovsky, Arkady. *The Invention of Russia: The Journey from Gorbachev's Freedom to Putin's War.* New York: Penguin, 2015.

Oushakine, Serguei Alex. "'We're Nostalgic But We're Not Crazy': Retrofitting the Past in Russia." *The Russian Review* 66 (July 2007): 451–82.

Parfyonov, Leonid. "'I'm No Hero, But It's Time to Call a Spade a Spade.'" Translation of Parfyonov's Listyev Prize acceptance speech. *Open Democracy,* November 26, 2010.

Putin, Vladimir. "New Year Address by Acting President Vladimir Putin." The Kremlin, December 31, 1999.

Rostova, Natalia. "How the media elected the president" ["Как пресса избирала президента"]. *Radio Svoboda,* July 3, 2016.

Saprykin, Yuri. "Yuri Saprykin talks with Konstantin Ernst and Anatoli Maksimov" ["Юрий Сапрыкин беседует с Константином Эрнстом и Анатолием Максимовым"]. *Afisha Daily,* December 19, 2005.

Stanley, Alessandra. "Russians Begin to Gild the Communist Past." *The New York Times,* December 30, 1995.

Yanchenkov, Vladimir. "Militants prepare their foreign passports" ["Боевики готовят загранпаспорта"]. *Trud,* January 6, 2000.

Yeltsin, Boris. "Chapter 1: December 31, 1999." In *Midnight Diaries.* Translated by Catherine Fitzpatrick. New York: PublicAffairs, 2000.

Yeltsin, Boris. "Statement." The Kremlin, December 31, 1999.

Yurchak, Alexei. *Everything Was Forever Until It Was No More: The Last Soviet Generation.* Princeton, NJ: Princeton University Press, 2005.

CHAPTER 2 | BEWARE OF DRAGONS

Author interviews with Heda Saratova, Tanya Lokshina, Elena Milashina, Svetlana Gannushkina, Oleg Orlov, Ekaterina Sokirianskaia, Lana Estemirova, Igor Kalyapin, Eliza Musaeva, Timur Akiev, Dzhanet Erezhebova, Ilyas Akhmadov, Timur Aliyev, Khassan Baiev, Veronika Silchenko.

Akhmedova, Marina. "A mountain woman's fate" ["Женщина горной судьбы"]. *Ogoniok,* no. 28, July 22, 2013.

Berg, Evgeny. Interview with Ruslan Kutaev. "'There are things that you must do no matter the consequences'" ["'Есть вещи, которые вне зависимости от последствий ты должен сделать'"]. Meduza, December 23, 2017.

Bullough, Oliver. *Let Our Fame Be Great: Journeys Among the Defiant People of the Caucasus.* New York: Basic Books, 2010.

Burasova, Anzhelika. "'I can't look on calmly at a person getting humiliated': Heda Saratova on the return of Russian women from Syria" ["'Смотреть, как человека унижают, не могу': Хеда Саратова о возврате из Сирии россиянок"]. Nn.ru, December 15, 2017.

Chizhova, Lyubov. Interview with Sergei Babinets. "'We are staying in Grozny'" ["'Мы останемся в Грозном'"]. *Radio Svoboda,* December 15, 2014.

Euronews. "Demonstrations in memory of Natalia Estemirova." Video footage taken July 16, 2009, published by No Comment TV on July 17, 2009. Online at https://youtu.be/_sNKIFh546M.

Feifer, Gregory. "Russian Rights Activist Battles On in Chechnya." *Radio Free Europe/Radio Liberty,* August 31, 2010.

Gall, Carlotta, and Thomas de Waal. *Chechnya: Calamity in the Caucasus.* New York: New York University Press, 1998.

Govorit Moskva. Interview with Heda Saratova. April 1, 2017.

Grozny TV. "On Constitution Day" ["Ко дню конституции"]. *Fulcrums [Точки опоры],* December 12, 2014. Online at https://youtu.be/CQ8MWKdzfdo.

Grozny TV. "Rally to protest the activities of faux human rights defenders is held in Grozny" ["В Грозном состоялся пикет против деятельности псевдоправозащитников"]. News segment, November 9, 2017.

Hassan, Hind. "Inside the Chechen Prison Where Gay Men Say They Were Tortured." *Vice News,* June 20, 2017.

Human Rights Watch. "'They Have Long Arms and They Can Find Me': Anti-Gay Purge by Local Authorities in Russia's Chechen Republic." May 26, 2017.

Human Rights Watch. "'You Dress According to Their Rules': Enforcement of an Islamic Dress Code for Women in Chechnya." March 10, 2011.

International Crisis Group. "Chechnya: The Inner Abroad." Europe Report no. 236, June 30, 2015.

Khachatrian, Diana. "The Children of ISIS" ["Дети ИГИЛ"]. *Takie Dela,* September 26, 2017.

Kramer, Andrew. "Reporting on People Who 'Don't Exist.'" *The New York Times,* April 23, 2017.

Kramer, Andrew, and Ellen Barry. "Chorus of Blame Follows Rights Worker's Death." *The New York Times,* July 16, 2009.

Lieven, Anatol. *Chechnya: Tombstone of Russian Power.* New Haven, CT: Yale University Press, 1998.

Milashina, Elena. "Honor killing: How a well-known LGBT activist's ambitions stirred a terrible ancient rite in Chechnya" ["Убийство чести: Как амбиции известного ЛГБТ-активиста разбудили в Чечне страшный древний обычай"]. *Novaya Gazeta,* April 1, 2017.

Milashina, Elena. "Prosecution of Chechen gays: The stories of surviving witnesses" ["Расправы над чеченскими геями: Публикуем истории выживших свидетелей"]. *Novaya Gazeta,* April 4, 2017.

Mirmaksumova, Aida. "From ISIS to Russia: Why Moscow stopped the program that allowed women and children who traveled to Iraq to return home" ["Из ИГИЛ в Россию. Почему Москва остановила программу по возвращению бежавших в Ирак женщин с детьми"]. *Nastoyascheye Vremya* (www.currenttime.tv), July 18, 2018.

Orlov, Petr. "High rank: Ramzan Khadyrov awarded Hero of Russia" ["Высокое звание: Рамзан Кадыров стал Героем России"]. *Rossiyskaya Gazeta,* December 30, 2004.

Politkovskaya, Anna. *A Dirty War: A Russian Reporter in Chechnya.* Translated by John Crowfoot. London: Harvill Press, 2001.

Politkovskaya, Anna. *A Russian Diary: A Journalist's Final Account of Life, Corruption, and Death in Putin's Russia.* Translated by Arch Tait. New York: Random House, 2007.

Saratova, Heda. "A word about Natasha" ["Слово о Наташе"]. *Chechen Human Rights Defender* [*Чеченский правозащитник*] 7, no. 21 (July 2009).

Walker, Shaun. *The Long Hangover: Putin's New Russia and the Ghosts of the Past.* New York: Oxford University Press, 2018.

Yaffa, Joshua. "Chechnya's ISIS Problem." *The New Yorker,* February 12, 2016.

Yaffa, Joshua. "Putin's Dragon." *The New Yorker,* February 8, 2016.

CHAPTER 3 | THE LAST FREE PRIEST

Author interviews with Vera Adelgeim, Viktor Yakovlev, Ioann Mukhanov, Andrey Kuraev, Vladimir Popov, Valentin Kurbatov, Sergey Bychkov, Svetlana Solodovnik, Petr Gusev.

Adelgeim, Pavel. *The Dogma of the Church in Canons and in Practice* [*Догмат о Церкви в канонах и практике*]. Pskov, Russia: Pskovskaya oblastnaya tipografiya, 2003.

Adelgeim, Pavel. *With my own eyes* [*Своими глазами*]. Moscow: Krestovozdvizhenskoye maloye pravoslavnoye bratstvo, 2010.

Burgess, John P. *Holy Rus': The Rebirth of Orthodoxy in the New Russia.* New Haven, CT: Yale University Press, 2017.

"The case of Father Pavel Adelgeim" ["Дело священника Павла Адельгейма"]. *Kontinent,* no. 115 (2003).

Filippov, Alexander. Interview with Vera Adelgeim. "Vera Mikhailovna Adelgeim on Father Pavel's murder: Direct hit to the heart" ["Вера Михайловна Адельгейм об убийстве отца Павла: Прямое попадание в сердце"]. Pravmir.ru, August 19, 2013.

Garrard, John, and Carol Garrard. *Russian Orthodoxy Resurgent: Faith and Power in the New Russia.* Princeton, NJ: Princeton University Press, 2008.

Gutsu, Roman. "Father Pavel's entire life from start to end was dedicated to God and the Church (Eulogy at the last rites)" ["Вся жизнь отца Павла от начала до конца была отдана Богу и Церкви (Слово на отпевании)"]. Pravmir.ru, August 12, 2013.

Kolymagin, Boris, and Alexandra Kolymagina. "Key events in church life in the press reflection" ["Основные события церковной жизни в зеркале прессы"]. *Kontinent*, no. 116 (2003).

Martemyanov, Maksim. "Frock discrimination: Pskov priest Pavel Adelgeim goes to court for his congregation" ["Рясовая дискриминация: Псковский священник Павел Адельгейм судится за свою паству"]. Lenta.ru, December 25, 2012.

Moiseyenko, Yuri. Interview with Pavel Adelgeim conducted in 2003. "Father Pavel Adelgeim: We now have a general secretary—I mean a patriarch" ["Отец Павел Адельгейм: Теперь у нас есть генеральный секретарь, то есть патриарх"]. *Novaya Gazeta*, August 7, 2013.

Moscow Patriarchate. "Transcript of Prime Minister V. Putin's conference with His Holiness Patriarch Kirill and leaders of Russia's traditional religious congregations" ["Стенограмма встречи председателя Правительства РФ В.В. Путина со Святейшим Патриархом Кириллом и лидерами традиционных религиозных общин России"]. February 8, 2012.

Racheva, Elena. "God forgives" ["Бог простит"]. *Novaya Gazeta*, May 13, 2014.

Racheva, Elena. "To each his own cross" ["Каждому свой крест"]. *Novaya Gazeta*, February 9, 2017.

Racheva, Elena. "Two weeks with Father Pavel Adelgeim" ["Две недели с отцом Павлом Адельгеймом"]. Snob, August 7, 2013.

Reiter, Svetlana, Anastasia Napalkova, and Ivan Golunov. "RBK Investigates: How the church funds itself" ["Расследование РБК: На что живет церковь"]. *RBK*, February 26, 2016.

Roschenia, Daria. "Father Pavel Adelgeim: Awaken. Rejoice." ["Отец Павел Адельгейм. Бодрствуйте. Радуйтесь."] Pravmir.ru, August 5, 2017.

Schipkov, Alexander. Interview with Pavel Adelgeim. "I was expelled from the seminary by Filaret Denisenko himself" ["Из семинарии меня выгонял лично Филарет Денисенко"]. Religare.ru, March 31, 2008.

Seddon, Max. "Putin and the Patriarch." *Financial Times*, August 22, 2019.

Semionov, Alexei. "Compatibility with spiritual life. Father Pavel Adelgeim: 'The symphony of Church and state is unnatural and detrimental for both'" ["Совместимость с духовной жизнью. Священник Павел Адельгейм: 'Симфония власти и Церкви противоестественна и губительна для обоих'"]. *Pskovskaya Guberniya*, no. 15 (April 2012).

Shiryaeva, Elena. Interview with Vera Adelgeim. "His Vera: Forty days without Father Pavel" ["Его Вера: Сорок дней без отца Павла"]. *Pskovskaya Guberniya*, no. 35 (September 2013).

Tayler, Jeffrey. "What Pussy Riot's 'Punk Prayer' Really Said." *The Atlantic*, November 8, 2012.

Voltskaya, Tatiana. "Ever against the flow: Recollections of Archpriest Pavel Adelgeim" ["Всегда наперекор: воспоминания протоиерея Павла Адельгейма"]. *Radio Svoboda*, March 11, 2010.

Yakovlev, Viktor. "Father Pavel Adelgeim: This code is called 'death to the parishes'" ["Священник Павел Адельгейм: Этот устав называется смерть приходам"]. *Pskovskaya Guberniya* 554, no. 32 (August 2011).

Yakovlev, Viktor. "'I, the accused, Father Pavel Adelgeim . . .'" ["'Я, обвиняемый, священник Павел Адельгейм . . .'"]. *Pskovskaya Guberniya* 545, no. 23 (June 2011).

Yakovlev, Viktor. Interview with Pavel Adelgeim. "One century of Russian Orthodoxy: From persecution to blood to embraces to death" ["Век русской Церкви: От гонений до крови до объятий до смерти"]. *Pskovskaya Guberniya* 453, no. 32 (August 2009).

CHAPTER 4 | KING OF THE PRIDE

Author interviews with Oleg Zubkov, Oksana Zubkova, Galina Perelovich, Abdureshit Dzhepparov, Alexander Shabanov.

Azar, Ilya. "'We're not highlanders, so don't take this approach with us': Crimean Tatars are learning to live in Russia" ["'Мы не горцы, с нами так не надо': Крымские татары учатся жить в России"]. Meduza, December 2, 2014.

Chepovskaya, Anastasia. "Crimean park: What the owner of Yalta's zoos is fighting for, and with whom" ["Парк крымского периода: С кем и за что борется владелец ялтинских зверинцев Олег Зубков"]. Lenta.ru, March 22, 2017.

"Crimea resident prepares his fighting lions for protecting the referendum" ["Житель Крыма подготовил боевых львов для защиты референдума"]. Life.ru, March 14, 2014.

Galustyan, Artem, Vadim Nikiforov, and Olesia Gerasimenko. "Crimean Tatar ego" ["Крымскотатарское эго"]. *Kommersant,* March 23, 2015.

Koteneva, Olga. "Tightening the valve: The gasification program for the peninsula's population centers will get cut by five billion rubles" ["Прикрутили вентиль: Программу газификации населенных пунктов полуострова урежут на пять миллиардов рублей"]. *Rossiyskaya Gazeta,* May 22, 2018.

Krutov, Mark. Interview with Oleg Zubkov. "Zubkov on Poklonskaya: 'I was the first to say she's a fool.'" ["Зубков о Поклонской: 'Я первый сказал, что она дура'"]. *Krym.Realii,* August 14, 2017.

Makovetsky, Leonid. "Emigration ideas of Taigan's owner find eager support in Crimea: 'The sooner the better!'" ["В Крыму горячо поддержали желание владельца парка 'Тайган' эмигрировать: 'Скорей бы!'"]. *Novy Den* (newdaynews.ru), February 7, 2017.

Mesnyanko, Anton. "Lion hunt" ["Охота на львов"]. *Radio Svoboda,* December 15, 2015.

Mesnyanko, Anton. "'Under Ukraine, authorities were reasonable'" ["'При Украине власти были адекватные'"]. *Radio Svoboda,* March 28, 2016.

Okrest, Dmitry. Interview with Abdureshit Dzhepparov. "'But if a Turkish squadron marched in . . .': Crimea and Tatars" ["'Вот если бы сюда зашла турецкая эскадра.' Крым и татары"]. *Spektr,* May 18, 2015.

Potapov, Egor. "To survive in spite of it all: How Crimean authorities tried to destroy Zubkov's parks" ["Выжить вопреки: Как власти Крыма пытались уничтожить парки Зубкова"]. *Krym.Realii,* September 30, 2017.

Prokopenko, Maria. "'Cursed silence'" ["'Проклятое молчание'"]. *Den* (day.kyiv.ua), September 27, 2017.

Putin, Vladimir. "Address by President of the Russian Federation." The Kremlin, March 18, 2014.

Samodelova, Svetlana. Interview with Oleg Zubkov. "Director of the closed Taigan Zoo gives the low-down on his conflict with authorities" ["Директор закрытого зоопарка 'Тайган' раскрыл подноготную конфликта с властями"]. MK.ru, December 17, 2015.

Shevchenko, Alexandra, and Inna Annitova. "Oleg Zubkov: 'I'm feeling subhuman in the Russian Crimea'" ["Олег Зубков: 'Чувствую себя недочеловеком в российском Крыму'"]. *Krym.Realii,* November 18, 2017.

Surgan, Alexandra. "Blood defenders: How the relatives of Crimea prisoners become activists" ["Кровные защитники: Как родственники заключенных в Крыму становятся активистами"]. *Krym.Realii,* April 9, 2018.

Yaffa, Joshua. "Reforming Ukraine After the Revolutions." *The New Yorker,* September 5, 2016.

Zhegulev, Ilya. "Myrrh-streaming and courage" ["Мироточение и мужество"]. Meduza, April 5, 2017.

Zubkov, Oleg. *I'm building a zoo* [*Я строю зоопарк*]. Kherson, Ukraine: Naddneprianochka, 2014.

Zubkov, Oleg. Personal website and blog. Online at http://olegzubkov.blogspot.com.

CHAPTER 5 | NOTES ON CAMP

Author interviews with Viktor Shmyrov, Tatiana Kursina, Yulia Kantor, Sergei Kovalev, Alexander Kalikh, Mikhail Meylac, Pavel Guryanov, Leonid Obukhov, Nailya Allakhverdieva, Ilya Rogotnev, Sergey Shevyrin.

Balmforth, Tom. "Russian Activists Rally Around Embattled Museum of Soviet Repression." *Radio Free Europe/Radio Liberty,* June 27, 2014.

Bukovsky, Vladimir. *To Build a Castle: My Life as a Dissenter.* Translated by Michael Scammell. New York: Viking Press, 1979.

"The crossing to liberty island" ["Переправа на остров свободы"]. Interview with Viktor Shmyrov. *Chelovecheskoye izmereniye,* no. 3 (December 2011).

Danilovich, Mikhail. "The new life of 'Perm-36'" ["Новая жизнь 'Перми-36'"]. *Radio Svoboda,* February 16, 2016.

Danilovich, Mikhail, and Robert Coalson. "Revamped Perm-36 Museum Emphasizes Gulag's 'Contribution to Victory.'" *Radio Free Europe/Radio Liberty,* July 25, 2015.

Etkind, Alexander. *Warped Mourning: Stories of the Undead in the Land of the Unburied.* Stanford, CA: Stanford University Press, 2013.

Grigorieva, Nadezhda. Interview with Mikhail Meylac. "Mikhail" ["Михаил"]. *Zvezda,* no. 8 (August 2002).

Kachkin, Sergei, dir. *Perm-36. Reflexion*. Documentary film. Russia: april film-lab, 2015.

Kozlov, Ivan. "'The flood of denunciations was unprecedented': How the assault on Perm's museum of political repressions unfolded" ["'Поток доносов был беспрецедентным': Как в Перми боролись с музеем истории политических репрессий"]. Meduza, November 10, 2014.

Kozlov, Ivan. "'They accuse us of inadequate maintenance of the camp complex'" ["'Нам предъявляют претензии за ненадлежащее содержание лагерного комплекса'"]. *Afisha Daily*, March 12, 2015.

Lavut, Evgeniya. Interview with Viktor Shmyrov. "'You're right, but you see, this was the only decision we could make': Interview with 'Perm-36' director" ["'Вы правы, но вы понимаете, мы не могли принять другого решения': интервью с директором 'Перми-36'"]. OpenRussia.org, March 7, 2015.

Morev, Gleb. *The Dissidents* [*Диссиденты*]. Moscow: AST, 2017.

Obukhov, Leonid. *Perm-36: Prehistory* [*Пермь-36: Предыстория*]. Perm, Russia: Memorial, 2018.

Racheva, Yelena, and Anna Artemieva. "Kum's revenge: The history of the standoff between Russia's main museum of repressions 'Perm-36' and the camp's former leadership" ["Реванш кума: История противостояния главного в России музея репрессий 'Пермь-36' и бывшего лагерного начальства"]. *Novaya Gazeta*, July 6, 2014.

Shmyrov, Viktor. "Perm-36: Rehabilitation of the repressions" ["Пермь-36. Реабилитация репрессий"]. *Zvezda*, December 13, 2016.

Shmyrov, Viktor. "13.8: On the history of Perm political camps" ["13.8. К истории пермских политлагерей"]. In *Years of terror: The online book of remembrance for the victims of political repressions* [*Годы террора: Электронная книга памяти жертв политических репрессий*]. Perm, Russia: Zdravstvuy, 1998.

Shteyner, Arseny. "A bid for freedom: Life and death of the Pilorama human rights forum" ["Век свободы не видать: Жизнь и смерть правозащитного форума 'Пилорама'"]. Lenta.ru, July 29, 2014.

Sokolov, Vladimir. "'Perm-36': Everything is different now ["'Пермь-36': Теперь всё по-другому"]. *Zvezda*, November 9, 2016.

Sokolov, Vladimir, and Evgenia Romanova. Interview with Tatiana Kursina. "'I still believe we haven't passed the point of no return.'" ["'Я и сейчас считаю, что точка невозврата не пройдена'"]. *Echo Moskvy Perm*, May 25, 2014.

Tumakova, Irina. Interview with Yulia Kantor. "'Perm-36': The museum of GULAG and the Ministry of Culture" ["'Пермь-36': музей ГУЛАГа и Минкульта"]. Fontanka.ru, October 30, 2016.

Zemskov, Viktor. "GULAG: Historical and sociological aspect" ["ГУЛАГ: Историко-социологический аспект"]. *Sotsiologicheskiye Issledovaniya*, no. 6 (1991).

CHAPTER 6 | HELL ON EARTH

Author interviews with Gleb Glinka, Mikhail Fedotov, Lana Zhurkina, Mikhail Gokhman, Dmitry Aleshkovsky, Ella Polyakova, Ksenia Sokolova, Svetlana Sergienko, Nikolay Polozov.

Albats, Yevgenia. "Doctor Liza: Children on the front lines" ["Доктор Лиза: Дети на линии фронта"]. Newtimes.ru, October 19, 2014.

"Doctor Liza: 'I have nothing to say to critics or advisors'" ["Доктор Лиза: 'Ни критикам, ни советчикам мне сказать нечего'"]. Interview with Elizaveta Glinka. Pravmir.ru, October 31, 2014.

Eroshok, Zoya. "Liza Glinka: 'I work with the outcast and the betrayed. And not everyone understands this about me" ["Лиза Глинка: 'Я работаю с отверженными и преданными. И не все меня в этом понимают'"]. *Novaya Gazeta,* December 25, 2016.

Glinka, Elizaveta. *Doctor Liza Glinka: "I always take the side of the weak." Diaries, conversations* [Доктор Лиза Глинка: "Я всегда на стороне слабого." Дневники, беседы]. Edited by Sergei Aleschenok. Moscow: AST, 2018.

Glinka, Elizaveta. "On life, on death, on love" ["Доктор Лиза: о жизни, о смерти, о любви"]. *Cosmopolitan Russia,* December 26, 2016.

Golovko, Oksana. Interview with Elizaveta Glinka. "Doctor Liza: Loneliness is the scariest thing" ["Доктор Лиза: Самое страшное—одиночество"]. Pravmir.ru, February 17, 2014.

"The hardest thing in life is to not hurt those who are weaker than you, to not snap at them" ["Самое трудное в жизни—не обидеть тех, кто слабее тебя, не накричать"]. Interview with Elizaveta Glinka. Pravmir.ru, January 17, 2007.

Krasnogorodskaya, Alexandra. Interview with Gleb Glinka. "She saw God's image in all" ["Она видела в каждом образ Божий"]. *Izvestia,* February 19, 2018.

The Kremlin. "Meeting of the Council on civil society and human rights" ["Заседание Совета по развитию гражданского общества и правам человека"]. October 14, 2014.

The Kremlin. "The president gives out state awards for outstanding achievements in philanthropy and human rights advocacy" ["Президент вручил Государственные премии за выдающиеся достижения в области благотворительной и правозащитной деятельности"]. December 8, 2016.

Kuzichev, Anatoly. Interview with Elizaveta Glinka. "'I'd take every politician to visit the I.C.U. rooms of the wounded children of Donetsk'" ["'Я бы каждого политика взяла в реанимацию, где лежат раненые дети Донецка'"]. Kommersant FM, October 20, 2014.

Nikitina, Yulia. Interview with Elizaveta Glinka. "Doctor Liza in Donetsk: It doesn't matter who my patients are" ["Доктор Лиза в Донецке: Мне все равно, кого лечить"]. Fontanka.ru, May 29, 2014.

Pogrebizhskaya, Elena, dir. *Doctor Liza* [Доктор Лиза]. Documentary film. REN TV, 2009.

Presidential Council for Civil Society and Human Rights. "Doctor Liza: In Memoriam" ["Памяти Доктора Лизы"]. The Kremlin, December 25, 2016.

Sokolova, Ksenia. Interview with Elizaveta Glinka. "Elizaveta Glinka: 'They should themselves be put under ground!'" ["Елизавета Глинка: 'Самих бы их закопать!'"]. Snob, November 7, 2012.

Sokolova, Ksenia. Interview with Elizaveta Glinka. "'Impotence is when a woman goes to a war zone to rescue children, and men talk shit about her!'" ["'Елизавета Глинка: Импотенция—это когда женщина ездит на войну спасать детей, а мужчины поливают ее за это дерьмом'"]. Snob, November 24, 2014.

Sudilovsky, Andrei, dir. *Elizaveta and Gleb Glinka: More than love [Елизавета и Глеб Глинки: Больше чем любовь]*. Documentary film. Rossiya K, 2018.

"Syrian doctors ask Doctor Liza to help procure medicine for the children" ["Сирийские врачи просят доктора Лизу помочь с лекарствами для детей"]. *Tass*, September 3, 2016.

Ulitskaya, Ludmila. "Doctor Liza: In Memoriam" ["Людмила Улицкая—памяти Доктора Лизы"]. OpenRussia.org, December 25, 2016.

Yershov, Evgeny. Interview with Elizaveta Glinka. "Doctor Liza: Death has taught me patience" ["Доктор Лиза: 'Смерть научила меня терпеть'"]. Pravmir.ru, May 17, 2012.

Zhuravskaya, Olga. "'Have you seen her in photographs? Forget them; they don't convey half her charm'" ["'Вы видели ее фотографии? Забудьте. Они не передают и половины очарования'"]. *Dozhd*, January 13, 2017.

CHAPTER 7 | SUBTLE CREATURES

Author interviews with Mikhail Shvydkoy, Anna Narinskaya, Alexey Chesnakov, Marina Davydova, Sergei Kapkov, Alexei Agranovich, Sophia Apfelbaum, Michael Idov, Yuri Bykov, Ivan Vyrypaev.

Aleksenko, Alexei. "Regarding Ivan Vyrypaev's open letter" ["Об открытом письме Ивана Вырыпаева"]. Snob, August 25, 2017.

Balmforth, Tom. "Russian Director Vows to Quit Cinema After 'Hysteria' over TV Spy Thriller." *Radio Free Europe/Radio Liberty,* October 17, 2017.

Bykov, Yuri. Public VKontakte post, October 13, 2017. Online at https://vk.com/wall-23793890_10837.

"'Free the director': The ballet's authors call for Kirill Serebrennikov's release on the 'Nureyev' opening night" ["'Свободу режиссеру'. На премьере 'Нуреева' авторы балета призвали освободить Кирилла Серебренникова"]. Meduza, December 9, 2017.

"Is this Russian director a criminal or a critic of the state?" *Vice News,* November 4, 2017.

Kashin, Oleg. Interview with Kirill Serebrennikov. "Near the Kremlin" ["Около Кремля"]. *Kommersant* video, April 28, 2010.

The Kremlin. "Meeting with cultural figures: Dmitri Medvedev visits the Multimedia Art Museum" ["Встреча с деятелями культуры: Дмитрий Медведев посетил Мультимедиа-арт музей"]. March 24, 2011.

Lipman, Maria. "Meet the Second-Rate Academic Who Is Vladimir Putin's Culture Cop." *The New Republic,* May 23, 2014.

"Moscow Theater Director Ordered Under House Arrest in Serebrennikov Case." *Radio Free Europe/Radio Liberty,* October 27, 2017.

Neumeyer, Joy. "Filming the Fifth Column: How Outspoken Director Yuri Bykov's New TV Show Landed Him in Hot Water." *Calvert Journal,* October 26, 2017.

Pomerantsev, Peter. *Nothing Is True and Everything Is Possible: The Surreal Heart of the New Russia.* New York: PublicAffairs, 2015.

Pomerantsev, Peter. "Putin's Rasputin." *London Review of Books,* October 20, 2011.

Serebrennikov, Kirill. "'I thought that we are staging this resonant, powerful project for our country, for our fatherland'" ["'Я думал, что мы для страны, для родины делаем такой яркий и мощный проект'"]. Speech given during a court hearing. Online on *Dozhd,* August 23, 2017.

"Serebrennikov's Embezzlement Case, Explained." *Moscow Times,* August 24, 2017.

Shermeneva, Evgeniya. "On 'Seventh Studio,' 'Platform,' and the Gogol Center: Account of the participant of the events" ["О 'Седьмой студии', 'Платформе' и Гоголь-центре от участника событий"]. *Medium/Cuttringger,* May 23, 2017.

Vyrypaev, Ivan. "Open letter in support of Kirill Serebrennikov" ["Открытое письмо драматурга и режиссера Ивана Вырыпаева в поддержку Кирилла Серебренникова"]. Snob, August 24, 2017.

Yaffa, Joshua. "The Rise and Fall of Russia's Most Acclaimed Theatre Director." *The New Yorker,* December 11, 2017.

Zygar, Mikhail. *All the Kremlin's Men: Inside the Court of Vladimir Putin.* New York: PublicAffairs, 2016.

EPILOGUE | FATHERS AND SONS

Author interviews with Ksenia Sokolova, Mikhail Meylac, Lev Gudkov, Danila Prilepa, Evgenia Merkulenko.

Agence France-Presse. "Renowned Russian Director Serebrennikov Freed from House Arrest." *The Guardian,* April 8, 2019.

Antonov, Evgeny. "'Straight from Our Homes to the Cemetery' Russia's COVID-19 Outbreak Isn't Limited to Big Cities—It's Spread to Rural Areas, Where a Lack of Doctors and Quality Healthcare Makes It Harder to Survive." *Meduza,* October 23, 2020.

Baunov, Alexander. "Sobyanin and Bogomolov: An invitation to the drama" ["Собянин и Богомолов. Приглашение к драме"]. Carnegie.ru, August 27, 2018.

"'Golden mask 2019': Two awards for Serebrennikov and a Pussy Riot arrest"

["'Золотая маска—2019': две награды для Серебренникова и задержание Pussy Riot"]. *Radio Svoboda,* April 16, 2019.

Higgins, Andrew. "The Theatrical Method in Putin's Vote Madness." *The New York Times,* July 1, 2020.

"Kirill Serebrennikov snags two 'Golden masks'" ["Кириллу Серебренникову достались две 'Золотые маски'"]. BBC, April 17, 2019.

Kolesnikov, Andrei. "Russians Find New Ways to Protest." *The Moscow Times,* May 2, 2019.

Kolesnikov, Andrei. "The Split in Russia's Civil Society." Carnegie.ru, April 29, 2019.

Krastev, Ivan, and Gleb Pavlovsky. "The Arrival of Post-Putin Russia." European Council on Foreign Relations (Ecfr.eu), March 2, 2018.

Levada Center. "Institutional Trust" ["Институциональное доверие"]. Press release, October 4, 2018.

Levada Center. "Presidential elections and politicians' trust" ["Президентское голосование и доверие политикам"]. Press release, April 11, 2018.

Lobanova, Vika, and Andrei Sakov. "Who is Danila Prilepa, who asked Putin about corruption?" ["Кто такой Данила Прилепа, спросивший у Путина про коррупцию?"]. *Afisha,* June 15, 2017.

Navalny, Alexei. "Open letter to Anna (Nyuta) Konstantinovna Federmesser" ["Письмо Анне Константиновне (Нюте) Федермессер"]. May 5, 2019. Online at https://navalny.com/p/6129.

"Open Letter from Priests in Defence of Prisoners in the 'Moscow case,'" Pravmir.com, September 22, 2019.

Petrova, Irina. "Do good, not harm: Director Bogomolov discusses the state of Moscow's theaters" ["Помогай и не навреди: Режиссер Богомолов рассказал, как живется театрам в Москве"]. Riafan.ru, August 27, 2018.

Rogov, Kirill. "Collaborators and revolutionaries" ["Коллаборанты и революционеры"]. Public Facebook post, May 7, 2019.

"A schoolboy asked Putin about corruption. The President didn't believe that he came up with the question himself" ["Школьник спросил Путина о коррупции. Президент не поверил, что тот сам придумал вопрос"]. Meduza, June 15, 2017.

"Serebrennikov wins the 2019 Golden Mask Award for best drama director" ["Серебренников получил 'Золотую маску—2019' как лучший драматический режиссер"]. *Tass,* April 16, 2019.

Sulim, Sasha. "'My conscience wouldn't have allowed me to stay home': Russian schoolchildren tell Meduza why they went to the street protests" ["'Мне бы совесть не позволила остаться дома': Российские школьники рассказали 'Медузе', почему они пошли на уличные акции"]. Meduza, March 27, 2017.

Svetova, Zoya. Interview with Nyuta Federmesser. "'I'm neither for nor against the government. I'm for the people who couldn't care less against it'" ["'Я не за власть и не против власти. Я—за людей, которым не до власти'"]. *Novaya Gazeta,* May 16, 2019.

Svetova, Zoya. Interview with Ksenia Sokolova. "'Liza Glinka would have told me, "Sokolova, you're a fool!"'" [Ксения Соколова: "Лиза Глинка сказала бы мне: 'Ты дура, Соколова!'"]. Mbk.sobchakprotivvseh.ru, August 9, 2018.

"'Thank you, Sobyanin, for my normal blood pressure': Muscovites ridicule the mayor's reelection campaign" ["'Спасибо Собянину за нормальное давление': в Москве смеются над предвыборной кампанией мэра"]. BBC, August 29, 2018.

Volkov, Denis. "'No Trust': What Russians Think About the Pension Reform Plan." Carnegie.ru, August 9, 2018.

Yaffa, Joshua. "As Russia Votes, Its Youth Are Open and Curious but Not Yet Insurrectionary." *The New Yorker,* March 17, 2018.

INDEX

—

PHOTO: © MAX AVDEEV

JOSHUA YAFFA is a correspondent for *The New Yorker* in Moscow. For his work in Russia, he has been named a fellow at New America, a recipient of the American Academy's Berlin Prize, and a finalist for the Livingston Award.

ABOUT THE TYPE

This book was set in Bembo, a typeface based on an old-style Roman face that was used for Cardinal) Pietro Bembo's tract *De Aetna* in 1495. Bembo was cut by Francesco Griffo (1450–1518) in the early sixteenth century for Italian Renaissance printer and publisher Aldus Manutius (1449–1515). The Lanston Monotype Company of Philadelphia brought the well-proportioned letterforms of Bembo to the United States in the 1930s.